STEM INVESTIGATIONS

for UPPER PRIMARY

integrating SCIENCE, MATHS and TECHNOLOGIES for real-world learning

Charlotte Forwood

macmillan education

TEACHER RESOURCE BOOK

CONTENTS

INTRODUCTION

STEM INVESTIGATIONS

BUILT WORLD

MANAGED WORLD

NATURAL WORLD

SUSTAINABLE WORLD

WHO WE ARE

→ GENERIC REPRODUCIBLES, TEMPLATES AND GRAPHIC ORGANISERS

ABOUT *STEM INVESTIGATIONS FOR UPPER PRIMARY*

STEM Investigations for Upper Primary **is designed to enable educators to implement inquiry-based investigations with a STEM approach. This resource provides 20 'real-world' challenges to inspire and motivate students. Each challenge is supported by an investigation into the key issues around the project, scaffolded by a comprehensive teaching plan and instructional model.**

STEM stands for Science, Technology, Engineering and Mathematics. *STEM Investigations* helps students use skills and learnings from all four STEM disciplines to question and problem solve in real-world contexts, using an inquiry-based instructional model. Each STEM investigation links explicitly to Science content and inquiry skills in the curriculum, as well as to Mathematics and Digital and/or Design Technologies. The Engineering component – that is, the practical application of science to solve real-world problems – is facilitated through a five-step design thinking process used in each investigation (see page 8).

REAL-WORLD CHALLENGES, DESIGN THINKING AND VOCABULARY BUILDING

By focusing on authentic real-world challenges and problems, *STEM Investigations* allows students to engage in a transdisciplinary approach to learning and problem solving – just as we all do in real life. Student challenges range from designing irrigated garden beds made from waste materials to creating an art installation based around the properties of light.

For each STEM investigation, students must first explore the key scientific concepts relating to the investigation before completing the challenge using a design thinking process (see pages 7–8). This process guides students through the different stages necessary to produce an end product or process relating to the original challenge. Stages include:

- empathising through learning about different points of view
- defining the issue
- ideating/creating different possible solutions
- prototyping
- testing their designs.

A key part of each STEM investigation is the development of students' subject-specific vocabulary (see pages 9–12). Students are encouraged to monitor their learning throughout the investigation and engage in evaluation and self-reflection at the conclusion of the challenge.

→ COMPONENTS OF STEM INVESTIGATIONS

STUDENT CARDS

For each STEM investigation, students are given a student card that sets out their challenge. They can work individually, in pairs or in groups. The student card outlines a description of the challenge, plus the key understandings, key skills, key actions, key vocabulary and design thinking stages involved.

TEACHER RESOURCE BOOK

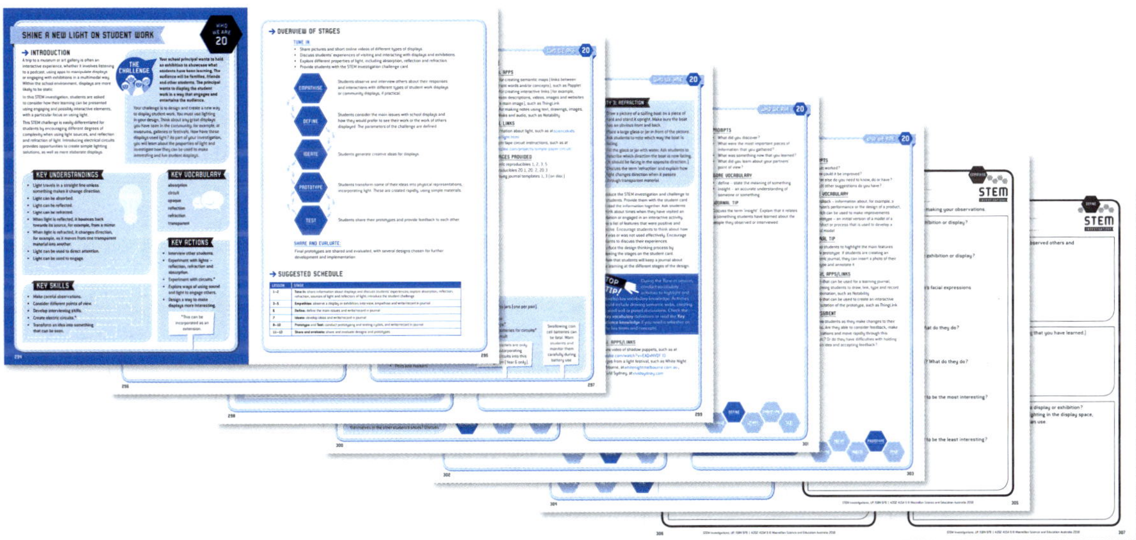

Each investigation is outlined in the Teacher Resource Book. The educator is provided with an overview of the challenge, and with curriculum links and detailed lesson plans, including suggestions for resources, technology use and assessment. Generic and investigation-specific reproducibles are also included.

DIGITAL RESOURCES DISC

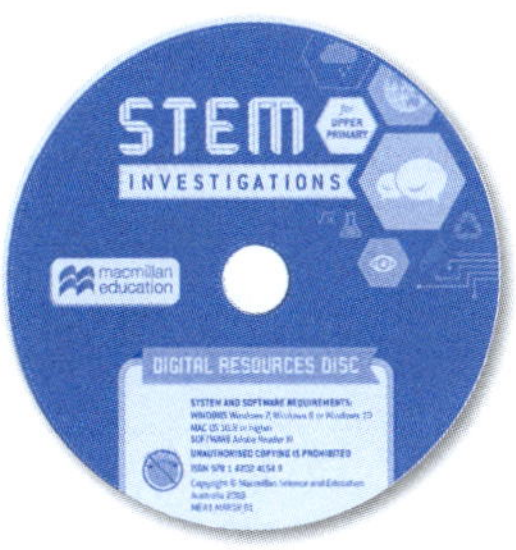

Helpful resources are included on the Digital Resources Disc, including PDFs of the student cards and Teacher Resource Book, templates so that educators can create their own STEM projects, and learning journal templates that can be printed or filled in electronically by students.

STEM SKILLS AND KNOWLEDGE, IN SCHOOL AND BEYOND

Discussions about the role of STEM in schools are ongoing, involving academics, business leaders and educators. Concern is widespread about the low levels of engagement in STEM subjects at school and university, and about poor performance compared with other countries, and the potential impact that this might have on the economic outlook. At the same time, there is real growth in STEM-related job opportunities, particularly in the fields of information and communications technology (ICT) and engineering.

THE BENEFITS OF BUILDING STEM SKILLS AND KNOWLEDGE

STEM knowledge and skills drive innovation and are important for economic growth, today and in the future. Employers are seeking graduates with a range of transdisciplinary skills, such as those developed in STEM subjects, and will continue to do so. In order to ensure today's students have the required skills for a changing future, schools need to develop students' STEM knowledge and skills from an early age. *STEM Investigations* offers a way to develop students' interdisciplinary STEM thinking.

The benefits of STEM are not just in the knowledge and skills specific to the individual disciplines of STEM. Benefits also include the learnings developed through the interplay of two or more of the STEM areas, as well as the development of general capabilities such as Critical and Creative Thinking.

Another benefit of engagement in STEM education is the development of collaborative skills. *STEM Investigations* encourages collaboration through small group work and regular peer feedback, and also through opportunities to interact with and interview school and local community members as part of the design thinking process.

Schools are addressing STEM competencies and attitudes in many different ways. Some programs incorporate the Arts and are referred to as STEAM or other similar acronyms. Many of the STEM investigations in this resource require artistic or visual design input.

THE IMPORTANCE OF REAL-WORLD RELEVANCE

As well as developing STEM knowledge and skills, students need to be aware of the importance of STEM in their lives. Many students perceive STEM subjects as too difficult or even irrelevant. Students are naturally curious from an early age. Harnessing and nurturing this curiosity throughout the primary years may lead to students having greater levels of confidence to engage with STEM subjects in secondary and tertiary education.

STEM Investigations tackles the issue of relevance by presenting authentic contexts. Real-world investigations provide students with opportunities to apply their knowledge and skills through sustained investigation and provide learning experiences that increase students' ability to transfer theoretical knowledge to the real world. Authentic experiences allow students to develop the four domains of learning:

- **cognitive** (associated with developing problem-solving skills)
- **affective** (relating to emotion and feeling)
- **psychomotor** (including expressing ideas through physical movement)
- **conative** (to do with striving and effort).

Authentic learning incorporates collaborative practices with opportunities for reflection, scaffolding and feedback at key points. *STEM Investigations for Upper Primary* provides authentic challenges that can be modified to consider the unique context and interests of the students and address such things as local conservation issues.

STEM AND THE WORKFORCE

Today, the STEM workforce covers a diverse range of jobs, including scientific and technical services, manufacturing, public administration and safety, and education and training. The unemployment rate for STEM-qualified adults is lower than for people with no STEM qualifications.

STEM jobs are growing at a faster rate than non-STEM jobs, and many current primary students will, in the future, work in STEM jobs that have not even been imagined today. The many benefits of a STEM education will be obvious, regardless of the future career a student chooses. Even employers in sectors that are not STEM focused value the skill set of STEM-qualified professionals. *STEM Investigations for Upper Primary* helps prepare students for the workforce of the future.

USEFUL RESOURCES

- **ACARA STEM report:** resources.australiancurriculum.edu.au/stemreport?section=15
- **STEM NSW resources, Australia:** stem-nsw.com.au
- **Students First, Australian Government initiative:** education.gov.au/support-science-technology-engineering-and-mathematics
- **STEM Learning UK resources:** stem.org.uk
- **The STEM Strategy, UK:** education-ni.gov.uk/articles/stem-strategy
- **STEM education data, National Science Foundation, USA:** nsf.gov/nsb/sei/edTool
- **Science, Technology, Engineering & Math (STEM), National Education Association, USA:** nea.org/home/stem.html
- **STEM education resources, New Zealand:** stemtec.aut.ac.nz/resources

THE DESIGN THINKING PROCESS

Design thinking is a process for developing solutions to problems. The design thinking process involves considering different points of view, exploring possibilities, thinking broadly but also within the scope of a challenge, and creating a solution that meets the needs of the people, group or organisation with the original problem.

Some of the key skills students develop through engagement with the design thinking process are:

- **observational skills** – learning to look carefully, make observations and identify patterns and trends
- **empathy** – considering something from different points of view
- **flexible thinking** – willingness to change ideas, opinions and solutions
- **narrative skills** – using language effectively to create a story to explain an issue, process, solution or product
- **creative thinking** – using imagination to generate a range of diverse ideas and solutions
- **evaluation skills** – reflecting on engagement with content, processes and product, and making constructive suggestions
- **synthesising skills** – using imagination to create new ideas, solutions and products
- **collaboration** – working with others, considering different ideas and opinions, compromising and being committed to a group task.

→ THE FIVE STAGES OF THE DESIGN THINKING PROCESS

There are many variations of the design thinking process. All involve creative solution-based thinking, but the stages of the process vary. The version used in *STEM Investigations for Upper Primary* was made famous by the Stanford University Design School, which used it to scaffold their students' learning and design approach. Five design thinking stages are used in *STEM Investigations for Upper Primary*: empathise, define, ideate, prototype and test.

EMPATHISE

During this stage, students focus on finding out different points of view. They look for patterns and trends in the information they initially find out.

DEFINE

The main focus of this stage is reframing the challenge. The initial challenge is usually quite open, so at this stage students learn how to define what needs to be done. This includes noting insights that have been generated.

IDEATE

The Ideate stage is all about generating lots of ideas. Students need to be flexible in their thinking and able to move beyond obvious ideas. At this stage, ideas are not judged; just generated and gathered.

PROTOTYPE

At this stage, students are asked to create a physical prototype of a solution. It is the stage where students need to get their ideas out of their heads and present them in a way that engages other students and helps them to understand the concept. When students create, it helps them to think and solve problems and disagreements. Students can role-play, make storyboards or use sticky notes. The most important feature is that viewers can interact with whatever is produced.

TEST

At this stage, students test their prototype to see if it meets the requirements of the audience or users. Students check to see if their prototype meets the criteria set at the start of the design process. They are given the opportunity to cycle through the Prototype and Test stages again.

USEFUL RESOURCES

- **Stanford University Design School:** dschool.stanford.edu
- **A Virtual Crash Course in Design Thinking:** dschool.stanford.edu/resources-collections/a-virtual-crash-course-in-design-thinking

UNDERSTANDING AND USING STEM VOCABULARY

The understanding and use of terms relating to an area of study, whether it be Science, Mathematics or another discipline, are incredibly important. Specific vocabulary is used to describe abstract scientific concepts, such as 'reversible' and 'absorption'. Discipline-specific vocabulary is also used to describe specific concrete objects, such as the science terms 'pipette' and 'LED'. One of the strengths of *STEM Investigations* is its emphasis on subject-specific vocabulary growth, which will result in improved comprehension and engagement.

ORAL LANGUAGE

Oral vocabulary has a key role in the development of comprehension and literacy skills. Rich oral language experiences are critical for vocabulary growth. Opportunities for speaking new vocabulary are a vital part of the vocabulary learning process, not only for general vocabulary acquisition but also for general academic vocabulary development. Students need multiple opportunities to read and use words in multiple contexts in order to own the words they see, hear and use (Forwood, 2013).

LEVELS OF KNOWING VOCABULARY

Words are not simply known or unknown. Dale (1965) outlined four stages of vocabulary development, ranging from no knowledge of a word to an ability to use and remember a word. These stages were later placed on a continuum by Stahl (1999), whereby students moved between no knowledge of a word's meaning to full and flexible knowledge of a word's meaning. Each of the four components makes a long-term contribution to vocabulary growth. Developing a deep understanding of new terms is a gradual process and requires students to be able to use words in different contexts.

The four levels of knowing vocabulary are:

DON'T KNOW THE WORD → HEARD OF THE WORD BUT DON'T KNOW WHAT IT MEANS → KNOW THE MEANING OF THE WORD IN ONE CONTEXT → KNOW THE MEANING OF THE WORD IN MULTIPLE CONTEXTS

VOCABULARY AND COMPREHENSION

Students need to know at least 95 per cent of words in a text in order to engage with and understand it (Schmitt, Jiang & Grabe, 2011). Science, along with History and Geography, is one of the subject areas with the highest number of subject-specific, or technical, terms. Many scientific terms are infrequently used and rarely used beyond the classroom.

Considerable research has shown that vocabulary levels are linked to general comprehension, reading comprehension, high-level thinking skills and attitude to school. Isabel Beck's three-tier model of vocabulary (see page 10) divides words into three levels (Beck & McKeown, 1985).

THREE-TIER MODEL OF VOCABULARY

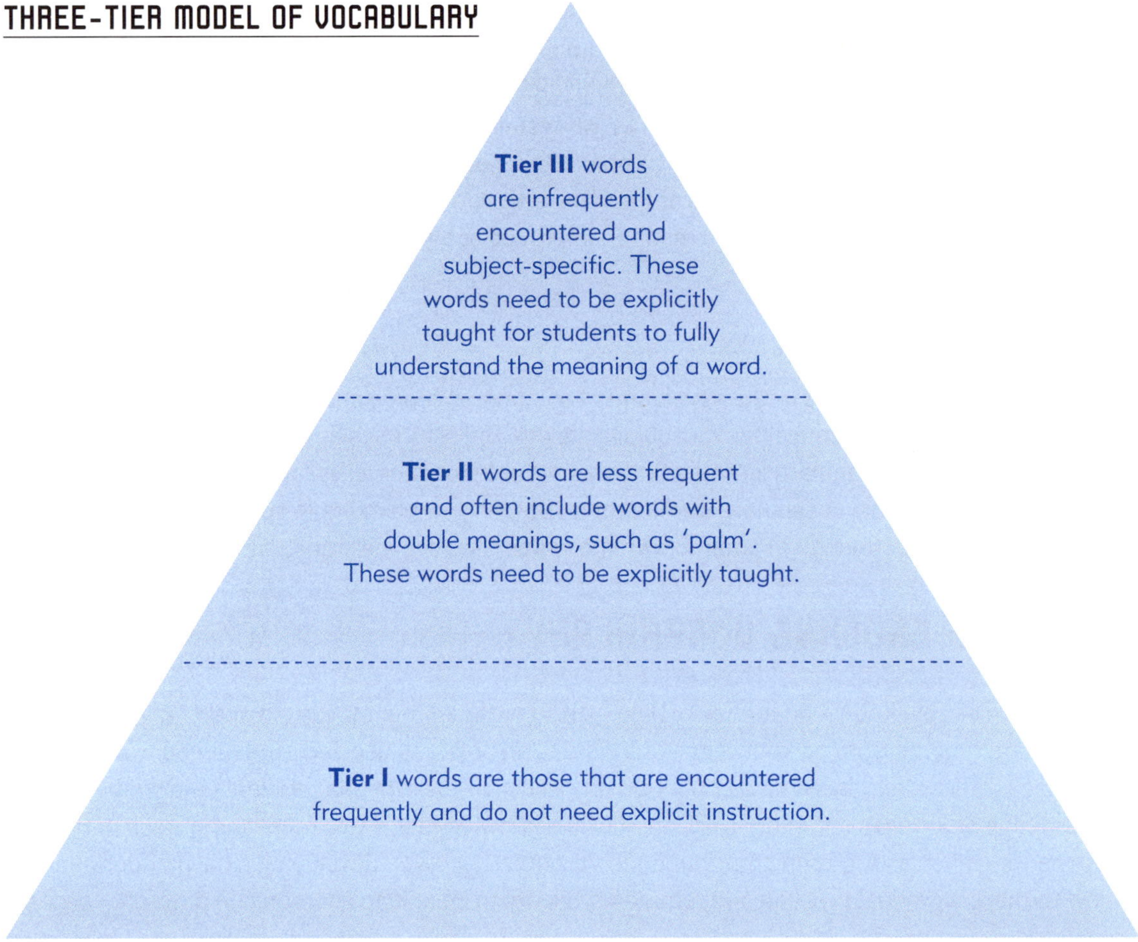

Understanding a word is more than just knowing its meaning. Understanding is also about knowing a word's associations with other words; for example, its category, synonyms, antonyms and word family. Students need multiple exposures to words, over time. They need to hear, see and write new words. Most importantly, words must be verbalised in order to be stored and retrieved correctly.

Students also need a well-developed vocabulary to use the high-level thinking skills necessary for developing STEM-related skills. A broad internalised vocabulary is important for a student to think about their thinking (metacognition) and articulate their ideas and observations with precision.

→ CONCEPTUAL AND INSTRUCTIONAL VOCABULARY

Understanding of conceptual and instructional science vocabulary has been linked to student attitudes to science. *STEM Investigations* explicitly teaches key instructional and conceptual vocabulary relating to each investigation, encouraging enhanced student engagement with the topic.

→ PRE-TESTING AND POST-TESTING VOCABULARY

STEM Investigations pre-tests key vocabulary knowledge at the Tune-in stage of each investigation and post-tests the same vocabulary at the Share and evaluate stage. Pre-testing understanding of key vocabulary relating to a unit of work provides information about the level of understanding of terminology for individual students, as well as that of the whole class. This can assist with targeting specific words for explicit instruction and additional practice. Including a post-test of the same words at the end of a unit of work provides students with tangible evidence of their learning and is also a way for teachers to monitor progress.

→ WAYS OF DEVELOPING VOCABULARY AND ORAL LANGUAGE

As already highlighted, it is important to develop students' STEM-related vocabulary and oral language skills. The following suggestions can support this skill development.

Marzano and Pickering (2005) provide a useful framework for building subject-specific vocabulary in their book *Building Academic Vocabulary: Teacher's Manual*. First, new words need to be discussed, with anecdotes and examples provided. Then students should write their own description of a word's meaning before drawing a picture or symbol that links to the word. The next stage is to compare terms, through different activities.

STEM Investigations can be used to develop subject-specific vocabulary in the following ways:

- **Key vocabulary list**: Before beginning a new unit of work, gauge students' understandings of words by providing them with a list of key words and asking them to indicate their level of understanding (see **Generic reproducible 1 – Key vocabulary table**).
- **Discuss and examine terms**: After the words have been identified, discuss them, providing anecdotes and examples. Then ask students to write their own description of a word's meaning before drawing a picture or symbol that links to the word.
- **Compare terms**: Various activities can be used to compare terms (see example activities below, such as sentence stems and semantic gradients).
- **Review words**: After students have been provided with opportunities to explore new words, they should review their initial descriptions and revise them, where relevant.

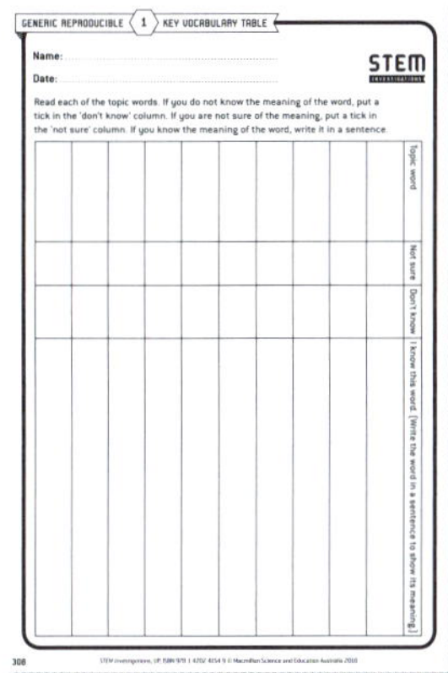
GENERIC REPRODUCIBLE 1 KEY VOCABULARY TABLE

STEM INVESTIGATIONS

Name:

Date:

Read each of the topic words. If you do not know the meaning of the word, put a tick in the 'don't know' column. If you are not sure of the meaning, put a tick in the 'not sure' column. If you know the meaning of the word, write it in a sentence.

Topic word	Not sure	Don't know	I know this word. (Write the word in a sentence to show its meaning.)

308

▲ Generic reproducible 1

SENTENCE STEMS

Use sentence stems such as 'These two words are similar because' and 'These two words are different because'. For example:

'Hot' and 'cold' are similar because they are both to do with temperature.
'Hot' and 'cold' are different because 'hot' relates to a high temperature and 'cold' relates to a low temperature.

SEMANTIC GRADIENTS

Sort words according to 'degrees' of meaning. For example:

hottest/boiling, warm, lukewarm, cold, freezing/coldest

DOUBLE BUBBLE

Identify similarities and differences between words (see **Generic reproducible 7 – Double bubble**).

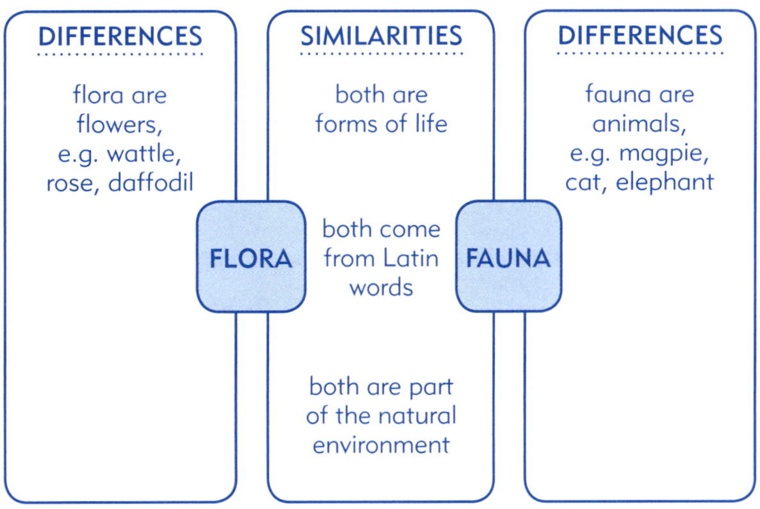

Double Bubble activity ▶

SEMANTIC MAPS

Make connections between the key word and other words or phrases.

▼ Semantic map

VOCABULARY HEXAGONS

Create a paper-based or software-generated mind map, or provide students with several copies of **Generic reproducible 8 – Vocabulary hexagons**. Students write each word they have generated onto a hexagon. They cut out and arrange the hexagons to connect related words. Create a wall display with the words and concepts. Students can add hexagons as they learn more related words and concepts.

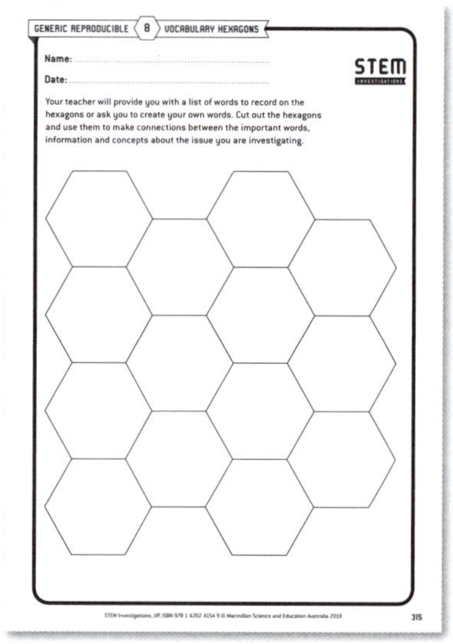
GENERIC REPRODUCIBLE 8 VOCABULARY HEXAGONS

STEM

Name:

Date:

Your teacher will provide you with a list of words to record on the hexagons or ask you to create your own words. Cut out the hexagons and use them to make connections between the important words, information and concepts about the issue you are investigating.

▲ Generic reproducible 8

OTHER WORD GAMES

Many word games can be played to increase word knowledge and consciousness. For examples, see the free vocabulary resources at the Marzano Research website.

REFERENCES AND RESOURCES

- Beck, IL & McKeown, MG 1985, 'Teaching vocabulary: Making the instruction fit the goal', *Educational Perspectives*, vol. 23(1), pp. 11–15
- Carrier, SJ, *Effective Strategies for Teaching Science Vocabulary*, learnnc.org/lp/pages/7079
- Dale, E 1965, 'Vocabulary measurement: Techniques and major findings', *Elementary English*, vol. 42, pp. 395–401
- Forwood, C 2013, 'Investigating Differences in Understanding of Vocabulary in Secondary Science', Curtin University of Technology, Perth, Australia, hdl.handle.net/20.500.11937/218
- Marzano, RJ & Carleton, L 2010, *Vocabulary Games for the Classroom*. Bloomington, IN: Marzano Research Laboratory
- Marzano, RJ, *Vocabulary Games for the Classroom Reproducibles*, Marzano Research, marzanoresearch.com/reproducibles/vocabulary_games
- Marzano, RJ & Pickering, DJ 2005, *Building Academic Vocabulary: Teacher's Manual*, Alexandria, VA: Association for Supervision and Curriculum Development
- Reading Rockets, *STEM Literacy*, readingrockets.org/reading-topics/stem-literacy
- Schmitt, N, Jiang X, & Grabe, W 2011, 'The percentage of words known in a text and reading comprehension', *The Modern Language Journal*, vol. 95(1), pp. 26–43. DOI: 10.1111/j.1540-4781.2011.01146.x
- Stahl, SA 1999, *Vocabulary Development*, Brookline, MA: Brookline Books

USING *STEM INVESTIGATIONS*

STEM Investigations **brings together three elements – student cards, a Teacher Resource Book and a Digital Resources Disc – to facilitate 20 individual investigations for Upper Primary students.**

Each investigation includes a set of student cards, which outline the challenge, the key learning, the important vocabulary and the main focus for each stage of the design thinking process. The accompanying Teacher Resource Book provides a framework for each of the 20 STEM investigations, including a range of resources and tasks to support the development of critical and creative thinking skills, design thinking skills, practical literacy and numeracy, visual literacy and digital technology use. The Digital Resources Disc contains digital copies of reproducibles, templates and rubrics, plus links to curated, third-party digital resources, to help teachers guide students through the investigations.

STUDENT CARDS

Each investigation consists of six copies of a double-sided student card. The card presents the challenge and guides students through the design thinking process.

The challenge Gives the challenge parameters and general guidance, including questions to consider. Also outlines the key scientific learning linked to the task.

Investigation name

Investigation theme

Investigation number

Key actions
Gives an overview of the main actions students will be expected to perform. Actions may also form part of student assessment.

Key vocabulary
Lists key terms that are important for understanding the concepts explored in the investigation. Definitions and ideas for developing challenge-related vocabulary are provided in the Teacher Resource Book.

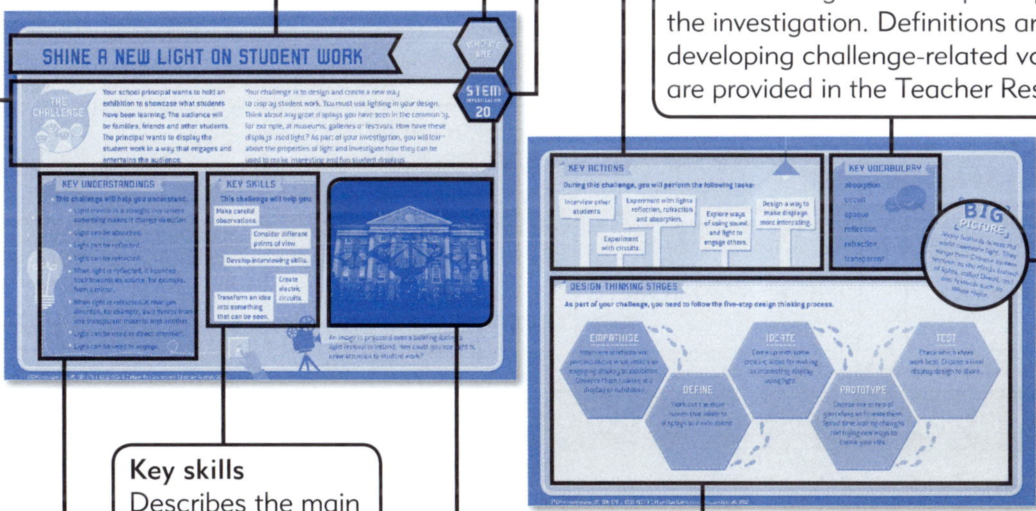

Key skills
Describes the main skills that will be developed. Also provides general information about the skills that will be assessed, formally or informally.

Image
Engages and hooks students into the investigation.

Big picture
A relevant quirky or light-hearted snippet of information that will spark student interest.

Key understandings Identifies the key curriculum-linked understandings associated with the challenge.

Design thinking stages
Gives an overview of the main activities associated with each stage of the design thinking process.

→ TEACHER RESOURCE BOOK

The Teacher Resource Book provides teachers with background information about each of the investigations, as well as structured activities and resources to teach the key concepts required for students to complete the challenge.

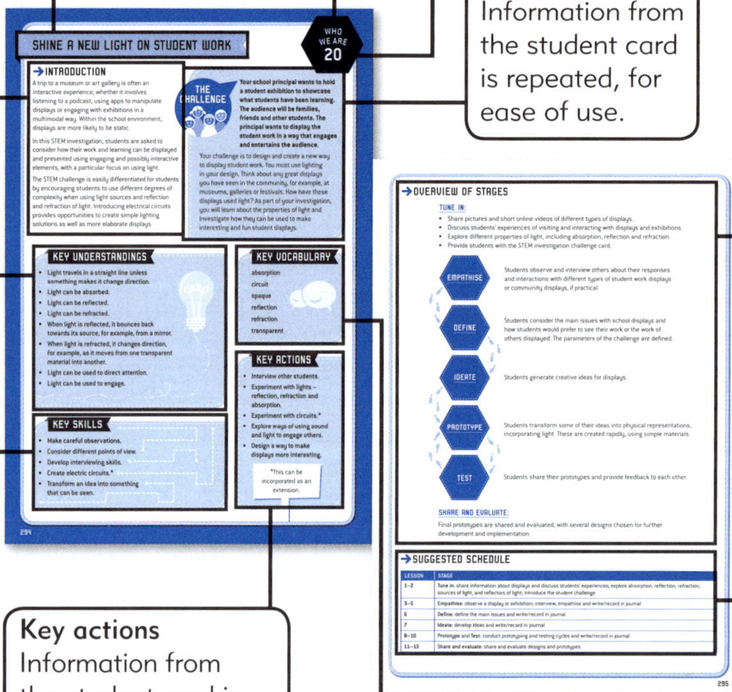

Investigation name

Investigation theme

Investigation number

Introduction
Gives background information relating to the challenge, including the focus of the investigation.

The challenge
Information from the student card is repeated, for ease of use.

Overview of stages
Gives an overview of the design thinking stages, with key actions for the investigation highlighted. Also gives an overview of the main components of the Tune-in stage, plus a final evaluation stage.

Key understandings
Information from the student card is repeated, for ease of use. Identifies the key curriculum-linked understandings associated with the challenge.

Key skills
Information from the student card is repeated, for ease of use. Describes the main skills that will be developed. Also provides general information about the skills that will be assessed, formally or informally.

Key actions
Information from the student card is repeated, for ease of use. Gives an overview of the main actions students will be expected to perform. Actions may also form part of student assessment.

Key vocabulary
Lists the key vocabulary from the student card, which are defined later, on the **Key science knowledge** page.

Suggested schedule
Helps teachers timetable the investigation. The initial sessions tune in the students to the investigation and introduce and/or develop the key science concepts required for the investigation. The rest of the sessions involve exploring, creating, evaluating and sharing solutions.

LESSON PLANNING AND DIFFERENTIATION

Each STEM investigation should take 12 to 16 sessions, depending on its scope, and the investigation can be completed over an extended period of time. This allows students time to reflect between sessions. Alternatively, the investigations could be completed as an intensive program of work over a one- or two-week period, although this depends on the focus of the investigation. Some investigations may require a specific amount of time to observe changes, such as growing plants.

The open-ended nature of each STEM investigation lends itself to differentiation. The initial sessions are clearly scaffolded to develop understanding of key science concepts, and they set up the criteria and limitations of the challenges clearly. The design thinking process provides scope to work at a pace and level suitable to individual skill and interest levels while still engaging in collaborative tasks.

INVESTIGATION THEMES

The 20 STEM investigations are grouped into five themes for ease of use and navigation:

- **BUILT WORLD** Topics such as simple machines, design of buildings, town planning and transportation
- **MANAGED WORLD** Topics such as human-made systems, communities and manufacturing.
- **NATURAL WORLD** Topics such as animal and plant life cycles, animal adaptations, geological changes, extreme events and chemical science
- **SUSTAINABLE WORLD** Topics such as sharing finite resources, interactions between the natural world and human societies, and global sustainability issues
- **WHO WE ARE** Topics such as human rights and responsibilities, community and cultural beliefs and values, social organisations, health issues, and art and creativity

Curriculum links
Lists major STEM links, along with links to other parts of the curriculum.

Getting ready for the investigation
A checklist to consider before beginning the investigation with students. Includes considerations for organisation, grouping of students, storage of materials for construction, sourcing of materials and preparation of resources.

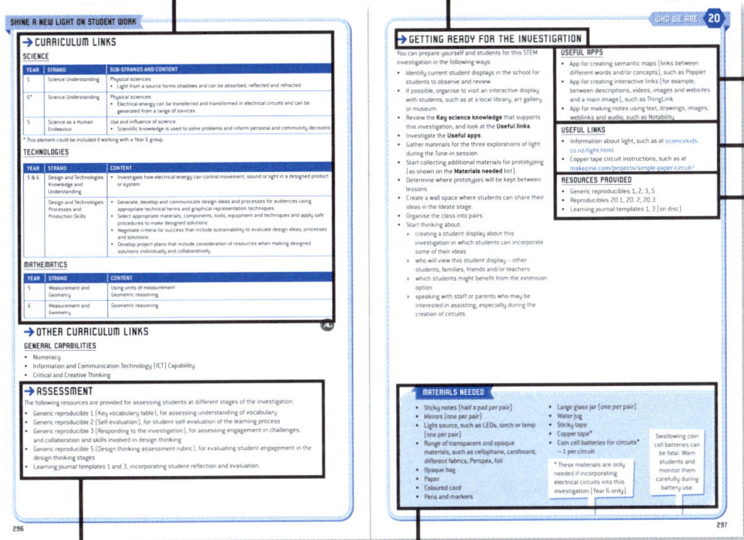

Useful apps
Suggests specific apps, but alternatives can be substituted. Most recommendations are free, although some require sign-up. In these cases, a class account could be created by the teacher to cover any age limitations.

Useful links
Provides links to third-party resources, including texts, images and videos that can be incorporated into activities.

Assessment resources
Lists resources for assessing students at different stages of the investigation.

Materials needed
Lists materials required for activities and to make prototypes or models.

Resources provided
Lists all generic reproducibles, investigation-specific reproducibles and learning journal templates used in the investigation.

Key science knowledge
An overview of the key science knowledge that is required for the investigation. Provides descriptions and elaborations of key concepts, as well as images, diagrams and infographics.

Tune-in session
Establishes students' prior knowledge and understanding of key concepts and vocabulary. Introduces the key understandings involved in the challenge.

Activities
Used to develop understanding of the key scientific concepts required for the challenge.

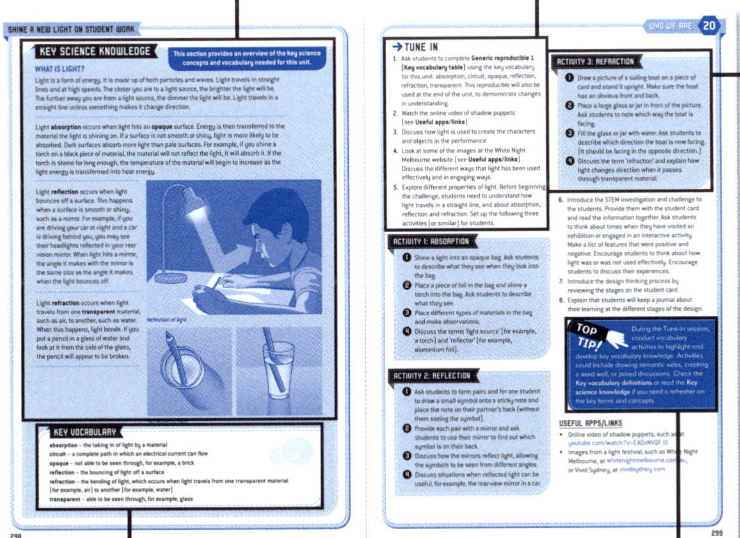

Key vocabulary
Definitions of key terms.

Top tip
Offers advice and tips, such as further activities and helpful resources.

BEGINNING THE INVESTIGATION

It is important to establish students' current knowledge and understandings of concepts and terminology at the start of the investigation. This will give teachers an insight into the prior knowledge students are bringing to the challenge.

At the Tune-in stage, students are asked to indicate their level of understanding of key conceptual and/or instructional vocabulary relating to the investigation. Following a Tune-in session or two, students are provided with a student card outlining their investigation. It is useful to review each section of the student card and link the information provided to the investigation.

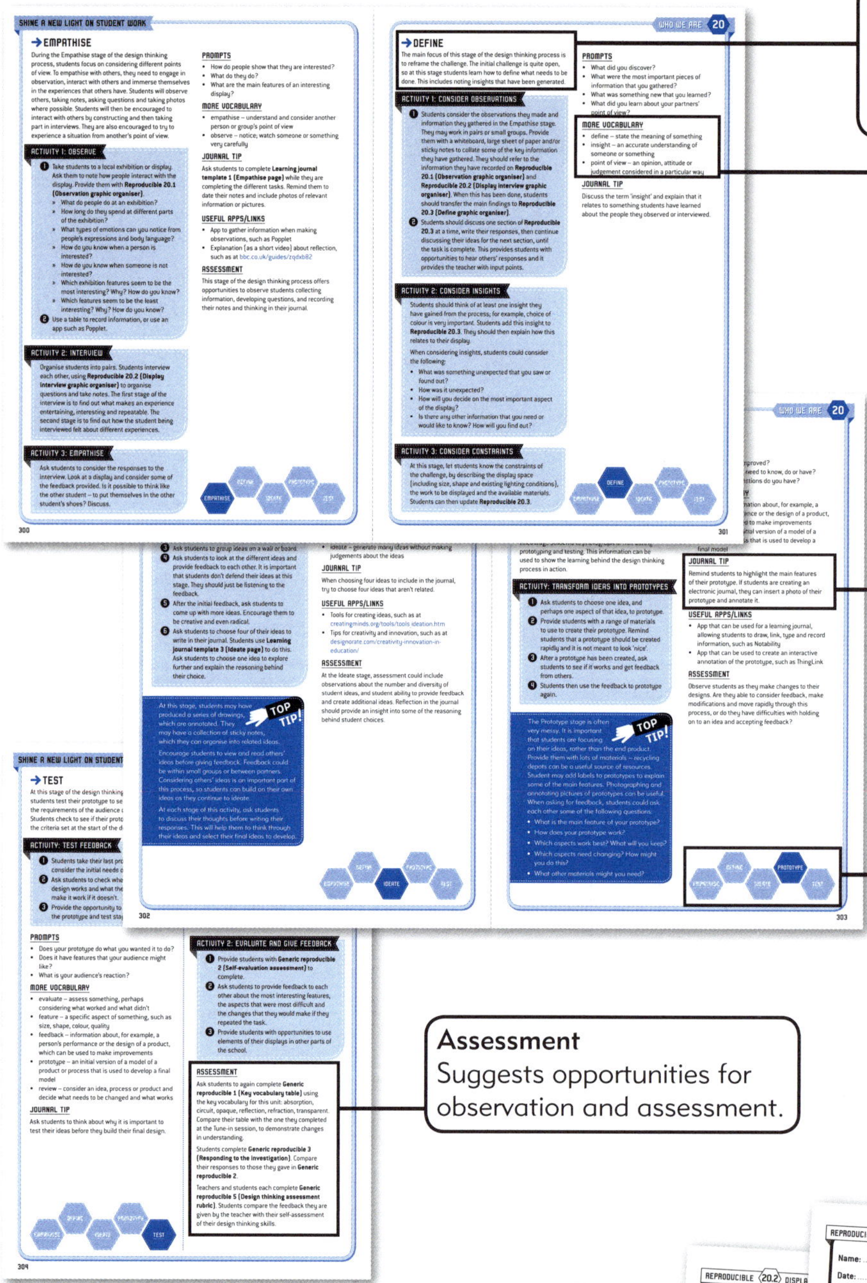

Design thinking stages
Each stage includes activities, including reproducible activity sheets and prompts.

More vocabulary
Defines design thinking vocabulary.

Journal tip
Students complete a learning journal template at each stage to show what they are learning and how they are reflecting on their learning.

Design thinking diagram
Shows what stage the student is at in the design thinking process.

Assessment
Suggests opportunities for observation and assessment.

REPRODUCIBLES

Investigation-specific reproducibles are included with the relevant investigation. Generic reproducibles and assessment rubrics can be found at the end of the Teacher Resource Book (see table opposite).

Each of the reproducibles can be used as an assessment task. These can be assessed informally, through observation and anecdotal records, or using rubrics, peer evaluation or self-evaluation.

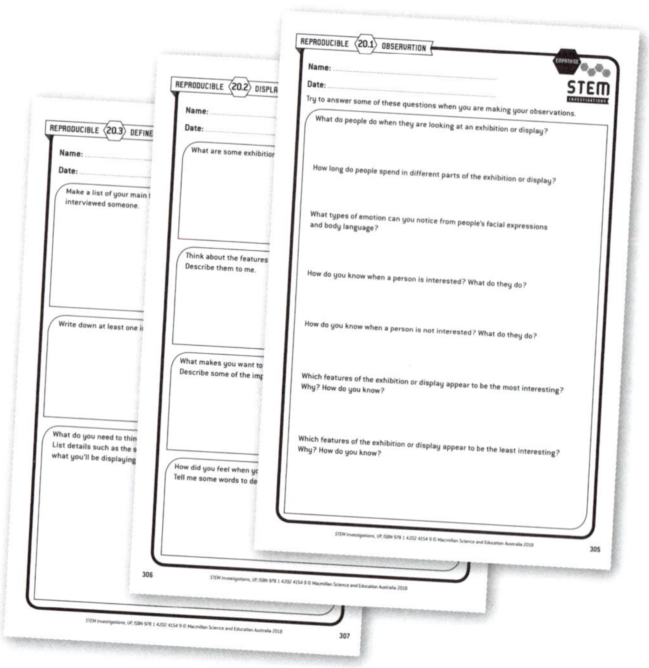

Generic reproducible number	Generic reproducible name	Description
1	Key vocabulary table	Used by students at the start and end of the investigation to determine their level of understanding of key vocabulary relating to the investigation. It provides tangible evidence of vocabulary development over the course of the investigation.
2	Self-evaluation	Focuses on the content, learning process and products produced with the investigation. Resources cater for a variety of purposes and student ability. Focuses on how a student's learning has changed, helps them evaluate their end product and provides them with the opportunity to consider improvements.
3	Responding to the investigation	Focuses on the content, learning process and products produced with the investigation. Resources cater for a variety of purposes and student ability. Focuses on feedback about the investigation topic and the design thinking process.
4	Key question table	Provides a template for guiding research. Students create micro-questions prior to beginning their research. These assist students to engage in focused searches by providing key words. The template provides space for note-taking and recording the source of information.
5	Design thinking assessment rubric	Used to evaluate student engagement in the different design thinking stages throughout the investigation.
6	In the frame	Used by students to assist with classifying and identifying relevant ideas.
7	Double bubble*	Used by students to scaffold comparisons between two objects, concepts or ideas. Students identify both similarities and differences.
8	Vocabulary hexagons**	Used by students to demonstrate their understandings of the relationships between words or concepts.
9	See, think, wonder***	Used by students when making observations and interpreting the information they see.
10	Group task organiser	Assists students to organise roles when completing collaborative tasks.

* A term coined by David Hyerle: dft.designsforthinking.com

** A SOLO Hexagons app is now available

*** A thinking routine from Harvard University's Project Zero: Visible Thinking: visiblethinkingpz.org.

DIGITAL RESOURCES DISC

The Digital Resources Disc includes PDFs of the cards and Teacher Resource Book, templates so that educators can create their own STEM projects, learning journal templates and a glossary booklet.

Learning journal templates
Can be printed out and filled in by students, or PDFs can be filled in electronically.

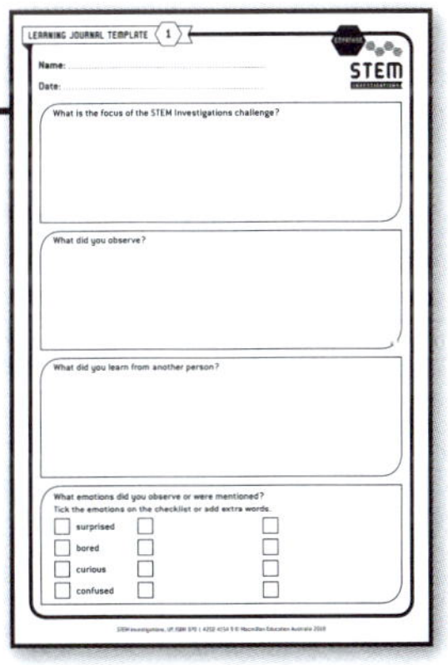

Digital Resources Disc

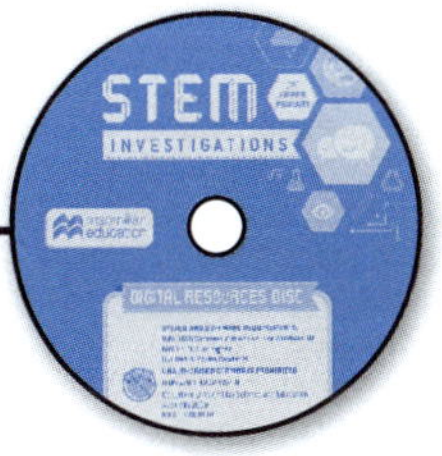

Glossary booklet

LEARNING JOURNAL TEMPLATES

Students can document and evaluate their learning at each stage of the investigation using the learning journal templates. They can be used to provide evidence of students' learning across the investigation.

Template number	Learning journal stage	Description
1	Empathise	Used by students to record some of the observations they make at the start of the investigation. They describe some of the things they have learned at the start of the investigation.
2	Define	Used by students to define the investigation by identifying relevant insights and actions.
3	Ideate	Used by students to record four different ideas that they have generated during the Ideate stage of the investigation.
4	Prototype and Test	Used by students to choose one idea to develop and test. They record their evaluations, as well as feedback from others.

INVESTIGATION OVERVIEWS AND CURRICULUM LINKS

THEME	NO.	PAGE	INVESTIGATION OVERVIEW	RESOURCES PROVIDED	SCIENCE CURRICULUM ALIGNMENT			TECHNOLOGY AND ENGINEERING CURRICULUM ALIGNMENT		MATHEMATICS CURRICULUM ALIGNMENT	OTHER CURRICULUM LINKS
					SCIENCE UNDERSTANDING	SCIENCE AS A HUMAN ENDEAVOUR	SCIENCE INQUIRY SKILLS	DIGITAL TECHNOLOGIES	DESIGN AND TECHNOLOGIES		
BUILT WORLD	**1**	22	**Chicken coop: yes or no?** In this STEM investigation, students are challenged to create a design for a chicken coop and consider the potential site for their coop. As part of the investigation, they will learn about different breeds of chickens, egg production, and animal welfare.	• Generic reproducibles 1, 2, 3 5 • Reproducibles 1.1, 1.2, 1.3 • Learning journal templates 1, 2, 3, 4 (on disc)	**Biological Sciences:** Living things have structural features and adaptations that help them to survive in their environment (Year 5) The growth and survival of living things are affected by physical conditions of their environment (Year 6)	✓		✓	✓	Number and Algebra Measurement and Geometry	**General Capabilities:** Literacy, Numeracy, Critical and creative thinking **Cross-curriculum priority:** Sustainability
BUILT WORLD	**2**	36	**Save the river from run-off ruin** In this STEM investigation, students are challenged to create a process or design that will help reduce erosion on a riverbank. As part of the investigation, they explore the process of erosion and the impact it can have on waterways and how wind and water affect the Earth's surface.	• Generic reproducibles 1, 2, 3, 5 • Reproducibles 2.1, 2.2, 2.3 • Learning journal templates 1, 2, 3, 4 (on disc)	**Earth and Space Sciences:** Sudden geological changes or extreme weather conditions can affect Earth's surface (Year 6)	✓	✓		✓	Number and Algebra	**General Capabilities:** Literacy, Numeracy, Information and Communication Technology (ICT) Capability, Critical and Creative Thinking
BUILT WORLD	**3**	50	**Design a quake-resistant building** In this STEM investigation, students are challenged to design and build a model of an earthquake-resistant building. As part of the investigation, they will find out about the structure of the Earth, the cause of earthquakes, flexible buildings and important features to think about when designing earthquake-resistant buildings.	• Generic reproducibles 1, 2, 3, 4, 5 • Reproducibles 3.1, 3.2, 3.3 • Learning journal templates 1, 2, 3, 4 (on disc)	**Earth and Space Sciences:** Sudden geological changes or extreme weather conditions can affect Earth's surface (Year 6)	✓	✓		✓	Measurement and Geometry	**General Capabilities:** Literacy, Numeracy, Information and Communication Technology (ICT) Capability, Critical and Creative Thinking
BUILT WORLD	**4**	64	**Plan a building that pleases the neighbours** In this STEM investigation, students are challenged to design a building that will cast the least amount of shadow, and test and model a prototype. As part of the investigation, they will learn about the relationship between light, objects and shadows.	• Generic reproducibles 1, 2, 3, 4, 5, 6 • Reproducibles 4.1, 4.2, 4.3, 4.4, 4.5 • Learning journal templates 1, 2, 3, 4 (on disc)	**Physical Sciences:** Light from a source forms shadows and can be absorbed, reflected and refracted (Year 5) **Earth and Space Sciences:** The Earth is part of a system of planets orbiting around a star (the Sun) (Year 5)	✓	✓		✓	Measurement and Geometry	**General Capabilities:** Literacy, Numeracy, Information and Communication Technology (ICT) Capability, Critical and Creative Thinking
MANAGED WORLD	**5**	80	**Invent a helpful product for a homeless person** In this STEM investigation, students are challenged to create a helpful product for a homeless person that has two purposes. Students learn about some of the issues associated with homelessness. As part of the investigation, they will learn about the production of natural materials and synthetic materials, and consider issues of sustainability.	• Generic reproducibles 1, 2, 3, 5 • Reproducibles 5.1, 5.2, 5.3 • Learning journal templates 1, 2, 3, 4 (on disc)	**Chemical Sciences:** Changes to materials can be reversible, such as melting, freezing and evaporating; or irreversible, such as burning and rusting (Year 6)	✓			✓	Number and Algebra Measurement and Geometry	**General Capabilities:** Literacy, Numeracy, Information and Communication Technology (ICT) Capability, Critical and creative thinking **Cross-curriculum priority:** Sustainability

THEME	NO.	PAGE	INVESTIGATION OVERVIEW	RESOURCES PROVIDED	SCIENCE CURRICULUM ALIGNMENT			TECHNOLOGY AND ENGINEERING CURRICULUM ALIGNMENT		MATHEMATICS CURRICULUM ALIGNMENT	OTHER CURRICULUM LINKS
					SCIENCE UNDERSTANDING	SCIENCE AS A HUMAN ENDEAVOUR	SCIENCE INQUIRY SKILLS	DIGITAL TECHNOLOGIES	DESIGN AND TECHNOLOGIES		
MANAGED WORLD	6	94	**Help recruit people to journey to Mars** In this STEM investigation, students are challenged to plan and create a presentation to help recruit 40 people for a mission to Mars. Their presentation must include designs for at least two living areas on the space craft. As part of the investigation, they will learn about the system of planets in our solar system, space travel and the impact of living beyond the Earth's atmosphere.	• Generic reproducibles 1, 2, 3, 5 • Reproducibles 6.1, 6.2, 6.3 • Learning journal templates 1, 2, 3, 4 (on disc)	**Earth and Space Sciences:** The Earth is part of a system of planets orbiting around a star (the Sun) (Year 5)	✓			✓	Number and Algebra Measurement and Geometry	**General Capabilities:** Literacy, Numeracy, Critical and Creative Thinking
MANAGED WORLD	7	108	**Power up your school disco!** In this STEM investigation, students are challenged to design one or two electrical circuits that can be used to run the lighting and sound at a disco, using a battery connected to a solar panel. As part of the investigation, they will learn about electrical circuits, conductors and insulators, as well as the best way to design and draw the parts of a circuit.	• Generic reproducibles 1, 2, 3, 4, 5 • Reproducibles 7.1, 7.2, 7.3 • Learning journal templates 1, 2, 3, 4 (on disc)	**Physical Sciences:** Electrical energy can be transferred and transformed in electrical circuits and can be generated from a range of sources (Year 6)	✓			✓	Measurement and Geometry	**General Capabilities:** Literacy, Numeracy, Information and Communication Technology (ICT) Capability, Critical and creative thinking
MANAGED WORLD	8	122	**Promote a business using bubbles** In this STEM investigation, students are challenged to design and build structured bubble modules that could stack together to make a display bubble castle. As part of the investigation, they will learn about the science of bubble solutions, the elasticity of bubbles, and surface tension.	• Generic reproducibles 1, 2, 3, 4, 5, 6, 9 • Reproducibles 8.1, 8.2, 8.3, 8.4, 8.5 • Learning journal templates 1, 2, 3, 4 (on disc)	**Chemical Sciences:** Solids, liquids and gases have different observable properties and behave in different ways (Year 5) Changes to materials can be reversible, such as melting, freezing, evaporating; or irreversible, such as burning and rusting (Year 6)	✓	✓	✓	✓	Measurement and Geometry	**General Capabilities:** Literacy, Numeracy, Information and Communication Technology (ICT) Capability, Critical and Creative Thinking
NATURAL WORLD	9	138	**Grow 'fast food' to sell at market** In this STEM investigation, students are challenged to design and create a greenhouse that will help them grow fast-growing plants to sell at market. As part of the investigation, they will learn how the growth and survival of living things is affected by the physical conditions of their environment.	• Generic reproducibles 1, 2, 3, 4, 5, 6 • Reproducibles 9.1, 9.2, 9.3 • Learning journal templates 1, 2, 3, 4 (on disc)	**Biological Sciences:** Living things have structural features and adaptations that help them to survive in their environment (Year 5) The growth and survival of living things are affected by physical conditions of their environment (Year 6)	✓	✓		✓	Number and Algebra Measurement and Geometry Statistics and Probability	**General Capabilities:** Literacy, Numeracy, Personal and Social Capability, Information and Communication Technology (ICT) Capability, Critical and Creative Thinking **Cross-curriculum priority:** Sustainability
NATURAL WORLD	10	152	**Make a plan to protect aquatic areas** In this STEM investigation, students investigate how a chemical contamination would affect plant and animal life within an aquatic environment and then design a solution to deal with the effects of this environmental disaster. As part of the investigation, they will learn about the importance of water for all living organisms and the effects of chemical spills.	• Generic reproducibles 1, 2, 3, 4, 5, 6, 8, 9 • Reproducibles 10.1, 10.2, 10.3 • Learning journal templates 1, 2, 3, 4 (on disc)	**Chemical Sciences:** Solids, liquids and gases have different observable properties and behave in different ways (Year 5) Changes to materials can be reversible, such as melting, freezing, evaporating; or irreversible, such as burning and rusting (Year 6) **Biological Sciences:** The growth and survival of living things are affected by physical conditions of their environment (Year 6)	✓	✓		✓	Statistics and Probability	**General Capabilities:** Literacy, Numeracy, Personal and Social Capability, Information and Communication Technology (ICT) Capability, Critical and Creative Thinking

THEME	NO.	PAGE	INVESTIGATION OVERVIEW	RESOURCES PROVIDED	SCIENCE CURRICULUM ALIGNMENT			TECHNOLOGY AND ENGINEERING CURRICULUM ALIGNMENT		MATHEMATICS CURRICULUM ALIGNMENT	OTHER CURRICULUM LINKS
					SCIENCE UNDERSTANDING	SCIENCE AS A HUMAN ENDEAVOUR	SCIENCE INQUIRY SKILLS	DIGITAL TECHNOLOGIES	DESIGN AND TECHNOLOGIES		
NATURAL WORLD	11	166	**Use sea water to save the village** In this STEM investigation, students are challenged to design and build a device to make safe drinking water from sea water (salt water). They must also calculate how much fresh water 13 people would need to survive for three days.	• Generic reproducibles 1, 2, 3, 4, 5 • Reproducibles 11.1, 11.2, 11.3 • Learning journal templates 1, 2, 3, 4 (on disc)	**Chemical Sciences:** Solids, liquids and gases have different observable properties and behave in different ways (Year 5) Changes to materials can be reversible, such as melting, freezing, evaporating; or irreversible, such as burning and rusting (Year 6) **Biological Sciences:** The growth and survival of living things are affected by physical conditions of their environment (Year 6)	✓	✓		✓	Number and Algebra	**General Capabilities:** Literacy, Numeracy, Personal and Social Capability, Critical and Creative Thinking
NATURAL WORLD	12	180	**Be the best weather presenter for the job** In this STEM investigation, students are challenged to put together a practical and fun weather presentation for younger students. As part of the investigation, they will learn all about extreme weather events, and the properties and behaviour of solids, liquids and gases.	• Generic reproducibles 1, 2, 3, 4, 5, 6 • Reproducibles 12.1, 12.2, 12.3 • Learning journal templates 1, 2, 3, 4 (on disc)	**Chemical Sciences:** Solids, liquids and gases have different observable properties and behave in different ways (Year 5) **Earth and Space Sciences:** Sudden geological changes and extreme weather events can affect Earth's surface (Year 6)	✓			✓	Measurement and Geometry	**General Capabilities:** Literacy, Numeracy, Information and Communication Technology (ICT) Capability, Critical and Creative Thinking
SUSTAINABLE WORLD	13	194	**Help animals cross the new road safely** In this STEM investigation, students are challenged to find a way for road designers to help animals to cross a new road. As part of the investigation, they will learn about animal habitats, food webs and ecosystems, and investigate what animals need to survive.	• Generic reproducibles 1, 2, 3, 4, 5, 6 • Reproducibles 13.1, 13.2, 13.3 • Learning journal templates 1, 2, 3, 4 (on disc)	**Biological Sciences:** Living things have structural features and adaptations that help them to survive in their environment (Year 5) The growth and survival of living things are affected by physical conditions of their environment (Year 6)	✓	✓		✓	Number and Algebra	**General Capabilities:** Literacy, Numeracy, Information and Communication Technology (ICT) Capability, Critical and Creative Thinking
SUSTAINABLE WORLD	14	208	**Create sustainable garden beds at school** In this STEM investigation, students are challenged to create a sustainable kitchen garden bed to grow food for students to use or sell. As part of the investigation, they will learn about sustainable gardening practices and how these can be applied to a school or home garden, as well as calculating capacity and volume.	• Generic reproducibles 1, 2, 3, 4, 5, 6, 9 • Reproducibles 14.1, 14.2, 14.3 • Learning journal templates 1, 2, 3, 4 (on disc)	**Biological Sciences:** Living things have structural features and adaptations that help them to survive in their environment (Year 5) The growth and survival of living things are affected by physical conditions of their environment (Year 6)	✓	✓		✓	Measurement and Geometry	**General Capabilities:** Literacy, Numeracy, Information and Communication Technology (ICT) Capability, Critical and Creative Thinking
SUSTAINABLE WORLD	15	222	**Plan and design a solar-panel uniform** In this STEM investigation, students are challenged to investigate the different occupations that could benefit from solar-panel clothing and then design a useful uniform for one occupation. As part of the investigation, they will find out how solar energy is converted to electrical energy.	• Generic reproducibles 1, 2, 3, 4, 5, 6 • Reproducibles 15.1, 15.2, 15.3 • Learning journal templates 1, 2, 3, 4 (on disc)	**Physical Sciences:** Electrical energy can be transferred and transformed in electrical circuits and can be generated from a range of sources (Year 6) Energy from a variety of sources can be used to generate electricity (Year 6)	✓			✓	Measurement and Geometry	**General Capabilities:** Literacy, Numeracy, Information and Communication Technology (ICT) Capability, Critical and Creative Thinking **Cross-curriculum priority:** Sustainability

THEME	NO.	PAGE	INVESTIGATION OVERVIEW	RESOURCES PROVIDED	SCIENCE CURRICULUM ALIGNMENT			TECHNOLOGY AND ENGINEERING CURRICULUM ALIGNMENT		MATHEMATICS CURRICULUM ALIGNMENT	OTHER CURRICULUM LINKS
					SCIENCE UNDERSTANDING	SCIENCE AS A HUMAN ENDEAVOUR	SCIENCE INQUIRY SKILLS	DIGITAL TECHNOLOGIES	DESIGN AND TECHNOLOGIES		
SUSTAINABLE WORLD	**16**	236	**Explore – and colonise – outside your world** In this STEM investigation, students are challenged to identify the most suitable planet or moon for colonisation and design a living pod for the first human colonists. As part of the investigation, they will explore the basic requirements for living things and key features of planets in our solar system.	• Generic reproducibles 1, 2, 3, 4, 5, 6 • Reproducibles 16.1, 16.2, 16.3 • Learning journal templates 1, 2, 3, 4 (on disc)	**Earth and Space Sciences:** The Earth is part of a system of planets orbiting around a star (the Sun) (Year 5)	✓	✓	✓	✓	Measurement and Geometry	**General Capabilities:** Literacy, Numeracy, Information and Communication Technology (ICT) Capability, Critical and Creative Thinking **Cross-curriculum priority:** Sustainability
WHO WE ARE	**17**	250	**Imagine humans of the future – on film** In this STEM investigation, students are challenged to design a human who could live on a warmer Earth in a world of extreme heat waves and superstorms. They must make a stop-motion animation that shows how the human would look and move. As part of the investigation, they will learn about body structures and behaviours that help animals to live in harsh environments on Earth today.	• Generic reproducibles 1, 2, 3, 4, 5, 6, 7 • Reproducibles 17.1, 17.2, 17.3 • Learning journal templates 1, 2, 3, 4 (on disc)	**Biological Sciences:** Living things have structural features and adaptations that help them to survive in their environment (Year 5) The growth and survival of living things are affected by physical conditions of their environment (Year 6) **Earth and Space Sciences:** Sudden geological changes or extreme weather conditions can affect Earth's surface (Year 6)	✓	✓	✓	✓	Measurement and Geometry Statistics and Probability	**General Capabilities:** Literacy, Numeracy, Personal and Social Capability, Information and Communication Technology (ICT) Capability, Critical and Creative Thinking
WHO WE ARE	**18**	264	**Think up an exciting dish that represents you** In this STEM investigation, students are challenged to design a unique dish that uses science to transform ingredients in a surprising way. As part of the investigation, they will learn about some of the science behind cooking, including chemical reactions.	• Generic reproducibles 1, 2, 3, 4, 5, 6 • Reproducibles 18.1, 18.2, 18.3, 18.4, 18.5 • Learning journal templates 1, 2, 3, 4 (on disc)	**Chemical Sciences:** Solids, liquids and gases have different observable properties and behave in different ways (Year 5) Changes to materials can be reversible or irreversible (Year 6)	✓			✓	Number and Algebra Measurement and Geometry	**General Capabilities:** Literacy, Numeracy, Information and Communication Technology (ICT) Capability, Critical and Creative Thinking
WHO WE ARE	**19**	280	**Colour your community with light** In this STEM investigation, students are challenged to design a large, colourful art installation using a light source and materials such as glass prisms, glass bottles and mirrors. As part of the investigation, they will learn about the properties of light, and about reflection, refraction and absorption.	• Generic reproducibles 1, 2, 3, 4, 5, 6 • Reproducibles 19.1, 19.2, 19.3 • Learning journal templates 1, 2, 3, 4 (on disc)	**Physical Sciences:** Light from a source forms shadows and can be absorbed, reflected and refracted (Year 5)	✓			✓	Measurement and Geometry	**General Capabilities:** Literacy, Numeracy, Information and Communication Technology (ICT) Capability, Critical and Creative Thinking
WHO WE ARE	**20**	294	**Shine a new light on student work** In this STEM investigation, students are challenged is to design and create a new way to display student work, using lighting in their design. As part of the investigation, students will learn about the properties of light and investigate how they can be used to make interesting and fun student displays.	• Generic reproducibles 1, 2, 3, 5 • Reproducibles 20.1, 20.2, 20.3 • Learning journal templates 1, 2, 3, 4 (on disc)	**Physical Sciences:** Light from a source forms shadows and can be absorbed, reflected and refracted (Year 5) Electrical energy can be transferred and transformed in electrical circuits and can be generated from a range of sources (Year 6)	✓			✓	Measurement and Geometry	**General Capabilities:** Literacy, Numeracy, Information and Communication Technology (ICT) Capability, Critical and Creative Thinking

AC

CHICKEN COOP: YES OR NO?

BUILT WORLD 1

→ INTRODUCTION

Sustainable gardens and chicken coops are becoming more common in schools. The schools are using produce from these gardens in canteens, cooking classes and to sell to the school community. As part of this, students can play a part in primary food production and sustainable practices, and also gain the skills and knowledge needed to keep domesticated animals.

In this STEM investigation, students will learn about chicken breeds and behaviours. They will find out about different breeds of chickens, egg production and animal welfare. Students will create a design for a chicken coop, taking into account the information they have collected, and consider the potential site for their coop.

THE CHALLENGE

Your school is setting up a sustainable garden area that could include chickens. Students would be able to collect any eggs for use in the school kitchen. The chickens would need to be housed in a chicken coop that is safe, secure and comfortable. What do you think? Chicken coop: yes or no?

Your challenge is to advise the school council about whether a chicken project is a good idea. You will need to present a plan that includes which chicken breeds to buy, how much the project would cost and a design for the chicken coop. Think about which breeds are suitable for handling and the size and number of eggs they might lay. As part of your investigation, you will learn about chicken behaviours and their health and wellbeing.

KEY UNDERSTANDINGS

- Animals belonging to the same species resemble each other and can breed among themselves.
- Humans can use selective breeding to change the characteristics of a particular type of domesticated animal.
- Different breeds of animal have different physical features and behaviours.
- Considering welfare issues is very important when keeping domesticated animals.

KEY VOCABULARY

behaviours

breed

broodiness

domesticated

selective breeding

KEY SKILLS

- Gather information.
- Make comparisons and summarise information.
- Make observations.
- Apply points about animal welfare to your design.

KEY ACTIONS

- Observe chicken behaviours.
- Compare features of different breeds of chicken.
- Design a chicken coop suitable for a school.
- Create a report advising the school council about a school chicken coop.

→ OVERVIEW OF STAGES

TUNE IN:

Students consider their prior knowledge about chickens, including breeds, behaviours, their origins and diet. They find out about the key features of chickens and learn about design features of chicken coops.

EMPATHISE

Students find out about chickens and different breeds. They learn about animal welfare and consider how the environment may affect chickens.

DEFINE

Students consider the information they know about chickens, including animal welfare. They work out the main requirements for designing a chicken coop.

IDEATE

Students generate ideas for making an original and functional chicken coop.

PROTOTYPE

Students choose one or two ideas to transform into physical representations (models). These are created rapidly, using simple materials.

TEST

As a class, prototypes are tested. When testing prototypes, students calculate the cost of building a chicken coop as well as ongoing costs for maintaining the chickens. Students share their prototypes and provide feedback to each other. They are given the opportunity to cycle through the Prototype and Test stages again.

SHARE AND EVALUATE:

Final prototypes are shared and evaluated, with opportunities for expert feedback. Students also provide a report to be shared with the school council, or a focus group.

→ SUGGESTED SCHEDULE

LESSON	STAGE
1–2	**Tune in:** state prior knowledge about chickens, observe chicken behaviours, explore chicken coop construction and introduce the student challenge
3–5	**Empathise:** learn about different chicken breeds and animal welfare, empathise and write/record in journal
6	**Define:** define the main issues, work out key requirements for designing a chicken coop and write/record in journal
7	**Ideate:** develop ideas and write/record in journal
8–10	**Prototype** and **Test:** conduct prototyping and testing cycles and write/record in journal
11–13	**Share and evaluate:** write a report, and share and evaluate designs and prototypes

CURRICULUM LINKS

The following tables show the key Science, Technologies and Mathematics curricula with which this STEM investigation is aligned.

SCIENCE

YEAR	STRAND	SUB-STRANDS AND CONTENT
5	Science Understanding	Biological sciences: • Living things have structural features and adaptations that help them to survive in their environment
6	Science Understanding	Biological sciences: • The growth and survival of living things are affected by physical conditions of their environment
5 & 6	Science as a Human Endeavour	Use and influence of science: • Scientific knowledge is used to solve problems and inform personal and community decisions

TECHNOLOGIES

YEAR	STRAND	CONTENT
5 & 6	Design and Technologies Processes and Production Skills	• Critique needs or opportunities for designing, and investigate materials, components, tools, equipment and processes to achieve intended designed solutions • Generate, develop and communicate design ideas and processes for audiences using appropriate technical terms and graphical representation techniques • Select appropriate materials, components, tools, equipment and techniques and apply safe procedures to make designed solutions • Develop project plans that include consideration of resources when making designed solutions individually and collaboratively
	Digital Technologies Processes and Production Skills	Acquire, store and validate different types of data, and use a range of software to interpret and visualise data to create information

MATHEMATICS

YEAR	STRAND	CONTENT
5 & 6	Measurement and Geometry	Using units of measurement
	Number and Algebra	Money and financial mathematics Number and place value

OTHER CURRICULUM LINKS

GENERAL CAPABILITIES

- Literacy
- Numeracy
- Critical and Creative Thinking

CROSS-CURRICULUM PRIORITIES

- Sustainability

ASSESSMENT

The following resources are provided for assessing students at different stages of the STEM investigations:

- Generic reproducible 1 (Key vocabulary table), for assessing understanding of vocabulary
- Generic reproducible 2 (Self-evaluation), for student self-evaluation of the learning process
- Generic reproducible 3 (Define graphic organiser), for assessing student engagement in the challenges, and the collaboration and skills involved in the design thinking stages
- Generic reproducible 5 (Design thinking assessment rubric), for evaluating student engagement in the design thinking stages
- Learning journal templates 1, 2, 3 and 4, for incorporating student reflection and evaluation

→ GETTING READY FOR THE INVESTIGATION

You can prepare yourself and students for this STEM investigation in the following ways:

- Identify groups of students who will work well together.
- Review the **Key science knowledge** that supports this investigation, and look at the **Useful links**.
- Investigate the **Useful apps**.
- Gather materials for completing the postbox task during the Tune-in session.
- Start collecting additional materials for prototyping (as shown on the **Materials needed** list).
- Determine where prototypes will be kept between lessons.
- Create a wall space where students can share their ideas in the Ideate stage.
- Organise the class into pairs.
- Start thinking about:
  - whether or not the school will be able to build a chicken coop – if so, will this investigation become a competition with monetary limits on construction and maintenance costs?
  - organising a visit to a chicken farm or perhaps a virtual visit using a web camera
  - websites for students to refer to when designing their chicken coop
  - gathering recycled materials or asking the school community to donate items
  - time and space constraints for this investigation
  - managing access to information about animal welfare, which may be confronting or distressing.

USEFUL APPS

- App for creating semantic maps (links between different words and/or concepts), such as Popplet or Inspiration
- App for creating interactive links (for example, between descriptions, videos, images and websites and a main image), such as ThingLink
- App for making notes using text, drawings, images, weblinks and audio, such as Notability
- App for creating multimedia presentations, such as Adobe Spark Video and iMovie
- Survey app such as Typeform (free for small surveys)
- Spreadsheet software such as Excel

USEFUL LINKS

- Examples of poultry behaviour, such as at poultryhub.org/production/husbandry-management/poultry-behaviour or youtube.com/watch?v=IEhHC58Q0Cc&feature=youtu.be&list=PL40aBCd034bCWLawEkj7kb14uYQ2aGHSq
- Normal behaviours of chickens, such as at articles.extension.org/pages/66175/normal-behaviors-of-chickens-in-small-and-backyard-poultry-flocks
- Checklist for building a chicken coop, such as at huckschickencoops.com/how-to-build-a-chicken-coop-a-step-by-step-checklist
- Examples of homemade chicken coops, such as at modernfarmer.com/2015/09/how-to-build-a-chicken-coop and bunnings.com.au/diy-advice/outdoor/pets-and-wildlife/how-to-build-a-diy-chicken-coop

RESOURCES PROVIDED

- Generic reproducibles 1, 2, 3, 5, 6
- Reproducibles 1.1, 1.2, 1.3
- Learning journal templates 1, 2, 3, 4 (on disc)

MATERIALS NEEDED

- Sticky notes (half a pad per pair)
- Paper
- Coloured card
- Pens and markers
- Sticky tape
- Pipe-cleaners
- Cardboard
- 4 shoe boxes
- Recycled materials or offcuts from a recycling outlet
- Balsa wood (optional)
- Hot glue gun and glue (optional)
- LEGO or other construction blocks (optional)

KEY SCIENCE KNOWLEDGE

This section provides an overview of the key science concepts and vocabulary needed for this unit.

SELECTIVE BREEDING

Chickens were **domesticated** more than 7000 years ago, and they would have looked very different to modern chickens. Humans began **selective breeding** of chickens to change parts of the birds' appearance, such as feathers, and to make chickens grow faster, bigger and to lay more eggs more often. Changes to chicken **behaviours** have also been made by selective breeding.

Some common **breeds** are:

Australorp – an Australian breed that lays all year round
Cochin – small and docile
Isa Brown – a great layer
Orpington – a very gentle breed
Silkie – very docile like Cochins; a small breed that lays small eggs and is often broody
Sussex – a good layer
Wyandotte – can be bossy with other hens, but manageable.

The size of eggs can be very different, depending on the chicken breed.

CHICKEN BEHAVIOURS

Chickens have different types of behaviour. For example, a mother hen teaches her chicks survival skills such as what to eat and where to find food. Social behaviours include activities with a pecking order, such as feeding, laying and dust-bathing. **Broodiness** is a breeding behaviour. Understanding the behaviours of chickens is an important part of their management and care.

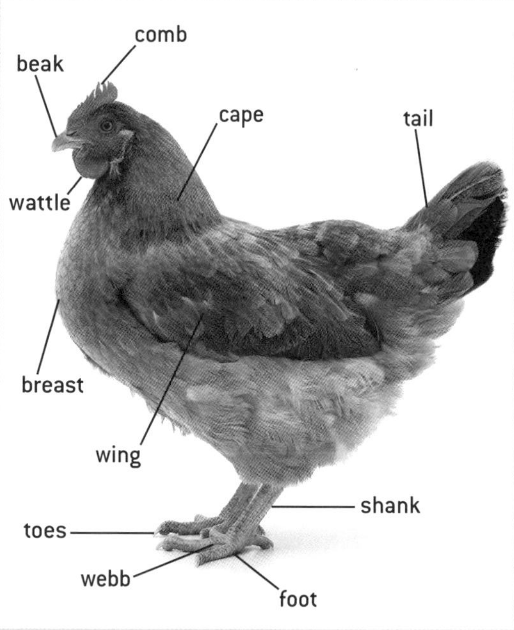

The physical features of a chicken

ANIMAL WELFARE

State education departments have guidelines for the keeping of animals in schools. These consider the health and safety of people and the welfare of the animals. It is important to check these guidelines, which will include information about:

- the size of the chicken coop (dependent on the number of chickens)
- whether to keep roosters (for breeding)
- what to do with newly hatched chickens
- the location of the coop in relation to nearby buildings
- secure storage of food and disposal of waste (to prevent rodents and disease).

Many councils won't allow roosters in built-up areas because their noise can disturb people living nearby.

KEY VOCABULARY

behaviours – responses an animal makes to a particular situation
breed – a group within a species of animal with characteristics that have been developed by humans
broodiness – a behaviour of chickens during which they sit for long periods on a nest (with or without eggs)
domesticated – tamed to be a pet, such as cats, or to be used in agriculture, such as cows
selective breeding – choosing which animals within a domesticated species to breed together, to develop certain characteristics

→ TUNE IN

1. Ask students to complete **Generic reproducible 1 (Key vocabulary table)** using the key vocabulary for this unit. This reproducible will also be used at the end of the unit, to demonstrate changes in understanding.
2. Prepare four shoe boxes (or similar) as postboxes. Label each box with one of the questions or instructions below. Provide each student with a piece of paper and ask them to divide it into quarters. Students write one question or instruction in each box, then fill in their ideas about each question or instruction. The questions and instructions are cut up and 'posted' into a box.
   - » Where do you think chickens originally came from? How many years do you think humans have been farming chickens?
   - » Make a list of foods that you think chickens eat.
   - » What are some of the behaviours of chickens?
   - » What do you know about different chicken breeds?
3. Ask groups to collate their responses on four large sheets, one for each question. The sheets will be referred to in subsequent lessons and annotated with new thinking or learning. Collaborative tools, such as Google Docs, could also be used for this task.
4. Before engaging in the challenge, students need to have an understanding of the features of chickens, typical chicken behaviours and the features of chicken coops.

ACTIVITY 1: FEATURES OF CHICKENS

1. Students draw a chicken and label its features, using their prior knowledge.
2. If possible, once completed, arrange for students to visit a chicken coop, observe and handle the chickens and then add any features they have missed or need to change on their original diagram. If there is no access to chicks or hens, ask students to look at pictures of hens and add any features they have missed or need to change.

TOP TIP!

During the Tune-in stage, conduct vocabulary activities to highlight and develop key vocabulary knowledge. Activities could include drawing semantic webs, creating a word wall or paired discussions. Check the **Key vocabulary** or read the **Key science knowledge** for a refresher on the key terms and concepts.

ACTIVITY 2: CHICKEN BEHAVIOURS

1. Introduce the term 'behaviour'. What does it mean? Give some examples.
2. Students observe the behaviours and movement of chickens (directly or online) over 10 minutes. If possible, visit a chicken coop. Alternatively, watch a video showing poultry behaviours (see **Useful apps/links**). Provide students with **Reproducible 1.1 (Chicken observation)** for recording their observations.
3. Students record their nominated chicken's position in the coop at the end of each minute and note the chicken's main behaviour for each minute. For example, '1 minute: Chicken scratched and pecked ground. 2 minutes: Chicken flapped its wings, then had a drink'.

ACTIVITY 3: CHICKEN COOPS

1. Students complete a 'think–pair–share' about what they think should be included in a chicken coop. Remind students to think about the chicken behaviours they have observed.
2. Collate a class list. Emphasise that this is a beginning 'think' – they will learn more about chickens in future lessons to refine their thinking.

5. Introduce the STEM investigation and challenge to the students. Provide them with the student card and read the information together. Ask students to think about some of the aspects of keeping chickens that they will need to learn about.
6. Introduce the design thinking process by reviewing the stages on the student card. Explain that students will keep a journal about their learning at the different stages of the design.

USEFUL APPS/LINKS

- Examples of poultry behaviour, such as at youtube.com/watch?v=lEhHC58Q0Cc&feature=youtu.be&list=PL40aBCd034bCWLawEkj7kb14uYQ2aGHSq

EMPATHISE

During the Empathise stage of the design thinking process, students focus on finding out about different points of view. To empathise with others, they need to research some of the issues relating to keeping chickens, as well as find out about the most suitable breeds for egg production. Students will take notes, ask questions, draw diagrams and take photos where relevant.

ACTIVITY 1: FIND OUT ABOUT CHICKEN BREEDS

1. Create a set of pictures of different chicken breeds (see **Useful apps/links**).
2. Place the pictures around the room or in a corridor and complete a gallery walk with the class. Provide students with the names of the chicken breeds on strips of paper or sticky notes. Groups of students walk through the gallery and stick the name of the chicken breed next to the picture.
3. At the end of the gallery walk, reveal the names of each of the chicken breeds. Discuss the similarities and differences students noticed between the breeds.
4. Ask pairs of students to find out some key information about a specific breed (see **Useful apps/links**). Share the information using a collaborative app such as Google Docs or Padlet.

ACTIVITY 2: LEARN ABOUT ANIMAL WELFARE

1. Watch a video or visit a website about chicken welfare (see **Useful apps/links**).
2. Ask students to discuss the impact that watching the video or reading the information has had on them. Discuss the term 'domesticated'. Make a class list of key considerations when raising chickens in a chicken coop at a school.
3. Ask students to consider the information they have collected and determine the most important insights they have had.

PROMPTS

- What did you find out about chicken breeds?
- What are some of the unusual breeds you learned about?
- What were some of the issues to do with keeping chickens?
- How did other people react to some of the issues with chicken farming?

MORE VOCABULARY

- empathise – understand and consider another person's or group's point of view
- point of view – an opinion, attitude or judgement considered in a particular way

JOURNAL TIP

Ask students to complete **Learning journal template 1 (Empathise page)** while they are completing the different tasks. Remind them to date their notes and include photos or drawings of relevant information.

USEFUL APPS/LINKS

- Tips about chicken breeds, such as at backyardchickencoops.com.au/top-20-chicken-breeds-for-your-backyard-coop or mypetchicken.com/chicken-breeds/breed-list.aspx
- Collaborative app, such as Google Docs or Padlet
- Information about hens and their welfare, such as at rspca.org.au/layer-hen-faq
- Video about chicken welfare on farms, such as at smh.com.au/national/10000-hens-to-a-hectare-is-no-free-range-accc-20130304-2fgxg.html

ASSESSMENT

This stage of the design thinking process offers opportunities to observe students collecting information, developing questions, and recording their notes and thinking in their journal.

EMPATHISE DEFINE IDEATE PROTOTYPE TEST

DEFINE

The main focus of this stage of the design thinking process is to reframe the challenge. The initial challenge is quite open, so at this stage students learn how to define what needs to be done. This includes noting insights that have been generated.

ACTIVITY 1: CONSIDER OBSERVATIONS

1. Students consider the information they gathered in the Empathise stage. They may work in pairs or small groups. Provide them with **Reproducible 1.2 (Chicken research)**, which they use to collate the information they have learned, and indicate what they still need to find out.
2. Students should discuss one section of **Learning journal template 2 (Define page)** at a time, write their responses, then continue discussing their ideas for the next section, until the task is complete. This provides students with opportunities to hear others' responses and also provides the teacher with input points.
3. Discuss some information students have learned about chicken breeds, welfare needs and the chicken coops. Provide students with the opportunity to research further. Ask them to write other information they would like to know, such as the best breeds for schools, tips for building a chicken coop (such as different structures) and how to look after chickens. Provide them with **Generic reproducible 4 (Key question table)** to assist them to record their questions, findings and sources.

ACTIVITY 2: CONSIDER INSIGHTS

Students think of at least one insight they have gained from the process; for example, some chicken breeds are able to produce more eggs than others and some lay eggs of a particular colour.

Students add this insight to **Learning journal template 2 (Define page)** and then write a brief explanation of what needs to be created.

When considering insights, students could think about the following:

- What was something unexpected that you saw or found out? How was it unexpected?
- How will you decide on the most important aspect of the chicken coop?
- Is there any other information that you need or would like to know? How will you find out?

ACTIVITY 3: CONSIDER CONSTRAINTS

At this stage, let students know the constraints of the challenge, by describing the time frame for completing the investigation, the materials available, whether one of the designs will be built as a full-scale model, whether there are cost constraints, who will be reading the reports and how the designs will be shared and evaluated. Students can then update **Learning journal template 2**.

PROMPTS

- What did you discover?
- What were the most important pieces of information that you gathered?
- What was something new that you learned?
- What other information do you need?

MORE VOCABULARY

- define – state the meaning of something
- insight – an accurate understanding of someone or something

JOURNAL TIP

Discuss the term 'insight'. Explain that it relates to something students have learned about the people and their responses to the surveys, as well as information gathered through research or excursions. You could refer to **Learning journal template 2**.

EMPATHISE DEFINE IDEATE PROTOTYPE TEST

→ IDEATE

The Ideate stage of the design thinking process is all about generating lots of ideas. Students need to be flexible in their thinking and able to move beyond obvious ideas. At this stage, ideas are not judged, just generated and gathered.

ACTIVITY: GENERATE IDEAS

1. Ask groups of students to draw or write their ideas for a chicken coop. Each new idea should be written or drawn on a separate piece of paper or sticky note.
2. Ask students to group ideas on a wall or board.
3. Ask students to look at the different ideas and provide feedback to each other. It is important that students don't defend their ideas at this stage. They should just be listening to the feedback.
4. After the initial feedback, ask students to come up with more ideas. Encourage them to be creative and even radical.
5. Ask students to choose four of their ideas to write in their journal. Students use **Learning journal template 3 (Ideate page)** to do this. Ask students to choose one idea to explore further and explain the reasoning behind their choice.

TOP TIP!

At this stage, students may have produced a series of annotated drawings about a chicken coop. They may have a collection of sticky notes, which they can organise into related ideas. Encourage students to view and read others' ideas before giving feedback. Feedback could be within small groups or between partners. Considering others' ideas is an important part of this process, so students can build on their own ideas as they continue to ideate.

At each stage of this activity, ask students to discuss their thoughts before writing their responses. This will help them to think through their ideas and select their final ideas to develop.

PROMPTS

- How do these ideas relate to the chickens' needs?
- How might you test your design?
- How can you make it easy to clean?
- How can you make it easy to access?
- What if you had to use different materials?

MORE VOCABULARY

- feedback – information about, for example, a person's performance or the design of a product, which can be used to make improvements
- ideate – generate many ideas without making judgements about the ideas

JOURNAL TIP

When choosing four ideas to include in the journal, students should try to choose ideas that aren't related, to show a range of ideas.

USEFUL APPS/LINKS

- Tools for creating ideas, such as at creatingminds.org/tools/tools_ideation.htm
- Tips for creativity and innovation, such as at designorate.com/creativity-innovation-in-education
- Examples of homemade chicken coops, such as at modernfarmer.com/2015/09/how-to-build-a-chicken-coop and bunnings.com.au/diy-advice/outdoor/pets-and-wildlife/how-to-build-a-diy-chicken-coop

ASSESSMENT

At the Ideate stage, assessment could include observations about the number and diversity of students' ideas, and their ability to provide feedback and create additional ideas. Reflection in the journal should provide an insight into some of the reasoning behind students' choices.

EMPATHISE · DEFINE · IDEATE · PROTOTYPE · TEST

→ PROTOTYPE

At this stage of the design thinking process, students are asked to create a physical prototype of a solution. It is the stage where students need to get their ideas out of their head and presented in a way that engages other students and helps them to understand the concept. When students create, it helps them to think and solve problems and disagreements. Students can role-play, make storyboards or use sticky notes when they prototype. The most important feature is that viewers can interact with whatever is produced.

Encourage students to photograph or film during the prototyping and testing stages. This information can be used to show the learning behind the design thinking process in action.

ACTIVITY: TRANSFORM IDEAS INTO PROTOTYPES

1. Students review the ideas generated at the Ideate stage. Provide them with an A3 copy of **Generic reproducible 6 (In the frame)** so they can organise their ideas into two sections: 'least relevant' and 'most relevant'. Students continue to cycle through this activity until they have an idea to start prototyping.
2. Provide students with a range of materials to create their prototype. LEGO or other construction blocks can be a good starting point for prototyping this sort of design before students move on to other materials. Remind students that a prototype should be created rapidly and is not meant to look 'nice'.
3. After a prototype has been created, ask students to see if it meets the original design challenge and get feedback from others.
4. Students then use the feedback to prototype again. Ask students to fill in the Prototype section of **Learning journal template 4 (Prototype and test page)**. See the **Journal tip** for further student guidance.

PROMPTS

- What worked?
- How could it be improved?
- What else do you need to know, do or have?
- What other suggestions do you have?

MORE VOCABULARY

- feedback – information about, for example, a person's performance or the design of a product, which can be used to make improvements
- prototype – an initial version of a model of a product or process that is used to develop a final model

JOURNAL TIP

Remind students to highlight the main features of their prototype. If they are creating an electronic journal, they can insert a photo and annotate it.

USEFUL APPS/LINKS

- App for creating interactive links (for example, between descriptions, videos, images and websites and a main image), such as ThingLink
- App for making notes using text, drawings, images, weblinks and audio, such as Notability

ASSESSMENT

Observe students as they make changes to their designs. Are they able to consider feedback, make modifications and move rapidly through this process? Or do they have difficulties with holding on to an idea and accepting feedback?

TOP TIP!

The Prototype stage is often very messy. It is important that students focus on their ideas, rather than the end product. Provide them with lots of materials – recycling depots can be a useful source. Students may add labels to explain some of the main features. Photographing and annotating pictures of prototypes can be useful.

To gain feedback, students could ask each other some of the following questions:

- What is the main feature of your chicken coop?
- How does it provide the best possible environment for chickens?
- Which aspects work best? What will you keep?
- Which aspects need changing? How might you do this?
- What other materials might you need?

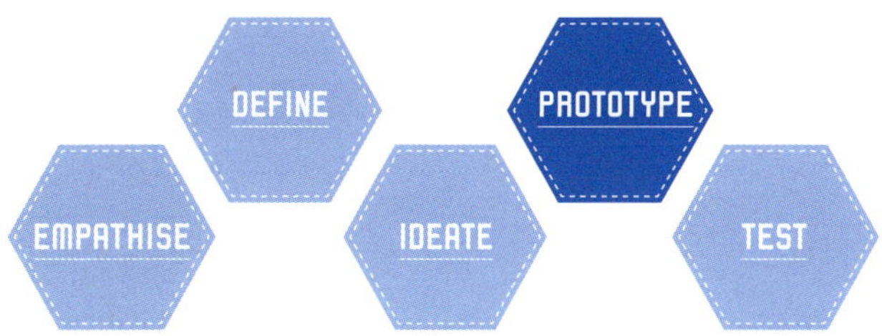

→ TEST

At this stage of the design thinking process, students test their prototype to see how it meets the criteria in the challenge. Students check to see if their prototype meets the criteria set at the start of the design process.

ACTIVITY: TEST FEEDBACK

1. Students take their last prototype and consider the needs of the chickens, as well as the space where the chicken coop would be placed.
2. Ask students to check whether or not their design works. If not, what do they need to do to make it work?
3. Provide the opportunity to cycle through the prototyping and testing stages again.
4. Ask students to calculate the costs of building their design. Demonstrate how to use a spreadsheet. Students will need to consider coop size, and materials quantity and cost.

Ask students to fill in the Test section of **Learning journal template 4 (Prototype and test page)**. See the **Journal tip** for further student guidance.

PROMPTS

- Does your prototype do what you wanted it to do?
- Are there other features you could add?
- What needs to be changed? What works well?

MORE VOCABULARY

- evaluate – assess something, perhaps considering what worked and what didn't
- feature – a specific aspect of something, such as size, shape, colour and quality
- feedback – information about, for example, a person's performance or the design of a product, which can be used to make improvements
- prototype – an initial version of a model of a product or process that is used to develop a final model
- review – consider an idea, process or product and decide what needs to be changed and what works

JOURNAL TIP

Ask students to think about why it is important to test their ideas before they build their final design.

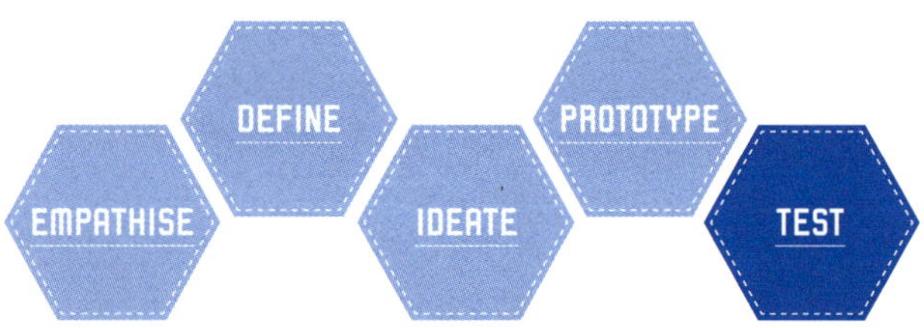

→ SHARE AND EVALUATE

At this stage of the investigation, students are provided with an opportunity to share their final design, as well as the processes involved in the investigation. Students evaluate their learning journals and their solutions.

ACTIVITY 1: BRING THE DESIGNS TOGETHER

1. Provide students with **Reproducible 1.3 (Chicken coop proposal)** to help them organise and update their information. Remind them that they need to give a final recommendation to the school council.
2. Students can create an iMovie or use Adobe Spark Video to demonstrate the process and thinking behind the designs. There should be an element of narration, where they are sharing their story about points of view, insights, prototyping and solutions.
3. Students should include their learning journals with the display so others can see the different stages of the design process.

ACTIVITY 2: EVALUATE AND GIVE FEEDBACK

1. Provide **Generic reproducible 2 (Self-evaluation)** for students to complete.
2. Ask students to provide feedback to each other about the most interesting features, the difficult aspects and the changes that they would make if they repeated the task.
3. Provide students with opportunities to share their designs with the wider community. This could include inviting a friend or family member with a chicken coop.

If the school decides to build a chicken coop, consider what to do with the eggs and how the chickens will be looked after on weekends and school holidays.

ASSESSMENT

Ask students to complete **Generic reproducible 1 (Key vocabulary table)** using the key vocabulary for this unit. Compare their table with the one they completed at the Tune-in stage.

Students complete **Generic reproducible 3 (Responding to the investigation)**. Compare their responses to those on **Generic reproducible 2**.

Teachers and students each complete **Generic reproducible 5 (Design thinking assessment rubric)**. Students compare the teacher's feedback with their self-assessment of their design thinking skills.

EMPATHISE

STEM INVESTIGATIONS

Name: ....

Date: ....

Observe a chicken for 10 minutes. Mark the position of your chicken in the diagram below at the end of each minute with the number 1, 2, 3, 4 and so on. In the table, record the main behaviours of the chicken during each minute.

Minute	Behaviours observed
1	
2	
3	
4	
5	
6	
7	
8	
9	
10	

STEM Investigations, UP, ISBN 978 1 4202 4154 9

Name: ....

Date: ....

Record in the table what you already know about chickens.
Add other categories in the last row. Write what you need to find out.

Category	What I already know	What I need to find out	Where I might find this information
Behaviours			
Welfare			
Coops			
Breeds			
Other			

STEM Investigations, UP, ISBN 978 1 4202 4154 9 © Macmillan Science and Education Australia 2018

REPRODUCIBLE 1.3 CHICKEN COOP PROPOSAL

STEM INVESTIGATIONS

Name: ....

Date: ....

Use this sheet to plan your proposal for building a chicken coop and keeping chickens.

Draw the design for your coop here.

Location of chicken coop	
Breed of chicken	
Reason for choice of breed	
Number of chickens	
Description of how chicks' and hens' needs would be met	
Expected egg production per day or week	
Proposed use of eggs	
Materials needed for ongoing care	
Cost of building coop	
Other information	
Final recommendation	

SAVE THE RIVER FROM RUN-OFF RUIN

BUILT WORLD 2

→ INTRODUCTION

The balance between our built world and the natural world can be a precarious one. Infrastructure, such as roads, is a part of modern living, but it does have an impact on the natural environment. Erosion and pollution are considerable problems for many natural environments.

In this STEM investigation, students are asked to create a process or design that will help reduce erosion on a riverbank, caused by a new road and drain. They explore the process of erosion and the impact it can have on waterways and the environment. They learn that erosion is usually a slow process, but extreme weather and human infrastructure can sometimes combine to speed up the process.

THE CHALLENGE

The local council has built a new road on a hill in your area. On rainy days, the water that falls on the road runs off into drainage pits. The run-off is released through a large drain pipe on the lower side of the road, and it flows downhill into a river. During some recent storms, the strong force of the run-off water washed away a lot of plants, causing erosion on the riverbank and washing soil and litter into the river.

Your challenge is to investigate ways to reduce future damage to the riverbank. You will need to prepare a report outlining the issue and your recommendations for fixing the problem. This will be presented to the council and your local junior rangers group. As part of your investigation, you will learn about erosion and how wind and water affect the Earth's surface.

KEY UNDERSTANDINGS

- Weathering is the wearing away of the Earth's surface.
- Water and wind can cause weathering and erosion.
- Plants and their roots help reduce the erosion of topsoil.
- Drains can reduce erosion by taking excess water away.

KEY VOCABULARY

deposition

erosion

run-off

silt

topsoil

weathering

KEY SKILLS

- Make careful observations.
- Consider different points of view.
- Collect and summarise information.

KEY ACTIONS

- Experiment with different soils.
- Explore how erosion occurs.
- Design a process or product to reduce erosion on a riverbank.

OVERVIEW OF STAGES

TUNE IN:

Students learn about different forms of erosion. They explore water erosion and how different soil types are affected. Students find out how different amounts of water force can affect the soils and the environment.

EMPATHISE

Students investigate people's responses to erosion. They gather pictures and information about erosion and record people's responses.

DEFINE

Students work out which materials and types of soil help reduce erosion. They identify the important elements of a successful design to reduce erosion in a river.

IDEATE

Students generate different designs to reduce erosion in a river. They sketch and label their designs.

PROTOTYPE

Students choose one or two ideas to transform into physical representations (models). These are created rapidly, using simple materials.

TEST

Students check which ideas work best. They choose a final design and create the final process or product. They are given the opportunity to cycle through the Prototype and Test stages again.

SHARE AND EVALUATE:

Final prototypes are shared and evaluated, with opportunities for expert feedback investigated.

SUGGESTED SCHEDULE

LESSON	STAGE
1–2	**Tune in:** explore soil types, erosion and related issues
3–5	**Empathise:** gather images and information about erosion and pollution relating to erosion and record others' responses to this information, and write/record in journal
6	**Define:** define the main issues and write/record in journal
7	**Ideate:** develop ideas and write/record in journal
8–10	**Prototype** and **Test:** conduct prototyping and testing cycles and write/record in journal
11–13	**Share and evaluate:** share and evaluate designs and prototypes

CURRICULUM LINKS

The following tables show the key Science, Technologies and Mathematics curricula with which this STEM investigation is aligned.

SCIENCE

YEAR	STRAND	SUB-STRANDS AND CONTENT
6	Science Understanding	Earth and space sciences: • Sudden geological changes and extreme weather events can affect Earth's surface
5 & 6	Science as a Human Endeavour	Nature and development of science: • Science involves testing predictions by gathering data and using evidence to develop explanations of events and phenomena
	Science Inquiry Skills	Questioning and predicting: • Processing and analysing data and information • Communicating

TECHNOLOGIES

YEAR	STRAND	CONTENT
5 & 6	Design and Technologies Processes and Production Skills	• Generate, develop and communicate design ideas and processes for audiences using appropriate technical terms and graphical representation techniques • Develop project plans that include consideration of resources when making designed solutions individually and collaboratively

MATHEMATICS

YEAR	STRAND	CONTENT
5 & 6	Number and Algebra	Number and place value Fractions and decimals

OTHER CURRICULUM LINKS

GENERAL CAPABILITIES

- Literacy
- Numeracy
- Information and Communication Technology (ICT) Capability
- Critical and Creative Thinking.

ASSESSMENT

The following resources are provided for assessing students at different stages of the STEM investigations:

- Generic reproducible 1 (Key vocabulary table), for assessing understanding of vocabulary
- Generic reproducible 2 (Self-evaluation), for student self-evaluation of the learning process
- Generic reproducible 3 (Responding to the investigation), for assessing student engagement in the challenges, and the collaboration and skills involved in the design thinking stages
- Generic reproducible 5 (Design thinking assessment rubric), for evaluating student engagement in the design thinking stages
- Learning journal templates 1, 2, 3 and 4, for incorporating student reflection and evaluation

GETTING READY FOR THE INVESTIGATION

You can prepare yourself and students for this STEM investigation in the following ways:

- Identify groups of students who will work well together.
- Review the **Key science knowledge** that supports this investigation, and look at the **Useful links**.
- Investigate the **Useful apps**.
- Gather materials for experimenting with soil types and water erosion during the Tune-in session.
- Start collecting images about weathering and erosion.
- Start collecting additional materials for prototyping (as shown on the **Materials needed** list).
- Determine where prototypes will be kept between lessons.
- Create a wall space where students can share their ideas in the Ideate stage, as well as a 3–2–1 display (see **Useful links**).
- Start thinking about:
  - » where exploration with soil and water will take place
  - » the roles of students and the teacher in the activities (for example, will the teacher pour the water or will students?)
  - » which experts can be invited to share information and provide feedback about designs
  - » whether or not the designs will be built or kept as drawings or multimedia presentations
  - » how and when the final designs will be displayed and who will be the audience
  - » whether or not to involve the local council in the process.

USEFUL APPS

- App for creating semantic maps (links between different words and/or concepts), such as Popplet
- App for creating interactive links (for example, between descriptions, videos, images and websites and a main image), such as ThingLink
- App for making notes using text, drawings, images, weblinks and audio, such as Notability
- App for creating multimedia presentations, such as Adobe Spark Video and iMovie
- Survey app such as Typeform (free for small surveys)

USEFUL LINKS

- A news video clip about storm erosion, such as at abc.net.au/btn/story/s4478709.htm
- A slideshow about erosion, such as at nps.gov/tica/learn/education/upload/Erosion.pptx
- A soil erosion experiment, such as at youtube.com/watch?v=im4HVXMGI68
- The 3–2–1 thinking routine, such as at pz.harvard.edu/resources/3-2-1-bridge

RESOURCES PROVIDED

- Generic reproducibles 1, 2, 3, 4, 5, 6
- Reproducibles 2.1, 2.2, 2.3
- Learning journal templates 1, 2, 3, 4 (on disc)

MATERIALS NEEDED

- Sticky notes (half a pad per group)
- Paper
- Coloured card
- Pens and markers
- Sticky tape
- Pipe-cleaners
- Cardboard
- String
- 4 trays per group
- Soil
- Grass
- Sponge cutouts (to represent trees)
- Blocks of wood (to elevate trays at one end)
- Watering can(s) with removable watering rose
- Sand
- Potting mix
- Clay soil
- Pebbles
- Small rocks
- Gravel
- Other soil mixtures
- Plastic cups
- 3 large plastic juice/soft-drink bottles per group

KEY SCIENCE KNOWLEDGE

This section provides an overview of the key science concepts and vocabulary needed for this unit.

WEATHERING AND EROSION

Weathering is the wearing away of rocks by natural forces such as wind and water. This creates much finer particles, which are easily moved by wind and water. The movement is called **erosion**. Soil erosion is erosion of the **topsoil** (the top layer of soil). This layer is very valuable because it is where plants obtain most of their nutrients. The plants protect topsoil from erosion by blocking the wind and by making the topsoil stable with their roots. Humans cause soil erosion by clearing plants (such as grasses and trees) from land and loosening the topsoil by digging it. If topsoil is exposed or heavily worked, it is likely to be eroded by **run-off** water during rain, and by windstorms and extreme weather events. The fine particles of **silt** that build up in waterways due to **deposition** can lead to further flooding, and the poor quality of the remaining soil will prevent plant regrowth.

Weathering of rocks can make spectacular landforms.

Windstorms cause erosion by moving large quantities of topsoil.

HOW CAN EROSION BE CONTROLLED?

The amount of soil erosion in an area also depends on factors such as the amount of topsoil, how much wind and rainfall occurs, and the slope of land. These factors need to be considered if land will be used for a new purpose, such as a road. Run-off needs to be controlled and the topsoil protected by covering it with materials suitable to its position.

For example, erosion in a riverbank environment could be controlled by:

- making sure there is good topsoil cover
- planting suitable grasses, shrubs and trees (for long-term erosion control)
- covering any bare areas with mesh or other suitable materials
- building litter traps and clearing them regularly
- removing silt from the bottom of waterways
- modifying large single drainpipes so that water escapes through several smaller points.

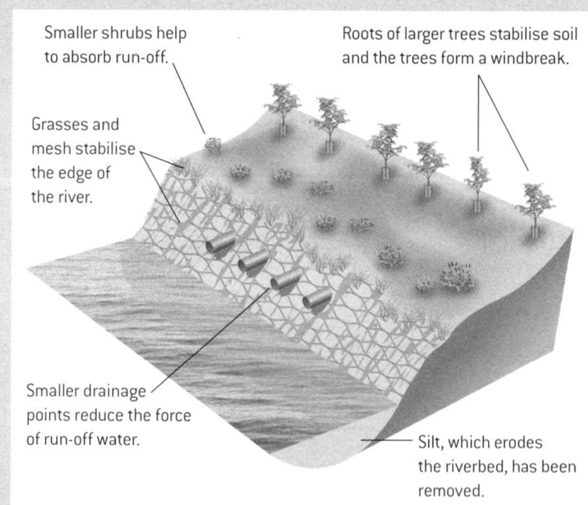

Drainage systems need to be planned so that erosion is controlled.

KEY VOCABULARY

deposition – the settling of eroded material in a different place

erosion – the movement of soil and weathered rock, usually by wind and water

run-off – water that moves off surfaces, such as roads, after rain

silt – a mixture of very fine particles (such as rock, soil and clay) that can sit at the bottom of a waterway or float in it, making the water cloudy

topsoil – the uppermost layer of soil (usually 5–20 cm thick), which contains most of the nutrients that plants need

weathering – the wearing away of rocks by the movement of wind and water

→ TUNE IN

1. Ask students to complete **Generic reproducible 1 (Key vocabulary table)** using the key vocabulary for this unit: deposition, erosion, run-off, silt, topsoil, weathering. This reproducible will also be used at the end of the unit, to demonstrate changes in understanding.
2. Watch a news video clip about storm erosion (see **Useful apps/links**).
3. Discuss how the action of the waves causes so much damage. Show images of changing coastlines.
4. Explore other forms of erosion, such as wind or water run-off. The US National Park Service has a slideshow that could be modified (see **Useful apps/links**).
5. Discuss the term 'deposition' and link it to leaf litter and pollution in the water. Ask students to share examples of deposition they have seen.

ACTIVITY 1: WATER EROSION

1. Have four trays prepared – one with bare soil, one with grass growing/covering, one with grass and small 'shrubs' (sponge cut-outs can be used), and one with grass cover and large 'trees' (sponges cut into tree shapes). Arrange the trays so that they slope (putting some blocks of wood under one end). Provide students with **Reproducible 2.1 (Soil erosion by water)**. Have students predict what they think will happen when water is poured onto the sloping trays from a watering can with a spray rose.
2. When everyone has written their predictions, have them observe what happens when the water is poured from a height of 40 cm. Discuss and record the observations.
3. Have the students predict what they think will happen when water is poured onto the sloping trays from a watering can with the spray rose removed so that there is a more solid stream of water.
4. When everyone has written their predictions, have them observe what happens when the water is poured from a height of 40 cm. Discuss the observations and record on **Reproducible 2.1**.
5. Provide students with time to use the information to explain what has happened. Follow this with a class discussion about the least and most effective ways of preventing erosion. Ask students to explain their choices.

ACTIVITY 2: RESISTING EROSION

1. Watch the video clip of the soil erosion experiment (see **Useful apps/links**). What would happen if different soil mixtures were tested? Are some soil mixes more stable?
2. Have available a range of soils (such as sand, potting mix, clay soil, rocks and gravel).
3. Have students work in groups of three or four. They should have three plastic juice or soft-drink bottles cut in half horizontally to use as trays with a suspended plastic cup under the spout.
4. Initially, have them test three individual samples. Provide them with **Reproducible 2.2 (Exploring soil mixtures)** to record their predictions, observations and explanations.
5. Ask students to create three mixes that they think will withstand the force of the water. Ask, 'Why have you chosen these mixes and what do you predict will happen when water is poured over them?' Pour water from a 40 cm height from a watering can without the rose. Which samples were the most effective at resisting the water force? Students update **Reproducible 2.2**.

6. Introduce the STEM investigation and challenge to the students. Provide them with the student card and read the information together. Ask students to think about what they have discovered about soil erosion and the force of water. Encourage students to think about how the damage could be limited.
7. Introduce the design thinking process by reviewing the stages on the student card.
8. Explain that students will keep a journal about their learning at the different stages of the design.

USEFUL APPS/LINKS

- A news video clip about storm erosion, such as at abc.net.au/btn/story/s4478709.htm
- A slideshow about erosion, such as at nps.gov/tica/learn/education/upload/Erosion.pptx
- A soil erosion experiment, such as at youtube.com/watch?v=im4HVXMGI68
- The 3–2–1 bridge thinking routine, such as at pz.harvard.edu/resources/3-2-1-bridge

EMPATHISE

During the Empathise stage of the design thinking process, students focus on finding out about different points of view. To empathise with others, they need to record responses to different stimuli about erosion, such as pictures. They also consider their own points of view. Students will observe, take notes, ask questions, draw diagrams and take photos where relevant.

ACTIVITY 1: THINK ABOUT EROSION

Provide students with pictures of weathering and the effects of erosion (see **Useful apps/links**), especially images that can be used to show the impact that it can have on individuals and communities. Ask students to complete a 3–2–1 bridge thinking routine (see **Useful apps/links**) using **Reproducible 2.3 (3–2–1 bridge thinking routine)** to record ideas.

After students have recorded their responses, create a 3–2–1 display for future reference. Collect students' reproducibles for comparison at the end of the investigation. (Repeat the activity at the conclusion of the challenge.)

ACTIVITY 2: FIND OUT WHAT OTHERS THINK

Ask students to find out others' reactions to erosion. Students collect pictures of erosion and statistics to create a short presentation. This could be a series of cards, slideshow or animation. They could also annotate images with facts using an app such as ThingLink. Students share their presentation with others and write the words people use to describe what they see and their responses.

Ask students to consider the key insights they have gathered from the two activities.

PROMPTS

- What were some of the emotional words people used?
- What new points of view did you learn?
- What were some of the different questions people had?
- How did a thinking routine help you find out people's ideas?

MORE VOCABULARY

- empathise – understand and consider another person's or group's point of view
- point of view – an opinion, attitude or judgement considered in a particular way

JOURNAL TIP

Ask students to complete **Learning journal template 1 (Empathise page)** while they are completing the different tasks. Remind them to date their notes and include photos or drawings of relevant information.

USEFUL APPS/LINKS

- Annotation app, such as ThingLink
- Images showing weathering and the effects of erosion, such as at nationalgeographic.com/science/earth/the-dynamic-earth/weathering-erosion and qld.gov.au/environment/land/soil/erosion/types
- The 3–2–1 bridge thinking routine, such as at pz.harvard.edu/resources/3-2-1-bridge

ASSESSMENT

This stage of the design thinking process offers opportunities to observe students collecting information, developing questions, and recording their notes and thinking in their journal.

DEFINE

The main focus of this stage of the design thinking process is to reframe the challenge. The initial challenge is quite open, so at this stage students learn how to define what needs to be done. This includes noting insights that have been generated.

ACTIVITY 1: CONSIDER OBSERVATIONS

1. Students consider the information they gathered in the Empathise stage. They may work in pairs or small groups. Provide them with a whiteboard, large sheet of paper and/or sticky notes to collate some of the key information they have gathered about people's responses to erosion. They also consider some of the information they gathered during the Tune-in activities about different types of erosion and its impact.
2. Students should discuss one section of **Learning journal template 2 (Define page)** at a time, write their responses, then continue discussing their ideas for the next section, until the task is complete. This provides students with opportunities to hear others' responses and also provides the teacher with input points.
3. Discuss information gathered about the impact of erosion on the environment. Provide students with the opportunity to research further. Ask them to write other information they would like to know, such as learning about different processes and materials that are used to reduce or prevent erosion, especially around water. Provide them with **Generic reproducible 4 (Key question table)** to assist them to record their questions, findings and sources.

ACTIVITY 2: CONSIDER INSIGHTS

Students think of at least one insight they have gained from the process; for example, the main source of erosion is water or run-off can cause considerable erosion.

Students add this insight to **Learning journal template 2 (Define page)** and then write a brief explanation of what needs to be created.

When considering insights, students could think about the following:

- What was something unexpected that you saw or found out? How was it unexpected?
- How will you decide on the most important aspect of reducing erosion and pollution in the river?
- Is there any other information that you need or would like to know? How will you find out?

ACTIVITY 3: CONSIDER CONSTRAINTS

At this stage, let students know the constraints of the challenge, by describing the materials available, the time frame for the investigation and the guidelines for testing designs, especially if students are incorporating soil and water into their designs. Students can then update **Learning journal template 2**.

PROMPTS

- What did you discover?
- What were the most important pieces of information that you gathered?
- What was something new that you learned?
- What other information do you need?

MORE VOCABULARY

- define – state the meaning of something
- insight – an accurate understanding of someone or something

JOURNAL TIP

Discuss the term 'insight'. Explain that it relates to something students have learned about the people and their responses to the surveys, as well as information gathered through research or excursions. You could refer to **Learning journal template 2**.

EMPATHISE DEFINE IDEATE PROTOTYPE TEST

IDEATE

The Ideate stage of the design thinking process is all about generating lots of ideas. Students need to be flexible in their thinking and be able to move beyond obvious ideas. At this stage, ideas are not judged, just generated and gathered.

ACTIVITY: GENERATE IDEAS

1. Ask groups of students to draw or write their ideas. Each new idea should be written or drawn on a separate piece of paper or sticky note.
2. Ask students to group ideas on a wall or board.
3. Ask students to look at the different ideas and provide feedback to each other. It is important that students don't defend their ideas at this stage. They should just be listening to the feedback.
4. After the initial feedback, ask students to come up with more ideas. Encourage them to be creative and even radical.
5. Ask students to choose four of their ideas to write in their journal. Students use **Learning journal template 3 (Ideate page)** to do this. Ask students to choose one idea to explore further and explain the reasoning behind their choice.

TOP TIP!

At this stage, students may have produced a series of annotated drawings about how erosion and pollution in the riverbank can be reduced. They may have a collection of sticky notes, which they can organise into related ideas.

Encourage students to view and read others' ideas before giving feedback. Feedback could be within small groups or between partners. Considering others' ideas is an important part of this process, so students can build on their own ideas as they continue to ideate.

At each stage of this activity, ask students to discuss their thoughts before writing their responses. This will help them to think through their ideas and select their final ideas to develop.

PROMPTS

- How do these ideas relate to erosion and pollution?
- How might you test your design?
- How can you make it represent a real riverbank?
- How can you demonstrate how it will reduce erosion?
- What if you had to use different materials?

MORE VOCABULARY

- feedback – information about, for example, a person's performance or the design of a product, which can be used to make improvements
- ideate – generate many ideas without making judgements about the ideas

JOURNAL TIP

When choosing four ideas to include in the journal, students should try to choose ideas that aren't related.

USEFUL APPS/LINKS

- Tools for creating ideas, such as at creatingminds.org/tools/tools_ideation.htm
- Tips for creativity and innovation, such as at designorate.com/creativity-innovation-in-education

ASSESSMENT

At the Ideate stage, assessment could include observations about the number and diversity of students' ideas, and their ability to create provide feedback and create additional ideas. Reflection in the journal should provide an insight into some of the reasoning behind students' choices.

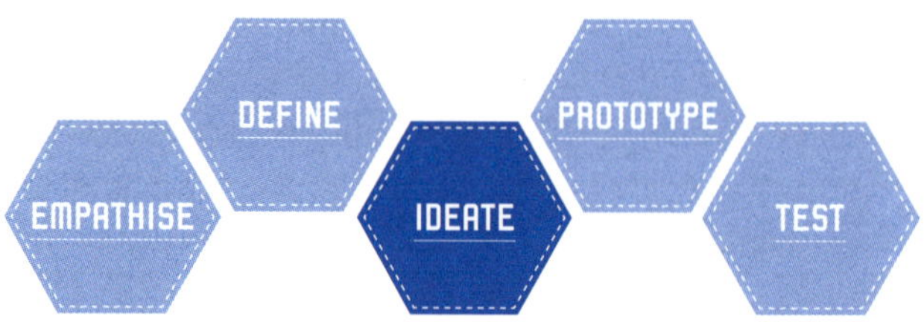

→ PROTOTYPE

At this stage of the design thinking process, students are asked to create a physical prototype of a process or structure that will reduce riverbank erosion. It is the stage where students need to get their ideas out of their head and presented in a way that engages other students and helps them to understand the ideas. When students create, it helps them to think and solve problems and disagreements. Students can role-play, make storyboards or use sticky notes when they prototype. The most important feature is that viewers can interact with whatever is produced.

Encourage students to photograph or film during the prototyping and testing stages. This information can be used to show the learning behind the design thinking process in action.

ACTIVITY: TRANSFORM IDEAS INTO PROTOTYPES

1. Students review the ideas generated at the Ideate stage. Provide them with an A3 copy of **Generic reproducible 6 (In the frame)** so they can organise their ideas into two sections: 'least relevant' and 'most relevant'. Students continue to cycle through this activity until they have an idea to start prototyping.
2. Provide students with a range of materials to use to create their prototype. Remind students that a prototype should be created rapidly and it is not meant to look 'nice'.
3. After a prototype has been created, ask students to see if it works and get feedback from others.
4. Students then use the feedback to prototype again.

Ask students to fill in the Prototype section of **Learning journal template 4 (Prototype and test page)**. See the **Journal tip** for further student guidance.

PROMPTS

- What worked?
- How could it be improved?
- What else do you need to know, do or have?
- What other suggestions do you have?

MORE VOCABULARY

- feedback – information about, for example, a person's performance or the design of a product, which can be used to make improvements
- prototype – an initial version of a model of a product or process that is used to develop a final model

JOURNAL TIP

Remind students to highlight the main features of their prototype. If students are creating an electronic journal, they can insert a photo of their prototype and annotate it.

USEFUL APPS/LINKS

- App that can be used for a learning journal, allowing students to draw, link, type and record information, such as Notability
- App that can be used to create an interactive annotation of the prototype, such as ThingLink

ASSESSMENT

Observe students as they make changes to their designs. Are they able to consider feedback, make modifications and move rapidly through this process? Or do they have difficulties with holding on to an idea and accepting feedback?

TOP TIP!

The Prototype stage is often very messy. It is important that students are focusing on their ideas, rather than the end product. Provide them with lots of materials – recycling depots can be a useful source of resources. Students may add labels to prototypes to explain some of the main features. Photographing and annotating pictures of prototypes can be useful.

To gain feedback, students could ask each other some of the following questions:

- What is the main feature of your prototype?
- How can you show the impact of erosion?
- Which aspects work best? What will you keep?
- Which aspects need changing? How might you do this?
- What other materials might you need?

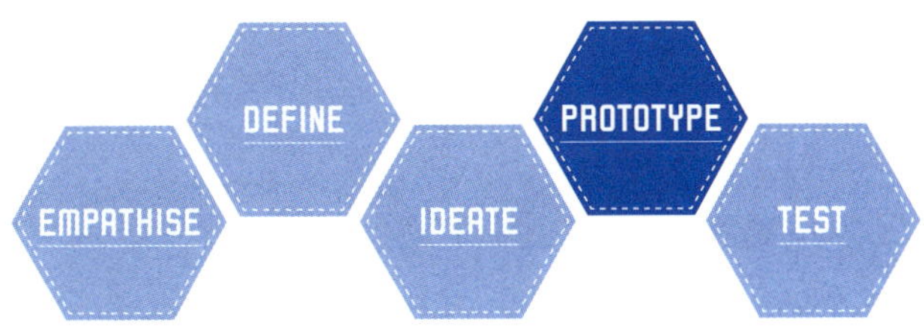

TEST

At this stage of the design thinking process, students test their prototype to see how it meets the criteria in the challenge. Students check to see if their prototype meets the criteria set at the start of the design process.

ACTIVITY: TEST FEEDBACK

1. Students take their last prototype and consider the original issues and the design brief.
2. Ask students to check whether or not their design works. If not, what do they need to do to make it work?
3. Provide students with the opportunity to cycle through the prototyping and testing stages again.

Ask students to fill in the Test section of **Learning journal template 4 (Prototype and test page)**. See the **Journal tip** for further student guidance.

PROMPTS

- Does your prototype do what you wanted it to do?
- Does it have additional features that might need changing or removing?

MORE VOCABULARY

- evaluate – assess something, perhaps considering what worked and what didn't
- feature – a specific aspect of something, such as size, shape, colour and quality
- feedback – information about, for example, a person's performance or the design of a product, which can be used to make improvements
- prototype – an initial version of a model of a product or process that is used to develop a final model
- review – consider an idea, process or product and decide what needs to be changed and what works

JOURNAL TIP

Ask students to think about why it is important to test their ideas before they build their final design.

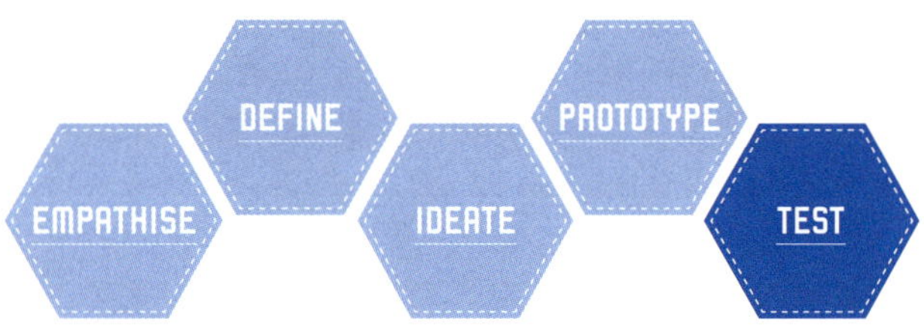

SHARE AND EVALUATE

At this stage of the investigation, students share their final design, as well as the processes involved in the investigation. Students evaluate their learning journals and their solutions.

ACTIVITY 1: BRING THE DESIGNS TOGETHER

1. Students can create an iMovie or use Adobe Spark Video to demonstrate the process and thinking behind the designs. There should be an element of narration, where they are sharing their points of view, insights, prototyping and solutions.
2. Students should include their learning journals with the display.

ACTIVITY 2: EVALUATE AND GIVE FEEDBACK

1. Provide students with **Generic reproducible 2 (Self-evaluation)** to complete.
2. Ask students to provide feedback to each other about the interesting features, the difficult aspects and possible changes.
3. Provide students with opportunities to share their designs. This could include inviting someone with experience managing waterways, an engineer, or a friend or family member with experience in this area.
4. Provide students with time to create final designs and write their report. The report should provide an overview of the investigation, annotated drawings or images, an explanation of the solution and clear links to the original design challenge.

ASSESSMENT

Provide students with another copy of **Reproducible 2.3 (3–2–1 bridge thinking routine)** and ask them to repeat the activity in the Empathise stage. Return the original and ask them to discuss the changes with a partner.

Ask students to again complete **Generic reproducible 1 (Key vocabulary table)** using the key vocabulary. Compare their table with the one they completed at the Tune-in stage, to demonstrate changes in understanding.

Students complete **Generic reproducible 3 (Responding to the investigation)**. Compare their responses to those on **Generic reproducible 2**.

Teachers and students each complete **Generic reproducible 5 (Design thinking assessment rubric)**. Students compare the teacher feedback with their self-assessment of their design thinking skills.

STEM INVESTIGATIONS

Name: ....

Date: ....

Predictions and observations with sprayed water

Sketch and label what is in each tray.				
What do you predict will happen to the soil?				
What did you observe?				

Predictions and observations with a solid stream of water

Sketch and label what is in each tray.				
What do you predict will happen to the soil?				
What did you observe?				

STEM Investigations, UP, ISBN 978 1 4202 4154 9 © Macmillan Science and Education Australia 2018

Name: ....

Date: ....

STEM INVESTIGATIONS

Choose three different types of soil, then predict the effect that water has on each of them. Can you explain what happened?

Soil type	Prediction	Observation	Explanation
1.			
2.			
3.			

Create three different soil mixtures and write the ingredients you used. Predict and observe the effect that water has on each of them. Can you explain what happened?

Soil mixture (describe ingredients)	Prediction	Observation	Explanation
1.			
2.			
3.			

EMPATHISE

STEM INVESTIGATIONS

Name: ....

Date: ....

Write three words that relate to what you know about erosion.

Write two questions you have about erosion.

1.)

2.)

Write one word that summarises what you know.

STEM Investigations, UP, ISBN 978 1 4202 4154 9 © Macmillan Science and Education Australia 2018

BUILT WORLD 3

DESIGN A QUAKE-RESISTANT BUILDING

→ INTRODUCTION

An earthquake is a natural phenomenon that occurs in many parts of the world. The magnitude, or size, of an earthquake can be measured using the Richter scale, where 1 is a tiny quake and 10 is the biggest quake possible. The magnitude of an earthquake does not necessarily predict the loss of life and destruction. For example, in 1999, an earthquake measuring 7.6 on the Richter scale killed just over 2000 people in Taiwan, but in 2005, an earthquake of the same magnitude killed more than 86 000 people in Pakistan. According to experts, many of the deaths in Pakistan could have been prevented if the buildings had been better designed and constructed.

In this STEM investigation, students are asked to consider the types of buildings that are more likely to resist an earthquake. They need to demonstrate their understandings of how an earthquake occurs, and why some buildings stay standing and others collapse. Students can make a shake table to test their designs, and other ways to test them can be developed.

This STEM challenge is easily differentiated for students by encouraging different groups to use different degrees of complexity when creating their buildings. Students could test different materials as well as designs.

THE CHALLENGE

The main risk to life during an earthquake is the collapse of poorly built buildings. After a devastating earthquake, volunteer organisations often work with local communities, helping them to rebuild. You want to join a junior volunteer team, but first you must impress the selection panel.

Your challenge is to design and build a model of an earthquake-resistant building. You may choose the type of building: a house, a public building such as a school or perhaps an apartment block. As part of your STEM investigation, you will find out about the structure of the Earth, the cause of earthquakes, flexible building, and important features to think about when designing earthquake-resistant buildings.

KEY UNDERSTANDINGS

- The Earth has five layers: inner core, outer core, lower mantle, upper mantle and crust.
- The Earth's crust is made up of many pieces, called tectonic plates.
- Tectonic plates move against each other.
- The surface where one plate slips past another is called the fault or fault plate.
- When plates slide against each other, this creates earthquakes.
- The hypocentre is the location below the Earth's crust where an earthquake starts.
- The epicentre is on the Earth's surface, directly above the hypocentre.
- Buildings that are flexible are more likely to withstand an earthquake.

KEY VOCABULARY

earthquake-resistant

epicentre

fault

hypocentre

magnitude

tectonic plate

KEY SKILLS

- Make careful observations.
- Consider different points of view.
- Develop research skills.
- Transform an idea into something that can be seen.

KEY ACTIONS

- Find out information from eyewitnesses of earthquakes.
- Experiment with different shapes and materials.
- Explore ways of making a structure strong and flexible.
- Design a way to create a building that can stay standing when the ground vibrates.

→ OVERVIEW OF STAGES

TUNE IN:

- Share an introductory video about earthquakes.
- Discuss students' understandings of what an earthquake is, how it occurs and the impact it can have, and establish prior knowledge.
- Explore the structure of the Earth, how earthquakes occur, the types of structures that can survive earthquakes and the science behind this.
- Provide students with the STEM Investigation challenge card.

EMPATHISE

Students find out information about earthquakes and buildings through eyewitness accounts.

DEFINE

Students consider the main issues with designing buildings that need to be earthquake-resistant. The parameters of the challenge are defined.

IDEATE

Students generate creative ideas for a building that is earthquake-resistant.

PROTOTYPE

Students transform some of their ideas into physical representations. These are created rapidly, using simple materials. Students can role-play, make storyboards or use sticky notes when they prototype.

TEST

Students share their prototypes and provide feedback to each other. They use a shake table or similar to test their buildings. They are given the opportunity to cycle through the Prototype and Test stages again.

SHARE AND EVALUATE:

Final prototypes are shared and evaluated, with opportunities for expert feedback.

→ SUGGESTED SCHEDULE

LESSON	STAGE
1–3	**Tune in**: share information about earthquakes; explore the structure of the Earth, how earthquakes occur and the features of buildings that survive earthquakes; introduce the student challenge
4–5	**Empathise**: learn about earthquakes through different eyewitness accounts over time; empathise and write/record in journal
6	**Define**: define the main issues and write/record in journal
7	**Ideate**: develop ideas and write/record in journal
8–10	**Prototype** and **Test**: conduct prototyping and testing cycles, and write/record in journal
11–13	**Share and evaluate**: share and evaluate designs and prototypes

CURRICULUM LINKS

The following tables show the key Science, Technologies and Mathematics curricula with which this STEM investigation is aligned.

SCIENCE

YEAR	STRAND	SUB-STRANDS AND CONTENT
6	Science Understanding	Earth and space sciences: • Sudden geological changes and extreme weather events can affect Earth's surface
6	Science as a Human Endeavour	Use and influence of science: • Scientific knowledge is used to solve problems and inform personal and community decisions
5 & 6	Science Inquiry Skills	Questioning and predicting Planning and conducting Processing and analysing data and information Evaluating Communicating

TECHNOLOGIES

YEAR	STRAND	CONTENT
5 & 6	Design and Technologies Knowledge and Understanding	• Investigate characteristics and properties of a range of materials, systems, components, tools and equipment, and evaluate the impact of their use
	Design and Technologies Processes and Production Skills	• Critique needs or opportunities for designing, and investigate materials, components, tools, equipment and processes to achieve intended designed solutions • Generate, develop and communicate design ideas and processes for audiences using appropriate technical terms and graphical representation techniques • Select appropriate materials, components, tools, equipment and techniques, and apply safe procedures to make designed solutions • Negotiate criteria for success that include sustainability to evaluate design ideas, processes and solutions • Develop project plans that include consideration of resources when making designed solutions individually and collaboratively

MATHEMATICS

YEAR	STRAND	SUB-STRANDS
5 & 6	Measurement and Geometry	Using units of measurement Geometric reasoning

OTHER CURRICULUM LINKS

GENERAL CAPABILITIES

- Literacy
- Numeracy
- Information and Communication Technology (ICT) Capability
- Critical and Creative Thinking

ASSESSMENT

The following resources are provided for assessing students at different stages of the STEM investigations:

- Generic reproducible 1 (Key vocabulary table), for assessing understanding of vocabulary
- Generic reproducible 2 (Self-evaluation), for student self-evaluation of the learning process
- Generic reproducible 3 (Responding to the investigation), for assessing student engagement in the challenge, and the collaboration and skills involved in the design thinking stages
- Generic reproducible 5 (Design thinking assessment rubric), for evaluating student engagement in the design thinking stages
- Learning journal templates 1, 2, 3 and 4, for incorporating student reflection and evaluation

GETTING READY FOR THE INVESTIGATION

You can prepare yourself and students for this STEM investigation in the following ways:

- Identify groups of students who will work well together.
- Investigate the **Useful apps**.
- If possible, open a class account for an app that creates multimedia presentations, such as Adobe Spark Video. (Students are not old enough to use an individual account so a class account should be used.)
- Review the **Key science knowledge** that supports this investigation, and look at the **Useful links**.
- Gather materials for the shake table, if building one.
- Start collecting materials for prototyping (as shown on the **Materials needed** list).
- Determine where prototypes will be kept between lessons.
- Create a wall space where students can share their ideas during the Ideate stage.
- Organise the class into pairs.
- Start thinking about:
  - » how the buildings will be evaluated, if not building a shake table
  - » who will view the designs
  - » who will provide expert feedback about the designs, and whether it will be provided in person or in digital form
  - » who could assist with building a shake table.

USEFUL APPS

- App for creating semantic maps (links between different words and/or concepts), such as Popplet
- App for creating multimedia presentations, such as Adobe Spark Video and iMovie
- App for creating interactive links (for example, between descriptions, videos, images and websites and a main image), such as ThingLink
- App for creating infographics, such as Canva

USEFUL LINKS

- Information about where earthquakes happen, such as information about the US Geological Survey at usgs.gov
- An introduction to earthquakes, such as at video.nationalgeographic.com.au/video/101-videos/earthquake-101?source=relatedvideo
- Information about the San Francisco earthquake of 1906, such as at sfmuseum.org/1906/06.html
- Information about earthquake-safe buildings and structures, such as at strucalc.com/designing-earthquake-safe-buildings-and-structures/
- Discussions about whether you can earthquake-proof a city, such as at bbc.com/news/science-environment-35810317
- Earthquake shake table instructions, such as at youtube.com/watch?v=6HgxiYBkh3U
- Information about how earthquakes are measured, such as at bbc.co.uk/schools/gcsebitesize/geography/natural_hazards/earthquakes_rev2.shtml
- Japanese pagodas during earthquakes, such as at youtube.com/watch?v=0tFWn_e71qc
- Information about the structure of the Earth, such as at natgeokids.com/au/discover/geography/physical-geography/structure-of-the-earth/

RESOURCES PROVIDED

- Generic reproducibles 1, 2, 3, 4, 5
- Reproducibles 3.1, 3.2, 3.3
- Learning journal templates 1, 2, 3, 4 (on disc)

MATERIALS NEEDED

- Sticky notes (half a pad per pair)
- Paper
- Coloured card
- Pens and markers
- Sticky tape
- Pipe-cleaners
- Cardboard
- Paperclips
- Other building materials, such as recyclable packaging, boxes, tubes
- For the shake table (link to instructions at **Useful links**):
  - » Cardboard box
  - » Strong card
  - » Rubber bands
  - » Zip tags (cable ties)
  - » Scissors
  - » Double-sided foam tape
  - » Battery pack with batteries
  - » Motor
  - » Gear
  - » Sticky foam circles
  - » Foam circle with the middle cut out
  - » Washer
  - » Craft sticks/icypole sticks

KEY SCIENCE KNOWLEDGE

This section provides an overview of the key science concepts and vocabulary needed for this unit.

WHAT CAUSES EARTHQUAKES?

The Earth is made up of several layers. One of these is the core, which is at the centre of the Earth and consists of molten lava. The crust is the surface layer of the Earth and consists of many pieces, called plates or **tectonic plates**.

An earthquake occurs when plates slide past each other along a break in the crust called a **fault**. Energy is transferred from one plate to another, causing the plates to vibrate. The **hypocentre** is the location beneath the Earth's crust where the earthquake started. The **epicentre** is the location on the Earth's surface (crust) directly above the hypocentre.

The most common way to measure earthquakes is the Richter scale. This scale measures their size, or **magnitude**.

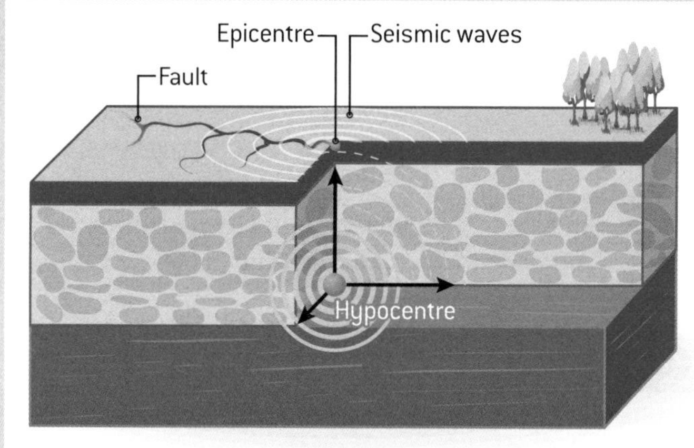

An earthquake starts at a hypocentre beneath the Earth. The epicentre is on the surface of the Earth.

HOW DO EARTHQUAKES CAUSE DAMAGE?

Many buildings collapse during an earthquake due to the way they were constructed and how tall they are. Some buildings are more **earthquake-resistant** than others. When the Earth vibrates, a structure made of rigid materials will vibrate quickly, like the earthquake vibrations, and it can snap. Tall buildings and those made with less rigid materials are more flexible. They sway more slowly than an earthquake's movement, so they are more likely to remain standing. Very tall buildings contain dampers, which help to control the shock of the vibrations. A damper reduces vibration, which occurs when there is an earthquake. There are different types of dampers. Some might be a large mass at the top of a building (a tuned mass damper). Others could be a series of plastic rings at the base of a building that absorb shock waves.

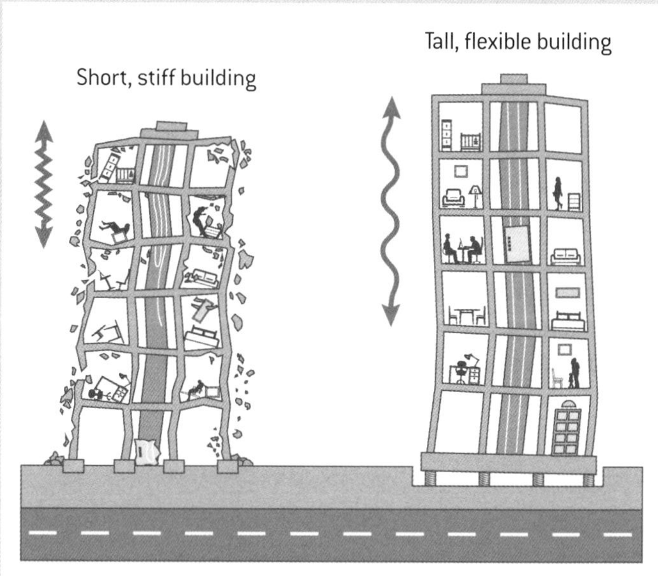

Taller buildings made with flexible materials and rubber springs sway slowly and are better at withstanding earthquakes. Short buildings made with stiff materials and concrete foundations vibrate quickly.

KEY VOCABULARY

earthquake-resistant – more likely to survive an earthquake than standard structures
epicentre – the point on the Earth's surface directly above the underground focus of an earthquake
fault – a break in the rocks that make up the Earth's crust (outer layer)
hypocentre – the point underground where an earthquake begins
magnitude – the size of an earthquake
tectonic plate – a massive slab of solid rock (part of the Earth's crust) that moves and sometimes fractures

→ TUNE IN

1. Ask students to complete **Generic reproducible 1 (Key vocabulary table)** using the key vocabulary for this unit: epicentre, fault, hypocentre, magnitude, earthquake-resistant, tectonic plate. This reproducible will also be used at the end of the unit to demonstrate changes in understanding.
2. Watch the National Geographic online video 'Earthquakes 101' (see **Useful apps/links**), or a similar introduction to earthquakes.
3. Discuss what students observed and learned.
4. Before engaging in the challenge, students need to have an understanding of the Earth's structure, how an earthquake occurs and some of the scientific concepts behind earthquake-resistant buildings. Set up the following three activities (or similar) for students.

ACTIVITY 1: THE EARTH'S STRUCTURE

1. Provide students with a link to information about the structure of the Earth (see **Useful apps/links**).
2. Ask students to create an infographic explaining the key features of the Earth's structure. They could draw the structure on paper, create their own diagrams on the computer, or use an app such as ThingLink to annotate an image found online and share their understandings.
3. Ask pairs of students to take turns explaining different features of the Earth's structure (for example, the core, the crust).

ACTIVITY 2: A PAGODA'S EARTHQUAKE-RESISTANT FEATURES

1. Watch an online video about what happens to Japanese pagodas during earthquakes (see **Useful apps/links**).
2. Discuss the key information presented in the video, focusing on the flexibility of the pagoda.
3. Provide students with paper, scissors and tape to experiment with simple, flexible designs.

ACTIVITY 3: SHAKE TABLE

1. Provide students with a link to an online video explaining how to make an earthquake shake table (see **Useful apps/links**). Give them the materials required to create the shake table (as shown in the online video). Decide how many shake tables to create and group students accordingly.
2. Ask students to follow the instructions in the video. Remind them to pause the video at the end of each instruction, and replay to check they understand the instruction.
3. If students are not able to complete this activity, brainstorm some ways that the class could create a machine to test the earthquake resistance of the buildings they are going to design.

5. Introduce the STEM investigation and challenge to the students. Provide them with the student card and read the information together.
6. Introduce the design thinking process by reviewing the stages on the student card.
7. Explain that students will keep a journal about their learning at the different stages of the design.

TOP TIP! During the Tune-in sessions, conduct vocabulary activities to highlight and develop key vocabulary knowledge. Activities could include drawing semantic webs, creating a word wall or paired discussions. Check **Key vocabulary** definitions or read the **Key science knowledge** if you need a refresher on the key terms and concepts.

USEFUL APPS/LINKS

- Japanese pagodas during earthquakes, such as at youtube.com/watch?v=0tFWn_e71qc
- Information about the structure of the Earth, such as at natgeokids.com/au/discover/geography/physical-geography/structure-of-the-earth/
- Instructions to make an earthquake shake table, such as at youtube.com/watch?v=6HgxiYBkh3U

→ EMPATHISE

During the Empathise stage of the design thinking process, students focus on considering different points of view. To empathise with others, they need to research some of the experiences that people have had. Students will take notes, ask questions, draw diagrams and take photos where relevant.

ACTIVITY 1: SAN FRANCISCO EARTHQUAKE EYEWITNESS, 1906

1. Provide students with the link to a boy's written observations and reflections on a large-magnitude earthquake in San Francisco in 1906 (see **Useful apps/links**). Read this together or in small groups.
2. Provide students with **Reproducible 3.1 (San Francisco eyewitness)** to record the key information and responses of Lloyd Head, the boy who wrote of his experiences.

ACTIVITY 2: NEPAL EARTHQUAKE EYEWITNESSES, 2015

1. Organise students into pairs and provide them with **Reproducible 3.2 (Nepal eyewitness)**.
2. Provide students with a link to the BBC News article 'Nepal Quake: Eyewitness Accounts' (see **Useful apps/links**). This article contains three eyewitness accounts of a 7.8 magnitude quake in Nepal in 2015. A second BBC News article (see **Useful apps/links**) gives seven eyewitness accounts of another quake in Nepal a few weeks later. Allocate each student pair a different eyewitness and ask them to record the key information on **Reproducible 3.2**.
3. Ask students to share different accounts between pairs.
4. Ask students, as a class, if they have experienced an earthquake or if they know of anyone who has. Organise time for people to speak with the class about their experiences.

Sensitivity is required here. Some students might not be prepared to discuss their personal experiences around earthquakes, or those of family members or friends.

ACTIVITY 3: EMPATHISE

1. Provide students with **Reproducible 3.3 (Eyewitness comparison)**. Ask them to consider the information provided by eyewitnesses from activities 1 and 2.
2. Students should record the similarities and differences of the eyewitnesses' experiences.
3. Ask students to generate words that describe how people felt. They can create a semantic map on paper or by using an app such as Popplet.

PROMPTS

- What feature of the earthquake made the most impact on your eyewitness? Why do you think this?
- What are some of the words people used to describe the earthquake?
- What were people concerned about?
- How did people react?

MORE VOCABULARY

- empathise – understand and consider another person's or group's point of view
- eyewitness – someone who has seen something happen
- point of view – an opinion, attitude or judgement considered in a particular way

JOURNAL TIP

Ask students to complete **Learning journal template 1 (Empathise page)** while they are completing the different tasks. Remind them to date their notes and include photos or illustrations of relevant information.

USEFUL APPS/LINKS

- App to gather information when making observations, such as Popplet
- Eyewitness account of the 1906 San Francisco earthquake, such as 'One Boy's Experience' at sfmuseum.net/1906/ew7.html
- Eyewitness accounts of the 2015 Nepal earthquake such as at bbc.com/news/world-asia-32467555 and bbc.com/news/world-asia-32704090

ASSESSMENT

This stage of the design thinking process offers opportunities to observe students collecting information, developing questions, and recording their notes and thinking in their journal.

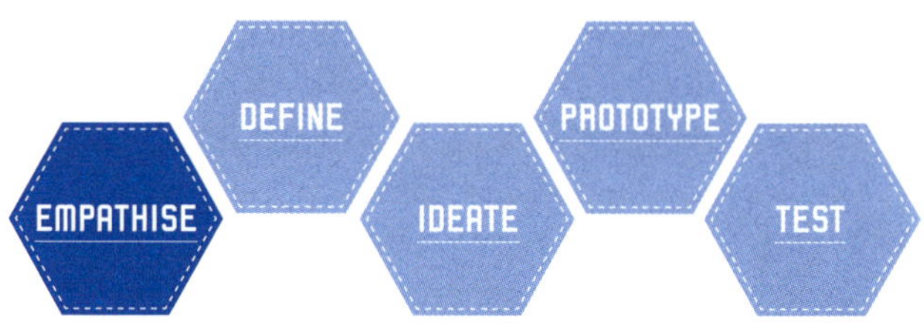

DEFINE

The main focus of this stage of the design thinking process is to reframe the challenge. The initial challenge is quite open, so at this stage students learn how to define what needs to be done. This includes noting insights that have been generated.

ACTIVITY 1: CONSIDER OBSERVATIONS

1. Students consider the information they gathered in the Empathise stage. They may work in pairs or small groups. Provide them with a whiteboard, large sheet of paper and/or sticky notes to collate some of their key information. They should refer to their information on **Reproducible 3.1 (San Francisco eyewitness graphic organiser)** and **Reproducible 3.2 (Nepal eyewitness graphic organiser)**. Students should then transfer the main findings to **Learning journal template 2 (Define page)**.
2. Students should discuss one section of **Learning journal template 2** at a time, write their responses and then continue discussing their ideas for the next section, until the task is complete. This provides students with opportunities to hear others' responses and it provides the teacher with input points.
3. Provide students with the opportunity to research further. Ask them to write other information they would like to know. Provide them with **Generic reproducible 4 (Key question table)** to assist them to record their questions, findings and sources.

ACTIVITY 2: CONSIDER INSIGHTS

Students should think of at least one insight they have gained from the process; for example, the shaking of a building is a very frightening experience. Students should add this insight to **Learning journal template 2**. They should then explain how this will affect the design of their model.

When considering insights, students could think about the following:

- What was something unexpected that you saw or found out? How was it unexpected?
- How will you decide on the most important aspect of your model?
- Is there any other information that you need or would like to know? How will you find out?

ACTIVITY 3: CONSIDER CONSTRAINTS

At this stage, let students know the constraints of the challenge by describing the types of materials that will be available and how students will test the building's flexibility when it is vibrated. Students can then update **Learning journal template 2**.

PROMPTS

- What did you discover?
- What were the most important pieces of information that you gathered?
- What was something new that you learned?
- What other information do you need?

MORE VOCABULARY

- define – state the meaning of something
- insight – an accurate understanding of someone or something

JOURNAL TIP

Discuss the term 'insight'. Explain that it relates to something students have learned about the people and situations they read about.

EMPATHISE DEFINE IDEATE PROTOTYPE TEST

→ IDEATE

The Ideate stage of the design thinking process is all about generating lots of ideas. Students need to be flexible in their thinking and be able to move beyond obvious ideas. At this stage, ideas are not judged, just generated and gathered.

ACTIVITY: GENERATE IDEAS

1. Ask groups of students to draw or write their ideas.
2. Each new idea should be written or drawn on a separate piece of paper or sticky note.
3. Ask students to group ideas on a wall or board.
4. Ask students to look at the different ideas and provide feedback to each other. It is important that students don't defend their ideas at this stage. They should just be listening to the feedback.
5. After the initial feedback, ask students to come up with more ideas. Encourage them to be creative and even radical.
6. Ask students to choose four of their ideas to write in their journal. Students use **Learning journal template 3 (Ideate page)** to do this. Ask students to choose one idea to explore further and explain the reasoning behind their choice.

TOP TIP!

At this stage, students may have produced a series of drawings that are annotated. They may have a collection of sticky notes, which they can organise into related ideas.

Encourage students to view and read others' ideas before giving feedback. Feedback could be within small groups or between partners. Considering others' ideas is an important part of this process, so students can build on their own ideas as they continue to ideate.

At each stage of this activity, ask students to discuss their thoughts before writing their responses. This will help them to think through their ideas and select their final ideas to develop.

PROMPTS

- How do your chosen ideas relate to earthquakes?
- How might you test your design?
- How can you make it more flexible?
- How can you make it a different shape?
- What if you had to use different materials?

MORE VOCABULARY

- feedback – information about, for example, a person's performance or the design of a product, which can be used to make improvements
- ideate – generate many ideas without making judgements about the ideas

JOURNAL TIP

When choosing four ideas to include in the journal, students should try to choose ideas that aren't related.

USEFUL APPS/LINKS

- Tools for creating ideas, such as at creatingminds.org/tools/tools_ideation.htm
- Tips for creativity and innovation, such as at designorate.com/creativity-innovation-in-education/

ASSESSMENT

At the Ideate stage, assessment could include observations about the number and diversity of students' ideas, and their ability to provide feedback and create additional ideas. Reflection in the journal should provide an insight into some of the reasoning behind students' choices.

EMPATHISE DEFINE IDEATE PROTOTYPE TEST

→ PROTOTYPE

At this stage of the design thinking process, students are asked to create a physical prototype of a solution. It is the stage where students need to get their ideas out of their head and presented in a way that engages other students and helps them to understand the concept. When students create, it helps them to think and solve problems and disagreements. Students can role-play, make storyboards or use sticky notes when they prototype. The most important feature is that viewers can interact with whatever is produced.

ACTIVITY: TRANSFORM IDEAS INTO PROTOTYPES

1. Ask students to choose one idea, and perhaps one aspect of that idea, to prototype.
2. Provide students with a range of materials to use to create their prototype. Remind students that a prototype should be created rapidly and is not meant to look 'nice'.
3. After a prototype has been created, ask students to see if it works and get feedback from others.
4. Students then use the feedback to prototype again.

Ask students to fill in the Prototype part of **Learning journal template 4 (Prototype and test page)**. See the **Journal tip** for further student guidance.

TOP TIP!

The Prototype stage is often very messy. It is important that students are focusing on their ideas, rather than the end product. Provide them with lots of materials – recycling depots can be a useful source of resources. Students may add labels to prototypes to explain some of the main features. Photographing and annotating pictures of prototypes can be useful.

To gain feedback, students could ask each other some of the following questions:

- What is the main feature of your prototype?
- How does your prototype work?
- Which aspects work best? What will you keep?
- Which aspects need changing? How might you do this?
- What other materials might you need?

PROMPTS

- What worked?
- How could it be improved?
- What else do you need to know, do or have?
- What other suggestions do you have?

MORE VOCABULARY

- feedback – information about, for example, a person's performance or the design of a product, which can be used to make improvements
- prototype – an initial version of a model of a product or process that is used to develop a final model

JOURNAL TIP

Remind students to highlight the main features of their prototype. If students are creating an electronic journal, they can insert a photo of their prototype and annotate it.

USEFUL APPS/LINKS

- App that can be used for a learning journal, allowing students to draw, link, type and record information, such as Notability
- App that can be used to create an interactive annotation of the prototype, such as ThingLink

ASSESSMENT

Observe students as they make changes to their designs. Are they able to consider feedback, make modifications and move rapidly through this process? Or do they have difficulties with holding on to an idea and accepting feedback?

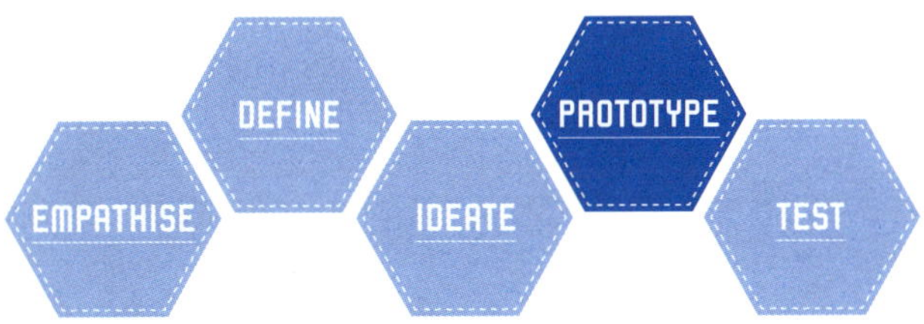

TEST

At this stage of the design thinking process, students test their prototype to see if it meets the requirements of the audience or user. Students check to see if their prototype meets the criteria set at the start of the design process.

ACTIVITY: TEST FEEDBACK

1. Students take their last prototype and consider the original design challenge.
2. Ask students to check whether or not their design works. If not, what do they need to do to make it work?
3. Provide the opportunity to cycle through the Prototype and Test stages again.

Ask students to fill in the Test part of **Learning journal template 4 (Prototype and test page)**. See the **Journal tip** for further student guidance.

PROMPTS

- Does your prototype do what you wanted it to do?
- Does it have additional features that might be useful in an earthquake-prone area?

MORE VOCABULARY

- evaluate – assess something, perhaps considering what worked and what didn't
- feature – a specific aspect of something, such as size, shape, colour, quality
- feedback – information about, for example, a person's performance or the design of a product, which can be used to make improvements
- prototype – an initial version of a model of a product or process that is used to develop a final model
- review – consider an idea, process or product and assess what works and what needs to be changed

JOURNAL TIP

Ask students to think about why it is important to test their ideas before they build their final design.

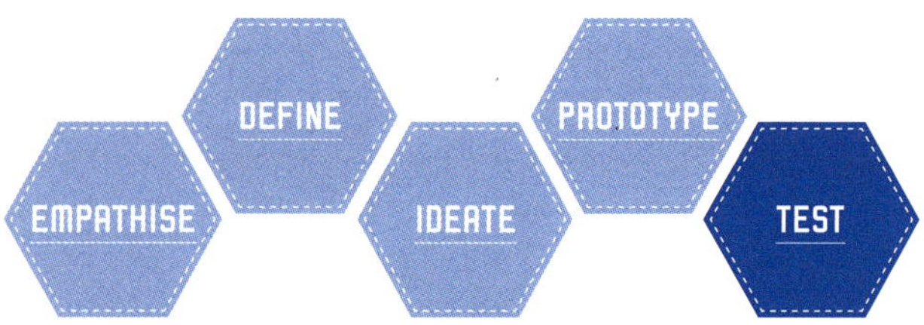

SHARE AND EVALUATE

At this stage of the investigation, students are provided with an opportunity to share their final design, as well as the processes involved in the investigation. Students evaluate their learning journals and their solutions.

ACTIVITY 1: BRING THE DESIGNS TOGETHER

1. Provide students with time to create their final designs.
2. Encourage them to film the process during prototyping and testing.
3. Students can create an iMovie or use Adobe Spark Video (via a teacher-created class account) to demonstrate the process and thinking behind the designs.
4. Students should include their learning journals with the display so others can see the different stages of the design process.

ACTIVITY 2: EVALUATE AND GIVE FEEDBACK

1. Provide students with **Generic reproducible 2 (Self-evaluation)** to complete.
2. Ask students to provide feedback to each other about the most interesting features, the aspects that were most difficult and the changes that they would make if they repeated the task.
3. Provide students with opportunities to share their designs with the wider community. This could include inviting someone from Engineers Without Borders, a parent with relevant experience or another external professional. It may be possible to share some of the videos with an expert for feedback about the designs.

ASSESSMENT

Ask students to again complete **Generic reproducible 1 (Key vocabulary table)** using the key vocabulary for this unit: epicentre, fault, hypocentre, magnitude, tectonic plate, earthquake-resistant. Compare their table with the one they completed at the Tune-in session, to demonstrate changes in understanding.

Students complete **Generic reproducible 3 (Responding to the investigation)**. Compare students' responses to those on **Generic reproducible 2**.

Teachers and students each complete **Generic reproducible 5 (Design thinking assessment rubric)**. Students compare the feedback they are given by the teacher with their self-assessment of their design thinking skills.

EMPATHISE

STEM INVESTIGATIONS

Name: ....

Date: ....

Read about Lloyd Head's account of the earthquake in San Francisco in 1906.
Use the table to write some notes about what he observed and heard.
Also write how he felt at the time.

Description of the earthquake (sounds, sights)	Words to describe how Lloyd felt during and after the earthquake

EMPATHISE

STEM INVESTIGATIONS

Name: ....

Date: ....

Read about one of the eyewitnesses to the earthquake in Nepal.
Think about the following questions and write some notes for each.

What did the person notice?

What did the person do?

What did the person think?

How might you have reacted in this situation?

STEM Investigations, UP, ISBN 978 1 4202 4154 9 © Macmillan Science and Education Australia 2018

EMPATHISE

STEM INVESTIGATIONS

Name: ....

Date: ....

List the main findings from your research and eyewitness accounts.

San Francisco earthquake 1906	Nepal earthquakes 2015

What are some similarities between the earthquakes?
What are some differences?

What do these accounts teach you to think about when designing an earthquake-resistant building?

PLAN A BUILDING THAT PLEASES THE NEIGHBOURS

BUILT WORLD 4

→ INTRODUCTION

Many people choose to work and live in cities, so buildings need to accommodate a lot of people without taking up much land. Tall buildings can do this, but their shadows can affect nearby buildings and land.

In this STEM investigation, students will learn about the impact of shadowing from tall buildings and will consider how decisions about building materials and building design can influence the amount of shadow that a building casts. They are challenged to design a tall building that casts minimal shadow.

Students who have completed **STEM Investigation 20 (Shine a new light on student work)** could use their understanding of reflection and refraction to incorporate materials that reflect and refract light.

THE CHALLENGE

Your mum works at a large building design business. Her team is designing a ten-storey (or higher) building for a piece of land that is surrounded by one-storey homes. The council will only approve the design if the team can demonstrate that the neighbours will not be bothered by shadows made by the building. Can you help?

Your challenge is to design a building that will cast the least amount of shadow. As part of your STEM investigation, you will learn about the relationship between light, objects and shadows, and you will apply this knowledge to your design. You will prove your design will not overshadow other homes by testing a model and recording the shadows that it forms.

KEY UNDERSTANDINGS

- Tall buildings cause shadows that vary in size and shape, depending on the time of day.
- Materials may absorb, reflect, refract and transmit light.
- Materials may be translucent, transparent or opaque.
- Opaque materials absorb light.
- Opaque materials create shadows where light has been absorbed.
- The position of the Sun determines the length of shadows, depending on the time of day.

KEY VOCABULARY

absorption

opaque

reflection

refraction

translucent

transmission

KEY SKILLS

- Make careful observations.
- Consider different points of view.
- Develop interviewing skills.
- Describe differences between transparent, translucent and opaque materials.
- Explain how shadows are formed.
- Collect information about building materials, light and shadowing.

KEY ACTIONS

- Interview other people.
- Experiment with light – reflection, refraction, transmission and absorption.
- Experiment with different materials and how they interact with light.
- Explore ways of creating buildings with minimal shadowing.
- Design a building with reduced shadowing.

→ OVERVIEW OF STAGES

TUNE IN:

Students learn about the concept of low shadowing from tall buildings. They explore properties of light and shadow. Students find out how light travels and about shadow shapes and lengths. They explore the properties of different materials in relation to light.

EMPATHISE

Students investigate the effect of shadow and shade on homes. They interview family and friends to discover their views on tall buildings built in suburban areas.

DEFINE

Students work out which materials and shapes are least likely to cast a shadow. They identify the important elements of a successful tall building.

IDEATE

Students generate different designs for a ten-storey building that casts the least amount of shadow. They sketch and label their designs.

PROTOTYPE

Students choose one or two ideas to transform into physical representations (models). These are created rapidly, using simple materials that simulate common building materials.

TEST

Students check which ideas work best. They choose a final design and create shadow drawings. They are given the opportunity to cycle through the Prototype and Test stages again.

SHARE AND EVALUATE:

Final prototypes are shared and evaluated, with opportunities for expert feedback investigated.

→ SUGGESTED SCHEDULE

LESSON	STAGE
1–2	**Tune in**: explore properties of light and shadows, and learn about the concept of low-shadow buildings
3–5	**Empathise**: interview and survey others about their experiences, knowledge and opinions about shadowing from tall buildings, and write/record in journal
6	**Define**: define the main issues and write/record in journal
7	**Ideate**: develop ideas and write/record in journal
8–10	**Prototype** and **Test**: conduct prototyping and testing cycles, and write/record in journal
11–13	**Share and evaluate:** share and evaluate designs and prototypes

CURRICULUM LINKS

The following tables show the key Science, Technologies and Mathematics curricula with which this STEM investigation is aligned.

SCIENCE

YEAR	STRAND	SUB-STRANDS AND CONTENT
5	Science Understanding	Physical sciences: • Light from a source forms shadows and can be absorbed, reflected and refracted
		Earth and space sciences: • The Earth is part of a system of planets orbiting around a star (the Sun)
	Science as a Human Endeavour	Use and influence of science: • Scientific knowledge is used to solve problems and inform personal and community decisions
	Science Inquiry Skills	Processing and analysing data and information

TECHNOLOGIES

YEAR	STRAND	CONTENT
5 & 6	Design and Technologies Knowledge and Understanding	• Investigate how electrical energy can control movement, sound or light in a designed product or system
	Design and Technologies Processes and Production Skills	• Generate, develop and communicate design ideas and processes for audiences using appropriate technical terms and graphical representation techniques • Select appropriate materials, components, tools, equipment and techniques and apply safe procedures to make designed solutions • Negotiate criteria for success that include sustainability to evaluate design ideas, processes and solutions • Develop project plans that include consideration of resources when making designed solutions individually and collaboratively

MATHEMATICS

YEAR	STRAND	CONTENT
5 & 6	Measurement and Geometry	Using units of measurement Geometric reasoning

AC

OTHER CURRICULUM LINKS

GENERAL CAPABILITIES

- Literacy
- Numeracy
- Information and Communication Technology (ICT) Capability
- Critical and Creative Thinking

ASSESSMENT

The following resources are provided for assessing students at different stages of the STEM investigations:

- Generic reproducible 1 (Key vocabulary table), for assessing understanding of vocabulary
- Generic reproducible 2 (Self-evaluation), for student self-evaluation of the learning process
- Generic reproducible 3 (Responding to the investigation), for assessing student engagement in the challenge, and the collaboration and skills involved in the design thinking stages
- Generic reproducible 5 (Design thinking assessment rubric), for evaluating student engagement in the design thinking stages
- Learning journal templates 1, 2, 3 and 4, for incorporating student reflection and evaluation

GETTING READY FOR THE INVESTIGATION

You can prepare yourself and students for this STEM investigation in the following ways:

- Identify groups of students who will work well together.
- Review the **Key science knowledge** that supports this investigation, and look at the **Useful links**.
- Investigate the **Useful apps**.
- Gather materials for the three activities in the Tune-in session.
- Start collecting additional materials for prototyping (as shown on the **Materials needed** list).
- Determine where prototypes will be kept between lessons.
- Create a wall space where students can share their ideas in the Ideate stage.
- Organise the class into pairs.
- Start thinking about:
  - » how the shadow size and shape cast by the prototypes will be evaluated
  - » who will act as the council, and 'approve' the designs.

USEFUL APPS

- App for making notes using text, drawings, images, weblinks and audio, such as Notability
- App for creating a learning journal, such as Book Creator
- App for creating semantic maps (links between different words and/or concepts), such as Popplet
- App for creating interactive links (for example, between descriptions, videos, images and websites and a main image), such as ThingLink
- App for creating multimedia presentations, such as Adobe Spark Video and iMovie
- Survey app such as Typeform (free for small surveys)

USEFUL LINKS

- An animation of the concept of low-shadow buildings, such as at youtube.com/watch?v=xgBCwhioUAM
- An explanation of shadow length change across the day, such as at youtube.com/watch?v=1SN1BOpLZAs
- A game that shows how the movement of a light source affects the size and shape of a shadow, such as at sciencekids.co.nz/gamesactivities/lightshadows.html

RESOURCES PROVIDED

- Generic reproducibles 1, 2, 3, 4, 5, 6
- Reproducibles 4.1, 4.2, 4.3, 4.4, 4.5
- Learning journal templates 1, 2, 3, 4 (on disc)

MATERIALS NEEDED

- Sticky notes (half a pad per pair)
- Paper
- Chalk
- Coloured card
- Pens and markers
- Sticky tape
- Pipe-cleaners
- Cardboard
- Opaque materials, such as wood, cardboard and fabric of light and dark colours
- Transparent materials, such as cellophane (clear or coloured), glass and clear plastic
- Translucent materials, such as frosted glass and plastic
- Light sources, such as torches
- Other materials to build prototypes, such as plastic construction blocks, recycled packaging and craft materials

KEY SCIENCE KNOWLEDGE

This section provides an overview of the key science concepts and vocabulary needed for this unit.

ALL ABOUT LIGHT

Light is a form of energy that humans can see. We are able to see light when it travels from a light source directly or via another object to our eyes.

Light travels in a straight line until it reaches an object. What happens next depends on the material the object is made from. The light might pass through the material, be **reflected**, be **refracted** or be **absorbed** – or it might do more than one of these things.

For example, objects appear to be different colours because they absorb some light energies and reflect others.

A **transparent** material will let light through it, but might reflect or refract light too.

Translucent materials reflect light and allow some light to pass through, but they do it in an unusual way. The light is scattered in many different directions. This means that a translucent object, or objects seen through it, appear to be cloudy or distorted.

When light reaches an **opaque** object, some of the light is absorbed (as heat) by the object while the rest of the light is reflected. A shadow appears on the other side of the object. See **STEM Investigation 20 (Shine a new light on student work)** for more information on light.

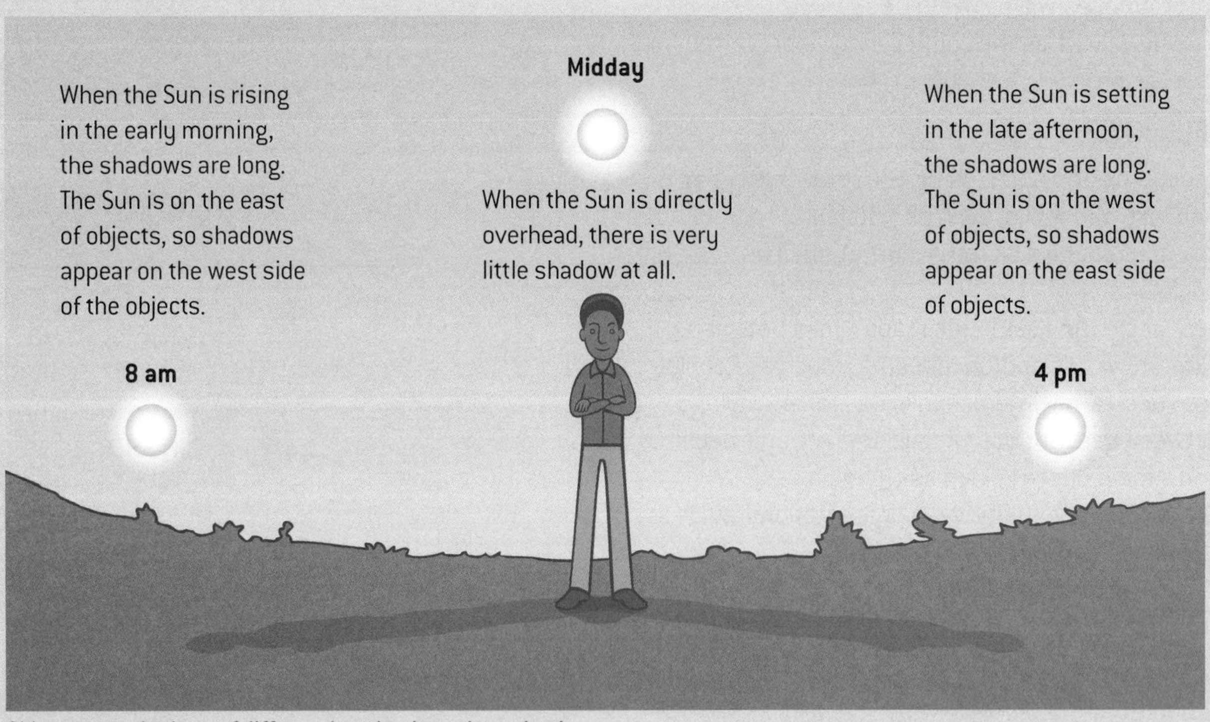

Objects cast shadows of different lengths throughout the day.

KEY VOCABULARY

absorption – the taking in of light by a material
opaque – does not allow light to travel through and therefore is not see-through
reflection – bouncing of light off a surface
refraction – the bending of light when it travels from one material (such as air) to another (such as water)
translucent – transmitting light so that objects can't be seen clearly – it is semi-transparent
transparent – see-through

→ TUNE IN

1. Ask students to complete **Generic reproducible 1 (Key vocabulary table)** using the key vocabulary for this unit: absorption, opaque, reflection, refraction, translucent, transparent. This reproducible will also be used at the end of the unit, to demonstrate changes in understanding.
2. Watch a video clip about a low-shadow building concept (see **Useful apps/links**).
3. Discuss students' prior knowledge of tall buildings and create an anchor chart using **Reproducible 4.1 (Anchor chart)** to describe their observations of shape, materials, height and shadows.
4. Explore different properties of light and shadow. Before engaging in the challenge, students need to have an understanding of how light travels in a straight line, how shadow length varies across the day and how the angle of a light source with the ground changes the shape of shadows.

ACTIVITY 1: LIGHT AND SHADOWS

1. Shine a torch and elicit the observation from the students that the light beam travels in a straight line.
2. Ask the students to view a variety of objects that are opaque (such as solid shape blocks), translucent (such as frosted plastic) and transparent (such as clear plastic) and make predictions about which objects will create shadows. Provide students with **Reproducible 4.2 (Transparent, translucent or opaque?)** to record their predictions and findings.
3. Test the predictions. In small groups, have students shine a torch towards the objects and observe if they can cast shadows or if the light can travel through the object.
4. Discuss the terms 'transparent', 'translucent' and 'opaque'.

ACTIVITY 2: TRACKING SHADOWS

1. Start with a riddle. Question: 'I follow you around in the day and I say goodbye to you at night. Who am I?' Answer: 'Your shadow.' Explain that the students will be tracking their shadow across the day.
2. Students work outside in pairs. Using chalk, one student stands in a sunny location while the other draws around their feet and then around their shadow. Students then note the time of day and the position of the Sun. Repeat at least twice more across the day.
3. Discuss the effect of the position of the Sun on the length of shadows across the day. Use the terms 'light source', 'opaque' and 'shadow'.
4. Consider showing a video clip about shadow length across the day (see **Useful apps/links**).

ACTIVITY 3: SHADOW SHAPES

1. Demonstrate that the distance between an object and the light source changes the size of the shadow cast, using an online game (see **Useful apps/links**).
2. Using opaque objects in a variety of shapes identified in **Reproducible 4.2**, have the students identify and describe the shadows they observe as they move a torch around the objects in a circular orbit. Provide students with **Reproducible 4.3 (Shadow shapes)** to record their observations.
3. Discuss their observations using the terms 'light source', 'opaque' and 'shadow'.

5. Introduce the STEM investigation and challenge to the students. Provide them with the student card and read the information together. Revisit **Reproducible 4.1** and add to students' ideas in a new colour to reflect their learning from the initial activities. Have students consider the impact of shadows on homes and gardens.
6. Introduce the design thinking process by reviewing the stages on the student card.
7. Explain that students will keep a journal about their learning at different stages of the design.

TOP TIP! During the Tune-in session, conduct vocabulary activities to highlight and develop key vocabulary knowledge. Activities could include drawing semantic webs, creating a word wall or paired discussions. Check the **Key vocabulary** definitions or read the **Key science knowledge** for a refresher on the key terms and concepts.

USEFUL APPS/LINKS

- An animation of the concept of low-shadow buildings, such as at youtube.com/watch?v=xgBCwhioUAM
- An explanation of shadow length change across the day, such as at youtube.com/watch?v=1SN1BOpLZAs
- A game that shows how the movement of a light source affects the size and shape of a shadow, such as at sciencekids.co.nz/gamesactivities/lightshadows.html

EMPATHISE

During the Empathise stage of the design thinking process, students focus on finding out about different points of view. To empathise with others, they need to research some of the experiences that people have had with shadowing, as well as their opinions. Students will create a survey, conduct an interview, take notes, ask questions, draw diagrams and take photos where relevant.

ACTIVITY 1: INTERVIEW FAMILY AND FRIENDS

Ask students to interview family members or friends about their perceptions of and/or experiences with shadowing by tall buildings. Provide students with **Reproducible 4.4 (Family and friends interview)** to record their notes. Students are provided with ideas for interview questions, as well as the opportunity to ask their own questions.

ACTIVITY 2: SURVEY THE WIDER COMMUNITY

Ask students to create a survey for another class, year level or the school community to find out their experiences, understandings and opinions about shadowing. The survey should have statements with a five-point scale using degrees of agreement or disagreement (such as 'strongly agree', 'agree', 'neither agree or disagree', 'disagree', 'strongly disagree'). Model how to create a statement. Ask pairs of students to write statements relating to the impact of shadowing. Provide them with **Reproducible 4.5 (Shadow survey plan)** to guide their statement creation. Each pair chooses one or two statements to be included in the class survey.

ACTIVITY 3: EMPATHISE

Ask students to consider the key insights they have gathered from the interviews and the surveys. Discuss these as a class.

PROMPTS

- What were some of the issues people raised?
- What new points of view did you find?
- What were some of the different opinions you discovered?
- How was interviewing a person different to using a survey?

MORE VOCABULARY

- empathise – understand and consider another person's or group's point of view
- point of view – an opinion, attitude or judgement considered in a particular way

JOURNAL TIP

Ask students to complete **Learning journal template 1 (Empathise page)** while they are completing the different tasks. Remind them to date their notes and include photos or drawings of relevant information.

USEFUL APPS/LINKS

- App for creating surveys, such as Typeform

ASSESSMENT

This stage of the design thinking process offers opportunities to observe students collecting information, developing questions, and recording their notes and thinking in their journal.

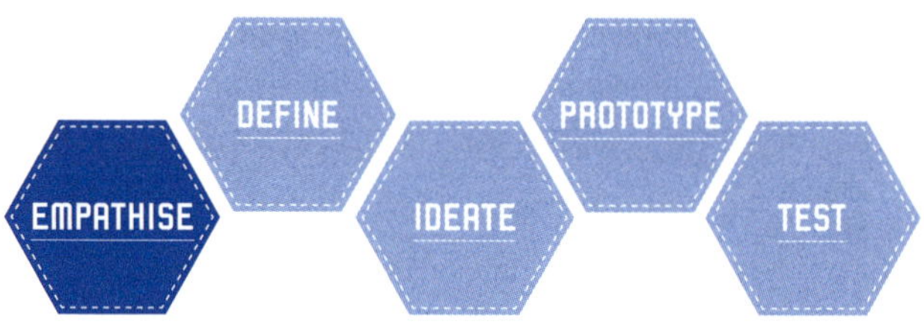

DEFINE

The main focus of this stage of the design thinking process is to reframe the challenge. The initial challenge is quite open, so at this stage students learn how to define what needs to be done. This includes noting insights that have been generated.

ACTIVITY 1: CONSIDER OBSERVATIONS

1. Students consider the information they gathered in the Empathise stage. They may work in pairs or small groups. Provide them with a whiteboard, large sheet of paper and/or sticky notes to collate some of the key information they have gathered about shadows, issues with shadowing, and the effect of different materials.
2. Students should discuss one section of **Learning journal template 2 (Define page)** at a time, write their responses, then continue discussing their ideas for the next section, until the task is complete. This provides students with opportunities to hear others' responses and also provides the teacher with input points.
3. Discuss information gathered about the impact of different materials on shadowing. Provide students with the opportunity to research further. Ask them to write other information they would like to know, such as learning about how architects and town planners take shadowing into consideration when designing and planning. Provide them with **Generic reproducible 4 (Key question table)** to assist them to record their questions, findings and sources.

ACTIVITY 2: CONSIDER INSIGHTS

Students think of at least one insight they have gained from the process; for example, materials can reflect, refract or absorb light.

Students add this insight to **Learning journal template 2**. They should then relate this insight to their design.

When considering insights, students could think about the following:

- What was something unexpected that you saw or found out? How was it unexpected?
- How will you decide on the most important aspect of reducing the issues of shadowing with tall buildings?
- Is there any other information that you need or would like to know? How will you find out?

ACTIVITY 3: CONSIDER CONSTRAINTS

At this stage, let students know the constraints of the challenge, by describing the materials available, time frame for the investigation and how to test shadowing with prototypes. Students can then update **Learning journal template 2**.

PROMPTS

- What did you discover?
- What were the most important pieces of information that you gathered?
- What was something new that you learned?
- What other information do you need?

MORE VOCABULARY

- define – state the meaning of something
- insight – an accurate understanding of someone or something

JOURNAL TIP

Discuss the term 'insight'. Explain that it relates to something students have learned about the people and their responses to the surveys, as well as information gathered through research or excursions. You could refer to **Learning journal template 2**.

→ IDEATE

The Ideate stage of the design thinking process is all about generating lots of ideas. Students need to be flexible in their thinking and able to move beyond obvious ideas. At this stage, ideas are not judged, just generated and gathered.

ACTIVITY: GENERATE IDEAS

1. Ask groups of students to draw or write their ideas.
2. Each new idea should be written or drawn on a separate piece of paper or sticky note.
3. Ask students to group ideas on a wall or board.
4. Ask students to look at the different ideas and provide feedback to each other. It is important that students don't defend their ideas at this stage. They should just be listening to the feedback.
5. After the initial feedback, ask students to come up with more ideas. Encourage them to be creative and even radical.
6. Ask students to choose four of their ideas to write in their journal. Students use **Learning journal template 3 (Ideate page)** to do this. Ask students to choose one idea to explore further and explain the reasoning behind their choice.

TOP TIP!

At this stage, students may have produced a series of annotated drawings about how shadowing of tall buildings can be minimised. They may have a collection of sticky notes, which they can organise into related ideas. Encourage students to view and read others' ideas before giving feedback. Feedback could be within small groups or between partners. Considering others' ideas is an important part of this process, so students can build on their own ideas as they continue to ideate.

At each stage of this activity, ask students to discuss their thoughts before writing their responses. This will help them to think through their ideas and select their final ideas to develop.

PROMPTS

- How do these ideas relate to shadowing?
- How might you test your design?
- How can you make it represent a real building?
- How can you make it demonstrate how light and therefore shadowing will affect surrounding buildings?
- What if you had to use different materials?

MORE VOCABULARY

- feedback – information about, for example, a person's performance or the design of a product, which can be used to make improvements
- ideate – generate many ideas without making judgements about the ideas

JOURNAL TIP

When choosing four ideas to include in the journal, students should try to choose ideas that aren't related, to show a range of ideas.

USEFUL APPS/LINKS

- Tools for creating ideas, such as at creatingminds.org/tools/tools_ideation.htm
- Tips for creativity and innovation, such as at designorate.com/creativity-innovation-in-education/

ASSESSMENT

At the Ideate stage, assessment could include observations about the number and diversity of students' ideas, and their ability to provide feedback and create additional ideas. Reflection in the journal should provide an insight into some of the reasoning behind students' choices.

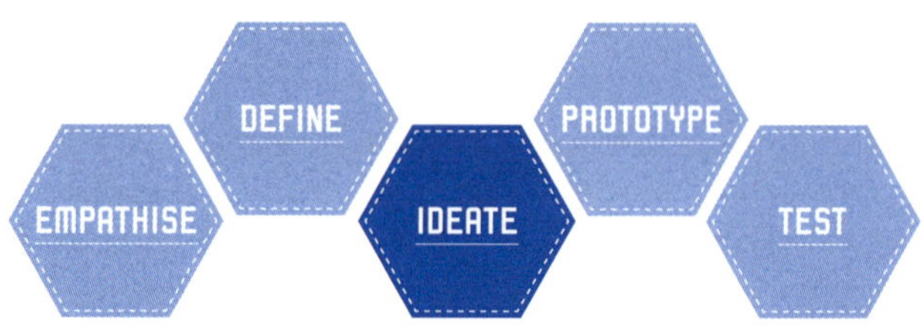

→ PROTOTYPE

At this stage of the design thinking process, students are asked to create a physical prototype of a building that demonstrates that the impact of shadowing has been considered. It is the stage where students need to get their ideas out of their head and presented in a way that engages other students and helps them to understand the concept. When students create, it helps them to think and solve problems and disagreements. Students can role-play, make storyboards or use sticky notes when they prototype. The most important feature is that viewers can interact with whatever is produced.

Encourage students to photograph or film during the prototyping and testing stages. This information can be used to show the learning behind the design thinking process in action.

ACTIVITY: TRANSFORM IDEAS INTO PROTOTYPES

1. Students review the ideas generated at the Ideate stage. Provide them with an A3 copy of **Generic reproducible 6 (In the frame)** so they can organise their ideas into two sections: 'least relevant' and 'most relevant'. Students continue to cycle through this activity until they have an idea to start prototyping.
2. Provide students with a range of materials to use to create their prototype. Remind students that a prototype should be created rapidly and is not meant to look 'nice'.
3. After a prototype has been created, ask students to see if it works and get feedback from others.
4. Students then use the feedback to prototype again.

Ask students to fill in the Prototype section of **Learning journal template 4 (Prototype and test page)**. See the **Journal tip** for further student guidance.

PROMPTS

- What worked?
- How could it be improved?
- What else do you need to know, do or have?
- What other suggestions do you have?

MORE VOCABULARY

- feedback – information about, for example, a person's performance or the design of a product, which can be used to make improvements
- prototype – an initial version of a model of a product or process that is used to develop a final model

TOP TIP!

The Prototype stage is often very messy. It is important that students are focusing on their ideas, rather than the end product. Provide them with lots of materials – recycling depots can be a useful source of resources. Students may add labels to prototypes to explain some of the main features. Photographing and annotating pictures of prototypes can be useful.

To gain feedback, students could ask each other some of the following questions:

- What is the main feature of your prototype?
- How can you show the impact of shadowing?
- Which aspects work best? What will you keep?
- Which aspects need changing? How might you do this?
- What other materials might you need?

JOURNAL TIP

Remind students to highlight the main features of their prototype. If students are creating an electronic journal, they can insert a photo of their prototype and annotate it.

USEFUL APPS/LINKS

- App for creating interactive links (for example, between descriptions, videos, images and websites and a main image), such as ThingLink
- App for making notes using text, drawings, images, weblinks and audio, such as Notability

ASSESSMENT

Observe students as they make changes to their designs. Are they able to consider feedback, make modifications and move rapidly through this process. Or do they have difficulties with holding onto an idea and accepting feedback?

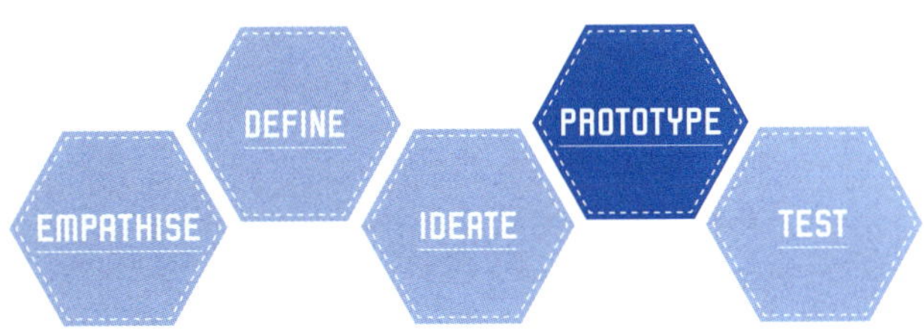

→ TEST

At this stage of the design thinking process, students test their prototype to see how it meets the criteria in the challenge. Students check to see if their prototype meets the criteria set at the start of the design process.

ACTIVITY: TEST FEEDBACK

1. Students take their last prototype and consider the initial needs of the council and residents.
2. Ask students to check whether or not their design works. If not, what do they need to do to make it work?
3. Provide the opportunity to cycle through the prototyping and testing stages again.

Ask students to fill in the Test part of **Learning journal template 4 (Prototype and test page)**. See the **Journal tip** for further student guidance.

PROMPTS

- Does your prototype do what you wanted it to do?
- Are there other features you could add?
- What needs to be changed?
- What works well?

MORE VOCABULARY

- evaluate – assess something, perhaps considering what worked and what didn't
- feature – a specific aspect of something, such as size, shape, colour and quality
- feedback – information about, for example, a person's performance or the design of a product, which can be used to make improvements
- prototype – an initial version of a model of a product or process that is used to develop a final model
- review – consider an idea, process or product and decide what needs to be changed and what works

JOURNAL TIP

Ask students to think about why it is important to test their ideas before they build their final design.

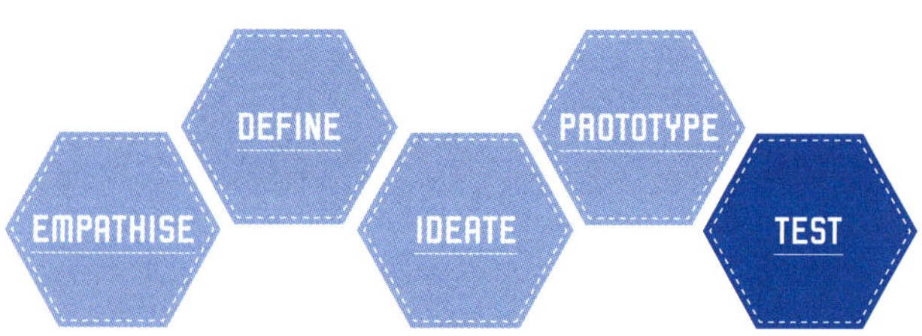

→ SHARE AND EVALUATE

At this stage of the investigation, students are provided with an opportunity to share their final design, as well as the processes involved in the investigation. Students evaluate their learning journals and their solutions.

ACTIVITY 1: BRING THE DESIGNS TOGETHER

1. Students can create an iMovie or use Adobe Spark Video to demonstrate the process and thinking behind the designs. There should be an element of narration, where they are sharing their story about points of view, insights, prototyping and solutions.
2. Students should include their learning journals with the display so others can see the different stages of the design process.

ACTIVITY 2: EVALUATE AND GIVE FEEDBACK

1. Provide students with **Generic reproducible 2 (Self-evaluation)** to complete.
2. Ask students to provide feedback to each other about the most interesting features, the aspects that were most difficult and the changes that they would make if they repeated the task.
3. Provide students with opportunities to share their designs with the wider community. This could include inviting a town planner, architect, or a friend or family member with relevant experience. It may be possible to share some of the videos with an expert for feedback about the designs.

ASSESSMENT

Ask students to again complete **Generic reproducible 1 (Key vocabulary table)**, using the key vocabulary for this unit: absorption, opaque, reflection, refraction, translucent, transparent. Compare their table with the one they completed at the Tune-in stage, to demonstrate changes in understanding.

Students complete **Generic reproducible 3 (Responding to the investigation)**. Compare their responses to those on **Generic reproducible 2**.

Teachers and students each complete **Generic reproducible 5 (Design thinking assessment rubric)**. Students compare the teacher feedback with their self-assessment of their design thinking skills.

STEM INVESTIGATIONS

Name: ....

Date: ....

Note the key features of some buildings you know.
Think about how their shapes affect the shadows they cast.

Height of tall buildings

3D shapes we recognise

Tall buildings we know

Shadows cast by tall buildings

Materials used in construction

TRANSPARENT, TRANSLUCENT OR OPAQUE?

Name: ....

Date: ....

STEM INVESTIGATIONS

Choose some objects and predict whether they are transparent, translucent or opaque. Then check to see if you are correct or not.

OBJECT	PREDICTION (✓)			CORRECT ANSWER
	Transparent	Translucent	Opaque	

STEM Investigations, UP, ISBN 978 1 4202 4154 9 © Macmillan Science and Education Australia 2018

Name: ....

Date: ....

STEM INVESTIGATIONS

SHAPE (name and draw)	**SHADOW** (describe and draw)

Name: ....

Date: ....

Interview at least two people. Find out their experiences, knowledge and opinions about the shadows that tall buildings make.

QUESTION	PERSON 1	PERSON 2
What are some of the problems with tall buildings and shadows?		
Can you describe a situation where shadowing has been a problem?		
What should councils do about tall buildings?		

STEM Investigations, UP, ISBN 978 1 4202 4154 9 © Macmillan Science and Education Australia 2018

EMPATHISE

STEM INVESTIGATIONS

Name: ....

Date: ....

Use this template to help you plan a survey about tall buildings and shadows.

Words associated with tall buildings and shadows:

Statements relating to tall buildings and shadows:

Choose your top two statements:

1)

2)

INVENT A HELPFUL PRODUCT FOR A HOMELESS PERSON

→ INTRODUCTION

People can become homeless for many reasons. A person may be considered homeless if their accommodation is inadequate or uncertain, or if they don't have control of their space for social relations. Some homeless people live in tents, cars or outdoors; others live in special accommodation. Homelessness can affect people in many different ways. It can make staying at school or keeping a job difficult. It can lead to long-term unemployment and chronic health issues.

In this STEM investigation, students are challenged to create a helpful product for a homeless person that has two purposes. Students learn about some of the issues associated with homelessness. They explore the properties of different materials as they consider how they can design a product using sustainable materials.

THE CHALLENGE

Your school is raising money for a charity that provides care packs to people who are homeless. You want to do more than raise money, and you've asked a family friend for advice. He is an industrial designer and has suggested that you design something extra for the care packs. If you design it, he'll make it – but he says it must be made from sustainable materials.

Your challenge is to design a product that can be used in two different ways. It might be a piece of clothing, a bag, a shelter and/or a comfort item. You will need to decide what kinds of material to use and why, considering the properties of different materials and their costs. As part of the investigation, you will learn about the production of natural materials and synthetic materials, and consider issues of sustainability.

KEY UNDERSTANDINGS

- People become homeless for different reasons.
- Basic needs of people include shelter, food and water, clothing and safety.
- Materials have different properties and degrees of absorption, elasticity and durability.
- Many materials can be recycled.
- PET is a strong synthetic material.
- rPET products are sustainable materials made from recycled PET.

KEY VOCABULARY

fibre

natural materials

properties

recycle

sustainable

synthetic materials

KEY SKILLS

- Evaluate information.
- Interview others.
- Consider different points of view.
- Generate and evaluate ideas.
- Refine ideas.

KEY ACTIONS

- Research the needs of people who are homeless.
- Interview people involved with supporting homeless people.
- Learn about sustainable materials.
- Design a product that has two different uses.

OVERVIEW OF STAGES

TUNE IN:

Students learn about homelessness, including facts about the number of homeless people, reasons why people become homeless and some of the issues they face. They also explore the properties of different materials to prepare to design a product for homeless people.

EMPATHISE

Students find out about some of the issues about homelessness from the point of view of homeless people. They interview organisations and people who support homeless people. They learn about products that have been designed to help homeless people.

DEFINE

Students think about the needs of homeless people and the design constraints regarding the use of sustainable materials. They consider the need to design a product with two uses.

IDEATE

Students generate ideas for a product that can have two uses.

PROTOTYPE

Students choose one or two ideas to transform ideas into physical representations (models). These are created rapidly, using simple materials.

TEST

Prototypes are tested. Students share their prototypes and provide feedback to each other. They are given the opportunity to cycle through the Prototype and Test stages again.

SHARE AND EVALUATE:

Students create their final prototype and prepare a pitch about their product. These are shared and evaluated, with opportunities for expert feedback. The possibility of creating an awareness event or expo could be explored.

SUGGESTED SCHEDULE

LESSON	STAGE
1–2	**Tune in**: learn about homelessness, explore the properties of materials and introduce the student challenge
3–5	**Empathise**: consider homelessness from the point of view of homeless people and the organisations supporting them, interview and research, and write/record in journal
6	**Define**: define the main issues about homelessness and the constraints of the design brief, and write/record in journal
7	**Ideate**: develop ideas and write/record in journal
8–10	**Prototype** and **Test**: conduct prototyping and testing cycles and write/record in journal
11–13	**Share and evaluate**: create a product pitch, and share and evaluate designs and prototypes

→ CURRICULUM LINKS

The following tables show the key Science, Technologies and Mathematics curricula with which this STEM investigation is aligned.

SCIENCE

YEAR	STRAND	SUB-STRAND AND CONTENT
6	Science Understanding	Chemical sciences: • Changes to materials can be reversible, such as melting, freezing and evaporating; or irreversible, such as burning and rusting
5 & 6	Science as a Human Endeavour	Use and influence of science: • Scientific understandings, discoveries and inventions are used to solve problems that directly affect people's lives

TECHNOLOGIES

YEAR	STRAND	CONTENT
5 & 6*	Design and Technologies Processes and Production Skills	• Critique needs or opportunities for designing, and investigate materials, components, tools, equipment and processes to achieve intended designed solutions • Generate, develop and communicate design ideas and processes for audiences using appropriate technical terms and graphical representation techniques • Negotiate criteria for success that include sustainability to evaluate design ideas, processes and solutions • Develop project plans that include consideration of resources when making designed solutions individually and collaboratively

* If students are making a model of their product.

MATHEMATICS

YEAR	STRAND	SUB-STRAND
5	Number and Algebra	Money and financial mathematics
5 & 6	Measurement and Geometry	Using units of measurement

→ OTHER CURRICULUM LINKS

GENERAL CAPABILITIES

- Literacy
- Numeracy
- Information and Communication Technology (ICT) Capability
- Critical and Creative Thinking

CROSS-CURRICULUM PRIORITIES

- Sustainability

→ ASSESSMENT

The following resources are provided for assessing students at different stages of the STEM investigations:

- Generic reproducible 1 (Key vocabulary table), for assessing understanding of vocabulary
- Generic reproducible 2 (Self-evaluation), for student self-evaluation of the learning process
- Generic reproducible 3 (Define graphic organiser), for assessing student engagement in the challenges, and the collaboration and skills involved in the design thinking stages
- Generic reproducible 5 (Design thinking assessment rubric), for evaluating student engagement in the design thinking stages
- Learning journal templates 1, 2, 3 and 4, for incorporating student reflection and evaluation

→ GETTING READY FOR THE INVESTIGATION

You can prepare yourself and students for this STEM investigation in the following ways:

- Identify groups of students who will work well together.
- Review the **Key science knowledge** that supports this investigation, and look at the **Useful links**.
- Investigate the **Useful apps**.
- Gather materials for the exploration of different materials during the Tune-in session.
- Start collecting additional materials for prototyping (as shown on the **Materials needed** list).
- Determine where prototypes will be kept between lessons.
- Create a wall space where students can share their ideas in the Ideate stage.
- Organise the class into pairs.
- Start thinking about:
  - » connecting with organisations that support homeless people
  - » organising a speaker or mentor
  - » finding useful school community contacts, such as social workers, charity employees and social entrepreneurs
  - » additional equipment that might be useful, such as sewing machines
  - » additional adult assistance for the prototyping stage
  - » the possibility of incorporating an awareness day, fundraiser or expo when sharing designs.

USEFUL APPS

- App for creating semantic maps (links between different words and/or concepts), such as Popplet
- App for creating interactive links (for example, between descriptions, videos, images and websites and a main image), such as ThingLink
- App for making notes using text, drawings, images, weblinks and audio, such as Notability
- App for creating multimedia presentations, such as Adobe Spark Video or iMovie
- App for creating surveys, such as Typeform
- App for sharing ideas, thoughts, questions and images, such as Padlet or Lino
- App for drawing shapes, inserting images, making annotations or adding to an inserted image, such as Drawisland

USEFUL LINKS

- Article about dual-use products for homeless people, such as at fastcompany.com/3055886/this-jacket-designed-for-refugees-transforms-into-a-tent and youtube.com/watch?v=hZuiJnar8ml
- Facts about homelessness, such as at homelessnessaustralia.org.au/sites/homelessnessaus/files/2017-07/Homelessness%20in%20Australiav2.pdf and huffingtonpost.com/bill-quigley/ten-facts-about-homelessn_b_5977946.html
- Information about waste and sustainability, such as at schoolsequella.det.nsw.edu.au/file/c860398f-225a-47ae-97ee-61860f08d04c/1/WastePrimary.zip/index.htm
- Fabrics information for teachers, such as at textileschool.com/articles/330/type-of-fabrics
- Information about rPET products, such as at waste2wear.com/faq and earthhero.com/whats-the-deal-with-rpet

RESOURCES PROVIDED

- Generic reproducibles 1, 2, 3, 5, 6
- Reproducibles 5.1, 5.2, 5.3
- Learning journal templates 1, 2, 3, 4 (on disc)

MATERIALS NEEDED

- Sticky notes (half a pad per group)
- Paper
- Coloured card
- Pens and markers
- Sticky tape
- Pipe-cleaners
- Cardboard
- Offcuts and recycled materials
- Small plastic pipes
- Different types of material, including cotton, silk, wool, acrylic (such as Perspex), elastane (such as Spandex), nylon, plastic
- Large paperclip
- Weight
- Dropper
- Water
- Ruler
- Sandpaper
- Containers made from a range of materials, such as plastic, cardboard, fabric, paper

KEY SCIENCE KNOWLEDGE

This section provides an overview of the key science concepts and vocabulary needed for this unit.

WHAT ARE SUSTAINABLE MATERIALS?

In science, a material is considered **sustainable** if it is sourced or made in a way that can be maintained and that causes minimal harm to the environment. Products made from sustainable materials have environmental, social and economic benefits. Like other products, they can be made from **natural**, **synthetic** or **recycled** materials, or combinations of these materials. All materials are composed of chemicals. They can consist of one type of chemical or a mixture of chemicals.

NATURAL MATERIALS

These materials come from living things or from the ground. Examples are wool from sheep, paper from trees, linen from plants (flax) and minerals such as metals. A natural material is not necessarily sustainable. For example, the growing and processing of cotton are not sustainable practices.

SYNTHETIC MATERIALS

These materials are made by people. They are manufactured from petroleum-based chemicals or by adding chemicals to plant extracts such as cellulose. Many synthetic materials are made by joining smaller synthetic units into chains called polymers. Nylon and polyesters are examples of synthetic polymer **fibres**.

BLENDED MATERIALS

These materials are a combination of two or more natural or synthetic materials. These blends have special **properties** such as being elastic, or crease- or water-resistant.

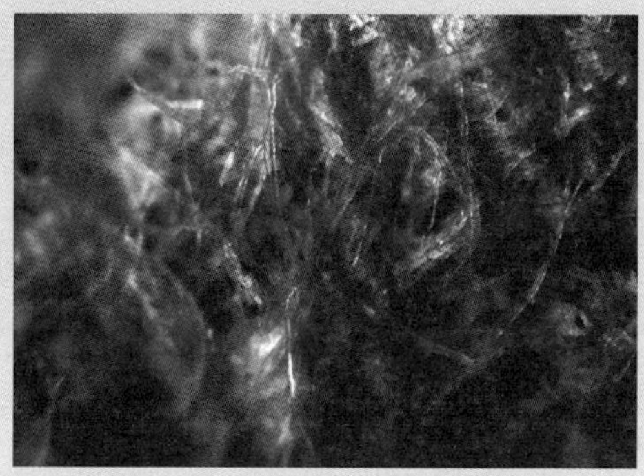

The fibres of tissue paper look like long, thin threads under a microscope.

RECYCLING ONE MATERIAL INTO ANOTHER

The process of recycling uses waste materials to manufacture a different product. PET (polyethylene terephthalate) is a polymer that can be heated and spun into fibres to create polyester fabric, or moulded and solidified to make containers such as plastic drink bottles. Recycled PET (rPET) can be used to make stretchy clothing, carpet and other fabric items. During manufacture, the original product undergoes changes that are not reversible. This means the changes made to them are permanent.

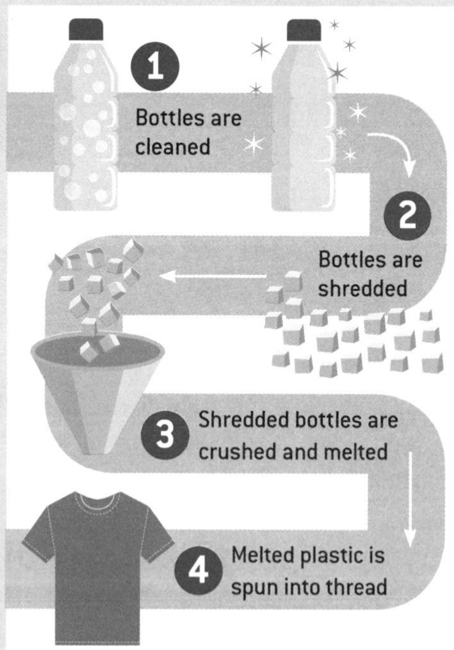

PET in plastic bottles can be recycled into rPET clothing.

REVERSIBLE AND IRREVERSIBLE CHANGE

Irreversible change to a substance or material means the change cannot be undone. Burning paper or cooking an egg are examples of irreversible changes. Sometimes in an irreversible change, new materials are made that are useful, such as in the making of plastics. Reversible change to a substance or material means the change can be undone or reversed. It may look or feel like a different material, but the change is reversible; for example, freezing juice to make an icypole.

KEY VOCABULARY

fibre – a natural or synthetic thread that may be manufactured into products such as fabric and fibreglass
natural materials – materials that come from plants, animals or the ground, for example, wool, cotton and gold
properties – characteristics that can be measured, such as elasticity and strength
recycled – make a different product, such as rPET, from a waste material
sustainable – able to be sourced or made while minimising harm to the environment
synthetic materials – materials manufactured by people, usually using petroleum products

→ TUNE IN

1. Ask students to complete **Generic reproducible 1 (Key vocabulary table)** using the key vocabulary.
2. Students work in groups of three to brainstorm and define the word 'sustainable'. Compare their definition to one from a dictionary. Have students repeat this for 'recycle'. Discuss how these two words are connected.
3. Ask groups of students to create a concept map about homelessness. Have them identify their knowledge, understandings and points of view.
4. Create a short slideshow with key facts about homelessness (see **Useful apps/links**). Ask students to return to their concept map with a different coloured pen and add new knowledge and questions.
5. Before engaging in the challenge, students need to know the difference between natural and synthetic materials, some properties of different materials, and that 'sustainable' products can be natural or synthetic.

ACTIVITY 1: MAGNIFIED FIBRES

1. Use very powerful magnifying glasses (or microscopes) and a selection of natural and synthetic fabrics (including open-weave fabrics).
2. Observe the length and roughness of the material's fibre. Ask students to compare and contrast what they see. (Natural fibres should be shorter and rougher.)

ACTIVITY 2: PHYSICAL PROPERTIES OF MATERIALS

1. Give student groups some natural and synthetic materials (see **Materials needed** list), a large paperclip and a weight. Different groups will test different physical properties and share results. Provide them with **Reproducible 5.1 (Properties of materials)**.
2. Explain that elasticity is the ability of a material to stretch and return to its original shape. Some groups will test this property by hanging the strips vertically, measuring, attaching a weight and measuring again. They should observe if the fabric returns to its original length.
3. Students test absorbency by putting two drops of water onto the centre of each fabric, then measuring the diameter of the absorbed water.
4. Students rub sandpaper across the material, each time in the same direction. Students record how many times they do this before the fibres show wear.
5. Discuss garments/items that could be made from elastic, absorbent and durable materials.

ACTIVITY 3: RECYCLING MATERIALS

1. Collect a range of (clean) containers made from plastic, cardboard, fabric and paper.
2. Explain that recycled synthetic products can be considered sustainable too. Introduce PET products and rPET. Reinforce that rPET uses synthetic PET materials that have been recycled and undergone permanent changes to make a different sustainable material.
3. Tell students that they need to choose some items to make a different useful object/device. Have them describe its function and useful properties.
4. Students could then peer assess and evaluate each object/device, and judge it on its creativity, usefulness and product design.

6. Introduce the STEM investigation and challenge to the students. Provide them with the student card and read the information together. Ask students to think about some of the main issues for homeless people and what they could design that would be helpful.
7. Introduce the design thinking process by reviewing the stages on the student card.
8. Explain that students will keep a journal about their learning at the different stages of the design.

TOP TIP! During the Tune-in stage, conduct vocabulary activities to highlight and develop key vocabulary knowledge. Activities could include drawing semantic webs, creating a word wall or paired discussions.

USEFUL APPS/LINKS

- Facts about homelessness, such as at http://www.homelessnessaustralia.org.au/sites/homelessnessaus/files/2017-07/Homelessness%20in%20Australiav2.pdf and huffingtonpost.com/bill-quigley/ten-facts-about-homelessn_b_5977946.html

→ EMPATHISE

During the Empathise stage of the design thinking process, students focus on finding out about different points of view. To empathise with others, they need to research some of the experiences that people have had with homelessness or working with homeless people. Students will take notes, ask questions, draw diagrams and take photos where relevant.

It is important to be mindful of some of the experiences people have had and the stories they might share.

ACTIVITY 1: FIND OUT ABOUT HOMELESSNESS

1. Provide students with an opportunity to learn about homelessness from the point of view of people who are or have been homeless. Be mindful that some of the issues could be confronting for students.
2. Provide students with **Reproducible 5.2 (Thinking about homelessness)**. Ask them to complete the first box ('What I think').
3. Watch a video clip or read a story about people's homeless experiences (see **Useful apps/links**).
4. Look at an interactive map about homelessness across regions, towns and cities in your country or state (see **Useful apps/links**).
5. Ask students to fill in the second box ('What I have learned') of **Reproducible 5.2**.
6. Have students return to **Reproducible 5.2** at the end of the investigation so they can complete the third box ('What I think now').

ACTIVITY 2: SUPPORTING HOMELESSNESS

1. Have students interview or request information from an organisation or individual working with homeless people.
2. If interviewing, ask students to create an interview checklist, with questions they would like to ask, as well as space for recording the interviewee's responses. If requesting information, ask the class to generate questions that can be asked via a class letter or email, or have pairs of students write a letter that can be sent via a class email account or via regular mail. If the class has a Twitter account, students can tweet their questions to specific organisations to gain a range of responses.

ACTIVITY 3: HELPFUL PRODUCTS

1. Watch some video clips about products for homeless people that can be used in two different ways (see **Useful apps/links**). Students compare the video clips and their understanding of needs for homeless people.
2. Ask students to consider the main issues for homeless people and compare them to their own living situation.

PROMPTS

- What are some important issues for homeless people?
- What are some organisations doing to support homeless people?
- What were some of the reasons for homelessness?
- How did you feel when finding out about other people's experiences?

MORE VOCABULARY

- empathise – understand and consider another person's or group's point of view
- point of view – an opinion, attitude or judgement considered in a particular way

JOURNAL TIP

Ask students to complete **Learning journal template 1 (Empathise page)** while they are completing the different tasks. Remind them to date their notes and include photos or pictures of relevant information.

USEFUL APPS/LINKS

- People's stories about homelessness, such as at theguardian.com/society/2017/aug/15/how-i-became-homeless-three-peoples-stories and huffingtonpost.com/mark-horvath/my-first-night-homeless_b_850145.html
- Interactive map showing homelessness in your region, such as at abc.net.au/interactives/homeless
- Products for refugees or homeless people, such as at youtube.com/watch?v=kKBLznclWq8 and youtube.com/watch?v=6va0_GPBAzA

ASSESSMENT

This stage of the design thinking process offers opportunities to observe students collecting information, developing questions, and recording their notes and thinking in their journal.

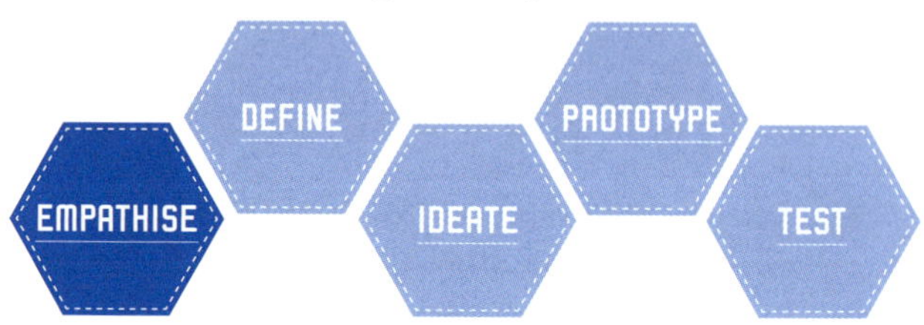

→ DEFINE

The main focus of this stage of the design thinking process is to reframe the challenge. The initial challenge is quite open, so at this stage students learn how to define what needs to be done. This includes noting insights that have been generated.

ACTIVITY 1: CONSIDER OBSERVATIONS

1. Students consider the information they gathered in the Empathise stage. They may work in pairs or small groups. Provide them with a whiteboard, large sheet of paper and/or sticky notes to collate some of the key information they have gathered, including the needs of homeless people.
2. Students should discuss one section of **Learning journal template 2 (Define page)** at a time, write their responses, then continue discussing their ideas for the next section, until the task is complete. This provides students with opportunities to hear others' responses and also provides the teacher with input points.
3. Discuss homelessness and the ways that people are supported. Provide students with the opportunity to research further. Ask them to write other information they would like to know, such as who experiences homelessness, what leads people to become homeless and how organisations help. Provide them with **Generic reproducible 4 (Key question table)** to assist them to record their questions, findings and sources.

ACTIVITY 2: CONSIDER INSIGHTS

Students think of at least one insight they have gained from the process; for example, safety is an important issue for homeless people and many different people become homeless (see **Useful apps/links**).

Students add this insight to **Learning journal template 2** and then write a brief explanation of what needs to be created.

When considering insights, students could think about the following:

- What was something unexpected that you saw or found out? How was it unexpected?
- How will you decide on the most important aspect of the product you are going to design?
- Is there any other information that you need or would like to know? How will you find out?

ACTIVITY 3: CONSIDER CONSTRAINTS

At this stage, let students know the constraints of the challenge, by describing the time frame, available materials and the inclusion of two uses for the product. Remind them that they need to design the product to be made from sustainable materials. Students can then update **Learning journal template 2**.

PROMPTS

- What did you discover?
- What were the most important pieces of information that you gathered?
- What was something new that you learned?
- What other information do you need?

MORE VOCABULARY

- define – state the meaning of something
- insight – an accurate understanding of someone or something

JOURNAL TIP

Discuss the term 'insight'. Explain that it relates to something students have learned about the people and their responses to the surveys, as well as information gathered through research or excursions. You could refer to **Learning journal template 2**.

USEFUL APPS/LINKS

- Information about supporting homeless people, such as at streetsmartaustralia.org/homelessness

EMPATHISE | **DEFINE** | IDEATE | PROTOTYPE | TEST

→ IDEATE

The Ideate stage of the design thinking process is all about generating lots of ideas. Students need to be flexible in their thinking and able to move beyond obvious ideas. At this stage, ideas are not judged, just generated and gathered.

ACTIVITY: GENERATE IDEAS

1. Ask students to write as many words as they can that represent the main needs for humans, such as 'eating', 'drinking', 'sleeping' and 'clothing'. Then ask them to choose one of these general words and write the names of products that meet these needs, such as 'cup', 'bowl' and 'cutlery' for the main need of eating. Finally, ask them to choose two of the main needs and to generate ideas for a product that could be designed to meet both of them.
2. Ask groups of students to draw or write their ideas. Each new idea should be written or drawn on a separate piece of paper or sticky note.
3. Ask students to group ideas on a wall or board.
4. Ask students to look at the different ideas and provide feedback to each other. It is important that students don't defend their ideas at this stage. They should just be listening to the feedback.
5. After the initial feedback, ask students to come up with more ideas. Encourage them to be creative and even radical.
6. Ask students to choose four of their ideas to write in their journal. Students use **Learning journal template 3 (Ideate page)** to do this. Ask students to choose one idea to explore further and explain the reasoning behind their choice.

TOP TIP!

At this stage, students may have produced a series of annotated drawings about products for homeless people. They may have a collection of sticky notes, which they can organise into related ideas. Encourage students to view and read others' ideas before giving feedback. Feedback could be within small groups or between partners. Considering others' ideas is an important part of this process, so students can build on their own ideas as they continue to ideate.

At each stage of this activity, ask students to discuss their thoughts before writing their responses. This will help them to think through their ideas and select their final ideas to develop.

PROMPTS

- How do these ideas relate to the needs of homeless people?
- How might you test your design?
- How can you make it easy to use?
- How can you make it easy to carry?
- What if you had to use different materials?

MORE VOCABULARY

- feedback – information about, for example, a person's performance or the design of a product, which can be used to make improvements
- ideate – generate many ideas without making judgements about the ideas

JOURNAL TIP

When choosing four ideas to include in the journal, students should try to choose four ideas that aren't related.

USEFUL APPS/LINKS

- Tools for creating ideas, such as at creatingminds.org/tools/tools_ideation.htm
- Tips for creativity and innovation, such as at designorate.com/creativity-innovation-in-education

ASSESSMENT

At the Ideate stage, assessment could include observations about the number and diversity of students' ideas, and their ability to provide feedback and create additional ideas. Reflection in the journal should provide an insight into some of the reasoning behind students' choices.

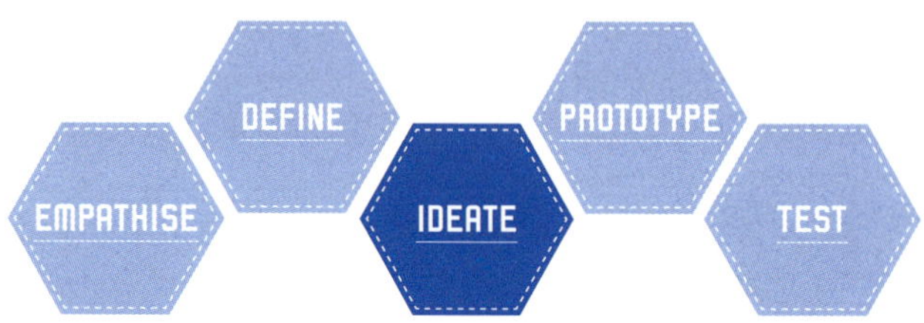

→ PROTOTYPE

At this stage of the design thinking process, students are asked to create a physical prototype of a solution. It is the stage where students need to get their ideas out of their head and presented in a way that engages other students and helps them to understand the concept. When students create, it helps them to think and solve problems and disagreements. Students can role-play, make storyboards or use sticky notes when they prototype. The most important feature is that viewers can interact with whatever is produced.

Encourage students to photograph or film during the prototyping and testing stages. This information can be used to show the learning behind the design thinking process in action.

ACTIVITY: TRANSFORM IDEAS INTO PROTOTYPES

1. Students review the ideas generated at the Ideate stage. Provide them with an A3 copy of **Generic reproducible 6 (In the frame)** so they can organise their ideas into two sections: 'least relevant' and 'most relevant'. Students continue to cycle through this activity until they have an idea to start prototyping.
2. Provide students with a range of materials to use to create their prototype. Remind students that a prototype should be created rapidly and is not meant to look 'nice'.
3. After a prototype has been created, ask students to see if it works and get feedback from others.
4. Students then use the feedback to prototype again.

Ask students to fill in the Prototype section of **Learning journal template 4 (Prototype and test page)**. See the **Journal tip** for further student guidance.

PROMPTS

- What worked?
- How could it be improved?
- What else do you need to know, do or have?
- What other suggestions do you have?

MORE VOCABULARY

- feature – a specific aspect of something, such as size, shape, colour and quality
- feedback – information about, for example, a person's performance or the design of a product, which can be used to make improvements
- prototype – an initial version of a model of a product or process that is used to develop a final model

JOURNAL TIP

Remind students to highlight the main features of their prototype. If students are creating an electronic journal, they can insert a photo of their prototype and annotate it.

USEFUL APPS/LINKS

- App for creating interactive links (for example, between descriptions, videos, images and websites and a main image), such as ThingLink
- App for making notes using text, drawings, images, weblinks and audio, such as Notability

ASSESSMENT

Observe students as they make changes to their designs. Are they able to consider feedback, make modifications and move rapidly through this process? Or do they have difficulties with holding on to an idea and accepting feedback?

TOP TIP!

In the Prototype stage, it is important that students are focusing on their ideas, rather than the end product. Provide them with lots of materials, such as different fabrics and recycled materials. Students may add labels to prototypes to explain some of the main features. Photographing and annotating pictures of prototypes can be useful.

To gain feedback, students could ask each other some of the following questions:

- What is the main feature of your prototype?
- What are its two main uses?
- Which aspects work best? What will you keep?
- Which aspects need changing? How might you do this?
- What other materials might you need?

EMPATHISE · DEFINE · IDEATE · **PROTOTYPE** · TEST

→ TEST

At this stage of the design thinking process, students test their prototype to see how it meets the criteria in the challenge.

ACTIVITY: TEST FEEDBACK

1. Students take their last prototype and consider the initial needs of their audience.
2. Ask students to check whether or not their design works. If not, what do they need to do to make it work?
3. Provide the opportunity to cycle through the prototyping and testing stages again.

Ask students to fill in the Test part of **Learning journal template 4 (Prototype and test page)**. See the **Journal tip** for further student guidance.

PROMPTS

- Does your prototype do what you wanted it to do?
- Does it have additional features that might need to be changed or removed?

MORE VOCABULARY

- evaluate – assess something, perhaps considering what worked and what didn't
- feature – a specific aspect of something, such as size, shape, colour and quality
- feedback – information about, for example, a person's performance or the design of a product, which can be used to make improvements
- prototype – an initial version of a model of a product or process that is used to develop a final model
- review – consider an idea, process or product and decide what needs to be changed and what works

JOURNAL TIP

Ask students to think about why it is important to test their ideas before they build their final design.

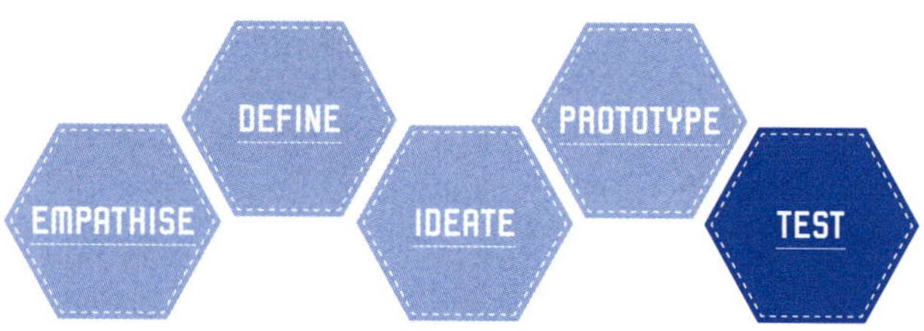

→ SHARE AND EVALUATE

At this stage of the investigation, students are provided with an opportunity to share their final designs, as well as the processes involved in the investigation. Students evaluate their learning journals and their solutions.

ACTIVITY 1: BRING THE DESIGNS TOGETHER

1. Provide students with **Reproducible 5.3 (Product pitch)** to help them plan their pitch. Ensure there is a time restriction for the pitch.
2. Students can create an iMovie or use Adobe Spark Video to demonstrate the process and thinking behind the designs. There should be some narration, where they are sharing points of view, insights, prototyping and solutions.
3. Students should include their learning journals with the display so others can see the different stages of the design process.

ACTIVITY 2: EVALUATE AND GIVE FEEDBACK

1. Provide students with **Generic reproducible 2 (Self-evaluation)** to complete.
2. Ask students to provide feedback to each other about the most interesting features, the aspects that were most difficult and the changes that they would make if they repeated the task.
3. Provide students with opportunities to share their designs. This could include inviting someone from an organisation supporting homelessness, or similar, or a friend or family member with relevant experience. It may be possible to share some of the videos with an expert for feedback.

ASSESSMENT

Ask students to again complete **Generic reproducible 1 (Key vocabulary table)** using the key vocabulary. Compare with the one completed at the Tune-in stage.

Have groups of students add more information to their initial concept map, using a different coloured pen, and consider if they can answer some of their initial questions. Ask students to return to **Reproducible 5.2 (Thinking about homelessness)** and complete the 'What I think now' box. Discuss the changes.

Students complete **Generic reproducible 3 (Responding to the investigation)**. Compare their responses to those on **Generic reproducible 2**.

Teachers and students each complete **Generic reproducible 5 (Design thinking assessment rubric)**. Students compare the teacher's feedback with their self-assessment of their design thinking skills.

STEM INVESTIGATIONS

Name: ....

Date: ....

Use this table to record information about how elastic, absorbent and durable your materials are.

HOW ELASTIC IS IT?			
Material	Initial length of material strip	Length of material strip with weight	Does it return to its original length after the weight is removed?

HOW ABSORBENT IS IT?	
Material	Width of absorbed water drops

HOW DURABLE IS IT?	
Material	Number of sandpaper rubs before fibres appear

STEM Investigations, UP, ISBN 978 1 4202 4154 9

EMPATHISE

STEM INVESTIGATIONS

Name: ....

Date: ....

In the first box, write what you think about homelessness.

When you have learned some more about homelessness, write about it in the second box.

At the end of your design challenge, write what you think about homelessness in the third box.

What I think

What I have learned

What I think now

STEM Investigations, UP, ISBN 978 1 4202 4154 9

STEM INVESTIGATIONS

Name: ....

Date: ....

Use this template to plan a pitch for the product you have designed.

Purpose of product
(highlighting two uses)

Materials used and
reason for choice of materials

Product name and picture

Special features
of the product

Other useful
information to
be included

HELP RECRUIT PEOPLE TO JOURNEY TO MARS

MANAGED WORLD 6

→ INTRODUCTION

The colonisation of Mars continues to be discussed as overpopulation, environmental concerns and decreasing resources challenge us. Many movies have tapped into our fascination with the colonisation of places beyond the Earth, including the 'red planet'.

Any future colonisation of Mars would require humans to undertake a long journey to get there. Humans have been living in space on the International Space Station for many years, with scientists continuously monitoring the impact on space travellers' health and wellbeing, as well as investigating the possibility of travelling to, and living, on other planets.

In this STEM investigation, students learn about the system of planets in our solar system, space travel and the impact of living beyond the Earth's atmosphere. They explore the key needs and activities of humans, and find out about the main characteristics and attributes associated with an adventurous challenge.

THE CHALLENGE

Your school class is attending a special presentation by a billionaire inventor. She is funding a project called MarsMMXL, which aims to start a human colony on Mars by 2040. To develop interest in her project she is holding a competition. All students in your country are invited to enter – and you want to win!

Your challenge is to plan and create a presentation to help recruit 40 people for the mission. The presentation should concentrate on the journey from Earth to Mars, such as how long the trip will take and the living conditions on the spacecraft. You will need to design at least two living areas, with features and tools that will help the recruits deal with living in microgravity. As part of this investigation, you will learn about the planets in our solar system, and all about gravity – or the lack of gravity – in space.

KEY UNDERSTANDINGS

- Gravitational forces pull all objects (including our atmosphere) towards the centre of the Earth.
- The gravitational pull of the Sun keeps all the other planets in our solar system in orbit around it.
- Mass is the amount of matter in an object. It stays the same, wherever an object is in space.
- Weight, which depends on gravitational pull, changes depending on where an object is in space.
- An astronaut's weight on the International Space Station is 90 per cent of their Earth weight.

KEY VOCABULARY

gravitational pull
gravity
mass
microgravity
orbit
weight

KEY SKILLS

- Gather and summarise information.
- Survey and interview others.
- Reflect on and evaluate information.
- Identify key attributes of space travellers.
- Understand key components of persuasive texts and dialogue.

KEY ACTIONS

- Interview others to gain insights into why people choose to do new and/or difficult things.
- Gather information about space travel and colonisation.
- Design parts of a spacecraft for travel to Mars.
- Create a persuasive presentation about space travel.

→ OVERVIEW OF STAGES

TUNE IN:

Students learn about life on the International Space Station. They consider the different conditions and explore the impact of gravity on astronauts, including the differences between mass and weight. Students learn about the solar system, the different orbits of Earth and Mars, and key features of space travel.

EMPATHISE

Students interview and survey others to find out about important everyday activities. They learn about the motivations behind people's choices to do new or different challenges and the attributes associated with being adventurous.

DEFINE

Students consider the key components of a persuasive text or talk. They determine the main elements of their spacecraft design, as well as their persuasive presentation.

IDEATE

Students generate ideas for their spacecraft design.

PROTOTYPE

Students choose one or two ideas to transform into physical representations (models). These are created rapidly, using simple materials.

TEST

Prototypes are tested through feedback from other students. Students need to consider the original challenge and whether or not they have met the criteria. They are given the opportunity to cycle through the Prototype and Test stages again.

SHARE AND EVALUATE:

Final prototypes are shared and evaluated, with opportunities for expert feedback. Students create a persuasive presentation to accompany their spacecraft design.

→ SUGGESTED SCHEDULE

LESSON	STAGE
1–2	**Tune in**: learn about gravity and life on the International Space Station, explore impact of space travel on humans and introduce the student challenge
3–5	**Empathise**: survey and interview others, empathise and write/record in journal
6	**Define**: define the main issues and write/record in journal
7	**Ideate**: develop ideas and write/record in journal
8–10	**Prototype** and **Test**: conduct prototyping and testing cycles and write/record in journal
11–13	**Share and evaluate**: share and evaluate designs and prototypes

CURRICULUM LINKS

The following tables show the key Science, Technologies and Mathematics curricula with which this STEM investigation is aligned.

SCIENCE

YEAR	STRAND	SUB-STRAND AND CONTENT
5	Science Understanding	Earth and space sciences: • The Earth is part of a system of planets orbiting around a star (the Sun)
	Science as a Human Endeavour	Nature and development of science: • Science involves testing predictions by gathering data and using evidence to develop explanations of events and phenomena, and reflects historical and cultural contributions
		Use and influence of science: • Scientific knowledge is used to solve problems and inform personal and community decisions

TECHNOLOGIES

YEAR	SUB-STRAND	CONTENT
5 & 6	Design and Technologies Understand How Design and Technologies Work	• Examine how people in design and technologies occupations address competing considerations, including sustainability in the design of products, services and environments for current and future use
	Design and Technologies Processes and Production Skills	• Generate, develop and communicate design ideas and processes for audiences using appropriate technical terms and graphical representation techniques • Develop project plans that include consideration of resources when making designed solutions individually and collaboratively

MATHEMATICS

YEAR	STRAND	SUB-STRAND
5	Measurement and Geometry	Using units of measurement
	Number	Fractions and decimals

OTHER CURRICULUM LINKS

GENERAL CAPABILITIES

- Literacy
- Numeracy
- Critical and Creative Thinking

ASSESSMENT

The following resources are provided for assessing students at different stages of the STEM investigations:

- Generic reproducible 1 (Key vocabulary table), for assessing understanding of vocabulary
- Generic reproducible 2 (Self-evaluation), for student self-evaluation of the learning process
- Generic reproducible 3 (Define graphic organiser), for assessing student engagement in the challenges, and collaboration and skills involved in the design thinking stages
- Generic reproducible 5 (Design thinking assessment rubric), for evaluating student engagement in the design thinking stages
- Learning journal templates 1, 2, 3 and 4, for incorporating student reflection and evaluation

→ GETTING READY FOR THE INVESTIGATION

You can prepare yourself and students for this STEM investigation in the following ways:

- Identify groups of students who will work well together.
- Review the **Key science knowledge** that supports this investigation, and look at the **Useful links**.
- Investigate the **Useful apps**.
- Gather materials for the toilet paper model during the Tune-in session.
- Start collecting additional materials for prototyping (as shown on the **Materials needed** list).
- Determine where prototypes will be kept between lessons.
- Create a wall space where students can share their ideas in the Ideate stage.
- Organise the class into pairs.
- Start thinking about:
  - » whether students will create a model of the spacecraft or just provide a plan
  - » which technology to use, such as Aurasma (this will need a class account)
  - » who will evaluate the presentations, and time limits for the presentations
  - » making contact with a space agency to investigate whether or not feedback can be given to students
  - » finding out if members of the school community can share their expertise
  - » where the Tune-in session can take place – it requires a large space.

USEFUL APPS

- App for creating semantic maps (links between different words and/or concepts), such as Popplet
- App for creating interactive links (for example, between descriptions, videos, images and websites and a main image), such as ThingLink
- App for making notes using text, drawings, images, weblinks and audio, such as Notability
- App for creating multimedia presentations, such as Adobe Spark Video and iMovie
- App for creating surveys, such as Typeform (free for small surveys)
- App for working collaboratively, such as Class OneNote – this allows teachers to create a single binder where students can work independently, collaborate and access resources
- App for creating floor plans, such as MS Visio Professional – this allows students to create floor plans, much like the Smart Art Graphics in MS Word
- App for sharing ideas, such as Padlet
- App for sharing presentations, such as QR Code Monkey
- App for creating augmented reality presentations, such as Aurasma
- App for creating images, blogs, infographics and narrated video presentations, such as Canva or Adobe Spark

USEFUL LINKS

- Information about the NASA Mars mission, such as at nasa.gov/content/journey-to-mars-overview
- General information about NASA, such as at nasa.gov/audience/forstudents/5-8/features/nasa-knows/index.html or (for students with additional needs) nasa.gov/audience/forstudents/k-4/stories/nasa-knows/index.html
- Resources about life in space, such as at esa.int/esaKIDSen/LifeinSpace.html
- A video clip about life on the International Space Station, such as at youtube.com/watch?v=pSTp2K0xlOM
- Video clips about gravity, such as at youtube.com/playlist?list=PLhz12vamHOnYXbP8_-PnzYDP3ibgdfH_4
- A tool to calculate your age on Mars, such as at exploratorium.edu/mars/yourage.php
- Ideas for further activities related to life on Mars, such as at mars.nasa.gov/classroom/pdfs/MSIP-MarsActivities.pdf and mars.nasa.gov/participate/funzone

RESOURCES PROVIDED

- Generic reproducibles 1, 2, 3, 4, 5, 6
- Reproducibles 6.1, 6.2, 6.3
- Learning journal templates 1, 2, 3, 4 (on disc)

MATERIALS NEEDED

- Sticky notes (half a pad per pair)
- Paper
- Coloured card
- Pens and markers
- Sticky tape
- Pipe-cleaners
- Cardboard
- Cardboard tubes
- Foil
- Wire
- Plastic bottles and cups
- Assorted recycled materials and offcuts

KEY SCIENCE KNOWLEDGE

This section provides an overview of the key science concepts and vocabulary needed for this unit.

A MISSION TO MARS?

Earth is one planet in a system of planets that **orbit** the Sun. The planets vary in size, mass, physical environment and atmosphere. These characteristics depend, in part, on planet formation, composition, location and distance from the Sun. NASA is currently pursuing a series of missions to Mars, the only planet considered feasible for human visitation. A private investor has also announced a proposed mission to Mars.

GRAVITY AND WEIGHT

For this STEM investigation, it is important that students and teachers understand the role of **gravity** on Earth and in space, and the experiences of space travel.

Gravity is the force that attracts any two objects towards each other. On Earth, we are able to walk, jump and breathe because the Earth's **gravitational pull** keeps our bodies, our atmosphere and other objects pulled towards the centre of the Earth. The larger an object is, the greater the gravitational pull. The gravitational pull of the Sun keeps all the other planets in orbit around it.

When the gravitational pull on an object changes, some characteristics of the object change as well. For example, a person's **mass** stays the same as they travel from the Earth to space and other planets (they have the same amount of matter). But their **weight** changes. A person's weight on the International Space Station is about 90 per cent of their Earth weight. This reduces to almost nothing in deep space.

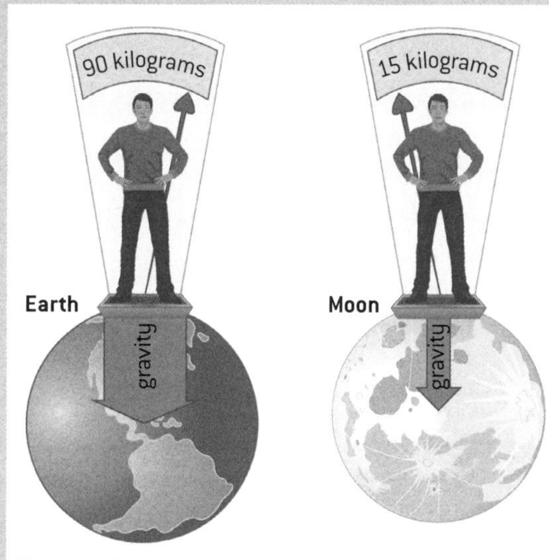

Our mass is the same wherever we are, but weight depends on gravitational pull.

MICROGRAVITY IN SPACE

Astronauts on the International Space Station, and those who will one day travel to Mars, will not experience zero gravity. They will experience **microgravity**. This very small amount of gravity causes objects and astronauts to appear to be floating. Actually, they are moving together with the spacecraft, through space.

Microgravity has many effects on the health of astronauts at the International Space Station, and this would also happen on the longer journey to Mars. The astronauts' muscles and bones weaken, blood flow to the astronauts' heads gives them a sensation of having a head cold, and they experience changes to their hearts and lungs.

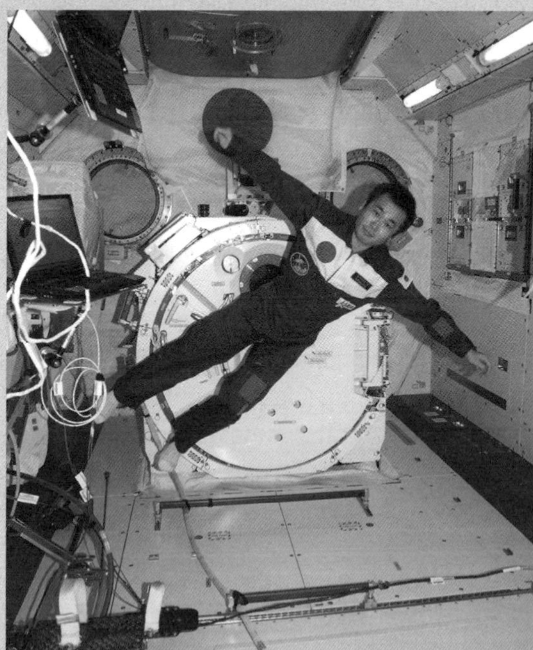

Life in a spacecraft is very different to life on Earth.

KEY VOCABULARY

gravitational pull – the force of attraction between objects
gravity – the force attracting an object towards the Earth, or another body in space
mass – the amount of matter in an object; it stays the same on Earth and in space
microgravity – a very small amount of gravity, such as what astronauts experience in space
orbit – move in a regular and repeating pattern around another object in space
weight – an amount that depends on gravitational pull; it changes depending on where an object is in space

→ TUNE IN

1. Ask students to complete **Generic reproducible 1 (Key vocabulary table)** using the key vocabulary for this unit. This reproducible will also be used at the end, to demonstrate changes in understanding.
2. Watch the video clip of life on the International Space Station (ISS) (see **Useful apps/links**). Have the students brainstorm their observations of the images and activities on a mindmap or a collaborative app, such as Padlet.
3. Explain that the ISS is still strongly affected by the Earth's gravitational pull. Have students predict what might happen to astronauts as they travel away from Earth.
4. Explore the differences between the Earth, space and Mars. Before the challenge, students need to understand the solar system, the distance and duration of the journey from Earth to Mars and the impact of space travel on humans.

ACTIVITY 1: MODELLING THE SOLAR SYSTEM

1. Locate a large area, such as a gym, to complete this task. Download the lesson plan and planet image cards (see **Useful apps/links**).
2. Mark a point in the middle of the room. This represents the Sun. Use a length of toilet roll to measure out the distance from the Sun to Neptune; for example, a toilet roll length of 45 sheets could represent 4.5 billion kilometres. Now, mark the relative position of the other planets along the length of toilet roll.
3. Next, measure out another toilet roll length just for Earth. Do this three more times, in different directions, so that the students can use the four points to draw, sketch or walk the orbit of the Earth around the Sun. Repeat for Mars.
4. Discuss how the travel distance from Earth to Mars varies due to the orbits.
5. Change the lesson focus to mathematics and use the scale model of the solar system to model fractions and decimals on a number line.

TOP TIP!

During the Tune-in stage, conduct vocabulary activities to highlight and develop key vocabulary knowledge. Activities could include drawing semantic webs, creating a word wall or paired discussions. Check the **Key vocabulary** definitions or read the **Key science knowledge** for a refresher on the key terms.

ACTIVITY 2: GRAVITY MATTERS

1. Watch a video clip about gravity (see **Useful apps/links**).
2. Explain the difference between mass and weight.
3. Have students weigh themselves or provide them with the average weight of a 12-year-old child (female: 42 kg, male: 40 kg). Help them to calculate the equivalent weight on the ISS, the Moon, on Mars and in deep space. Provide **Reproducible 6.1 (Weight in space)** to record the information.

ACTIVITY 3: LIFE ON THE ISS

1. Watch a video clip about life on the ISS.
2. Discuss the differences between life on Earth and life on the ISS, based on students' observations, and compare these to their brainstorms at the beginning of the unit.
3. Explain the different impacts of gravity and microgravity on the Earth and on the ISS.

5. Introduce the STEM investigation and challenge to the students. Watch a video clip about travel to Mars (see **Useful apps/links**).
6. Provide students with the student card and read the information together. Ask students about advertisements that have persuaded them to do or buy something. List some facts and details that might persuade someone to join the expedition.
7. Introduce the design thinking process by reviewing the stages on the student card. Explain that students will keep a journal about their learning at different stages of the design.

USEFUL APPS/LINKS

- Lesson plan for a toilet paper model of the solar system, such as at astrosociety.org/wp-content/uploads/2017/03/D2-Toilet_Paper_Solar_System.pdf
- Planet image cards, such as at cse.ssl.berkeley.edu/AtHomeAstronomy/act09_imagecards.html
- Video clip about life on the ISS, such as at youtube.com/watch?v=pSTp2K0xlOM, youtube.com/watch?v=tgRMAVoHRbk or youtube.com/watch?v=SGP6Y0Pnhe4
- Video clip about gravity, such as at youtube.com/watch?v=IjRIB6TuMOU or youtube.com/playlist?list=PLhz12vamH0nYXbP8_-PnzYDP3ibgdfH_4
- Video clip about travel to Mars, such as at youtube.com/watch?v=d0OHJrqIJqY

→ EMPATHISE

During the Empathise stage of the design thinking process, students focus on finding out about different points of view. To empathise with others, they need to research some of the experiences that people have had, especially when considering something new or different. They will find out about the attributes that people associate with being adventurous. Students will take notes, ask questions, draw diagrams and take photos where relevant.

ACTIVITY 1: FIND OUT ABOUT EVERYDAY ACTIVITIES

1. Students find out about the everyday activities that people engage in, so that they can incorporate the activities into their spacecraft design.
2. Ask students to create a survey, or interview people about important everyday activities. These could be categorised; for example, 'health', 'leisure', 'communication', 'work' and 'organisation'.
3. If surveying, students can use an online survey tool. Results from each pair or group of students can then be collated into a class set of results and used as reference material when designing the spacecraft.

ACTIVITY 2: FIND OUT ABOUT ATTRIBUTES

1. In this activity, students learn about what motivates people to try something new or attempt a difficult challenge.
2. Provide students with **Reproducible 6.2 (Personal attributes)**. Explain the term 'attribute' and discuss the words in the personal attributes list. Ask students to share examples of when this attribute is evident, either in their own lives or the world around them.
3. Ask students to cut out the cards on **Reproducible 6.2**. They choose a partner or family member to interview. Students present the cards and explain the different terms. They ask their interviewee to choose the five main attributes they associate with being adventurous and to explain their choices.
4. Create a display with the main attributes that interviewees chose. Students may like to use an augmented reality app (see **Useful apps/links**) to link written examples or short podcasts or videos that explain the importance of each attribute.
5. Ask students to consider the information collected about important everyday activities and decide as a class which three activities must be provided for in their spacecraft design. (They may include other activities too.)

PROMPTS

- What were the main everyday activities that people thought were important?
- What are some of the more unusual activities people suggested?
- What were some of the key attributes people associated with a sense of adventure?
- What were some of the examples people provided about different attributes?

MORE VOCABULARY

- attribute – a quality associated with someone
- empathise – understand and consider another person's or group's point of view
- point of view – an opinion, attitude or judgement considered in a particular way

JOURNAL TIP

Ask students to complete **Learning journal template 1 (Empathise page)** while they are completing the different tasks. Remind them to date their notes and include photos and drawings of relevant information.

USEFUL APPS/LINKS

- App for creating interactive links (for example, between descriptions, videos, images and websites and a main image), such as ThingLink
- App for creating surveys, such as Typeform or Survey Monkey
- App for creating augmented reality presentations, such as Aurasma

ASSESSMENT

This stage of the design thinking process offers opportunities to observe students collecting information, developing questions, and recording their notes and thinking in their journal.

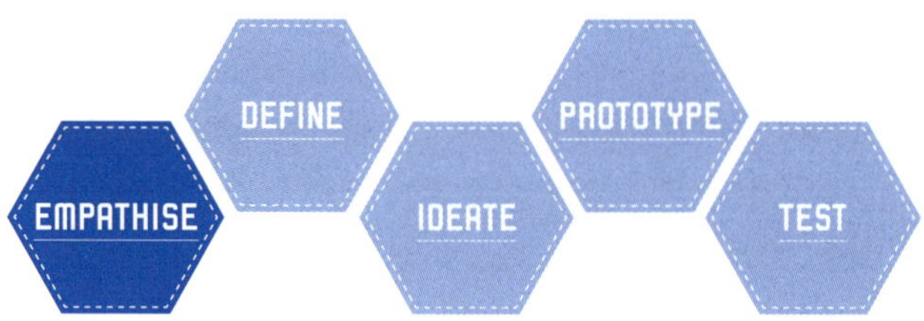

→ DEFINE

The main focus of this stage is to reframe the challenge and define what needs to be done. This includes noting insights that have been generated.

ACTIVITY 1: CONSIDER OBSERVATIONS

1. Students consider the information they gathered in the Empathise stage. They may work in pairs or small groups. Provide a whiteboard, large sheet of paper and/or sticky notes to collate the key information. Have students brainstorm a list of words to do with the challenge and collate them using an online app, such as Padlet. These words may be used in their persuasive presentation.
2. Students should discuss one section of **Learning journal template 2 (Define page)** at a time, write their responses, then continue discussing their ideas for the next section, until the task is complete.
3. Discuss how people persuade. Provide students with an example of a persuasive text and presentation. Consider the key features, such as strong imagery, use of persuasive words and tone. Create an accessible list or display for students to refer to. Ask students to write other information they would like to know, such as information about travel and life in space. Provide them with **Generic reproducible 4 (Key question table)** to assist them to record their questions, findings and sources.

ACTIVITY 2: CONSIDER INSIGHTS

Students think of at least one insight they have gained from the process; for example, it is important to include space for leisure activities or time alone.

Students add this insight to **Learning journal template 2** and write what needs to be created.

When considering insights, students could think about the following:

- What was something unexpected that people shared? How was it unexpected?
- How will you decide on key persuasive words?
- How will you decide on the most important aspects of your spacecraft design?
- Is there any other information that you need or would like to know? How will you find out?

Provide students with **Reproducible 6.3 (New recruit presentation plan)** to help guide their investigation. Explain that this table should help them with planning their presentation and that it can be added to as the investigation progresses.

ACTIVITY 3: CONSIDER CONSTRAINTS

At this stage, let students know the constraints of the challenge, by describing the timeframe, the materials available, how the presentations will be evaluated and who the audience will be, the availability of technology, whether or not students will build models of their spacecrafts and, if so, size limitations.

Students can then update **Learning journal template 2**.

PROMPTS

- What did you discover?
- What were the most important pieces of information that you gathered?
- What was something new that you learned?
- What other information do you need?

MORE VOCABULARY

- define – state the meaning of something
- insight – an accurate understanding of someone or something

JOURNAL TIP

Discuss the term 'insight'. Explain that it relates to something students have learned about the people and their responses to the surveys, as well as information gathered through research or excursions. You could refer to **Learning journal template 2**.

USEFUL APPS/LINKS

- App for sharing ideas, such as Padlet

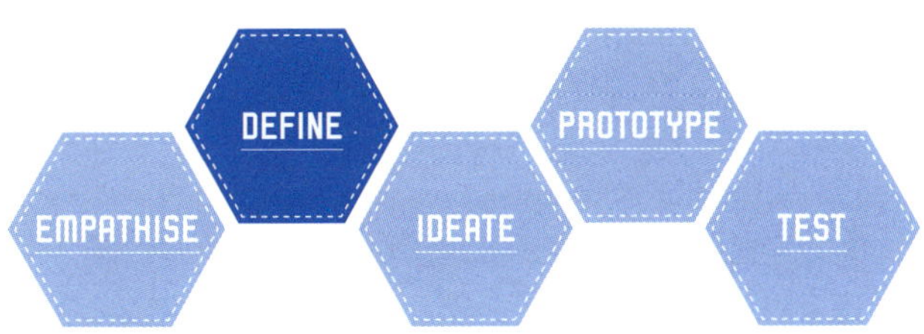

→ IDEATE

The Ideate stage of the design thinking process is all about generating lots of ideas. Students need to be flexible in their thinking and able to move beyond obvious ideas. At this stage, ideas are not judged, just generated and gathered.

ACTIVITY: GENERATE IDEAS

1. Ask groups of students to draw or write their ideas. Each new idea should be written or drawn on a separate piece of paper or sticky note.
2. Ask students to group ideas on a wall or board.
3. Ask students to look at the different ideas and provide feedback to each other. It is important that students don't defend their ideas at this stage. They should just be listening to the feedback.
4. After the initial feedback, ask students to come up with more ideas. Encourage them to be creative and even radical.
5. Ask students to choose four of their ideas to write in their journal. Students use **Learning journal template 3 (Ideate page)** to do this. Ask students to choose one idea to explore further and explain the reasoning behind their choice.

TOP TIP!

At this stage, students may have produced a series of annotated drawings about space travel and spacecraft design. They may have a collection of sticky notes, which they can organise into related ideas.

Encourage students to view and read others' ideas prior to giving feedback. Feedback could be within small groups or between partners. Considering others' ideas is an important part of this process, so students can build on their own ideas as they continue to ideate.

At each stage of this activity, ask students to discuss their thoughts before writing their responses. This will help them to think through their ideas and select their final ideas to develop.

PROMPTS

- How do these ideas relate to the everyday activities that recruits will need to do?
- How do these ideas incorporate some of the challenges of space travel?
- How might you test your design?
- How can you make it more comfortable for the recruits?
- What if you had to use different materials?

MORE VOCABULARY

- feedback – information about, for example, a person's performance or the design of a product, which can be used to make improvements
- ideate – generate many ideas without making judgements about the ideas

JOURNAL TIP

When choosing four ideas to include in the journal, students should try to choose four ideas that aren't related.

USEFUL APPS/LINKS

- Tools for creating ideas, such as at creatingminds.org/tools/tools_ideation.htm
- Tips for creativity and innovation, such as at designorate.com/creativity-innovation-in-education

ASSESSMENT

At the Ideate stage, assessment could include observations about the number and diversity of students' ideas, and their ability to provide feedback and create additional ideas. Reflection in the journal should provide an insight into some of the reasoning behind students' choices.

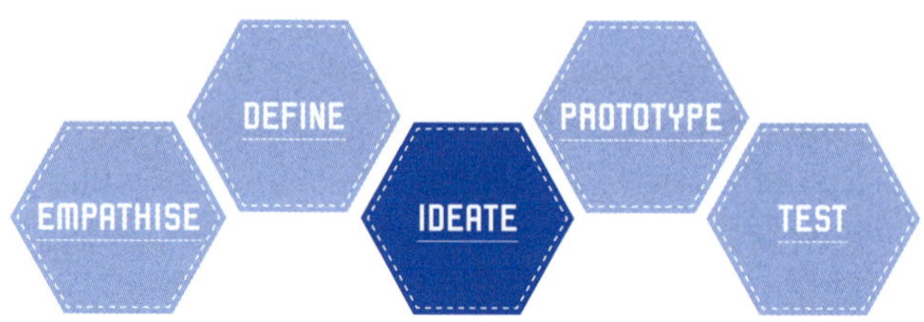

→ PROTOTYPE

At this stage of the design thinking process, students are asked to create a physical prototype of a solution. It is the stage where students need to get their ideas out of their head and presented in a way that engages other students and helps them to understand the concept. When students create, it helps them to think and solve problems and disagreements. Students can role-play, make storyboards or use sticky notes when they prototype. The most important feature is that viewers can interact with whatever is produced.

Encourage students to photograph or film during the prototyping and testing stages. This can be used to show the learning behind the design thinking process.

ACTIVITY: TRANSFORM IDEAS INTO PROTOTYPES

1. Students review the ideas generated at the Ideate stage. Provide them with an A3 copy of **Generic reproducible 6 (In the frame)** so they can organise their ideas into two sections: 'least relevant' and 'most relevant'. Students continue to cycle through this activity until they have an idea to start prototyping.
2. Ask students to draw some of the spaces for the spacecraft, incorporating the three activities identified earlier. They could include aspects of activities such as eating, sleeping, cleaning, leisure, work and time out.
3. After students have created some initial drawings, provide them with a range of materials to create their prototype. Remind students that a prototype should be created rapidly and is not meant to look 'nice'.
4. After a prototype has been created, ask students to see if it works and get feedback from others.
5. Students use the feedback to prototype again.

Ask students to fill in the Prototype part of **Learning journal template 4 (Prototype and test page)**. See the **Journal tip** for further student guidance.

PROMPTS

- What worked?
- How could it be improved?
- What else do you need to know, do or have?
- What other suggestions do you have?

MORE VOCABULARY

- feedback – information about, for example, a person's performance or the design of a product, which can be used to make improvements
- prototype – an initial version of a model of a product or process that is used to develop a final model

JOURNAL TIP

Remind students to highlight the main features of their prototype. If students are creating an electronic journal, they can insert a photo of their prototype and annotate it.

USEFUL APPS/LINKS

- App for creating interactive links (for example, between descriptions, videos, images and websites and a main image), such as ThingLink
- App for making notes using text, drawings, images, weblinks and audio, such as Notability

ASSESSMENT

Observe students as they make changes to their designs. Are they able to consider feedback, make modifications and move rapidly through this process? Or do they have difficulties with holding on to an idea and accepting feedback?

TOP TIP!

The Prototype stage is often very messy. It is important that students are focusing on their ideas, rather than the end product. Provide them with lots of materials – recycling depots can be a useful source. Students may add labels to explain some of the main features. Photographing and annotating pictures of prototypes can be useful.

To gain feedback, students could ask each other some of the following questions:

- What is the main feature of your prototype?
- How does the prototype meet the needs of the recruits?
- Which aspects work best? What will you keep?
- Which aspects need changing? How might you do this?
- What other materials might you need?

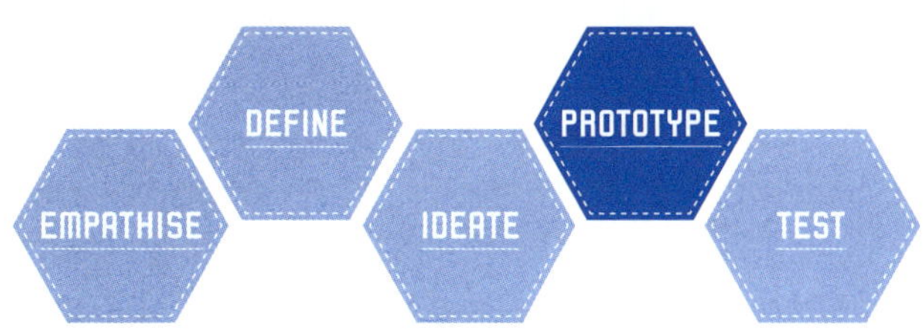

→ TEST

At this stage of the design thinking process, students test their prototype to see how it meets the criteria in the challenge. Students check to see if their prototype meets the criteria set at the start of the design process.

ACTIVITY: TEST FEEDBACK

1. Students take their last prototype and consider the initial needs of their audience. Ask them to create a checklist to ensure that they have followed the guidelines.
2. Ask students what they need to change to meet audience needs.
3. Provide the opportunity to cycle through the prototyping and testing stages again. Include opportunities to share prototypes and share and listen to feedback.

Ask students to fill in the Test part of **Learning journal template 4 (Prototype and test page)**. See the **Journal tip** for further student guidance.

PROMPTS

- Does your prototype do what you wanted it to do?
- Does it have additional features that make the design more useful?
- Does it have features that are not necessary?

MORE VOCABULARY

- evaluate – assess something, perhaps considering what worked and what didn't
- feature – a specific aspect of something, such as size, shape, colour and quality
- feedback – information about, for example, a person's performance or the design of a product, which can be used to make improvements
- prototype – an initial version of a model of a product or process that is used to develop a final model
- review – consider an idea, process or product and decide what needs to be changed and what works

JOURNAL TIP

Ask students to think about why it is important to test their ideas before they build their final design.

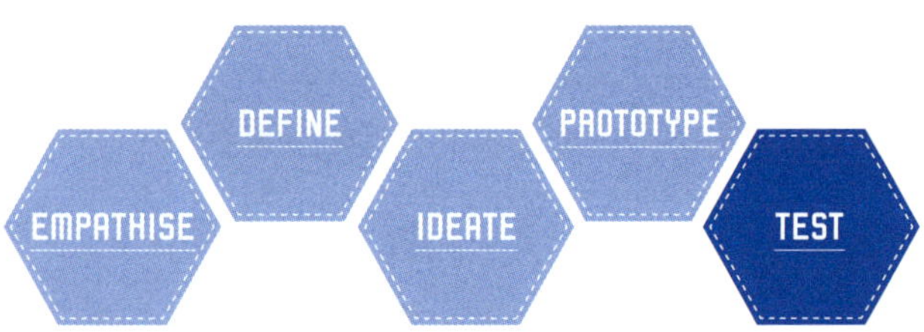

→ SHARE AND EVALUATE

At this stage of the investigation, students are provided with an opportunity to share their final design, as well as the processes involved in the investigation. Students evaluate their learning journals and their solutions.

ACTIVITY 1: BRING THE DESIGNS TOGETHER

1. Provide students with a time limit for their presentation and remind them of useful persuasion techniques.
2. Students can create an iMovie or use Adobe Spark Video to demonstrate the process and thinking behind the designs. There should be an element of narration, where they are sharing their story about points of view, insights, prototyping and solutions.
3. Students should include their learning journals with the display so others can see the different stages of the design process.

ACTIVITY 2: EVALUATE AND GIVE FEEDBACK

1. Provide students with **Generic reproducible 2 (Self-evaluation)** to complete.
2. Ask students to provide feedback to each other about interesting features, difficult aspects and changes that they would make if they repeated the task.
3. Provide students with opportunities to share their designs with the wider community. This could include inviting a friend or family member with relevant experience. It may be possible to share some of the videos with an expert for feedback about the designs.

ASSESSMENT

Ask students to again complete **Generic reproducible 1 (Key vocabulary table)** using the key vocabulary for this unit. Compare their table with the one they completed at the Tune-in stage, to demonstrate changes in understanding.

Students complete **Generic reproducible 3 (Responding to the investigation)**. Compare their responses to those on **Generic reproducible 2**.

Teachers and students each complete the **Generic reproducible 5 (Design thinking assessment rubric)**. Students compare the feedback they are given by the teacher with their self-assessment of their design thinking skills.

Name: ....

Date: ....

STEM INVESTIGATIONS

Use your own mass or find out the average mass of a boy or girl of a particular age. Your teacher will help you to calculate and record weight on the International Space Station, the Moon, Mars and in deep space.

Place	Mass (kilograms)	Multiplied by	Weight (kilograms)
Earth		1.0	
International Space Station		0.9	
Moon		0.16	
Mars		0.38	
Deep space		0	

1. Why does a person's weight change in different parts of space?

2. What adventures and challenges in space could happen because of this?

Name: ....

Date: ....

Cut out the cards and discuss the meanings of the words and phrases.
Use the cards to identify important attributes of adventurous people.

courageous	enthusiastic
dedicated	hard-working
self-directed	communicative
visionary	creative
caring	grateful
optimistic	empathetic
empowered	energetic
risk taking	humble

 STEM Investigations, UP, ISBN 978 1 4202 4154 9

Name: ....

Date: ....

Use this table to help you plan your presentation.
You will need to add information as you continue the investigation.

List three essential everyday activities or needs that your spacecraft design will address.	
List other activities or needs to be included.	
Describe at least two living areas.	
Draw your spacecraft design on a separate page and label the main features.	Design completed ☐
List some key personal attributes required by people wishing to travel to Mars.	
Write some general information people need to know about space travel.	
Write some specific information people need to know about space travel to Mars.	
Write some important information people need to know about life on Mars.	
Note some images to include in your presentation.	
List important persuasive words to include in your presentation.	
Describe the tools you will use to create your presentation, such as a multimedia slideshow.	

STEM Investigations, UP, ISBN 978 1 4202 4154 9 © Macmillan Science and Education Australia 2018

POWER UP YOUR SCHOOL DISCO!

MANAGED WORLD 7

→ INTRODUCTION

Electricity is a part of everyday life that most of us take for granted. The expectation is to have unlimited access. As we use more powered devices, demands on power sources are increasing. It is important that infrastructure, such as powerlines, is maintained to avoid power blackouts. Solar panels and a battery is an alternative power source, but the stored electricity in this kind of battery can power only simple electrical circuits, not the large, complicated circuits of a whole home or school.

In this STEM investigation, students are asked to design one or two electrical circuits that can be used to run the lighting and sound at a disco, using a battery connected to a solar panel. They will explore the components of electrical circuits. They will design and create new circuits using standard symbols and terminology.

THE CHALLENGE

You are part of a team organising the school graduation disco, which will be held in your school hall. The principal has just found out that there will be no electricity for the area that night, due to work on local powerlines. Luckily, a parent can donate a solar panel and battery usually used for camping. Your team will need to work out how to use it to power the disco lighting and music.

Your challenge is to plan a creative and fun design for the disco lights and music speakers. All lights and speakers need to be powered by an electrical circuit that is connected to the battery, and you should use no more than two circuits for your entire light and sound plan. As part of your investigation, you will learn about electrical circuits, conductors and insulators, as well as the best way to design and draw the parts of a circuit.

KEY UNDERSTANDINGS

- Electricity is a form of energy.
- Potential energy is energy available to do something, such as in a battery.
- Kinetic energy is energy that is doing something.
- Conductors are materials that allow electrical energy to flow freely through them. Metal is an example of a conductor.
- Insulators are materials that stop or reduce the flow of electrical energy. Plastic is an example of an insulator.

KEY VOCABULARY

battery
component
current
electrical circuit
electricity
switch

KEY SKILLS

- Make careful observations.
- Consider different points of view.
- Collect and summarise information.
- Explain the difference between conductors and insulators.
- Describe and demonstrate how an electrical circuit works.
- Use standard symbols for designing electrical circuits.

KEY ACTIONS

- Collect information through interviews and discussion.
- Measure and create a scale drawing of a disco space.
- Design an electrical circuit using standard symbols.
- Build an electrical circuit.

→ OVERVIEW OF STAGES

TUNE IN:

Students learn about electrical circuits. They explore how to draw circuits, using standard symbols. They learn about conductors and insulators and the impact they have on the transfer of electrical energy through a circuit. They also find out about the impact of increasing the number of components, such as globes, on a circuit.

EMPATHISE

Students learn about lighting design and music at discos by asking friends or family members about their experiences.

DEFINE

Students consider the constraints of the investigation. They measure the length, width, perimeter and area of the space to be used for a disco and consider how many lights and speakers would be needed. Students create a bird's-eye view map of the hall, which can be used to identify the location of the different components of the design.

IDEATE

Students generate ideas for how to create one or two circuits to provide lighting and sound to a disco. They sketch and label their designs.

PROTOTYPE

Students choose one or two of their ideas and build a prototype to test using appropriate materials to simulate lights and sound.

TEST

As a class, prototypes are tested. Students share their prototypes and provide feedback to each other. They are given the opportunity to cycle through the Prototype and Test stages again.

SHARE AND EVALUATE:

Final prototypes are shared and evaluated, with opportunities for expert feedback.

→ SUGGESTED SCHEDULE

LESSON	STAGE
1–2	**Tune in**: learn about electrical circuits, explore conductors, insulators and batteries, and introduce the student challenge
3–4	**Empathise**: learn about lighting design and music at discos, create a wish list and write/record in journal
5–6	**Define**: define the main issues, measure and draw a bird's-eye view map of the venue, and write/record in journal
7	**Ideate**: develop ideas and write/record in journal
8–10	**Prototype** and **Test**: conduct prototyping and testing cycles and write/record in journal
11–13	**Share and evaluate**: share and evaluate designs and prototypes

CURRICULUM LINKS

The following tables show the key Science, Technologies and Mathematics curricula with which this STEM investigation is aligned.

SCIENCE

YEAR	STRAND	SUB-STRAND AND CONTENT
6	Science Understanding	Physical sciences: • Electrical energy can be transferred and transformed in electrical circuits, and can be generated from a range of sources
5 & 6	Science as a Human Endeavour	Use and influence of science: • Scientific knowledge is used to solve problems and inform personal and community decisions

TECHNOLOGIES

YEAR	STRAND	CONTENT
5 & 6	Design and Technologies Knowledge and Understanding	• Investigate how electrical energy can control movement, sound or light in a designed product or system • Investigate characteristics and properties of a range of materials, systems, components, tools and equipment, and evaluate the impact of their use
	Design and Technologies Processes and Production Skills	• Generate, develop and communicate design ideas and processes for audiences using appropriate technical terms and graphical representation techniques • Critique needs or opportunities for designing, and investigate materials, components, tools, equipment and processes to achieve intended design solutions • Develop project plans that include consideration of resources when making designed solutions individually and collaboratively

MATHEMATICS

YEAR	STRAND	SUB-STRAND
6	Measurement and Geometry	Using units of measurement

OTHER CURRICULUM LINKS

AC

GENERAL CAPABILITIES

- Literacy
- Numeracy
- Information and Communication Technology (ICT) Capability
- Critical and Creative Thinking

ASSESSMENT

The following resources are provided for assessing students at different stages of the STEM investigations:

- Generic reproducible 1 (Key vocabulary table), for assessing understanding of vocabulary
- Generic reproducible 2 (Self-evaluation), for student self-evaluation of the learning process
- Generic reproducible 3 (Define graphic organiser), for assessing student engagement in the challenges, and the collaboration and skills involved in the design thinking stages
- Generic reproducible 5 (Design thinking assessment rubric), for evaluating student engagement in the design thinking stages
- Learning journal templates 1, 2, 3, and 4, for incorporating student reflection and evaluation

GETTING READY FOR THE INVESTIGATION

You can prepare yourself and students for this STEM investigation in the following ways:

- Identify groups of students who will work well together.
- Review the **Key science knowledge** that supports this investigation, and look at the **Useful links**.
- Investigate the **Useful apps**.
- Gather materials for exploring conductors and insulators, and creating electrical circuits during the Tune-in session.
- Start collecting additional materials for prototyping (as shown on the **Materials needed** list).
- Determine where prototypes will be kept between lessons.
- Create a wall space where students can share their ideas in the Ideate stage.
- Organise the class into pairs.
- Start thinking about:
  - » which materials will be available to students
  - » whether limitations will be set regarding the amount of material available to students
  - » safety issues, such as working with coin batteries
  - » how each group will store its circuits – small tubs with lids are useful
  - » whether or not students will create a small working model (diorama) of the disco, or just provide drawings and the electrical circuit
  - » how the investigations will be shared beyond the classroom
  - » ways of collecting offcuts of copper tape or wire.

USEFUL APPS

- App for creating semantic maps (links between different words and/or concepts), such as Popplet
- App for creating interactive links (for example, between descriptions, videos, images and websites and a main image), such as ThingLink
- App for making notes using text, drawings, images, weblinks and audio, such as Notability
- App for creating multimedia presentations, such as Adobe Spark Video or iMovie
- App for creating surveys, such as Typeform
- App for engaging in collaborative tasks, such as Class OneNote
- App for creating floor plans and circuit drawings following standard conventions, such as MS Visio Professional
- App for creating an online discussion group that is closed to outside members, such as Padlet

USEFUL LINKS

- Simple explanation of electricity and circuits, such as at discoverykids.com/articles/how-do-electric-circuits-work or (for students with additional needs) bbc.co.uk/bitesize/ks2/science/physical_processes/electrical_circuits/read/1/
- Further explanation of electricity and circuits, such as at bbc.co.uk/bitesize/ks3/science/energy_electricity_forces/electric_current_voltage/revision/1/ Difference between static and current electricity, such as at explainthatstuff.com/electricity.html
- Concepts of series and parallel circuits, such as at youtube.com/watch?v=XSukRnxGy5c
- Information on solar panels and solar electricity (extension), such as at youtube.com/watch?v=xKxrkht7CpY and energymatters.com.au/education/solar-kids-teens
- How to create your own circuit components, such as at youtube.com/watch?v=INBYuA6KoLA

RESOURCES PROVIDED

- Generic reproducibles 1, 2, 3, 4, 5
- Reproducibles 7.1, 7.2, 7.3
- Learning journal templates 1, 2, 3, 4 (on disc)

MATERIALS NEEDED

- Sticky notes (half a pad per pair)
- Paper
- Coloured card
- Pens and markers
- Sticky tape
- Pipe-cleaners
- Cardboard
- Conductive materials, such as paperclips, foil, coins
- Insulating materials, such as plastic, rubber bands, cork
- Copper tape
- Mini whiteboards and markers (optional – instead of paper)
- Mini LED lights for circuits
- Poster or handout with standard electrical circuit symbols
- Coin batteries
- Switches
- Buzzers

Swallowing coin cell batteries can be fatal. Warn students and monitor them carefully during battery use.

KEY SCIENCE KNOWLEDGE

This section provides an overview of the key science concepts and vocabulary needed for this unit.

ELECTRICITY

Electricity is a type of energy. In this investigation, the focus is on **current** electricity, or the flow of electrical energy.

Two types of energy are potential and kinetic energy. Potential energy is stored energy such as in a battery – it is energy available to do something. Kinetic energy is moving energy, or energy that is doing something, such as being used when a **switch** operates a light.

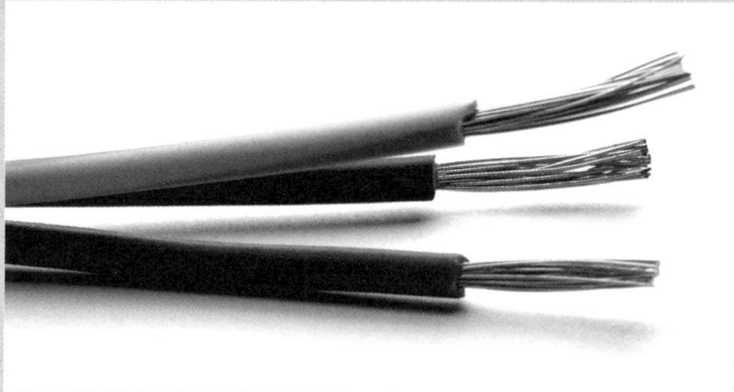

Electrical wires are coated with a layer of plastic, which is an insulator.

CONDUCTORS AND INSULATORS

Electricity does not move equally through all materials. Some materials, called **conductors**, allow electricity to flow easily. Materials with high electrical conductivity include metals and water. Other materials, called **insulators**, stop or reduce the flow of electricity. Insulating materials include rubber, plastic and glass. The electrical wires in your home are made of metal wires (conductors) wrapped in plastic (an insulator). This means that accidental contact with them is unlikely to lead to electrocution.

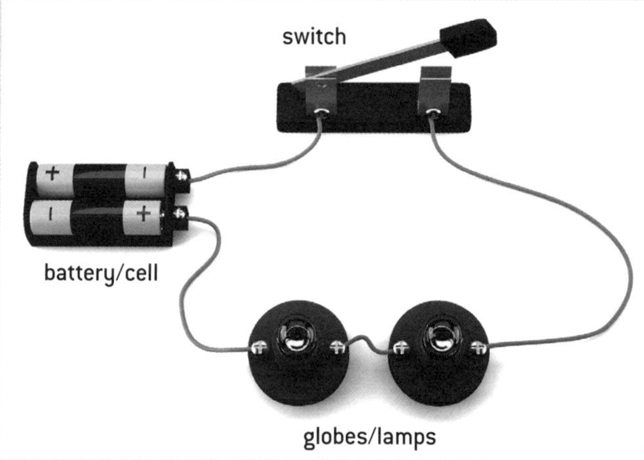

This electrical circuit has been set up so that a battery can supply energy to two globes. In this picture, the switch is open so the circuit is broken.

ELECTRICAL CIRCUITS

An **electrical circuit** is a loop in which electrical energy flows. When a circuit is closed, the energy flows around the circuit continuously. The energy flow can be stopped by breaking the circuit. A switch is used to open (break) or close (complete) the electrical circuit.

The battery used for a particular circuit must be able to supply enough energy for the devices (such as globes and speakers) in that circuit.

Electrical circuits are drawn using standard symbols to represent the circuit **components**. These symbols are drawn in the correct order to show the structure of a circuit. For this investigation, the students will use symbols for wires, batteries, globes, buzzers and switches.

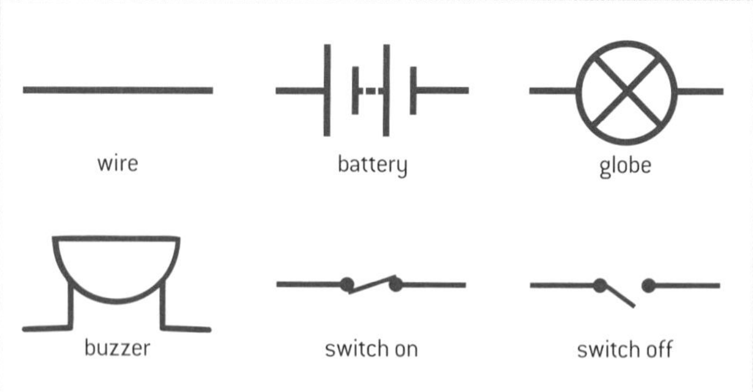

Circuit components have standard symbols.

KEY VOCABULARY

component – part of an electrical circuit, such as a battery, switch or buzzer
conductor – a material that allows the flow of electrical energy
current – a flow of electrical energy
electrical circuit – a continuous loop in which electrical energy flows
insulator – a material that limits the flow of electrical energy
switch – a component that can be used to break or complete an electrical circuit

→ TUNE IN

1. Ask students to complete **Generic reproducible 1 (Key vocabulary table)** using the key vocabulary for this unit. This reproducible will also be used at the end of the unit to demonstrate changes in understanding.
2. Discuss where students have observed electricity. Elicit that electricity occurs naturally (in muscles, lightning) and in human-made circuits in their homes, schools and cars. Explain that the focus of this investigation will be on electrical circuits.
3. Watch a video clip about electricity (see **Useful apps/links**).
4. Explore the properties of electrical circuits. Before engaging in the challenge, students need to understand that current electricity is the flow of electrical energy around a circuit, that materials are conductors or insulators and that there is a standard way to draw a circuit.

ACTIVITY 1: CREATE AND DRAW A CIRCUIT

1. Show a brief video clip about simple circuits (see **Useful apps/links**).
2. Model how to use your school's equipment to make the same simple circuit and draw it using the standard symbols.
3. Have the students draw more complex circuits using switches, globes and buzzers.
4. Discuss the terms 'circuit' (continuous loop in which electrical energy flows) and 'components' (for example, switches, globes, buzzers, wires, batteries). Note the importance of a complete or closed circuit.

ACTIVITY 2: CONDUCTORS AND INSULATORS

1. Show the students conductors (such as coins, aluminum foil, paperclips) and insulators (such as rubber bands, pieces of polystyrene cup, cork) and have them make predictions about the impact of these if included in a circuit.
2. Have students create a simple circuit to test their predictions.
3. Discuss the terms 'insulator' (material that limits the flow of electrical energy) and 'conductors' (material that allows the flow of electrical energy). Consider when it would be important to understand the difference between these (for example, safety considerations).

ACTIVITY 3: CIRCUITS AND BATTERIES

1. Demonstrate a simple circuit with one battery and one globe. Ask students to predict what will happen to the brightness of the globe if you add another globe, and test the prediction. (It will decrease in brightness.)
2. Ask students to investigate the effects of adding increasing numbers of components or batteries to the circuit.
3. Discuss why engineers and electricians need to consider the size of a battery when designing an electrical circuit in a home or school (for example, so that the circuit can work as designed).

5. Introduce the STEM investigation and challenge to the students. Provide them with the student card and read the information together. Remind students that the electricity will be limited and so they must only include the most important elements and keep their design simple.
6. Introduce the design thinking process by reviewing the stages on the student card. Explain that students will keep a journal about their learning at the different stages of the design.

TOP TIP!

Some students might find it challenging to visualise the standard circuit drawings and recreate their original circuits. It can be helpful to have the students sketch their created circuit or photograph it and then draw the circuit again alongside the sketch using standard symbols.

During the Tune-in stage, conduct vocabulary activities to highlight and develop key vocabulary knowledge. Check the **Key vocabulary** or read the **Key science knowledge** for a refresher on the key terms and concepts.

USEFUL APPS/LINKS

- Video clip about electricity, such as at splash.abc.net.au/home#!/media/2190951/how-electricity-works
- Video clip about simple circuits, such as at youtube.com/watch?v=zSSkZ9F7Bng

→ EMPATHISE

During the Empathise stage of the design thinking process, students focus on finding out about different points of view. To empathise with others, they need to research some of the experiences that people have had. Students will take notes, ask questions, draw diagrams and take photos where relevant.

ACTIVITY 1: FIND OUT IMPORTANT FEATURES

1. Ask students to create a short set of interview questions about discos. They should include questions that investigate the following, as well as any other features they feel are important:
   - types, colour, size and position of lighting
   - position and types of sound.
2. Students interview a partner and, if possible, a family member. It may even be possible to conduct an interview with students from a partner school, using email or an app such as Google Hangout.
3. Provide students with **Reproducible 7.1 (Disco interview)** for recording their questions and interviewees' responses.

ACTIVITY 2: MAKE A WISH LIST

1. Ask students to find pictures of lighting arrangements and create a collection of pictures using a collaborative app such as Padlet, or make a wall display.
2. Ask students to discuss the different images and which appeal or don't appeal, and why.
3. Complete a think–pair–share activity to generate a class disco wish list. Individual students consider three or four key elements of a disco. Pairs of students share their ideas with each other and then generate a new list, with three or four elements. Finally, group pairs of students and ask them to generate their top three or four features. Collate the responses and display them for future reference during the investigation.

Ask students to consider the key insights they have gathered from the two activities.

PROMPTS

- What features of discos are most popular?
- What are some important points to consider when designing lighting and sound for a disco?
- What are some aspects of a disco that you hadn't considered?
- Were there any surprise features?

MORE VOCABULARY

- empathise – understand and consider another person's or group's point of view
- feature – a specific aspect of something, such as size, shape, colour and quality
- point of view – an opinion, attitude or judgement considered in a particular way

JOURNAL TIP

Students complete **Learning journal template 1 (Empathise page)** while they are completing the different tasks. Remind them to date their notes and include photos or pictures of relevant information.

USEFUL APPS/LINKS

- App for creating an online discussion group that is closed to outside members, such as Padlet
- App for interviewing other people, such as an email app or Google Hangout

ASSESSMENT

This stage of the design thinking process offers opportunities to observe students collecting information, developing questions, and recording their notes and thinking in their journal.

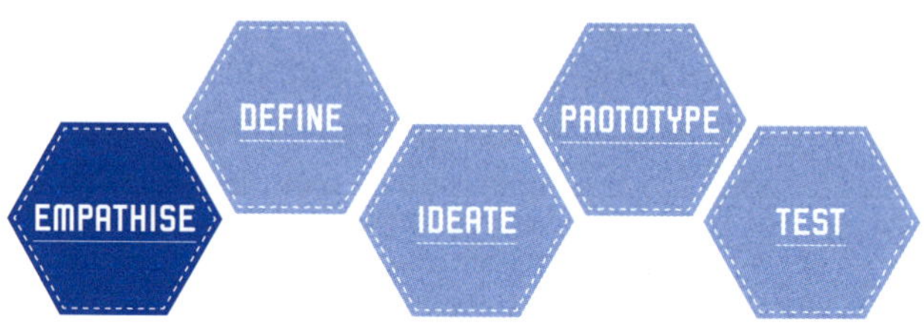

→ DEFINE

The main focus of this stage of the design thinking process is to reframe the challenge. The initial challenge is quite open, so at this stage students learn how to define what needs to be done, such as which features of lighting and sound to include and the restriction to two electrical circuits. Students also note insights that have been generated.

ACTIVITY 1: CONSIDER OBSERVATIONS

1. Students consider the information they gathered in the Empathise stage. They may work in pairs or small groups. Provide them with a whiteboard, large sheet of paper and/or sticky notes to collate some of the key information they have gathered. Students focus on the different features that have been highlighted by their interviewees.
2. Students should discuss one section of **Learning journal template 2 (Define page)** at a time, write their responses, then continue discussing their ideas for the next section, until the task is complete. This provides students with opportunities to hear others' responses and also provides the teacher with input points.
3. Discuss the most popular features of discos and whether or not they could be included in the design challenge. Provide students with the opportunity to research further. Ask them to write down other information they would like to know, such as different ways of incorporating lights and switches into electrical circuits. Provide them with **Generic reproducible 4 (Key question table)** to assist them to record their questions, findings and sources.

ACTIVITY 2: CONSIDER INSIGHTS

Students think of at least one insight they have gained from the process; for example, the position of lights is important, or having different coloured lights creates a good atmosphere.

Students add this insight to **Learning journal template 2 (Define page)** and then write a brief explanation of what needs to be created.

When considering insights, students could think about the following:

- What was something unexpected that you saw or found out? How was it unexpected?
- How will you decide on the most important aspect of the disco light and sound design?
- Is there any other information that you need or would like to know? How will you find out?

ACTIVITY 3: CONSIDER CONSTRAINTS

At this stage, let students know the constraints of the challenge, by describing the materials available and perhaps the limitations, the timeframe for the investigation, the standard symbols to be used in the circuit and safety issues.

Ask students to gather information about the space they are designing the lighting and sound circuit(s) for. They will need to measure the length, width, perimeter and area of the space. Students need to create a bird's-eye view scale drawing of the space, which includes the location of lights and speakers, as well as doors, windows and any other important features.

Students can then update **Learning journal template 2**.

PROMPTS

- What did you discover?
- What were the most important pieces of information that you gathered?
- What was something new that you learned?
- What other information do you need?

MORE VOCABULARY

- define – state the meaning of something
- feature – a specific aspect of something, such as size, shape, colour and quality
- insight – an accurate understanding of someone or something

JOURNAL TIP

Discuss the term 'insight'. Explain that it relates to something students have learned about the people and their responses to the surveys, as well as information gathered through research or excursions. You could refer to **Learning journal template 2**.

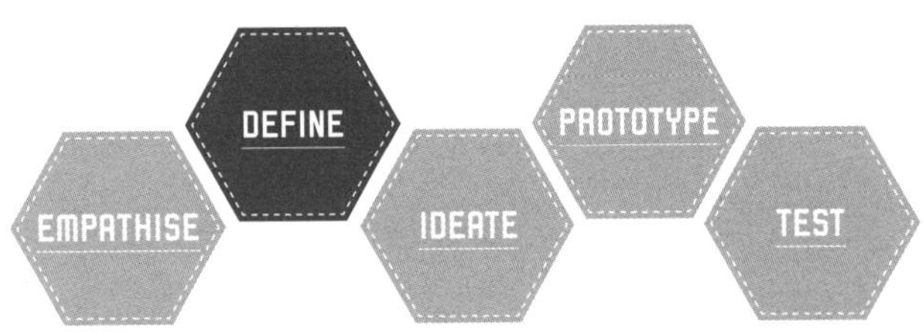

→ IDEATE

The Ideate stage of the design thinking process is all about generating lots of ideas. Students need to be flexible in their thinking and able to move beyond obvious ideas. At this stage, ideas are not judged, just generated and gathered.

ACTIVITY: GENERATE IDEAS

1. Ask groups of students to draw or write their ideas. Each new idea should be written or drawn on a separate piece of paper or on a sticky note.
2. Ask students to group ideas on a wall or board.
3. Ask students to look at the different ideas and provide feedback to each other. It is important that students don't defend their ideas at this stage. They should just be listening to the feedback.
4. After the initial feedback, ask students to come up with more ideas. Encourage them to be creative and even radical.
5. Ask students to choose four of their ideas to write down in their journal. Students use **Learning journal template 3 (Ideate page)** to do this. Ask students to choose one idea to explore further and explain the reasoning behind their choice.

TOP TIP!

At this stage, students may have produced a series of annotated drawings about electrical circuits incorporating light and sound. They may have a collection of sticky notes, which they can organise into related ideas.

Encourage students to view and read others' ideas before giving feedback. Feedback could be within small groups or between partners. Considering others' ideas is an important part of this process, so students can build on their own ideas as they continue to ideate.

At each stage of this activity, ask students to discuss their thoughts before writing their responses. This will help them to think through their ideas and select their final ideas to develop.

PROMPTS

- How do these ideas relate to the design challenge?
- How might you test your design?
- How many circuits have you included?
- What impact will the number of lights have on your circuit?
- What would happen if you added more or less lights?
- What if you had to use different or fewer materials?

MORE VOCABULARY

- feature – a specific aspect of something, such as size, shape, colour and quality
- feedback – information about, for example, a person's performance or the design of a product, which can be used to make improvements
- ideate – generate many ideas without making judgements about the ideas

JOURNAL TIP

When choosing four ideas to include in the journal, students should try to choose four ideas that aren't related.

USEFUL APPS/LINKS

- Tools for creating ideas, such as at creatingminds.org/tools/tools_ideation.htm
- Tips for creativity and innovation, such as at designorate.com/creativity-innovation-in-education

ASSESSMENT

At the Ideate stage, assessment could include observations about the number and diversity of students' ideas, and their ability to provide feedback and create additional ideas. Reflection in the journal should provide an insight into some of the reasoning behind students' choices.

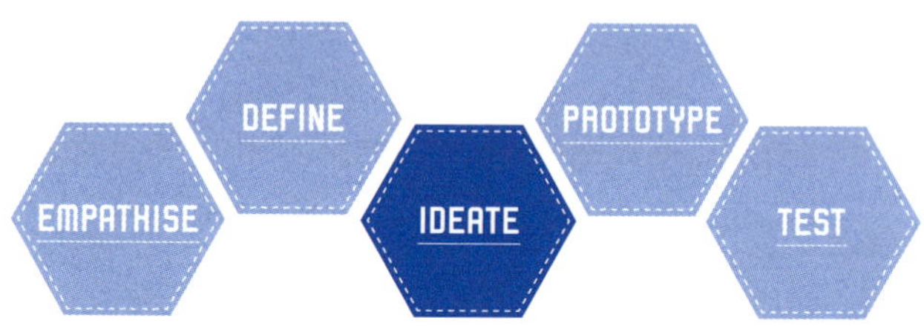

→ PROTOTYPE

At this stage of the design thinking process, students are asked to create a physical prototype of a solution. It is the stage where students need to get their ideas out of their head and presented in a way that engages other students and helps them to understand the concept. When students create, it helps them to think and solve problems and disagreements. Students can role-play, make storyboards or use sticky notes when they prototype. The most important feature is that viewers can interact with whatever is produced.

Encourage students to photograph or film during the prototyping and testing stages. This information can be used to show the learning behind the design thinking process in action.

ACTIVITY: TRANSFORM IDEAS INTO PROTOTYPES

1. Students review the ideas generated at the Ideate stage. Provide them with **Reproducible 7.2 (Circuit comparison)** to help them evaluate their designs, two at a time. Students take two designs to compare and consider the key features.
2. Provide students with a range of materials to create their prototype. Remind students that a prototype should be created rapidly and is not meant to look 'nice'.
3. After a prototype has been created, ask students to see if it works and get feedback from others.
4. Students then use the feedback to prototype again. The number of opportunities to prototype may depend on the availability of materials.

Ask students to fill in the Prototype part of **Learning journal template 4 (Prototype and test page)**. See the **Journal tip** for further student guidance.

PROMPTS

- What worked?
- How could it be improved?
- What else do you need to know, do or have?
- What other suggestions do you have?

MORE VOCABULARY

- feedback – information about, for example, a person's performance or the design of a product, which can be used to make improvements
- prototype – an initial version of a model of a product or process that is used to develop a final model

TOP TIP!

The Prototype stage is often very messy. It is important that students are focusing on their ideas, rather than the end product. It may be possible to find offcuts of copper tape, wire or other conductive materials for circuit making. When prototyping the electrical circuits, students should have a drawing of the circuit, using standard symbols, before creating the circuit. Photographing and annotating pictures of prototypes can be useful, especially when identifying any issues with the electrical circuit.

To gain feedback, students could ask each other some of the following questions:

- How does your electrical circuit work?
- Which aspects work best? What will you keep?
- Which aspects need changing? How might you do this?
- What other materials might you need?

JOURNAL TIP

Remind students to highlight the main features of their prototype. If students are creating an electronic journal, they can insert a photo of their prototype and annotate it.

USEFUL APPS

- App for making notes using text, drawings, images, weblinks and audio, such as Notability
- App for creating floor plans and circuit drawings following standard conventions, such as MS Visio Professional

ASSESSMENT

Observe students as they make changes to their designs. Are they able to consider feedback, make modifications and move rapidly through this process? Or do they have difficulties with holding on to an idea and accepting feedback?

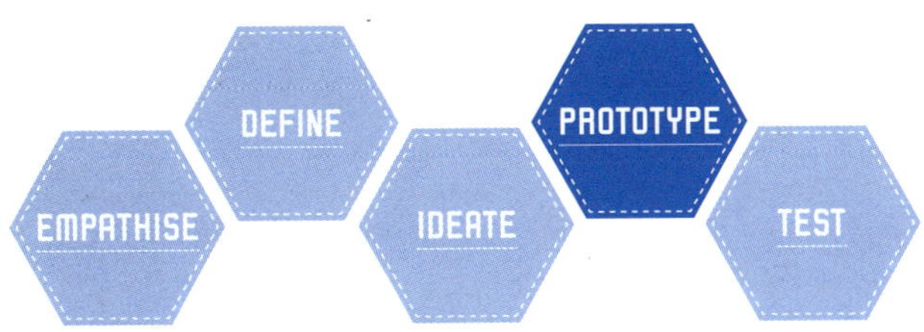

→ TEST

At this stage of the design thinking process, students test their prototype to see how it meets the criteria in the challenge. Students check to see if their prototype meets the criteria set at the start of the design process. There should be no more than two circuits in the design and it should include lighting and sound.

ACTIVITY: TEST FEEDBACK

1. Students take their last prototype and consider the initial design challenge.
2. Ask students to check whether or not their design works and what they need to do to make it work if it doesn't.
3. Provide the opportunity to cycle through the Prototype and Test stages again.

Ask students to fill in the Test part of **Learning journal template 4 (Prototype and test page)**. See the **Journal tip** for further student guidance.

PROMPTS

- Does your prototype do what you wanted it to do?
- Does it have additional features such as extra lighting or flashing lights?
- Does the prototype feature some of the items on the class wish list?

MORE VOCABULARY

- evaluate – assess something, perhaps considering what worked and what didn't
- feature – a specific aspect of something, such as size, shape, colour and quality
- feedback – information about, for example, a person's performance or the design of a product, which can be used to make improvements
- prototype – an initial version of a model of a product or process that is used to develop a final model
- review – consider an idea, process or product and decide what needs to be changed and what works

JOURNAL TIP

Ask students to think about why it is important to test their ideas before they build their final design.

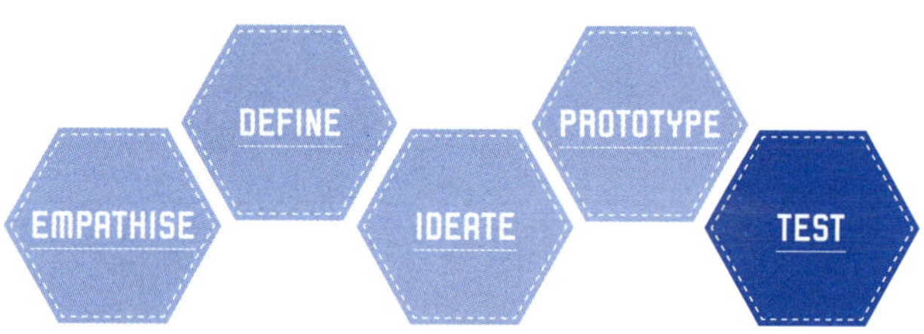

→ SHARE AND EVALUATE

At this stage of the investigation, students are provided with an opportunity to share their final design, as well as the processes involved in the investigation. Students evaluate their learning journals and their solutions.

ACTIVITY 1: BRING THE DESIGNS TOGETHER

1. Provide students with **Reproducible 7.3 (Final circuit design)** for organising their final circuit. They will need to include a drawing of their circuit(s), the materials, any help needed, the role of each person and how it meets the original design brief.
2. Students can create an iMovie or use Adobe Spark Video to demonstrate the process and thinking behind the designs. There should be an element of narration, where they are sharing their story about points of view, insights, prototyping and solutions.
3. Students should include their learning journals with the display so others can see the different stages of the design process.

ACTIVITY 2: EVALUATE AND GIVE FEEDBACK

1. Provide students with **Generic reproducible 2 (Self-evaluation)**.
2. Ask students to provide feedback to each other about interesting features, difficult aspects and any changes they would make.
3. Provide students with opportunities to share their designs. This could include inviting someone from an events company, an electrician or electrical engineer, or a friend or family member with relevant experience. It may be possible to share some of the videos with an expert for feedback about the designs.

ASSESSMENT

Ask students to again complete **Generic reproducible 1 (Key vocabulary table)** using the key vocabulary. Compare their table with the one they completed at the Tune-in stage, to demonstrate changes in understanding.

Students complete **Generic reproducible 3 (Responding to the investigation)**. Compare their responses to those on **Generic reproducible 2**.

Teachers and students each complete **Generic reproducible 5 (Design thinking assessment rubric)**. Students compare the feedback they are given by the teacher with their self-assessment of their design thinking skills.

EMPATHISE

STEM INVESTIGATIONS

Name: ....

Date: ....

Question	**Response:** Interviewee 1	**Response:** Interviewee 2

PROTOTYPE

STEM INVESTIGATIONS

Name: ....

Date: ....

Compare two of your circuit designs to decide which one is better.
Think of some questions to help you compare the two circuits.

	Circuit 1	Circuit 2
Draw a picture of the circuit (using standard symbols).		
Does the circuit include a switch?		
Does the circuit include lights? How many?		
Does the circuit include sound?		

STEM Investigations, UP, ISBN 978 1 4202 4154 9 © Macmillan Science and Education Australia 2018

DEFINE

STEM INVESTIGATIONS

Name: ....

Date: ....

Use this template to help you plan your final design.

Draw your circuit(s) here using standard symbols.
Include a key for the symbols.

List the materials you need to complete your circuit, as well as the number of each needed.	
What help might you need?	
Describe each person's role here.	
Does your design meet the original design brief?	☐
Write other useful information here.	

Ask your teacher to sign off on your design before you create your circuit(s).

Teacher: .... **Date:** ....

STEM Investigations, UP, ISBN 978 1 4202 4154 9 © Macmillan Science and Education Australia 2018

PROMOTE A BUSINESS USING BUBBLES

→ INTRODUCTION

Being an entrepreneur requires many skills. Entrepreneurs have lots of ideas and they look for ways to use them in their business. This investigation uses elements of art and science to support a business idea.

In this STEM investigation, students are asked to design and create a bubble castle to help promote a children's party business. They explore the science behind bubbles. They consider their different forms and how bubbles can be connected to create new designs.

THE CHALLENGE

Your aunt has a new business idea. She wants to hold bubble parties, where kids can blow bubbles, play with them and even make things with bubbles. She decides that the best way to promote the business is to build a structured bubble castle at the local shopping centre. She wants your help.

Your challenge is to design and build structured bubble modules that could stack together to make a display bubble castle. You must make the bubble solution and any tools, bubble blowers and structural support yourself. Is it possible to make bubbles that are not spheres? (Think about the building blocks of a castle wall.) As part of your investigation, you will learn about the science of bubble solutions, the elasticity of bubbles and surface tension.

KEY UNDERSTANDINGS

- A bubble is a thin skin of liquid that surrounds air.
- Water has strong surface tension, which means that it is difficult for bubbles to form from water alone.
- A solution of detergent and water has a weaker surface tension and more surface elasticity.
- Glycerine can be used to make bubbles stronger and last for longer.
- Bubbles can take the form of different geometric solids.
- Geometric solids include spheres, cubes, cuboids, triangular prisms, triangle-based pyramids and square-based pyramids.

KEY VOCABULARY

detergent
elasticity
geometric solid
solution
sphere
surface tension

KEY SKILLS

- Make observations and conduct interviews.
- Consider different points of view.
- Make predictions.
- Evaluate predictions.
- Create a fair test.

KEY ACTIONS

- Collect information through observation and interviews.
- Experiment with different bubble blowers and bubble mixtures.
- Design a structured bubble castle.

→ OVERVIEW OF STAGES

TUNE IN:

Students learn about bubbles and the science of surface tension. They explore how bubbles are made and how different bubbles can be formed. Students find out how to join bubbles together and create bubbles that are not spheres. They explore different bubble solutions.

EMPATHISE

Students find out about how people respond when playing with bubbles by observing their behaviour and interviewing them.

DEFINE

Students consider their observations of people interacting with bubbles, as well as the science behind bubbles, and then create a design brief.

IDEATE

Students generate ideas for how to build a bubble castle that is engaging and possible to create. They sketch and label their designs.

PROTOTYPE

Students choose one or two ideas to transform into physical representations (models). These are created rapidly, using simple materials.

TEST

As a class, students test their prototypes. Students share their prototypes and provide feedback to each other. They are given the opportunity to cycle through the Prototype and Test stages again.

SHARE AND EVALUATE:

Final prototypes are shared and evaluated, with opportunities for expert feedback investigated. Students consider whether or not their designs could be scaled up for a demonstration in a shopping centre.

→ SUGGESTED SCHEDULE

LESSON	STAGE
1–2	**Tune in**: watch a video clip about bubbles, explore the science of bubbles and introduce the student challenge
3–5	**Empathise**: observe and interview people about playing with bubbles, empathise and write/record in journal
6	**Define**: define the main focus of the challenge, create a design brief and write/record in journal
7	**Ideate**: develop ideas and write/record in journal
8–10	**Prototype** and **Test**: conduct prototyping and testing cycles and write/record in journal
11–13	**Share and evaluate**: share and evaluate designs and prototypes

CURRICULUM LINKS

The following tables show the key Science, Technologies and Mathematics curricula with which this STEM investigation is aligned.

SCIENCE

YEAR	STRAND	SUB-STRANDS AND CONTENT
5	Science Understanding	Chemical sciences: • Solids, liquids and gases have different observable properties and behave in different ways
6	Science Understanding	Chemical sciences: • Changes to materials can be reversible or irreversible
5 & 6	Science as a Human Endeavour	Nature and development of science: • Science involves testing predictions by gathering data and using evidence to develop explanations of events and phenomena
	Science Inquiry Skills	Questioning and predicting: • Processing and analysing data and information • Communicating

TECHNOLOGIES

YEAR	STRAND	CONTENT
5 & 6	Design and Technologies Knowledge and Understanding	• Investigate characteristics and properties of a range of materials, systems, components, tools and equipment and evaluate the impact of their use
	Design and Technologies Processes and Production Skills	• Generate, develop and communicate design ideas and processes for audiences using appropriate technical terms and graphical representation techniques • Select appropriate materials, components, tools, equipment and techniques and apply safe procedures to make designed solutions • Develop project plans that include consideration of resources when making designed solutions individually and collaboratively
	Digital Technologies Processes and Production Skills	• Collect, manage and analyse data • Acquire, store and validate different types of data, and use a range of software to interpret and visualise data to create information • Collaborate and manage • Plan, create and communicate ideas and information, including collaboratively online, applying agreed ethical, social and technical protocols

MATHEMATICS

YEAR	STRAND	CONTENT
5 & 6	Measurement and Geometry	Using units of measurement Shape

OTHER CURRICULUM LINKS

GENERAL CAPABILITIES

- Literacy
- Numeracy
- Information and Communication Technology (ICT) Capability
- Critical and Creative Thinking

ASSESSMENT

AC

The following resources are provided for assessing students at different stages of the STEM investigations:

- Generic reproducible 1 (Key vocabulary table), for assessing understanding of vocabulary
- Generic reproducible 2 (Self-evaluation), for student self-evaluation of the learning process
- Generic reproducible 3 (Responding to the investigation), for assessing student engagement in challenges, and the collaboration and skills involved in the design thinking stages
- Generic reproducible 5 (Design thinking assessment rubric), for evaluating student engagement in the design thinking stages
- Learning journal templates 1, 2, 3 and 4, for incorporating student reflection and evaluation

GETTING READY FOR THE INVESTIGATION

You can prepare yourself and students for this STEM investigation in the following ways:

- Identify groups of students who will work well together.
- Review the **Key science knowledge** that supports this investigation, and look at the **Useful links**.
- Investigate the **Useful apps**.
- Gather materials for creating bubbles and experiment with bubble shapes and bubble mixture during the Tune-in session. Prepare the glycerine mixture in advance – it needs to be left overnight before use.
- Start collecting additional materials for prototyping (as shown on the **Materials needed** list).
- Determine where prototypes will be kept between lessons.
- Create a wall space where students can share their ideas in the Ideate stage.
- Organise the class into pairs.
- Start thinking about:
  - » where the experiments with bubbles will take place, as it is likely to be messy and wet
  - » consider which groups to observe playing with bubbles, how this will be explained to the groups involved and the materials required
  - » how students will share their designs (in real time or using a multimedia presentation)
  - » whether or not it is possible to create a large-scale bubble castle in a public place
  - » people who might provide feedback about the bubble castle designs.

USEFUL APPS

- App for creating semantic maps (links between different words and/or concepts), such as Popplet
- App for creating interactive links (for example, between descriptions, videos, images and websites and a main image), such as ThingLink
- App for making notes using text, drawings, images, weblinks and audio, such as Notability
- App for creating multimedia presentations, such as Adobe Spark Video and iMovie
- App for creating surveys, such as Typeform (free for small surveys)

USEFUL LINKS

- Properties of solids, liquids and gases (revision), such as at bbc.co.uk/education/guides/z2wmxnb/revision/2
- The ingredients of detergents and a description of solvents, such as at bbc.co.uk/schools/gcsebitesize/science/add_gateway_pre_2011/chemical/detergentsrev1.shtml
- Bubble mix recipes, such as at questacon.edu.au/outreach/programs/science-circus/videos/bubble-mix-recipe
- Close-up images of bubbles, such as at pxhere.com/en/photos?q=bubbles
- A bubbles theme page (including ideas and links), such as at cln.org/themes/bubbles.html
- A recipe for homemade giant bubbles, such as at happyhooligans.ca/homemade-giant-bubbles
- Instructions for a sock bubble blower (which makes masses of interlinked small bubbles in a tubular shape), such as at housingaforest.com/rainbow-bubble-snakes

RESOURCES PROVIDED

- Generic reproducibles 1, 2, 3, 4, 5, 6, 9
- Reproducibles 8.1, 8.2, 8.3, 8.4, 8.5
- Learning journal templates 1, 2, 3, 4 (on disc)

MATERIALS NEEDED

- Sticky notes (half a pad per pair)
- Paper
- Coloured card
- Pens and markers
- Sticky tape
- Pipe-cleaners
- Cardboard
- Straws
- Detergent
- Water
- Containers for water
- Containers for bubble solution
- Small bubble blowers
- Soft wire
- Wool
- Stopwatch/timer
- Glycerine
- Eye-droppers

KEY SCIENCE KNOWLEDGE

This section provides an overview of the key science and maths concepts and vocabulary needed for this unit.

PROPERTIES OF A BUBBLE

A bubble is a thin skin of liquid surrounding air. Bubbles that are made of just water don't form easily, because water has a strong **surface tension**. This means that the water molecules are attracted much more to each other than to the air. Adding a **detergent** to water makes a **solution** that has less surface tension, which makes bubbles easier to form. The skin of these bubbles is a layer of water sandwiched between layers of detergent. It has good **elasticity**, allowing it to stretch rather than burst immediately.

The colours of a bubble can be seen because of the way that light is reflected from the skin's outer and inner surfaces. As the bubble skin becomes thinner, a dark band forms on top of the bubble, just before it pops.

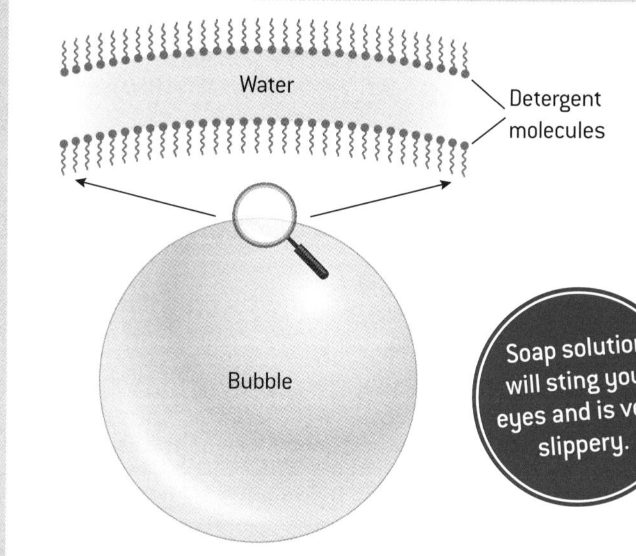

The skin of a bubble consists of two layers of detergent molecules around a layer of water.

Soap solution will sting your eyes and is very slippery.

BUBBLE SOLUTIONS

The simplest bubble solution consists of nine parts water and one part detergent (see **Useful links**). This provides elasticity and some strength, so bubbles can last for quite a while. Adding a teaspoon of glycerine to the solution will slow down evaporation, making the bubbles last for even longer.

GEOMETRIC SHAPES

Geometric solids can be used as basic building blocks. Common geometric solids include **spheres**, cubes, cuboids, triangular prisms, triangle-based pyramids and square-based pyramids.

To build a castle, it's best to use cubes and cuboids that have one side length in common (e.g. cubes of 10 cm × 10 cm × 10 cm and cuboids 10 cm × 10 cm × 20 cm) so that the parts can be easily put together. Triangular prisms or pyramids could be used to top the walls or to make roofs. Their dimensions should also be based on a common length (e.g. 10 cm).

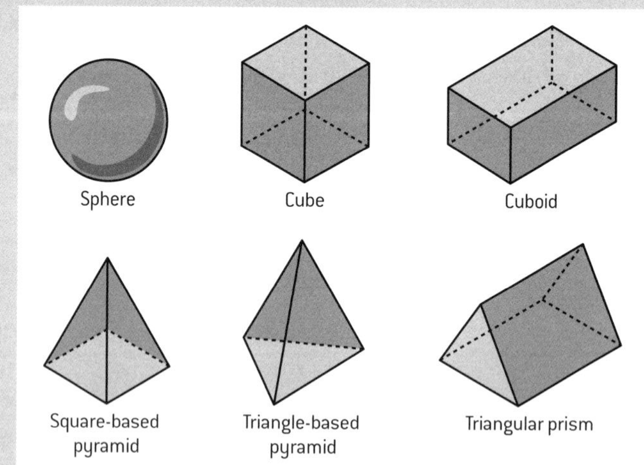

Common geometric shapes

KEY VOCABULARY

detergent – a water-soluble cleaning agent; its molecules attract oil and grease at one end and water at the other

elasticity – the ability to stretch

geometric solid – a three-dimensional solid such as a sphere, cube or pyramid

solution – a mixture containing substances that are evenly spread throughout

sphere – a geometric solid such as a ball or globe

surface tension – the skin-like property of the surface of a liquid, which is caused by the attraction the liquid particles have for each other

→ TUNE IN

1. Ask students to complete **Generic reproducible 1 (Key vocabulary table)** using the key vocabulary for this unit. This reproducible will also be used at the end of the unit, to demonstrate changes in understanding.
2. Ask students what they know about bubbles. Look at some images of a bubble going through the stages of being whole and finally popping. Observe some bubble close-up images (see **Useful apps/links**). What do students notice? Discuss their observations.
3. Watch a video clip of a bubble landing on a cactus (see **Useful apps/links**). Discuss why the bubble burst. What other factors can cause this?
4. Students need to have an understanding of surface tension, geometric solids and solutions.

ACTIVITY 1: BUBBLE EXPLORATION

1. Provide small containers of water and plastic straws and ask students to predict what will happen when they blow through the straw into the water. How long do they think the bubbles will last? Students record their predictions and observations in part 1 of **Reproducible 8.1 (Bubble observations)**.
2. Add some detergent to each water container and have the students stir the liquid with their straws. Explain that a solution is a mixture where the ingredients are evenly mixed. Again, students record their predictions and observations in part 2 of **Reproducible 8.1**. Discuss observations and predictions. Why was there a difference?

ACTIVITY 2: MAKING BUBBLE BLOWERS

1. Have a selection of materials (such as straws, pipe-cleaners, wool and wire) and small containers of bubble solution for each group.
2. Ask students to make bubble blowers, experimenting with different shapes and materials. Provide **Reproducible 8.2 (Bubble blowers)** to record process and results.
3. Each group demonstrates their bubble blowers to the class.
4. Discuss the bubbles made – were there any cubes or triangular prisms? Which materials made the best bubble blower for size of bubbles? Did the bubbles last long?
5. Ask students to complete **Reproducible 8.2**.

ACTIVITY 3: THE BEST BUBBLE MIXTURE

1. This experiment helps students to determine the solution that makes the strongest bubbles. Emphasise the need for fair testing – students change one variable, and test and compare to a control. Provide student pairs with a copy of **Reproducible 8.3 (Bubble experiment).**
2. Provide each pair with a pipe-cleaner, to make into a bubble blower, and a shallow container for solution. The control bubble mix is nine parts water and one part dishwashing detergent. The students use this mixture to blow a bubble, and then catch it on their bubble blower. They time how long it lasts and repeat at least 10 times.
3. Have two containers (one with glycerine and the other with detergent) and several eye-droppers. Students decide which and how many drops of ingredients to add to their control solution.
4. Students again blow a bubble, catch it and time how long it lasts. This is repeated 10 times and the results entered into **Reproducible 8.3**. How do the times compare to the control?
5. Students can then add ingredients to their solution, or rinse and dry their container and add ingredients to the fresh control solution. They then test and record again.
6. After at least four trials, have the students present their best mix. Which mixtures produce stronger bubbles?

5. Introduce the STEM investigation and challenge to the students. Provide them with the student card and read the information together. Ask students to write about their experiences with bubbles, and the best conditions for bubble blowing.
6. Introduce the design thinking process by reviewing the stages on the student card.
7. Explain that students will keep a journal about their learning at the different stages of the design.

TOP TIP! Conduct vocabulary activities to highlight and develop key vocabulary knowledge. Activities could include drawing semantic webs, creating a word wall or paired discussions.

USEFUL APPS/LINKS

- Close-up images of bubbles, such as at pxhere.com/en/photos?q=bubbles
- Bubble landing on a cactus, such as at giphy.com/gifs/art-cactus-bubble-bursting-McWTxnpVZp6IG

→ EMPATHISE

During the Empathise stage of the design thinking process, students focus on finding out about different points of view. To empathise with others, they need to research some of the experiences that people have had. Students will take notes, ask questions, draw diagrams and take photos where relevant.

ACTIVITY 1: OBSERVE

In this activity, students observe how people interact with bubbles. Provide different groups of people with bubble solution and bubble blowers. These could be homemade or bought. The people to observe may be other students in the playground, family members or friends.

Provide students with **Generic reproducible 9 (See, think, wonder)** for recording their observations of things such as facial expressions, responses and interactions.

ACTIVITY 2: INTERVIEW

Ask students to interview other students and/or their families and friends about their experiences playing with bubbles. Provide them with **Reproducible 8.4 (Bubble play interview)** for them to record the responses of different people.

Ask students to consider the information they have gathered through observation and interviews. Use the **Prompts** to start a class discussion.

PROMPTS

- What were some of the expressions people used?
- What were some of the things people liked doing with the bubble blowers?
- Were there any aspects of bubble blowing that people didn't enjoy?
- How did people use their bubble blowers?

MORE VOCABULARY

- empathise – understand and consider another person or group's point of view
- point of view – an opinion, attitude or judgement considered in a particular way

JOURNAL TIP

Ask students to complete **Learning journal template 1 (Empathise page)** while they are completing the different tasks. Remind them to date their notes and include photos or drawings of relevant information.

ASSESSMENT

This stage of the design thinking process offers opportunities to observe students collecting information, developing questions, and recording their notes and thinking in their journal.

REPRODUCIBLE 8.4 BUBBLE PLAY INTERVIEW

EMPATHISE

STEM INVESTIGATIONS

Name: ....

Date: ....

Write some of your interviewee responses in the bubbles.

134

STEM Investigations, UP, ISBN 978 1 4202 4154 9 © Macmillan Education Australia 2018

Reproducible 8.4 (Bubble play interview)

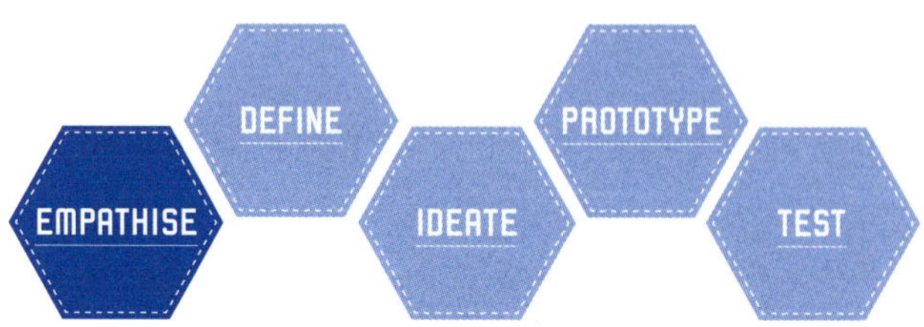

→ DEFINE

The main focus of this stage of the design thinking process is to reframe the challenge. The initial challenge is quite open, so at this stage students learn how to define what needs to be done. This includes noting insights that have been generated.

ACTIVITY 1: CONSIDER OBSERVATIONS

1. Students consider the information they gathered in the Empathise stage. They may work in pairs or small groups of students. Provide them with a whiteboard, large sheet of paper and/or sticky notes to collate some of the key information they have gathered. Students should consider some of the possible limitations they observed, as well as any positive points.
2. Students should discuss one section of **Learning journal template 2 (Define page)** at a time, write their responses, then continue discussing their ideas for the next section, until the task is complete. This provides students with opportunities to hear others' responses and provides the teacher with input points.
3. Discuss information gathered about bubbles – how they are created, the effect of changing the ingredients of the bubble solutions and how others interact with bubbles. Provide students with the opportunity to research further. Ask them to write other information they would like to know, such as different bubble mix recipes, materials for making bubble blowers and ways to construct more unusual bubble blower shapes. Provide them with **Generic reproducible 4 (Key question table)** to assist them to record their questions, findings and sources.

PROMPTS

- What did you discover?
- What were the most important pieces of information that you gathered?
- What was something new that you learned?
- What other information do you need?

MORE VOCABULARY

- define – state the meaning of something
- insight – an accurate understanding of someone or something

ACTIVITY 2: CONSIDER INSIGHTS

Students think of at least one insight they have gained from the process; for example, different-shaped bubble blowers affect the form and size of bubbles.

Students add this insight to **Learning journal template 2**. Provide students with **Reproducible 8.5 (Bubble castle design brief)**, which will direct their design and can be customised.

When considering insights, students could think about the following:

- What was something unexpected that you saw or found out? How was it unexpected?
- How will you decide on the most important aspect of creating the bubble castle?
- Is there any other information that you need or would like to know? How will you find out?

ACTIVITY 3: CONSIDER CONSTRAINTS

At this stage, let students know the constraints of the challenge, by describing the materials available, the size parameters, and when and how the bubble castles will be demonstrated.

Students can then update **Learning journal template 2**.

JOURNAL TIP

Discuss the term 'insight'. Explain that it relates to something students have learned about the people and their responses to the surveys, as well as information gathered through research or excursions. You could refer to **Learning journal template 2**.

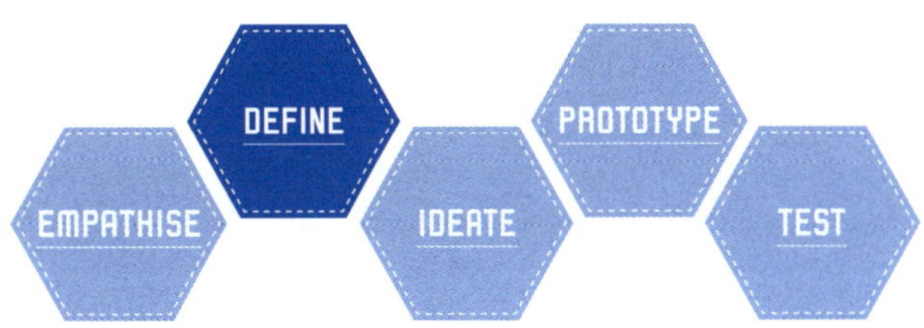

→ IDEATE

The Ideate stage of the design thinking process is all about generating lots of ideas. Students need to be flexible in their thinking and able to move beyond obvious ideas. At this stage, ideas are not judged, just generated and gathered.

ACTIVITY: GENERATE IDEAS

1. Ask groups of students to draw or write their ideas. Each new idea should be written or drawn on a separate piece of paper or sticky note.
2. Ask students to group ideas on a wall or board.
3. Ask students to look at the different ideas and provide feedback to each other. It is important that students don't defend their ideas at this stage. They should just be listening to the feedback.
4. After the initial feedback, ask students to come up with more ideas. Encourage them to be creative and even radical.
5. Ask students to choose four of their ideas to write in their journal. Students use **Learning journal template 3 (Ideate page)** to do this. Ask students to choose one idea to explore further and explain the reasoning behind their choice.

TOP TIP!

At this stage, students may have produced a series of annotated drawings about their bubble castle. They may have a collection of sticky notes, which they can organise into related ideas.

Encourage students to view and read others' ideas before giving feedback. Feedback could be within small groups or between partners. Considering others' ideas is an important part of this process, so students can build on their own ideas as they continue to ideate.

Have students determine the best size for the castle wall components by starting with sides of 5 cm and working their way up until the construction can no longer support bubbles. Plastic straws and pipe-cleaners are ideal materials to use.

At each stage of this activity, ask students to discuss their thoughts before writing down their responses. This will help them to think through their ideas and select their final ideas to develop.

PROMPTS

- How do these ideas relate to the design brief?
- How might you test your design?
- How can you make it more stable?
- How can you make it more interesting?
- If you could use different materials, what would you choose to use?

MORE VOCABULARY

- feedback – information about, for example, a person's performance or the design of a product, which can be used to make improvements
- ideate – generate many ideas without making judgements about the ideas

JOURNAL TIP

When choosing four ideas to include in the journal, students should try to choose ideas that aren't related, to show a range of ideas.

USEFUL APPS/LINKS

- Tools for creating ideas, such as at creatingminds.org/tools/tools_ideation.htm
- Tips for creativity and innovation, such as at designorate.com/creativity-innovation-in-education

ASSESSMENT

At the Ideate stage, assessment could include observations about the number and diversity of students' ideas, and their ability to provide feedback and create additional ideas. Reflection in the journal should provide an insight into some of the reasoning behind students' choices.

EMPATHISE | DEFINE | IDEATE | PROTOTYPE | TEST

→ PROTOTYPE

At this stage of the design thinking process, students are asked to create a physical prototype of how the bubble castle might look. It is the stage where students need to get their ideas out of their head and presented in a way that engages other students and helps them to understand the ideas. When students create, it helps them to think and solve problems and disagreements. Students can role-play, make storyboards or use sticky notes when they prototype. The most important feature is that viewers can interact with whatever is produced.

Encourage students to photograph or film during the prototyping and testing stages. This information can be used to show the learning behind the design thinking process in action.

ACTIVITY: TRANSFORM IDEAS INTO PROTOTYPES

1. Students review the ideas generated at the Ideate stage. Provide them with an A3 copy of **Generic reproducible 6 (In the frame)** so they can organise their ideas into two sections: 'least relevant' and 'most relevant'. Students continue to cycle through this activity until they have an idea to start prototyping.
2. Provide students with a range of materials to use to create their prototype. Remind students that a prototype should be created rapidly and is not meant to look 'nice'.
3. After a prototype has been created, ask students to see if it works and get feedback from others.
4. Students then use the feedback to prototype again.

Ask students to fill in the Prototype section of **Learning journal template 4 (Prototype and test page)**. See the **Journal tip** for further student guidance.

PROMPTS

- What worked?
- How could it be improved?
- What else do you need to know, do or have?
- What other suggestions do you have?

MORE VOCABULARY

- feedback – information about, for example, a person's performance or the design of a product, which can be used to make improvements
- prototype – an initial version of a model of a product or process that is used to develop a final model

JOURNAL TIP

Remind students to highlight the main features of their prototype. If students are creating an electronic journal, they can insert a photo of their prototype and annotate it.

USEFUL APPS/LINKS

- App for creating interactive links (for example, between descriptions, videos, images and websites and a main image), such as ThingLink
- App for making notes using text, drawings, images, weblinks and audio, such as Notability

ASSESSMENT

Observe students as they make changes to their designs. Are they able to consider feedback, make modifications and move rapidly through this process? Or do they have difficulties with holding onto an idea and accepting feedback?

TOP TIP!

The Prototype stage is often very messy, particularly when dealing with bubbles and bubble mixture. It is important that students are focusing on their ideas, rather than the end product. Provide them with lots of materials – recycling depots can be a useful source of resources. Students may add labels to prototypes to explain some of the main features. Photographing and annotating pictures of prototypes can be useful. Students may initially create their prototypes with cardboard, pipe-cleaners or straws. It will then be important to prototype with bubble mixture and different-shaped bubble blowers, remembering to video-record the process because the bubbles may not last long.

To gain feedback, students could ask each other some of the following questions:

- What is the main feature of your prototype?
- How does it work?
- Which aspects work best? What will you keep?
- Which aspects need changing? How might you do this?
- What other materials might you need?

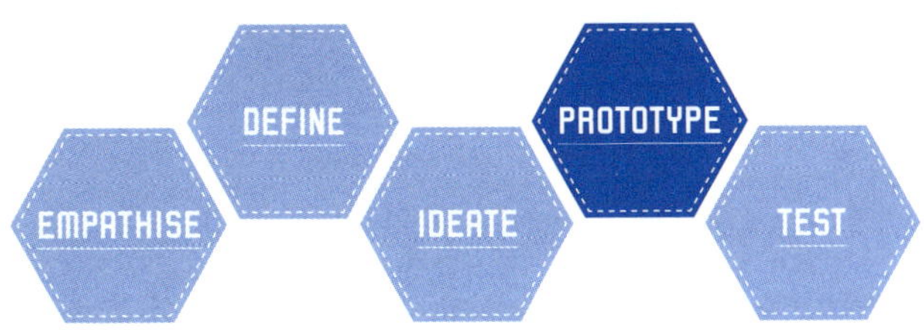

→ TEST

At this stage of the design thinking process, students test their prototype to see how it meets the criteria in the challenge. Students check to see if their prototype meets the criteria set at the start of the design process.

ACTIVITY: TEST FEEDBACK

1. Students take their last prototype and consider the initial design brief.
2. Ask students to check whether or not their design works. If not, what do they need to do to make it work?
3. Provide the opportunity to cycle through the prototyping and testing stages again.

Ask students to fill in the Test part of **Learning journal template 4 (Prototype and test page)**. See the **Journal tip** for further student guidance.

PROMPTS

- Does your prototype do what you wanted it to do?
- Are there other features you could add?
- What needs to be changed?
- What works well?

MORE VOCABULARY

- evaluate – assess something, perhaps considering what worked and what didn't
- feature – a specific aspect of something, such as size, shape, colour and quality
- feedback – information about, for example, a person's performance or the design of a product, which can be used to make improvements
- prototype – an initial version of a model of a product or process that is used to develop a final model
- review – consider an idea, process or product and decide what needs to be changed and what works

JOURNAL TIP

Ask students to think about why it is important to test their ideas before they build their final design.

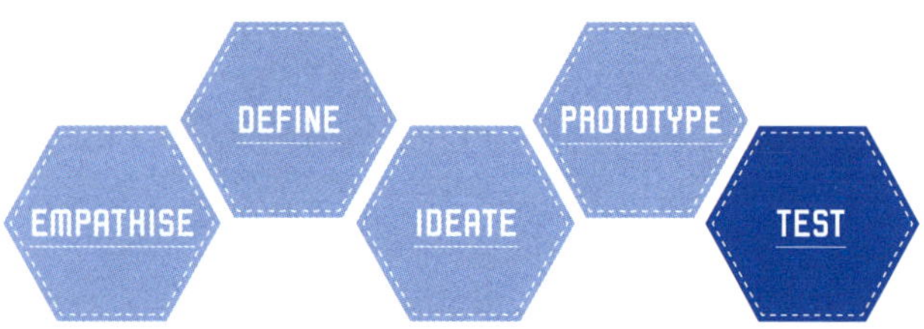

→ SHARE AND EVALUATE

At this stage of the investigation, students are provided with an opportunity to share their final design, as well as the processes involved in the investigation. Students evaluate their learning journals and their solutions.

ACTIVITY 1: BRING THE DESIGNS TOGETHER

1. Students can create an iMovie or use Adobe Spark Video to demonstrate the process and thinking behind the designs. There should be an element of narration, where they are sharing their story about points of view, insights, prototyping and solutions.
2. Students should include their learning journals with the display so others can see the different stages of the design process.

ACTIVITY 2: EVALUATE AND GIVE FEEDBACK

1. Provide students with the **Generic reproducible 2 (Self-evaluation)** to complete.
2. Ask students to provide feedback to each other about the most interesting features, the aspects that were most difficult and the changes that they would make if they repeated the task.
3. Provide students with opportunities to share their designs. This could include inviting someone from a party business, an architect, or perhaps a friend or family member. It may be possible to share some of the videos with an expert for feedback about the designs.

ASSESSMENT

Ask students to again complete **Generic reproducible 1 (Key vocabulary table)** using the key vocabulary for this unit: detergent, elasticity, geometric solid, solution, sphere, surface tension. Compare their table with the one they completed at the Tune-in stage, to demonstrate changes in understanding.

Students complete **Generic reproducible 3 (Responding to the Investigation)**. Compare their responses to those on **Generic reproducible 2**.

Teachers and students each complete **Generic reproducible 5 (Design thinking assessment rubric)**. Students compare the teacher feedback they are given with their self-assessment of their design thinking skills.

BUBBLE OBSERVATIONS

Name: ....

Date: ....

STEM INVESTIGATIONS

PART 1

What do you predict will happen when you blow into the straw?

What did you observe?

PART 2

How long do you think the bubbles will last?

What did you observe?

Name: ....

Date: ....

STEM INVESTIGATIONS

1. Write the shapes of the different bubble blowers in the left column of the table. Predict what the bubble will be like for each shape and write it in the second column. Then record what you observed in the last column.

Shape	What do you think the bubble will look like?	What did you observe?

2. Which materials made the best bubble blowers and which made the worst? Consider both the bubble's size and how long it lasted for the different bubble blowers.

....

....

....

Explain your answer.

....

....

....

3. What do you think would be the best combination of shape and material for a bubble blower?

....

....

....

....

STEM Investigations, UP, ISBN 978 1 4202 4154 9 © Macmillan Science and Education Australia 2018

Name: ....

Date: ....

STEM INVESTIGATIONS

Use this table to record the time your bubbles take to pop for each mixture.

TEST NUMBER	Time bubble takes to pop for ...			
	... control mixture. INGREDIENTS: water and detergent AMOUNTS:	... control mixture plus detergent or glycerine. INGREDIENTS: AMOUNTS:	... previous mixture plus additional ingredient. INGREDIENTS: AMOUNTS:	... new mixture. INGREDIENT(S): AMOUNT(S):
1				
2				
3				
4				
5				
6				
7				
8				
9				
10				

REPRODUCIBLE 8.4 BUBBLE PLAY INTERVIEW

EMPATHISE

STEM INVESTIGATIONS

Name: ....

Date: ....

Write some of your interviewee responses in the bubbles.

STEM Investigations, UP, ISBN 978 1 4202 4154 9 © Macmillan Science and Education Australia 2018

DEFINE

STEM INVESTIGATIONS

Name: ....

Date: ....

Create a design brief for your bubble castle by completing these sentences.

The bubble castle must include the following features (for example, tower, turrets):

The bubble castle must meet these size guidelines:

The bubble castle should be able to:

Additional information:

STEM Investigations, UP, ISBN 978 1 4202 4154 9 © Macmillan Science and Education Australia 2018

GROW 'FAST FOOD' TO SELL AT MARKET

NATURAL WORLD 9

→ INTRODUCTION

Farmers' markets have become very popular as more people understand the importance of buying foods that are grown locally and sustainably. Many foods sold in supermarkets today have a high carbon footprint. Animal products account for the most food-generated greenhouse gases, and transporting foods long distances uses considerable energy. Processed foods use water, energy and other resources, and also need to be packaged, transported and sometimes refrigerated. Food factories often generate waste, which has an impact on the environment. By buying fresh foods at farmers' markets, people are choosing to support sustainability.

In this STEM investigation, students need to think about ways to grow 'fast food' in a sustainable way. They are asked to find out about fast-growing edible plants, such as herbs and sprouts, that can be sold at farmers' markets, and they are required to demonstrate how to grow plants quickly and sustainably.

THE CHALLENGE

Your school is hosting a farmers' market. People usually go to farmers' markets to buy fresh, local produce. You want to make some money quickly, so you decide to sell some home-grown food at the market. You'll need a steady supply of fresh produce – and you'll need to grow it fast!

Your challenge is to design and create a greenhouse that will help you grow fast-growing plants to sell at market. Think about ways to make the project sustainable; for example, you could use seeds from your plants to keep growing more plants . Also, keep in mind who might buy your produce. Could the way it is grown help sell your produce? As part of your STEM investigation, you will learn how the growth and survival of living things is affected by the physical conditions of their environment.

KEY UNDERSTANDINGS

- Plants need water and sunlight to grow.
- Plants transform light energy into chemical energy that they can use to grow.
- Some plants grow more quickly than others.
- A plant's environment can affect how it grows and survives.
- A greenhouse can help plants grow faster.
- Sustainable gardening includes harvesting seeds from plants to grow new plants.

KEY VOCABULARY

conditions

food choices

food production

greenhouse

nutrient

sustainable

KEY SKILLS

- Make careful observations.
- Consider different points of view.
- Develop research skills.
- Create environments to grow fast-growing edible plants.

KEY ACTIONS

- Find out about the best conditions for growing plants.
- Learn about automated watering systems.
- Explore ways to create ideal growing conditions.
- Find out about fast-growing edible plants.
- Create a greenhouse for growing edible plants.
- Grow edible plants to sell.

OVERVIEW OF STAGES

TUNE IN:

- Watch a time-lapse video showing plant growth.
- Explore different parts of plants. Students create a three-dimensional display to demonstrate their understanding.
- Explore plant growing times and conditions, and how greenhouses work. Students replicate a fast-growing plant experiment using simulated greenhouse conditions.

EMPATHISE

Students conduct surveys to find out about the kinds of fresh foods different people like or expect to buy at a farmers' market (for example, sustainable foods and local foods) and how much people are prepared to pay.

DEFINE

Students consider the main issues that relate to the needs of plants, and how greenhouses work. They also consider the information gathered in the surveys.

IDEATE

Students generate creative ideas for making a greenhouse. They consider sustainability issues and costs. Students choose what they might grow, and predict how much they could grow, the production costs and how much they could sell the produce for.

PROTOTYPE

Students transform some of their ideas into physical representations. These are created rapidly, using simple materials. Students can role-play, make storyboards or use sticky notes when they prototype.

TEST

Students share their prototypes and provide feedback to each other. Students check which ideas work best, then choose a final design to build. They calculate how many greenhouses (on what scale) they would need to build to make a profit.

SHARE AND EVALUATE:

Final prototypes are shared and evaluated, with opportunities for expert feedback.

SUGGESTED SCHEDULE

LESSON	STAGE
1–4	**Tune in**: pre-test key vocabulary, watch time-lapse video showing plant growth, explore different parts of plants and create a three-dimensional display to demonstrate understanding Explore plant growing times and conditions, explore how greenhouses work and replicate a fast-growing plant experiment using simulated greenhouse conditions
5–6	**Empathise**: survey people about fresh food choices and likes, and find out about origins of foods
7	**Define**: define the main issues relating to the choice of plants to grow and greenhouse building, and write/record in journal
8–9	**Ideate**: develop ideas for a greenhouse and write/record in journal
10–14	**Prototype** and **Test**: conduct prototyping and testing cycles, and write/record in journal
15–16	**Share and evaluate**: share and evaluate designs and prototypes

CURRICULUM LINKS

The following tables show the key Science, Technologies and Mathematics curricula with which this STEM investigation is aligned.

SCIENCE

YEAR	STRAND	SUB-STRANDS AND CONTENT	
5	Science Understanding	Biological sciences: • Living things have structural features and adaptations that help them to survive in their environment	
6	Science Understanding	Biological sciences: • The growth and survival of living things are affected by physical conditions of their environment	
5 & 6	Science as a Human Endeavour	Use and influence of science: • Scientific knowledge is used to solve problems and inform personal and community decisions	
	Science Inquiry Skills	Questioning and predicting Processing and analysing data and information	Planning and conducting Communicating

TECHNOLOGIES

YEAR	STRAND	CONTENT
5 & 6	Design and Technologies Knowledge and Understanding	• Investigate how and why food and fibre are produced in managed environments and prepared to enable people to grow and be healthy
	Design and Technologies Processes and Production Skills	• Critique needs or opportunities for designing, and investigate materials, components, tools, equipment and processes to achieve intended designed solutions • Generate, develop and communicate design ideas and processes for audiences using appropriate technical terms and graphical representation techniques • Select appropriate materials, components, tools, equipment and techniques, and apply safe procedures to make designed solutions • Negotiate criteria for success that include sustainability to evaluate design ideas, processes and solutions • Develop project plans that include consideration of resources when making designed solutions individually and collaboratively

MATHEMATICS

YEAR	STRAND	SUB-STRANDS
5 & 6	Number and Algebra	Number and place value Fractions and decimals Money and financial mathematics
	Measurement and Geometry	Using units of measurement Geometric reasoning
	Statistics and Probability	Chance Data representation and interpretation

OTHER CURRICULUM LINKS

GENERAL CAPABILITIES

- Literacy
- Numeracy
- Personal and Social Capability
- Information and Communication Technology (ICT) Capability
- Critical and Creative Thinking

CROSS-CURRICULUM PRIORITIES

- Sustainability

This STEM investigation also contains links to Humanities and Social Sciences – Economics and Business (Years 5 and 6).

ASSESSMENT

The following resources are provided for assessing students at different stages of the STEM investigations:

- Generic reproducible 1 (Key vocabulary table), for assessing understanding of vocabulary
- Generic reproducible 2 (Self-evaluation), for student self-evaluation of the learning process
- Generic reproducible 3 (Responding to the investigation), for assessing student engagement in the challenge, and the collaboration and skills involved in the design thinking stages
- Generic reproducible 5 (Design thinking assessment rubric), for evaluating student engagement in the design thinking stages
- Learning journal templates 1, 2, 3 and 4, for incorporating student reflection and evaluation

GETTING READY FOR THE INVESTIGATION

You can prepare yourself and students for this STEM investigation in the following ways:

- Identify groups of students who will work well together.
- Review the **Key science knowledge** that supports this investigation, and look at the **Useful links**.
- Investigate the **Useful apps**.
- Gather materials for the seed-growing experiments.
- Start collecting additional materials for prototyping (as shown on the **Materials needed** list).
- Determine where prototypes will be kept between lessons.
- Create a wall space where students can share their ideas in the Ideate stage.
- Organise the class into pairs or small groups.
- Create display space for information about plants and growth.
- Start thinking about:
  - which seeds students could use
  - where they can obtain the seeds
  - how frequently the seeds need watering
  - managing watering over weekends
  - materials they may need to build their greenhouse
  - who they might interview to find out about food preferences.
- Consider whether or not to discuss automated watering systems – some students may wish to explore this aspect of growing food.

USEFUL APPS

- App for creating a learning journal, such as Book Creator
- App for creating semantic maps (links between different words and/or concepts), such as Popplet
- App for creating interactive links (for example, between descriptions, videos, images and websites and a main image), such as ThingLink
- App for making notes using text, drawings, images, weblinks and audio, such as Notability
- App for creating multimedia presentations, such as Adobe Spark Video and iMovie
- Survey app such as Typeform (free for small surveys)

USEFUL LINKS

- Information about the life cycle of plants, such as at scienceforkidsclub.com/plant-lifecycle.html
- A time-lapse video of plants growing, such as at vimeo.com/69225705
- Plant parts and other information, such as at bbc.co.uk/bitesize/ks2/science/living_things/plants/read/1/
- An explanation of photosynthesis, such as at photosynthesisforkids.com
- An animated teacher resource on photosynthesis, such as at youtube.com/watch?v=zD_49VPxpRQ
- Food choices and how they relate to sustainable food, such as at uq.edu.au/sustainability/sustainable-food
- Information about where food comes from, such as at abc.net.au/btn/story/s4425894.htm
- A game about photosynthesis, such as at splash.abc.net.au/home#!/media/1388663/photosynthesis-builder

RESOURCES PROVIDED

- Generic reproducibles 1, 2, 3, 4, 5, 6
- Reproducibles 9.1, 9.2, 9.3
- Learning journal templates 1, 2, 3, 4 (on disc)

MATERIALS NEEDED

- Sticky notes (half a pad per pair)
- Paper
- Coloured card
- Pens and markers
- Sticky tape
- Pipe-cleaners
- Cardboard
- Recycled plastic bottles
- Plastic wrap
- Edible plant seeds
- Potting mix
- Thermometer
- Jugs
- Pipes
- Straws
- Perspex or clear card
- Sprout seeds (or similar)
- Cotton wool
- Containers, such as egg cartons
- Glass bowls or other clear glass containers

Students will also need access to water.

KEY SCIENCE KNOWLEDGE

This section provides an overview of the key science concepts and vocabulary needed for this unit.

PLANTS, FOOD AND SUSTAINABLE FOOD PRODUCTION

Knowledge of a plant's life cycle, (see diagram), is important in an understanding of **food production**.

During their lifetimes, plants produce the energy they need to live, grow and reproduce. They do this in the process of photosynthesis. A plant takes in carbon dioxide through stomata (small holes in their leaves). The root of the plant absorbs water and **nutrients** from the soil, and transports them to the leaves. The plant's leaves contain chlorophyll, which makes leaves green. The combination of chlorophyll, nutrients, water, carbon dioxide and sunlight is turned into glucose (a type of sugar) and oxygen. The plants use the glucose as a source of energy and release the oxygen into the atmosphere.

Plenty of nutrients, sunlight and water are all **conditions** that help plants to grow faster. A **greenhouse** also helps plants to grow faster because the energy of the sun that travels through the glass or plastic in a greenhouse is changed to heat energy. Greenhouses help to control the temperature inside. Artificial heating and lighting inside a greenhouse means that photosynthesis can continue for longer and at an increased rate. Additional carbon dioxide is released into the atmosphere so the rate of photosynthesis is increased. A greenhouse also offers protection from wind, rain and hail, as well as keeping pests from eating the food or flowers being grown inside.

Where and how plants are grown and harvested can affect the environment. **Sustainable** foods include those that have been grown or sourced locally, have not been processed in a factory, avoid packaging and have been produced in a way that considers the environment. These factors are among the things that people consider when making **food choices**.

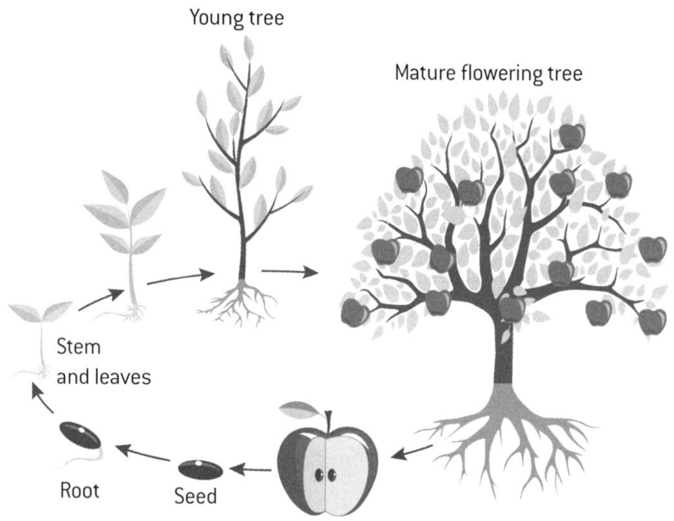

The life cycle of plants

- A seed is planted or falls into the soil.
- The seed starts to sprout. This is called germination.
- A root emerges from the seed as it starts to grow.
- The stem and leaves of the plant break through the soil and continue to grow.
- The plant needs to be pollinated before fruit or vegetables can grow. This happens when bees, animals or the wind transfer pollen from one plant to another.
- The pollen sticks to the reproductive part of the plant. This creates flowers, which contain the plant's seeds. The seeds are eventually released into the air or fall to the ground and the whole cycle begins again.

KEY VOCABULARY

conditions – factors that affect something, such as the soil, nutrients, sunlight and water that plants need

food choices – choices that consumers make when deciding which foods to buy, to do with things such as its ingredients, where and how it is made or grown, who is selling it and how much it costs

food production – the work of a number of businesses to study, grow, process, transport, store and sell food

greenhouse – a building made of glass or plastic that protects plants from the weather

nutrient – a substance that is needed for life and growth

sustainable – able to be continued while minimising harm to the environment

→ TUNE IN

1. Ask students to complete **Generic reproducible 1 (Key vocabulary table)** using the key vocabulary for this unit: conditions, food choices, food production, greenhouse, nutrient, sustainable.
2. Watch a time-lapse video showing plants growing (see **Useful apps/links**).
3. Discuss what is happening, including what is common to each plant shown. Talk about the life cycle of a plant.
4. Provide a link to a diagram of a plant, showing the different parts of the plant (see **Useful apps/links**).
5. Groups of students create a three-dimensional wall display by making different plants and labelling the key features: stem, roots, leaf, flower, seeds.
6. Set up the following three activities.

ACTIVITY 1: HOW FAST PLANTS GROW

1. Provide students with **Reproducible 9.1 (Plant growing times)**. Students cut up the cards and group them according to the length of time they predict it takes to grow.
2. Students explain the reasoning for their groupings, then use the internet or books to find out if their groupings are accurate.

ACTIVITY 2: PLANTS IN DIFFERENT CONDITIONS

1. Read about photosynthesis and look at diagrams showing the process or an online video (see **Useful apps/links**).
2. Discuss the key components of photosynthesis: water, sunlight and carbon dioxide.
3. Set up the following experiment:
   - Place sprout seeds in cotton wool within a container, such as an egg carton. Create four separate containers.
   - Place the first container in a dark place with no light or water.
   - Place the second in a dark place with water.
   - Place the third in a well-lit place with no water.
   - Place the fourth in a well-lit place with water.
4. Discuss why the experiment has been set up with four different containers. Provide students with **Reproducible 9.2 (Plant observations table)**. Ask students to make observations every day about each of the containers, for at least a week.
5. At the end of the experiment, ask students to discuss their results and encourage them to set up their own experiments.

ACTIVITY 3: FEATURES OF A GREENHOUSE

1. Look at images of greenhouses and discuss their features. Explain to students what happens to light when it passes through a greenhouse and is trapped as heat. Read about a simple greenhouse experiment (see **Useful apps/links**). If there is time, carry out this experiment at school.
2. Discuss how light creates heat. Discuss examples such as the sun, a bedside lamp, a torch or a fire.
3. Set up a new sprout growing experiment. This time, have two containers – one with access to light and water, and the other with light, water and a glass covering. (This could be a glass bowl, container or cloche.) Provide students with another copy of **Reproducible 9.2** and ask them to record their observations each day, for at least a week.
4. Discuss the findings and compare similarities and differences with the original experiment in Activity 2.

Note: Activities 1 and 2 can be run simultaneously, especially if there is limited time for the investigation.

7. Introduce the STEM investigation and challenge to the students. Provide them with the student card and read through the information together. Ask students to think about foods that people like and can be grown quickly. Discuss seasonal foods too.
8. Introduce the design thinking process by reviewing the stages on the student card. Explain that students will keep a journal about their learning at the different stages of the design.

USEFUL APPS/LINKS

- A time-lapse video showing plants growing, such as at vimeo.com/69225705
- A diagram of a plant, showing the different parts of the plant, such as at bbc.co.uk/bitesize/ks2/science/living_things/plants/read/3/
- A game about photosynthesis, such as at splash.abc.net.au/home#!/media/1388663/photosynthesis-builder
- A simple greenhouse experiment, such as at education.com/activity/article/Observe_Greenhouse_Effect/

→ EMPATHISE

During the Empathise stage of the design thinking process, students focus on considering different points of view. To empathise with others, they need to engage in observation, interact with others and immerse themselves in the experiences that others have. Students will observe others, taking notes, asking questions and taking photos where possible. Students interview people to find out what sorts of foods they might buy from a farmers' market and how much they would be prepared to pay.

ACTIVITY 1: FIND OUT ABOUT PEOPLE'S PREFERENCES

Students create a survey to find out the kinds of fresh foods people like, which foods they would buy at a farmers' market and how much they would be prepared to pay. Students could also ask whether or not people are willing to pay more or less at a farmers' market and why. Include some examples of fast-growing foods, such as sprouts and herbs, for people to comment on. Students can create a handwritten survey, or use a free app (see **Useful apps/links**).

ACTIVITY 2: FIND OUT WHERE FRESH FOODS COME FROM

1. Students investigate where different fresh foods have originated. Create a list of fresh foods, then arrange a visit to a local supermarket or greengrocer to find out the origin of the foods. Students use **Reproducible 9.3 (Food origins table)** to record their information.
   If there is a local farmers' market, some students may be able to gather information about where the foods sold there come from and share their findings with the class.
2. Discuss some of the issues with food production and its impact, including the environmental costs of importing foods that are not in season. Visit some websites with information about sustainable food and where food comes from (see **Useful apps/links**).

ACTIVITY 3: EMPATHISE

Ask students to consider which fresh foods are the most popular and which fast-growing foods people might be interested in purchasing. Students rank the foods in order of popularity and note which of these foods are fast growing.

Direct students to the **Learning journal template 1 (Empathise page)**.

PROMPTS

- What were the most popular fresh foods?
- What were the least popular fresh foods?
- Which fast-growing foods do people like to eat?
- How did people respond to growing home-grown or locally sourced food?
- What did you learn about sustainable food?

MORE VOCABULARY

- empathise – understanding and considering another person's or group's point of view
- point of view – an opinion, attitude or judgement considered in a particular way
- sustainable – able to be continued while minimising harm to the environment

JOURNAL TIPS

Ask students to complete **Learning journal template 1 (Empathise page)** while they are completing the different activities. Remind them to date their notes and include photos of relevant information or pictures.

USEFUL APPS/LINKS

- A survey app such as Typeform
- Information about sustainable food, such as at uq.edu.au/sustainability/sustainable-food
- Information about where food comes from, such as at abc.net.au/btn/story/s4425894.htm

ASSESSMENT

This stage of the design thinking process offers opportunities to observe students collecting information, developing questions, and recording their notes and thinking in their journal.

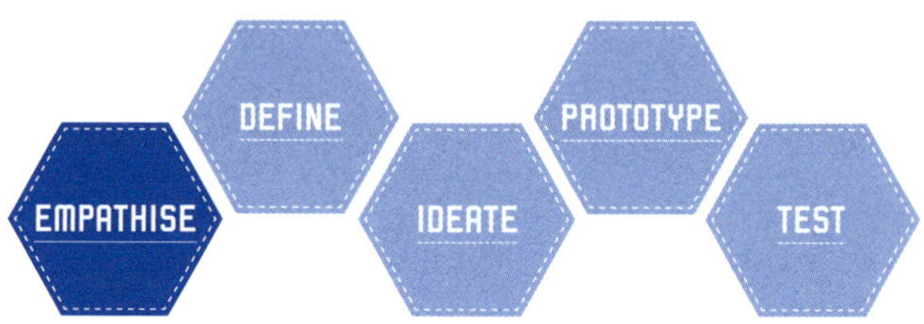

DEFINE

The main focus of this stage of the design thinking process is to reframe the challenge. The initial challenge is quite open, so at this stage students learn how to define what needs to be done. This includes noting insights that have been generated.

ACTIVITY 1: CONSIDER OBSERVATIONS

1. Students consider the information they gathered in the Empathise stage. They may work in pairs or small groups. Provide them with a whiteboard, large sheet of paper and/or sticky notes to collate some of their key information. Students sort the feedback from the survey and discuss their findings. They prioritise the foods and discuss which 'fast foods' could be investigated.
2. Students should discuss one section of **Learning journal template 2 (Define page)** at a time, write their responses and then continue discussing their ideas for the next section, until the task is complete. This provides students with opportunities to hear others' responses and it provides the teacher with input points.
3. Discuss the exploration of greenhouses in the Tune-in sessions. Provide students with the opportunity to research further. Ask them to list things they would like to know, such as growing times and conditions for different foods, information about greenhouse construction and the cost of growing different foods. Provide them with **Generic reproducible 4 (Key question table)** to assist them to record their questions, findings and sources.

ACTIVITY 2: CONSIDER INSIGHTS

Students think of at least one insight they have gained from the process; for example, people suggesting fresh foods that hadn't been considered by the students. Students add this insight to **Learning journal template 2 (Define page)**. They should then relate the insight to their greenhouse design plans.

When considering insights, students could think about the following:

- What was something unexpected that you saw or found out? How was it unexpected?
- How will you decide on which food to grow?
- How will you decide which type of greenhouse to design?
- Is there any other information that you need or would like to know? How will you find out?

ACTIVITY 3: CONSIDER CONSTRAINTS

At this stage, let students know the constraints of the challenge by describing the schedule for the investigation, materials available and budget restrictions (in terms of how much money students can spend if they wish to use additional materials). Students can then update **Learning journal template 2**.

PROMPTS

- What did you discover?
- What were the most important pieces of information that you gathered?
- What was something new that you learned?
- What other information do you need?

MORE VOCABULARY

- define – state the meaning of something
- insight – an accurate understanding of someone or something

JOURNAL TIP

Discuss the term 'insight'. Explain that it relates to something students have learned about the people and their responses to the surveys, as well as information gathered through research or excursions. You could refer to **Learning journal template 2**.

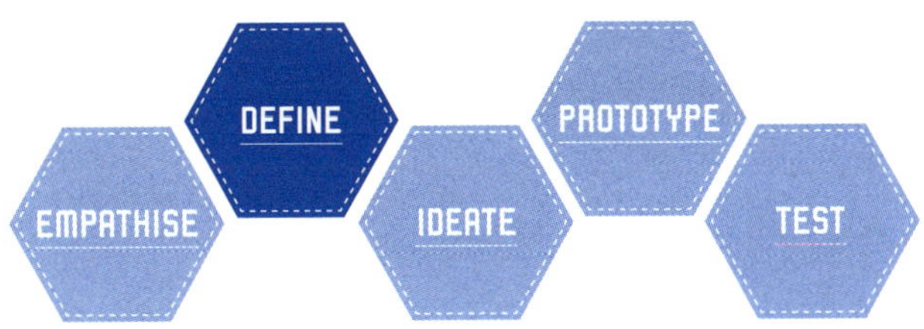

→ IDEATE

The Ideate stage of the design thinking process is all about generating lots of ideas. Students need to be flexible in their thinking and be able to move beyond obvious ideas. At this stage, ideas are not judged, just generated and gathered.

ACTIVITY: GENERATE IDEAS

1. Ask groups of students to draw or write their ideas.
2. Each new idea should be written or drawn on a separate piece of paper or sticky note.
3. Ask students to group ideas on a wall or board.
4. Ask students to look at the different ideas and provide feedback to each other. It is important that students don't defend their ideas at this stage. They should just be listening to the feedback.
5. After the initial feedback, ask students to come up with more ideas. Encourage them to be creative and even radical.
6. Ask students to choose four of their ideas to write in their journal. Students use **Learning journal template 3 (Ideate page)** to do this. Ask students to choose one idea to explore further and explain the reasoning behind their choice.

TOP TIP!

At this stage, students may have produced a series of drawings about the types of plants they would grow in each of their greenhouse designs. These drawings should be annotated. They may have a collection of sticky notes, which they can organise into related ideas.

Encourage students to view and read others' ideas before giving feedback. Feedback could be within small groups or between partners. Considering others' ideas is an important part of this process, so students can build on their own ideas as they continue to ideate.

At each stage of this activity, ask students to discuss their thoughts before writing down their responses. This will help them to think through their ideas and select their final ideas to develop.

PROMPTS

- How do your chosen ideas relate to growing plants quickly?
- How do these ideas relate to the type of food you would like to grow?
- How might you test your design?
- What can you do to make the greenhouse easy to move to different spaces if necessary?
- How can you make it easy to access and water the plants?
- What would you do if you had to use different materials?

MORE VOCABULARY

- feedback – information about, for example, a person's performance or the design of a product, which can be used to make improvements
- ideate – generate many ideas without making judgements about the ideas

JOURNAL TIP

When choosing four ideas to include in the journal, students should try to choose four ideas that aren't related, to show a range of ideas.

USEFUL APPS/LINKS

- Tools for creating ideas, such as at creatingminds.org/tools/tools_ideation.htm
- Tips for creativity and innovation, such as at designorate.com/creativity-innovation-in-education/

ASSESSMENT

At the Ideate stage, assessment could include observations about the number and diversity of students' ideas, and their ability to provide feedback and create additional ideas. Reflection in the journal should provide an insight into some of the reasoning behind students' choices.

EMPATHISE · DEFINE · **IDEATE** · PROTOTYPE · TEST

PROTOTYPE

At this stage of the design thinking process, students are asked to create a physical prototype of the greenhouse. It is the stage where students need to get their ideas out of their head and presented in a way that engages other students and helps them to understand the concept. When students create, it helps them to think and solve problems and disagreements. Students can role-play, make storyboards or use sticky notes. The most important feature is that viewers can interact with whatever is produced.

Encourage students to photograph or film during the prototyping and testing stages. This information can be used to show the learning behind the design thinking process in action.

ACTIVITY: TRANSFORM IDEAS INTO PROTOTYPES

1. Students review the ideas generated at the Ideate stage. Provide them with an A3 copy of **Generic reproducible 6 (In the frame)** so they can organise their ideas into two sections: least relevant and most relevant. Students continue to cycle through this activity until they have an idea to start prototyping.
2. Provide students with a range of materials to use to create their prototype. Remind students that a prototype should be created rapidly and it is not meant to look 'nice'.
3. After a prototype has been created, ask students to see if it works and get feedback from others.
4. Students then use the feedback to prototype again.

Ask students to fill in the Prototype part of **Learning journal template 4 (Prototype and Test page)**. See the **Journal tip** for further student guidance.

PROMPTS

- What worked?
- How could it be improved?
- What else do you need to know, do or have?
- What other suggestions do you have?

MORE VOCABULARY

- feedback – information about, for example, a person's performance or the design of a product, which can be used to make improvements
- prototype – an initial version of a model of a product or process that is used to develop a final model

JOURNAL TIP

Remind students to highlight the main features of their prototype. If students are creating an electronic journal, they can insert a photo of their prototype and annotate it.

USEFUL APPS/LINKS

- App for creating interactive links (for example, between descriptions, videos, images and websites and a main image), such as ThingLink
- App for making notes using text, drawings, images, weblinks and audio, such as Notability

ASSESSMENT

Observe students as they make changes to their designs. Are they able to consider feedback, make modifications and move rapidly through this process? Or do they have difficulties with holding onto an idea and accepting feedback?

TOP TIP!

The Prototype stage is often very messy. It is important that students are focusing on their ideas, rather than the end product. Provide them with lots of materials, such as recycled packaging and Perspex. Students may add labels to prototypes to explain some of the main features. Photographing and annotating pictures of prototypes can be useful.

To gain feedback, students could ask each other some of the following questions:

- What is the main feature of your prototype?
- How does your prototype work?
- Which aspects work best? What will you keep?
- Which aspects need changing? How might you do this?
- What other materials might you need?

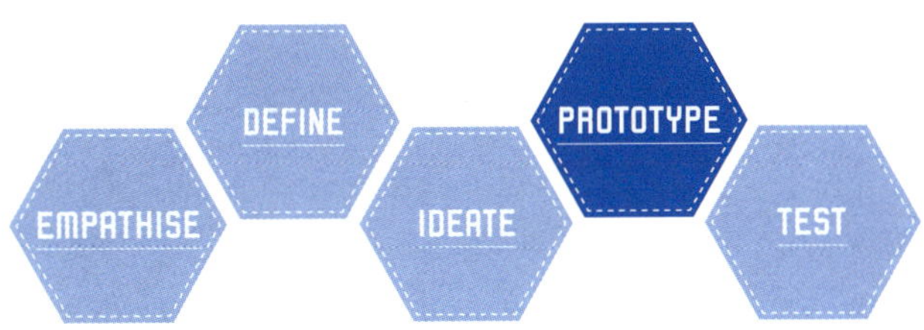

→ TEST

At this stage of the design thinking process, students test their prototype to see if it meets the requirements of the user. Students check to see if their prototype meets the criteria set at the start of the design process.

ACTIVITY: TEST FEEDBACK

1. Students take their last prototype and consider how it meets the criteria in the challenge.
2. Ask students to check whether or not their design works. If not what do they need to do to make it work?
3. Provide the opportunity to cycle through the Prototype and Test stages again.
4. Students complete their final design.

Ask students to fill in the Test part of **Learning journal template 4 (Prototype and test page)**. See the **Journal tip** for further student guidance.

PROMPTS

- Does your prototype do what you wanted it to do?
- Are there other features you could add?
- What needs to be changed?
- What works well?

MORE VOCABULARY

- evaluate – assess something, perhaps considering what worked and what didn't
- feature – a specific aspect of something, such as size, shape, colour, quality
- feedback – information about, for example, a person's performance or the design of a product, which can be used to make improvements
- prototype – an initial version of a model of a product or process that is used to develop a final model
- review – consider an idea, process or product and assess what works and what needs to be changed

JOURNAL TIP

Ask students to think about why it is important to test their ideas before they build their final design.

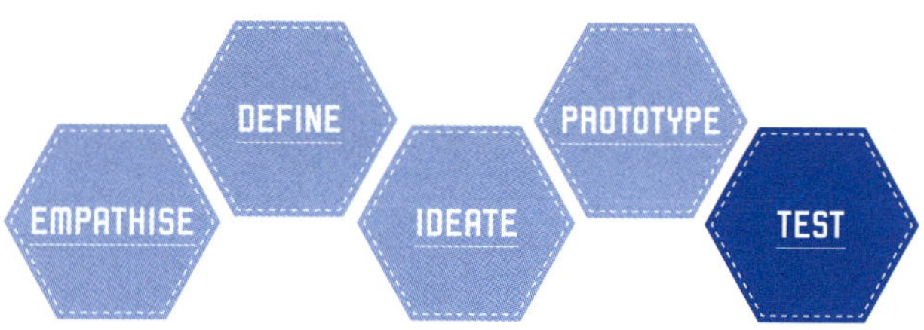

→ SHARE AND EVALUATE

Students can share their final design, as well as the processes involved in the investigation. Students evaluate their learning journals and their solutions.

ACTIVITY 1: BRING THE DESIGNS TOGETHER

1. Provide students with time to create final designs. Students can create an iMovie or use Adobe Spark Video to demonstrate the process and thinking behind the designs. There should be an element of narration, where they are sharing their points of view, insights, prototyping and solutions.
2. Students should include their learning journals with the display so others can see the different stages of the design process.

ACTIVITY 2: EVALUATE AND GIVE FEEDBACK

1. Provide students with **Generic reproducible 2 (Self-evaluation)** to complete.
2. Ask students to provide feedback to each other about the most interesting features, the aspects that were most difficult and the changes that they would make if they repeated the task.
3. Provide students with opportunities to share their designs with the wider community. It may be possible to share some of the videos with an expert for feedback.

Students could set up their own farmers' market to sell their produce to the school community. If the school does not already have a food garden, they could look into starting one or developing a current garden further.

ASSESSMENT

Ask students to complete **Generic reproducible 1 (Key vocabulary table)** using the key vocabulary for this unit: sustainable, conditions, food choices, food production, greenhouse, nutrient. Compare their table with the one they completed at the Tune-in session. Students complete **Generic reproducible 3 (Responding to the investigation)**. Compare students' responses to those on **Generic reproducible 2**.

Teachers and students each complete **Generic reproducible 5 (Design thinking assessment rubric)**. Students compare the feedback from the teacher with their self-assessment of their design thinking skills.

Name: ....

Date: ....

STEM INVESTIGATIONS

Cut out these cards and organise the foods into three different groups:

- slow-growing foods (9 or more weeks to grow)
- medium-growing foods (4 to 8 weeks to grow)
- fast-growing foods (up to 3 weeks to grow)

lettuce	corn
mint	radishes
carrots	turnips
potatoes	cress
tomatoes	apples
spinach	thyme

Name: ....

Date: ....

STEM INVESTIGATIONS

Use this table to record your observations about the plants you are growing.

		Description of container conditions (e.g. water, no light)			
OBSERVATIONS	Day 1				
	Day 2				
	Day 3				
	Day 4				
	Day 5				
	Day 6				
	Day 7				

STEM Investigations, UP, ISBN 978 1 4202 4154 9 © Macmillan Science and Education Australia 2018

EMPATHISE

STEM INVESTIGATIONS

Name: ....

Date: ....

Write down the names of the fresh foods you are investigating in your local area. Find out where the food has come from – is it local or from another country?

Fresh food item	Origin (where it was grown)

STEM Investigations, UP, ISBN 978 1 4202 4154 9

MAKE A PLAN TO PROTECT AQUATIC AREAS

NATURAL WORLD 10

→ INTRODUCTION

Aquatic environments occur in both the natural and built worlds. An aquatic environment may be an ocean or an estuary (where the river meets the sea), or a lake, dam or inland stream. Aquatic environments can be freshwater or saltwater. Each of these environments has a wide range of plant and animal life. Good water quality is an essential part of healthy aquatic environments.

Water pollution can happen naturally or be caused by humans. A dead animal in a stream or river can affect the quality of water. Petrol can leak from boats and other water craft. Chemical spills can occur due to accidents involving ships transporting oil and other resources. Water quality can be affected by pollution from industry, and by litter.

In this STEM investigation, students are asked to consider how they could clean up a chemical spill, and to design a process or piece of equipment that could help to clean up a chemical spill.

This STEM challenge is easily differentiated for Year 5 and Year 6 students by encouraging different groups to use different degrees of complexity when investigating chemical properties and materials. Students could also be provided with opportunities to test different materials and designs.

THE CHALLENGE

Aquatic environments are home to a wide range of plant and animal species, all of which rely on clean, healthy water to survive. Sadly, human activity can cause pollution, which does great harm to aquatic environments. Members of your local community are worried that a chemical spill will happen in your area. They think the local council is not prepared for this potential danger.

Your challenge is to investigate how a chemical contamination would affect the plant and animal life within an aquatic environment near your community, and then design a solution to deal with the effects of this environmental disaster. Think of the best way to present your research and designed solutions to council members, other students, parents or local community members. As part of your challenge, you will learn about the importance of water for all living organisms and the effects of chemical spills.

KEY UNDERSTANDINGS

- Water is important for all living organisms.
- There are different types of aquatic environments, such as estuarine (rivermouth), marine (sea), and inland waterways.
- Water can be fresh water or salt water.
- Chemical spills have an impact on water quality.
- Some chemical reactions can be reversed.

KEY VOCABULARY

aquatic
disperse
dissolve
pollution
viscosity
water quality

KEY SKILLS

- Make careful observations.
- Consider different points of view.
- Develop research skills.
- Create prototypes of processes or products to reverse a chemical spill.

KEY ACTIONS

- Find out information about chemical spills.
- Learn about different aquatic environments.
- Learn about organisations that protect aquatic environments.
- Learn how different substances behave in water.

→ OVERVIEW OF STAGES

TUNE IN:

- Pre-test vocabulary relating to this challenge.
- Show students images of different aquatic environments.
- Identify students' prior knowledge about aquatic environments with a brainstorming task.
- Use Google Maps to explore different aquatic environments.
- Explore different chemical reactions and determine whether they can be reversed or not.

EMPATHISE

Students find out about aquatic environments and some of the ways in which they are threatened.

DEFINE

Students consider the main issues with protecting aquatic environments and how to manage the effects of a chemical spill.

IDEATE

Students generate ideas for protecting and cleaning up an aquatic environment.

PROTOTYPE

Students transform some of their ideas into physical representations. These are created rapidly, using simple materials. Students can role-play, make storyboards or use sticky notes when they prototype.

TEST

Students share their prototypes and provide feedback to each other. They use synthesised environments to test their ideas. They are given the opportunity to cycle through the Prototype and Test stages again.

SHARE AND EVALUATE:

Final prototypes are shared and evaluated, with opportunities for expert feedback.

→ SUGGESTED SCHEDULE

LESSON	STAGE
1–4	**Tune in**: pre-test vocabulary, explore images of different aquatic environments and explore using Google Maps, establish prior knowledge, explore different chemical reactions with water and determine whether they can be reversed or not
5–6	**Empathise**: find out about aquatic environments and some of the ways in which they are threatened
7	**Define**: define the main issues about water pollution relating to chemical spills, and write/record in journal
8	**Ideate**: generate ideas for protecting and cleaning up an aquatic environment, and write/record in journal
9–12	**Prototype** and **Test**: conduct prototyping and testing, use synthesised environments to test, and write/record in journal
13–14	**Share and evaluate**: share and evaluate designs and prototypes

CURRICULUM LINKS

The following tables show the key Science, Technologies and Mathematics curricula with which this STEM investigation is aligned.

SCIENCE

YEAR	STRAND	SUB-STRANDS AND CONTENT
5	Science Understanding	Chemical sciences: • Solids, liquids and gases have different observable properties and behave in different ways
6	Science Understanding	Chemical sciences: • Changes to materials can be reversible or irreversible Biological sciences: • The growth and survival of living things are affected by physical conditions of their environment
7*	Science Understanding	Chemical sciences: • Mixtures, including solutions, contain a combination of pure substances that can be separated using a range of techniques
5 & 6	Science as a Human Endeavour	Use and influence of science: • Scientific knowledge is used to solve problems and inform personal and community decisions
	Science Inquiry Skills	Planning and conducting • Processing and analysing data and information • Communicating

* This understanding could be developed as an extension for students within the context of their experiment.

TECHNOLOGIES

YEAR	STRAND	CONTENT
5 & 6	Design and Technologies Processes and Production Skills	• Critique needs or opportunities for designing, and investigate materials, components, tools, equipment and processes to achieve intended designed solutions • Generate, develop and communicate design ideas and processes for audiences using appropriate technical terms and graphical representation techniques • Select appropriate materials, components, tools, equipment and techniques, and apply safe procedures to make designed solutions • Negotiate criteria for success that include sustainability to evaluate design ideas, processes and solutions • Develop project plans that include consideration of resources when making designed solutions individually and collaboratively

MATHEMATICS

YEAR	STRAND	CONTENT
5	Statistics and Probability	Data representation and interpretation
6	Statistics and Probability	Data representation and interpretation Chance

OTHER CURRICULUM LINKS

GENERAL CAPABILITIES

- Literacy
- Numeracy
- Personal and Social Capability
- Information and Communication Technology (ICT) Capability
- Critical and Creative Thinking

ASSESSMENT

AC

The following resources are provided for assessing students at different stages of the investigation:

- Generic reproducible 1 (Key vocabulary table), for assessing understanding of vocabulary
- Generic reproducible 2 (Self-evaluation), for student self-evaluation of the learning process
- Generic reproducible 3 (Responding to the investigation), for assessing student engagement in the challenges, and the collaboration and skills involved in the design thinking stages
- Generic reproducible 5 (Design thinking assessment rubric), for evaluating student engagement in the design thinking stages
- Learning journal templates 1, 2, 3 and 4, for incorporating student reflection and evaluation

→ GETTING READY FOR THE INVESTIGATION

You can prepare yourself and students for this STEM investigation in the following ways:

- Identify groups of students who will work well together.
- Investigate the **Useful apps**.
- Review the **Key science knowledge** that supports this investigation, and look at the **Useful links**.
- Gather materials for creating synthesised aquatic environments, such as large tubs for water.
- Start collecting additional materials for prototyping (as shown on the **Materials needed** list).
- Determine where prototypes will be kept between lessons.
- Create a wall space where students can make a word wall to share their ideas from the Tune-in session and the Ideate stage.
- Organise the class into pairs.
- Start thinking about:
  - » whether students will focus on preventing chemical spills, treating a chemical spill or a combination of both
  - » who will provide expert feedback to the students and if this will be face-to-face
  - » which water environment(s) will be explored, for example, a lake, river or ocean
  - » the safety aspects of the different liquids to be explored.

USEFUL APPS

- App for creating a learning journal, such as Book Creator
- App for creating semantic maps (links between different words and/or concepts), such as Popplet
- App for creating interactive links (for example, between descriptions, videos, images and websites and a main image), such as ThingLink
- App for making notes using text, drawings, images, weblinks and audio, such as Notability
- App for creating multimedia presentations, such as Adobe Spark Video and iMovie

USEFUL LINKS

- Identifying plant features and requirements for plant life, such as at bbc.co.uk/guides/z98jpbk
- Online video about marine life affected by pollution, such as at youtube.com/watch?v=cwTDvqaqPIM
- How to clean oil from penguin feathers, such as at bbc.com/news/magazine-15272040
- Responses to oil and chemical spills, such as at oceanservice.noaa.gov/hazards/spills/
- Information about Australia's water resources, such as at csiro.au/en/Research/Environment/Water
- Causes and effects of ocean pollution, such as at conserve-energy-future.com/causes-and-effects-of-ocean-pollution.php
- An example of field-testing water quality, such as at lrrpublic.cli.det.nsw.edu.au/lrrSecure/Sites/Web/about_fieldwork/lo/Water/documents/water_testing.pdf

RESOURCES PROVIDED

- Generic reproducibles 1, 2, 3, 4, 5, 6, 8, 9
- Reproducibles 10.1, 10.2, 10.3
- Learning journal templates 1, 2, 3, 4 (on disc)

MATERIALS NEEDED

- Sticky notes (half a pad per pair)
- Paper
- Coloured card
- Pens and markers
- Sticky tape
- Pipe-cleaners
- Cardboard
- Tubs and other water containers, such as large bowls
- Jugs
- Cleaning materials, such as paper towel, tea towels
- Absorbent materials, such as paper towel, sponges
- Paperclips
- Plastic items, such as bottles, Perspex, overhead projector sheets
- Sieves or strainers
- Disposable plastic spoons for stirring
- Chemicals/substances for Tune-in activity (student use): cooking oil, engine oil, washing liquids, paint, copper filings, iron filings, soil
- Chemicals for Tune-in activity (teacher use): bleach, methylated spirits, liquid fertiliser

Take care when using the chemicals. It is strongly advised that you seek advice from school leaders about which chemicals may be used and the spaces to use them in. Ensure everyone is aware of and follows clear guidelines for working with, observing use of and disposing of chemicals.

KEY SCIENCE KNOWLEDGE

This section provides an overview of the key science concepts and vocabulary needed for this unit.

AQUATIC ENVIRONMENTS AND CHEMICAL POLLUTION

An **aquatic** environment is a body of water and the living things in it. This could be in fresh water, for example, a river, stream, pond or lake. It could also be in salt water, for example, an ocean or an estuary, where a river reaches an ocean.

Aquatic environments are always changing. Plants and animals must adapt to conditions such as waves, depth and flow of water, and how salty or muddy the water is. These conditions affect **water quality**, which in turn can be affected by weather patterns, the seasons and human activity.

Aquatic and land-based plants and animals have the same requirements to survive, grow and reproduce. They need shelter, food, oxygen (from the air or **dissolved** in water) and an energy source (usually the sun).

Pollution in aquatic environments can be caused by substances such as oil, plastics and waste from factories and farms. The box below shows some ways that living things in aquatic environments are affected by pollution such as an oil spill. These spills can sometimes be treated by using special chemicals to **disperse** the oil.

The pollution of an aquatic environment, such as the dumping of polluted water from factories into a river, can affect all the living things in the environment.

Possible effects of chemical pollution on living things

- Fish might die from lack of oxygen in the water. Underwater plants may no longer have enough light.
- Birds, fish, shellfish and mammals might die or be unable to reproduce after eating or absorbing polluted water.
- Animals that can still reproduce may have fewer babies survive, for example turtles.
- Animals that eat affected plants may be poisoned.
- Affected animals might have weakened immune systems and so die more easily from other diseases.
- Water birds with chemicals on their feathers may no longer be able to fly, swim, find food or control their body temperature.

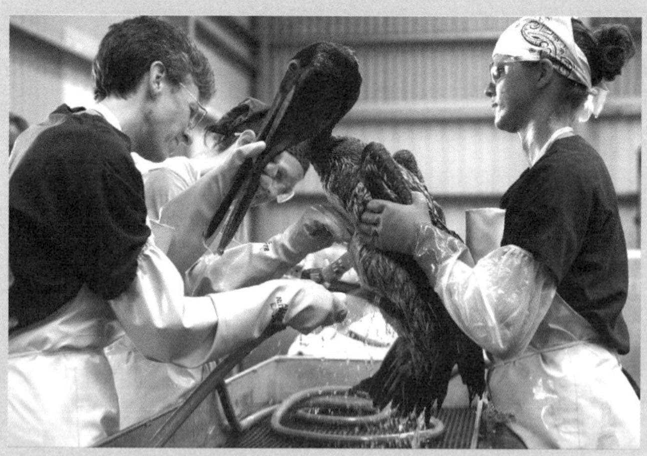

This pelican was rescued after an oil spill and is having the oil removed from its feathers.

KEY VOCABULARY

aquatic – relating to water
disperse – separate and spread out
dissolve – mix with water and become part of the water as a solution
pollution – the presence of one or more substances that are harmful to their environment
viscosity – how easily a liquid (water) flows; for example, water has lower viscosity than honey
water quality – the condition of water, which includes physical, chemical and biological characteristics

→ TUNE IN

1. Ask students to complete **Generic reproducible 1 (Key vocabulary table)** using the key vocabulary for this unit.
2. To establish prior knowledge, ask students to individually brainstorm what they know about aquatic environments. Prompts could include:
   - What is an aquatic environment?
   - Can you list different types of aquatic environments?
   - What life can be found in water?
   - Do plants and animals that live in water have the same requirements for life as land-based species?
   - What do we know about water?
3. Look at some short videos or images showing different aquatic environments. Ask students to brainstorm words they associate with aquatic environments. Ask them to either create a paper-based or software-generated mind map, or provide them with several copies of **Generic reproducible 8 (Vocabulary hexagons)**. (See page 17 for how to use this reproducible.)

ACTIVITY 1: WATER POLLUTION

1. Provide students with an image of polluted water.
2. Provide them with **Reproducible 10.1 (Water issues)**. Ask students to write what they see in the image, some of the issues for the plants and animals in the environment, and questions they have relating to the image.
3. Discuss different observations and responses.
4. Students complete the visible thinking routine in **Generic reproducible 9 (See, think, wonder)**.

ACTIVITY 2: LOCAL AQUATIC ENVIRONMENTS

1. Use Google Maps or topographical maps to find bodies of water close to the school. Investigate the characteristics of the environment(s), making hypotheses about water type (salty or fresh), water quality, life within the water and surrounding life dependent upon the water.
2. Select a plant or animal from this environment to investigate in detail. Is it indigenous to the region, native to your location but introduced to the region, or an introduced species? Why do you think it is thriving in this location? Identify the conditions that make this environment suitable for your selected species to survive.
3. Ask students to research community groups to determine if any organisation is doing field work and data collection to help protect this environment.

ACTIVITY 3: HOW SUBSTANCES BEHAVE IN WATER

1. Brainstorm the types of substances that might pollute water.
2. In small groups, students develop an experiment to see how these substances behave in water. Encourage the use of a range of substances, and share results among the class.
3. Explore different properties, such as viscosity and smell. Behaviours to examine could include dissolving, floating/sinking and response to stirring. Students could also investigate removing the substances, for example, by filtering and absorbing.

Be mindful of the safety precautions required when choosing substances. Some should only be used by adults (see suggested list in the **Materials needed** section). Chemicals should only be smelled from a distance.

4. Ask students which substances they think would be easy to remove from the water and which would be more difficult. How would this work in a real aquatic environment?
5. Provide students with **Reproducible 10.2 (Substances in water)**. Students use this to plan their experiment, develop hypotheses and record their observations.
6. Students record the results in a way that can be shared with others and accessed for reference during the inquiry. This could be done through a class blog or in hard copy and displayed around the classroom.

4. Introduce the STEM investigation and challenge. Provide students with the student card and read the information together. Ask them to think about some of the issues to do with protecting aquatic environments and cleaning up chemical spills.
5. Introduce the design thinking process by reviewing the stages on the student card.
6. Explain that students will keep a journal about their learning at the different stages of the design.

USEFUL APPS/LINKS

- Harvard Visible Thinking – Project Zero: visiblethinkingpz.org/VisibleThinking_html_files/03_ThinkingRoutines/03c_Core_routines/SeeThinkWonder/SeeThinkWonder_Routine.html

→ EMPATHISE

During the Empathise stage of the design thinking process, students focus on considering different points of view. To empathise with others, they need to engage in observation, interact with others and immerse themselves in the experiences that others have. Students will observe others, taking notes, asking questions and taking photos where possible.

ACTIVITY 1: FIND OUT

1. Provide students with a link to an online video or news story about an oil spill (see **Useful apps/links**).
2. Ask students to consider what they see and the impact that the spill has had, or may have, on plants and animals.
3. Provide **Reproducible 10.3 (Chemical spills)** for students to record information provided in the video.
4. Provide students with text or video about another chemical spill, for example from mining or firefighting (see **Useful apps/links**).
5. Ask students to consider what they find out in the text or video and the impact that the spill has had, or may have, on plants and animals.
6. Students continue to use **Reproducible 10.3** to record information provided in the text.

ACTIVITY 2: EMPATHISE

Ask students to make a list of the main issues that were common to both examples of a chemical spill.

Direct students to **Learning journal template 1 (Empathise page)**.

PROMPTS

- How did the water quality change?
- What are some of the ways animals were affected?
- What are some of the ways plants were affected?
- What were the main causes of the chemical spill in each scenario?
- How might these events have been prevented or their impact limited?
- How do you and other people feel about the impact of the chemical spills?

MORE VOCABULARY

- empathise – understand and consider another person's or group's point of view
- impact – the effect that something has on another thing
- observe – notice; watch someone or something very carefully
- point of view – an opinion, attitude or judgement considered in a particular way

JOURNAL TIPS

Students complete **Learning journal template 1 (Empathise page)** while they are completing the different tasks. Remind them to date their notes and include photos or illustrations of relevant information.

USEFUL APPS/LINKS

- Australian oil spill news story, such as at abc.net.au/btn/story/s2515241.htm
- US oil rig explosion news story, such as at abc.net.au/btn/story/s2893099.htm
- Oil spill facts, such as at conserve-energy-future.com/interesting-oil-spill-facts.php
- Gulf of Mexico oil spill news story, such as at news.nationalgeographic.com/news/2014/04/140408-gulf-oil-spill-animals-anniversary-science-deepwater-horizon-science/
- Firefighting foam spill news story, such as at couriermail.com.au/news/queensland/queensland-government/brisbane-river-site-of-chemical-spill-now-below-acceptable-levels/news-story/b71aeab5b94556630c0e51d3f7b9365f
- Mining site chemical spill news story, such as at abc.net.au/7.30/content/2015/s4322068.htm

ASSESSMENT

This stage of the design thinking process offers opportunities to observe students collecting information, developing questions, and recording their notes and thinking in their journal.

EMPATHISE DEFINE IDEATE PROTOTYPE TEST

DEFINE

The main focus of this stage of the design thinking process is to reframe the challenge. The initial challenge is quite open, so at this stage students learn how to define what needs to be done. This includes noting insights that have been generated.

ACTIVITY 1: CONSIDER OBSERVATIONS

1. Students consider the information they gathered in the Empathise stage. They may work in pairs or small groups. Provide them with a whiteboard, large sheet of paper and/or sticky notes to collate some of their key information.
2. Students should discuss one section of **Learning journal template 2 (Define page)**, write their responses and then continue discussing their ideas for the next section, until the task is complete. This provides students with opportunities to hear others' responses and it provides the teacher with input points.
3. Provide students with the opportunity to research further. Ask them to write other information they would like to know. Provide them with **Generic reproducible 4 (Key question table)** to assist them to record their questions, findings and sources. Explain that a micro-question is a small question that will help students research and answer the bigger question they are considering. Micro-questions should be answerable.

ACTIVITY 2: CONSIDER INSIGHTS

Students think of at least one insight they have gained from the process; for example, an oil spill can block out plants' access to light or make swimming difficult for animals. Students add this insight to **Learning journal template 2 (Define page)**. They should then relate their insight to their design.

When considering insights, students could think about the following:

- What was something unexpected that you saw or found out? How was it unexpected?
- How will you decide on the most important aspect of your design?
- Is there any other information that you need or would like to know? How will you find out?

ACTIVITY 3: CONSIDER CONSTRAINTS

At this stage, let students know the constraints of the challenge by describing the types of materials they will have access to, the different aquatic environment(s) to consider and safety issues with handling liquids. Students can then update **Learning journal template 2**.

TOP TIP! Before considering an environmental pollution investigation, students would benefit from studying the natural conditions of the chosen aquatic environment, mapping key features and identifying seasonal or tidal changes. This knowledge will support students to develop their predictions about the impact of environmental contamination, as well as helping them consider the unique interventions required for recovery.

PROMPTS

- What did you discover?
- What were the most important pieces of information that you gathered?
- What was something new that you learned?
- What other information do you need?

MORE VOCABULARY

- define – state the meaning of something
- insight – an accurate understanding of someone or something

JOURNAL TIPS

Discuss the term 'insight'. Explain that it relates to something students have learned about the people and situations they read about. You could refer to **Learning journal template 2**.

EMPATHISE DEFINE IDEATE PROTOTYPE TEST

→ IDEATE

The Ideate stage of the design thinking process is all about generating lots of ideas. Students need to be flexible in their thinking and be able to move beyond obvious ideas. At this stage, ideas are not judged, just generated and gathered.

ACTIVITY: GENERATE IDEAS

1. Ask groups of students to draw or write their ideas.
2. Each new idea should be written or drawn on a separate piece of paper or sticky note.
3. Ask students to group ideas on a wall or board.
4. Ask students to look at the different ideas and provide feedback to each other. It is important that students don't defend their ideas at this stage. They should just be listening to the feedback.
5. After the initial feedback, ask students to come up with more ideas. Encourage them to be creative and even radical.
6. Ask students to choose four of their ideas to write in their journal. Students use **Learning journal template 3 (Ideate page)** to do this. Ask students to choose one idea to explore further and explain the reasoning behind their choice.

TOP TIP!

At this stage, students may have produced a series of annotated drawings. They may have a collection of sticky notes, which they can organise into related ideas.

Encourage students to view and read others' ideas before giving feedback. Feedback could be within small groups or between partners. Considering others' ideas is an important part of this process, so students can build on their own ideas as they continue to ideate.

At each stage of this activity, ask students to discuss their thoughts before writing their responses. This will help them to think through their ideas and select their final ideas to develop.

PROMPTS

- How do your chosen ideas relate to protecting or cleaning up the aquatic environment?
- How might you test your design?
- How can you make it similar to a real environment?
- How can you make it a safe test?
- What if you had to use different materials?
- What other materials could you use?

MORE VOCABULARY

- feedback – information about, for example, a person's performance or the design of a product, which can be used to make improvements
- ideate – generate many ideas without making judgements about the ideas

JOURNAL TIP

When choosing four ideas to include in the journal, students should try to choose ideas that aren't related, to show a range of ideas.

USEFUL APPS/LINKS

- Tools for creating ideas, such as at creatingminds.org/tools/tools_ideation.htm
- Tips for creativity and innovation, such as at designorate.com/creativity-innovation-in-education/

ASSESSMENT

At the Ideate stage, assessment could include observations about the number and diversity of students' ideas, and their ability to provide feedback and create additional ideas. Reflection in the journal should provide an insight into some of the reasoning behind students' choices.

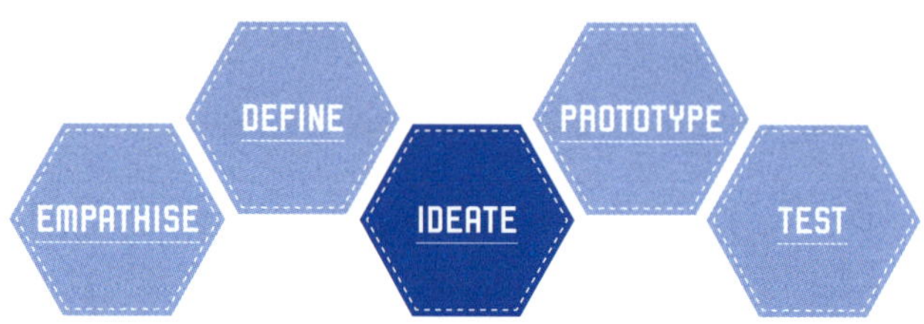

PROTOTYPE

At this stage of the design thinking process, students are asked to create a physical prototype of a solution. It is the stage where students need to get their ideas out of their head and presented in a way that engages other students and helps them to understand the ideas. When students create, it helps them to think and solve problems and disagreements. Students can role-play, make storyboards or use sticky notes when they prototype. The most important feature is that viewers can interact with whatever is produced.

Encourage students to photograph or film during the prototyping and testing stages. This information can be used to show the learning behind the design thinking process in action.

ACTIVITY: TRANSFORM IDEAS INTO PROTOTYPES

1. Students review the ideas generated at the Ideate stage. Provide them with an A3 copy of **Generic reproducible 6 (In the frame)** so they can organise their ideas into two sections: least relevant and most relevant. Students continue to cycle through this activity until they have an idea to start prototyping.
2. Provide students with a range of materials to use to create their prototype. Remind students that a prototype should be created rapidly and is not meant to look 'nice'.
3. After a prototype has been created, ask students to see if it works and get feedback from others.
4. Students then use the feedback to prototype again.

Ask students to fill in the Prototype part of **Learning journal template 4 (Prototype and test page)**. See the **Journal tip** for further student guidance.

TOP TIP!

The Prototype stage is often very messy. This challenge uses water so consider how this can be managed. It is important that students are focusing on their ideas, rather than the end product. Provide them with lots of materials – recycling depots can be a useful source of resources. Students may add labels to prototypes to explain some of the main features. Photographing and annotating pictures of prototypes can be useful.

To gain feedback, students could ask each other some of the following questions:

- What is the main feature of your prototype?
- How does your prototype work?
- Which aspects work best? What will you keep?
- Which aspects need changing? How might you do this?
- What other materials might you need?

PROMPTS

- What worked?
- How could it be improved?
- What else do you need to know, do or have?
- What other suggestions do you have?

MORE VOCABULARY

- feedback – information about, for example, a person's performance or the design of a product, which can be used to make improvements
- prototype – an initial version of a model of a product or process that is used to develop a final model

JOURNAL TIP

Remind students to highlight the main features of their prototype. If students are creating an electronic journal, they can insert a photo of their prototype and annotate it.

USEFUL APPS/LINKS

- App for creating a learning journal, such as Book Creator
- App for creating interactive links (for example, between descriptions, videos, images and websites and a main image), such as ThingLink
- App for making notes using text, drawings, images, weblinks and audio, such as Notability

ASSESSMENT

Observe students as they make changes to their designs. Are they able to consider feedback, make modifications and move rapidly through this process? Or do they have difficulties with holding on to an idea and accepting feedback?

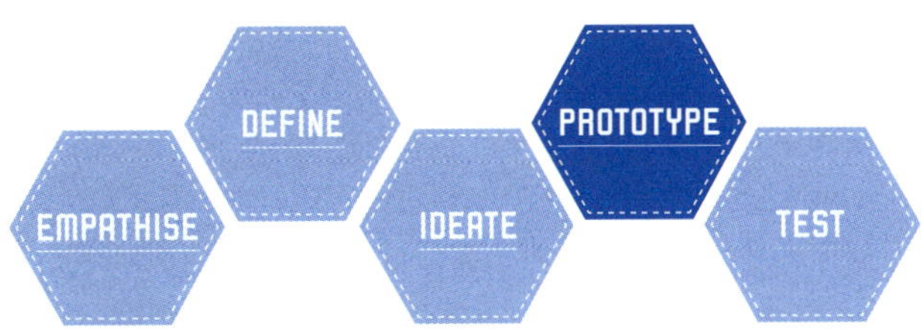

→ TEST

At this stage of the design thinking process, students test their prototype to see if it meets the criteria set at the start of the design process.

ACTIVITY: TEST FEEDBACK

1. Students take their last prototype and consider the original design challenge.
2. Ask students to check whether or not their design works. If not, what do they need to do to make it work?
3. Provide the opportunity to cycle through the Prototype and Test stages again.
4. Students complete their final design.

Ask students to fill in the Test part of **Learning journal template 4 (Prototype and test page)**. See the **Journal tip** for further student guidance.

PROMPTS

- Does your prototype do what you wanted it to do?
- Are there other features you could add?
- What needs to be changed?
- What works well?

MORE VOCABULARY

- evaluate – assess something, perhaps considering what worked and what didn't
- feature – a specific aspect of something, such as size, shape, colour, quality
- feedback – information about, for example, a person's performance or the design of a product, which can be used to make improvements
- prototype – an initial version of a model of a product or process that is used to develop a final model
- review – consider an idea, process or product and decide what needs to be changed and what works

JOURNAL TIP

Ask students to think about why it is important to test their ideas before they build their final design.

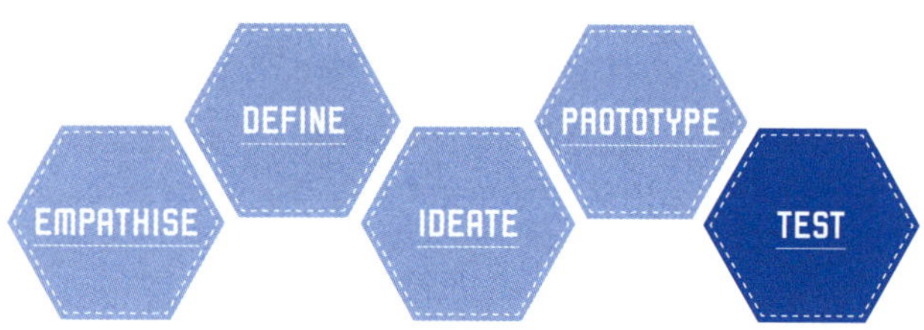

→ SHARE AND EVALUATE

At this stage of the investigation, students are provided with an opportunity to share their final design, as well as the processes involved in the investigation. Students evaluate their learning journals and their solutions.

ACTIVITY 1: BRING THE DESIGNS TOGETHER

1. Provide students with time to create final designs. Students can create an iMovie or use Adobe Spark Video to demonstrate the process and thinking behind the designs. There should be an element of narration, where they are sharing points of view, insights, prototyping and solutions, and relating this to the aquatic environment that has been focused on.
2. Students should include their learning journals with the final design so others can see the different stages of the design process.

ACTIVITY 2: EVALUATE AND GIVE FEEDBACK

1. Provide students with **Generic reproducible 2 (Self-evaluation)** to complete.
2. Ask students to provide feedback to each other about the most interesting features, the aspects that were most difficult and the changes that they would make.
3. Provide students with opportunities to share their designs with the wider community. This could include inviting someone from the local council, water authority, environmental agency, or a parent with relevant experience or another external professional. It may be possible to share some of the videos with an expert for feedback about the designs.

ASSESSMENT

Ask students to again complete **Generic reproducible 1 (Key vocabulary table)** using the key vocabulary for this unit: aquatic, disperse, dissolve, pollution, viscosity, water quality. Compare their table with the one they completed at the Tune-in session, to demonstrate changes in understanding.

Students complete **Generic reproducible 3 (Responding to the investigation)**. Compare their responses to those on **Generic reproducible 2**.

Teachers and students each complete **Generic reproducible 5 (Design thinking assessment rubric)**. Students compare the feedback they are given by the teacher with their self-assessment of their design thinking skills.

STEM INVESTIGATIONS

Name: ....

Date: ....

What do you see?

What might be some issues for animal life?

Find and add an image here, or draw what you saw.

What else do you want to know about this image?

What might be some issues for plant life?

Name: ....

Date: ....

STEM INVESTIGATIONS

Write the name of each substance that is placed in the water.
What happens? Record your observations.

SUBSTANCE	OBSERVATIONS

STEM Investigations, UP, ISBN 978 1 4202 4154 9 © Macmillan Science and Education Australia 2018

EMPATHISE

STEM INVESTIGATIONS

Name: ....

Date: ....

	VIDEO CLIP	TEXT
What do you see?		
What is the impact on animals?		
What is the impact on plants?		
Write at least one question relating to each scenario.		

USE SEA WATER TO SAVE THE VILLAGE

→ INTRODUCTION

Fresh water is essential to human life, so a reliable and safe source is important. Cyclones can wreak havoc on large areas of land, destroying vegetation and homes, and polluting fresh water sources. In this STEM investigation, students are asked to create a desalination unit that can be used to make safe drinking water from sea water. Students will find out why fresh water is important and how sea water can be used to make fresh water.

THE CHALLENGE

You are a volunteer in a remote village on a tropical island. When a cyclone hits, flood waters destroy the village and pollute all of the island's fresh water sources. You and the twelve villagers have no safe drinking water.

Your challenge is to design and build a device to make safe drinking water from the island's biggest natural resource: sea water. You have only some basic materials available, and your device must be quick and easy to build – you need water now. Also, you must calculate how much fresh water you and the twelve villagers will need to survive for the three days until you are rescued.

KEY UNDERSTANDINGS

- The water cycle describes how water moves through the Earth's surface, the atmosphere and underground.
- Living things need fresh water to survive.
- Water makes up about 60 per cent of the average human's body.
- Humans need around 2 litres of fresh drinking water per day.
- Humans need a minimum of 15 litres of fresh water per day for drinking, washing and cleaning.
- Potable water is water that is safe to use for drinking or food preparation, without the risk of health issues.

KEY VOCABULARY

condensation

desalination

distillation

evaporation

potable

states of matter

KEY SKILLS

- Classify items as solids, liquids or gases.
- Describe the words used to explain the changes in matter, for example, solid melting into a liquid.
- Explain how desalination works.
- Make careful observations.

KEY ACTIONS

- Gather information about drinking water.
- Demonstrate how desalination works.
- Create a desalination unit to make fresh water from salt water.

→ OVERVIEW OF STAGES

TUNE IN:

Students explore the three main states of matter (solid, liquid and gas) and how things can change from one state to another. Students research why fresh water is important for living things. They explore the desalination process, learning how salt water can be changed into drinking water after a natural disaster such as a cyclone.

EMPATHISE

Students find out about some of the issues involved when a community's drinking water becomes unsafe.

DEFINE

Students consider what desalination is and the materials available to create a desalination unit. Students calculate how much the desalination unit would need to generate to support them and the twelve villagers.

IDEATE

Students generate ideas about how to change salt water into fresh water. They sketch and label their designs.

PROTOTYPE

Students choose one or two ideas to transform into physical representations (models). These are created rapidly, using simple materials. Students can role-play, make storyboards or use sticky notes when they prototype.

TEST

Students share their prototypes and provide feedback to each other. Students check which ideas work best, then choose a final design to build. They are given the opportunity to cycle through the Prototype and Test stages again.

SHARE AND EVALUATE:

Final prototypes are shared and evaluated, with opportunities for expert feedback investigated. Students consider whether or not their designs could be scaled up to meet the demands of the people on the island.

→ SUGGESTED SCHEDULE

LESSON	STAGE
1–2	**Tune in**: learn about the water cycle and cyclones, and explore states of matter and desalination
3–5	**Empathise**: find out about issues with water when there has been a natural disaster, and how these issues are managed, and write/record in journal
6	**Define**: define the main issues and write/record in journal
7	**Ideate**: develop ideas and write/record in journal
8–10	**Prototype** and **Test**: conduct prototyping and testing cycles, and write/record in journal
11–13	**Share and evaluate**: share and evaluate designs and prototypes

CURRICULUM LINKS

The following tables show the key Science, Technologies and Mathematics curricula with which this STEM investigation is aligned.

SCIENCE

YEAR	STRAND	SUB-STRANDS AND CONTENT
5	Science Understanding	Chemical sciences: • Solids, liquids and gases have different observable properties and behave in different ways
6	Science Understanding	Chemical sciences: • Changes to materials can be reversible, such as melting, freezing and evaporating; or irreversible, such as burning and rusting Biological sciences: • The growth and survival of living things are affected by physical conditions of their environment
5 & 6	Science as a Human Endeavour	Nature and development of science: • Science involves testing predictions by gathering data and using evidence to develop explanations of events and phenomena
	Science Inquiry Skills	Questioning and predicting Processing and analysing data and information Communicating

TECHNOLOGIES

YEAR	STRAND	CONTENT
5 & 6	Design and Technologies Processes and Production Skills	• Generate, develop and communicate design ideas and processes for audiences using appropriate technical terms and graphical representation techniques • Develop project plans that include consideration of resources when making designed solutions individually and collaboratively

MATHEMATICS

YEAR	STRAND	CONTENT
5 & 6	Number and Algebra	Number and place value Fractions and decimals

OTHER CURRICULUM LINKS

GENERAL CAPABILITIES

- Literacy
- Numeracy
- Personal and Social Capability
- Critical and Creative Thinking

ASSESSMENT

The following resources are provided for assessing students at different stages of the STEM investigations:

- Generic reproducible 1 (Key vocabulary table), for assessing understanding of vocabulary
- Generic reproducible 2 (Self-evaluation), for student self-evaluation of the learning process
- Generic reproducible 3 (Responding to the investigation), for assessing student engagement in the challenge, and the collaboration and skills involved in the design thinking stages
- Generic reproducible 5 (Design thinking assessment rubric), for evaluating student engagement in the design thinking stages
- Learning journal templates 1, 2, 3 and 4, for incorporating student reflection and evaluation

→ GETTING READY FOR THE INVESTIGATION

You can prepare yourself and students for this STEM investigation in the following ways:

- Identify groups of students who will work well together.
- Review the **Key science knowledge** that supports this investigation, and look at the **Useful links**.
- Investigate the **Useful apps**.
- Gather materials for exploring changes in states of matter, as well as desalination.
- Start collecting additional materials for prototyping (as shown on the **Materials needed** list).
- Determine where prototypes will be kept between lessons.
- Create a wall space where students can share their ideas in the Ideate stage.
- Organise the class into pairs.
- Start thinking about:
  - » a heating source to heat the water for desalination
  - » any time constraints on the investigation
  - » how students will share their learning and desalination units
  - » who can be invited to provide feedback to students about their designs.

USEFUL APPS

- App for making notes using text, drawings, images, weblinks and audio, such as Notability
- App for creating a learning journal, such as Book Creator
- App for creating semantic maps (links between different words and/or concepts), such as Popplet
- App for creating interactive links (for example, between descriptions, videos, images and websites and a main image), such as ThingLink
- App for creating multimedia presentations, such as Adobe Spark Video and iMovie
- Survey app such as Typeform (free for small surveys)

USEFUL LINKS

- General information about cyclones, such as at sage.unsw.edu.au/currentstudents/ug/projects/Darmawan/Cyclone.html and australiangeographic.com.au/topics/science-environment/2011/02/cyclones-facts-and-figures
- Cyclones and problems with access to drinking water, such as at bbc.com/news/world-asia-31917913
- An animation of the water cycle, such as at pmm.nasa.gov/education/videos/water-cycle-animation
- States of matter and changes in states of matter, such as at idahoptv.org/sciencetrek/topics/matter/facts.cfm
- Information about desalination, such as at water.usgs.gov/edu/drinkseawater.html
- The damage done by cyclones, such as at abc.net.au/btn/story/s3127773.htm
- States of matter sorter, such as at abcya.com/states_of_matter.htm
- Things to consider after a cyclone, flood or other disaster, such as at healthywa.wa.gov.au/Articles/U_Z/Water-safety-after-cyclones-floods-and-other-disasters
- Instructions to make a solar still for distillation, such as at capriplus3.com/2015/06/how-to-make-solar-still-desalination-kids.html

RESOURCES PROVIDED

- Generic reproducibles 1, 2, 3, 4, 5
- Reproducibles 11.1, 11.2, 11.3
- Learning journal templates 1, 2, 3, 4 (on disc)

MATERIALS NEEDED

- Sticky notes (half a pad per pair)
- Paper
- Coloured card
- Pens and markers
- Sticky tape
- Pipe-cleaners
- Cardboard
- 2 bowls per group: one large, one small
- 1 mug per group
- 2 small rocks per group
- 1 large, black plastic sheet per group, for covering the large bowl
- Cardboard box with flaps intact (per group)
- Ice: cubes and crushed
- Plastic cups
- Plates
- Spoons
- Eye-droppers
- Kettle

KEY SCIENCE KNOWLEDGE

This section provides an overview of the key science concepts and vocabulary needed for this unit.

CYCLONES AND DRINKING WATER

A cyclone is a type of storm that happens in tropical areas. Cyclones are also known as typhoons or hurricanes. Cyclones can cause a lot of damage to the places where people live, which can affect water supplies. If power systems are damaged, then water treatment plants can no longer supply **potable** water to residents. Floods caused by cyclones can allow waste to enter water supplies and introduce microbes such as bacteria and viruses.

THREE STATES OF MATTER

There are three main **states of matter**: solid, liquid and gas.

Solids are made up of particles that are tightly packed. They have a fixed shape.

Liquids have more space between their particles than solids do, and the particles are not evenly spaced. They have the shape of any container they are poured into.

Gas particles are even more widely and unevenly spaced. They have the shape of any container they are poured into. Matter can move from one state to another:

- When a solid is heated, it becomes a liquid. This is called melting.
- When a liquid is heated, it becomes a gas. This is called **evaporation**.
- When a gas is cooled, it becomes a liquid. This is called **condensation**.
- When a liquid is cooled, it becomes a solid. This is called freezing.

Changes in states of matter occur naturally as part of the water cycle.

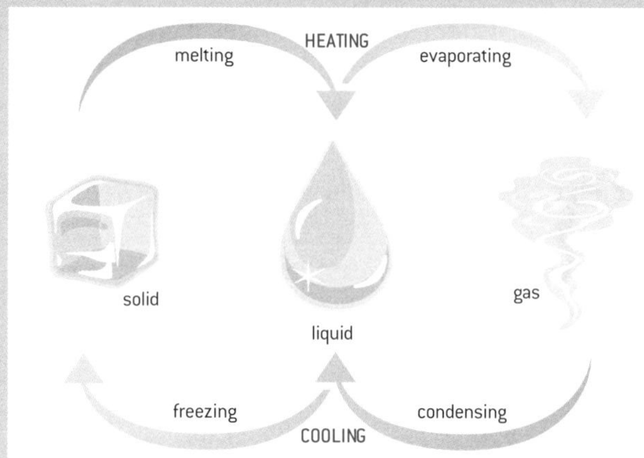

Water exists in different states of matter: as a solid, liquid and gas.

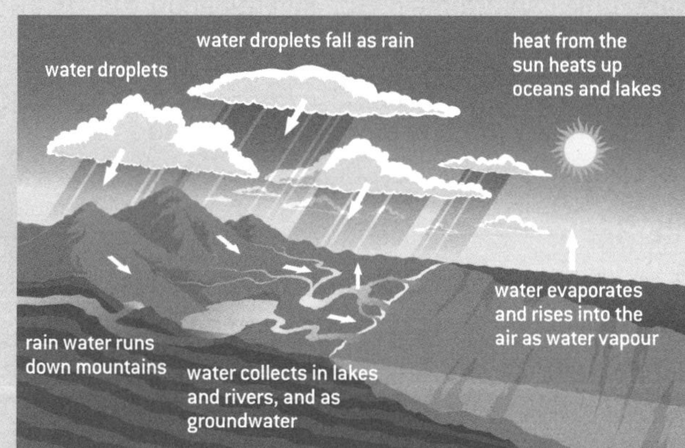

Water changes state during the water cycle.

MAKING DRINKING WATER FROM SEA WATER

Desalination is a process in which fresh water is made from salt water. One method of desalination is called **distillation**.

During distillation, salt water is heated until the water evaporates (becomes steam). The steam is then cooled until it becomes liquid water. The drinkable water is collected in a different container and the salt remains in the original container.

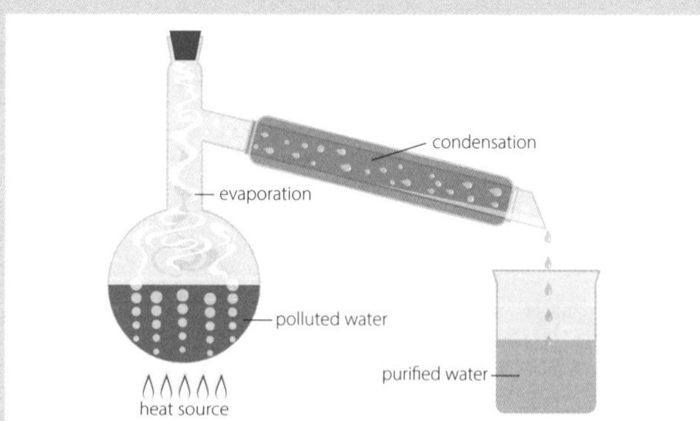

How distillation works

KEY VOCABULARY

condensation – the change from a gas into a liquid (for example, steam into water)
desalination – the removal of salt from water (for example, using distillation)
distillation – the process of evaporating a liquid and condensing it to remove impurities
evaporation – the change from a liquid into a gas (for example, water into steam)
potable – drinkable
states of matter – the different arrangements that particles can take (for example, solid, liquid and gas)

→ TUNE IN

1. Ask students to complete **Generic reproducible 1 (Key vocabulary table)** using the key vocabulary for this unit: condensation, desalination, distillation, evaporation, potable, states of matter. This reproducible will also be used at the end of the unit, to demonstrate changes in understanding.
2. Watch a video clip about the damage done by cyclones (see **Useful apps/links**).
3. Discuss what a tropical cyclone is and its impact on land, including islands. Discuss different terminology, such as 'cyclone', 'hurricane' and 'typhoon'.
4. Provide a link to general information about tropical cyclones (see **Useful apps/links**). Create a class semantic map with information about cyclones.
5. Students consider the impact that a cyclone might have on the wellbeing of people living on a tropical island. Ask students to consider what might be impacted, such as housing and the water supply.
6. Before engaging in the challenge, students need to have an understanding of states of matter, changes of state, cyclones, desalination and the water cycle.

ACTIVITY 1: WATER CYCLE

1. Watch an animation of the water cycle (see **Useful apps/links**).
2. Pause the video at different points to discuss what can be seen. Discuss the terms 'evaporation', 'condensation' and 'precipitation', and highlight them in the video clip.

ACTIVITY 2: STATES OF MATTER

1. Provide students with **Reproducible 11.1 (States of matter)**. Students cut out the cards and categorise the objects shown on the cards as solids, liquids or gases. When they have finished, students add other examples of each state of matter.
2. Using the **Key science knowledge** as a guide, have students model the three main states of matter. They can pack together like a solid, move apart slightly like a liquid, and move further apart and randomly like a gas.
3. Provide students with a link to an online game to sort items according to state of matter (see **Useful apps/links**).

ACTIVITY 3: SALTY TO FRESH

1. Give students the opportunity to explore the desalination process. Provide materials to assemble solar distillation equipment, and some instructions (see **Useful apps/links**).
2. Ensure the following key terms are used and discussed during the experiment: 'condensation', 'desalination', 'distillation', 'evaporation'. The main focus of the task is for students to observe and understand how water in salt water can be evaporated, leaving the salt behind, then condensed, so the resulting water is salt free.
3. Encourage students to photograph the experiment at different stages and annotate or describe their observations.

7. Introduce the STEM investigation and challenge to the students. Provide them with the student card and read the information together. Ask students to think about the scientific processes they will need to use to complete the challenge, as well as the purpose of the challenge.
8. Introduce the design thinking process by reviewing the stages on the student card.
9. Explain that students will keep a journal about their learning at the different stages of the design.

TOP TIP! During the Tune-in session, conduct vocabulary activities to highlight and develop key vocabulary knowledge. Activities could include drawing semantic webs, creating a word wall or paired discussions. Check the **Key vocabulary** definitions or read the **Key science knowledge** for a refresher on the key terms and concepts.

USEFUL APPS/LINKS

- An animation of the water cycle, such as at pmm.nasa.gov/education/videos/water-cycle-animation
- The damage done by cyclones, such as at abc.net.au/btn/story/s3127773.htm
- General information about cyclones, such as at sage.unsw.edu.au/currentstudents/ug/projects/Darmawan/Cyclone.html and australiangeographic.com.au/topics/science-environment/2011/02/cyclones-facts-and-figures
- States of matter sorter, such as at abcya.com/states_of_matter.htm
- Instructions to make a solar still for distillation, such as at capriplus3.com/2015/06/how-to-make-solar-still-desalination-kids.html

EMPATHISE

During the Empathise stage of the design thinking process, students focus on considering different points of view. To empathise with others, they need to research some of the experiences that people have had. Students will take notes, ask questions, draw diagrams and take photos where relevant. Consider recent global weather events, such as Hurricane Irma, to make the investigation more current.

ACTIVITY 1: LITTLE OR NO WATER

1. Read about some of the issues for survivors of a cyclone such as Cyclone Pam in Vanuatu (see **Useful apps/links**).
2. Read about some things to consider if there has been a cyclone, flood or disaster (see **Useful apps/links**). Students ask others in their class how they would react if they had no drinking water. They can use **Reproducible 11.2 (Without water)** to record different people's responses.

ACTIVITY 2: MANAGING WATER ISSUES

1. Pairs of students find out about some of the ways that people manage water issues following natural disasters. Students also find out about other important uses of fresh water. Students use **Reproducible 11.3 (Solving water problems)** to record their findings.
2. Pairs of students join another pair of students to share some of the key information they have located. Students choose one or two points to share with the class.

ACTIVITY 3: EMPATHISE

Ask students to consider how people feel when they don't have fresh water and some of the impacts this has on people's lives. They rank the impacts in order, from most important to least important.

Direct students to **Learning journal template 1 (Empathise page)**.

PROMPTS

- What are some of the main issues when there has been a cyclone?
- What were some of the words people used to describe how they would feel if they didn't have access to fresh water?
- How have some people coped with water issues when there have been natural disasters such as cyclones?

MORE VOCABULARY

- empathise – understand and consider another person's or group's point of view
- point of view – an opinion, attitude or judgement considered in a particular way

JOURNAL TIP

Ask students to complete **Learning journal template 1 (Empathise page)** while they are completing the different tasks. Remind them to date their notes and include photos or drawings of relevant information.

USEFUL APPS/LINKS

- Cyclones and problems with access to drinking water, such as at bbc.com/news/world-asia-31917913
- Things to consider following a cyclone, flood or other disaster, such as at healthywa.wa.gov.au/Articles/U_Z/Water-safety-after-cyclones-floods-and-other-disasters

ASSESSMENT

This stage of the design thinking process offers opportunities to observe students collecting information, developing questions, and recording their notes and thinking in their journal.

EMPATHISE DEFINE IDEATE PROTOTYPE TEST

→ DEFINE

The main focus of this stage of the design thinking process is to reframe the challenge. The initial challenge is quite open, so at this stage students learn how to define what needs to be done. This includes noting insights that have been generated.

ACTIVITY 1: CONSIDER OBSERVATIONS

1. Students consider the information they gathered in the Empathise stage. They may work in pairs or small groups. Provide them with a whiteboard, large sheet of paper and/or sticky notes to collate some of the key information they have gathered about issues with water pollution and access to drinking water when there has been a cyclone.
2. Students should discuss one section of **Learning journal template 2 (Define page)** at a time, write their responses, then continue discussing their ideas for the next section, until the task is complete. This provides students with opportunities to hear others' responses and also provides the teacher with input points.
3. Discuss the information gathered about water pollution. Provide students with the opportunity to research further. Ask them to write down other information they would like to know, such as learning about the process of desalination. Provide them with **Generic reproducible 4 (Key question table)** to assist them to record their questions, findings and sources.

ACTIVITY 2: CONSIDER INSIGHTS

Students think of at least one insight they have gained from the process; for example, fresh water is not just needed for drinking – it is also essential for good hygiene.

Students add this to **Learning journal template 2**. They should then relate this insight to their design.

When considering insights, students could think about the following:

- What was something unexpected that you saw or found out? How was it unexpected?
- How will you decide on the most important aspect of providing usable water?
- Is there any other information that you need or would like to know? How will you find out?

ACTIVITY 3: CONSIDER CONSTRAINTS

At this stage, let students know the constraints of the challenge, by describing the materials available for creating the desalination unit, the time frame for completing the challenge, safety issues with heating for evaporation and how the units will be tested. Students can then update **Learning journal template 2**.

PROMPTS

- What did you discover?
- What were the most important pieces of information that you gathered?
- What was something new that you learned?
- What other information do you need?

MORE VOCABULARY

- define – state the meaning of something
- insight – an accurate understanding of someone or something

JOURNAL TIP

Discuss the term 'insight' and explain that it relates to something students have learned about the people and their responses to the surveys, as well as information gathered through research or excursions. You could refer to **Learning journal template 2**.

EMPATHISE DEFINE IDEATE PROTOTYPE TEST

→ IDEATE

The Ideate stage of the design thinking process is all about generating lots of ideas. Students need to be flexible in their thinking and able to move beyond obvious ideas. At this stage, ideas are not judged, just generated and gathered. Students generate ideas relating to the creation of a desalination unit, using a limited range of materials.

ACTIVITY: GENERATE IDEAS

1. Ask groups of students to draw or write their ideas about how their desalination unit might look and work. Each new idea should be written or drawn on a separate piece of paper or sticky note.
2. Ask students to group ideas on a wall or board.
3. Ask students to look at the different ideas and provide feedback to each other. It is important that students don't defend their ideas at this stage. They should just be listening to the feedback.
4. After the initial feedback, ask students to come up with more ideas. Encourage them to be creative and even radical.
5. Ask students to choose four of their ideas to write in their journal. Students use **Learning journal template 3 (Ideate page)** to do this. Ask students to choose one idea to explore further and explain the reasoning behind their choice.

TOP TIP!

At this stage, students may have produced a series of annotated drawings of desalination methods. They may have a collection of sticky notes, which they can organise into related ideas.

Encourage students to view and read others' ideas before giving feedback. Feedback could be within small groups or between partners. Considering others' ideas is an important part of this process, so students can build on their own ideas as they continue to ideate.

At each stage of this activity, ask students to discuss their thoughts before writing their responses. This will help them to think through their ideas and select their final ideas to develop.

PROMPTS

- How do your chosen ideas relate to creating usable water?
- How might you test your design?
- How can you make it easy to use?
- How can you make it possible to build with common materials?
- What if you had to use different materials?

MORE VOCABULARY

- feedback – information about, for example, a person's performance or the design of a product, which can be used to make improvements
- ideate – generate many ideas without making judgements about the ideas

JOURNAL TIP

When choosing four ideas to include in the journal, students should try to choose ideas that aren't related, to show a range of ideas.

USEFUL APPS/LINKS

- Tools for creating ideas, such as at creatingminds.org/tools/tools_ideation.htm
- Tips for creativity and innovation, such as at designorate.com/creativity-innovation-in-education

ASSESSMENT

At the Ideate stage, assessment could include observations about the number and diversity of students' ideas, and their ability to provide feedback and create additional ideas. Reflection in the journal should provide an insight into some of the reasoning behind students' choices.

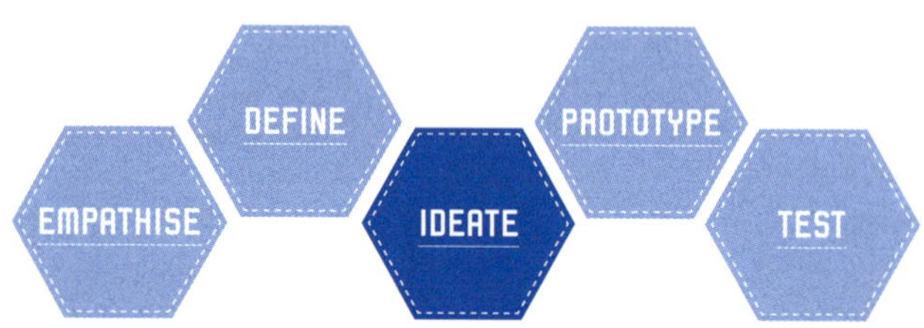

→ PROTOTYPE

At this stage of the design thinking process, students are asked to create a physical prototype of a desalination unit. It is the stage where students need to get their ideas out of their head and presented in a way that engages other students and helps them to understand the ideas. When students create, it helps them to think and solve problems and disagreements. Students can role-play, use LEGO, make a storyboard or use sticky notes when they prototype. The most important feature is that viewers can interact with whatever is produced.

Encourage students to photograph or film during the prototyping and testing stages. This information can be used to show the learning behind the design thinking process in action.

ACTIVITY: TRANSFORM IDEAS INTO PROTOTYPES

1. Ask students to choose one or two desalination unit design ideas to prototype. They need to make a scaled representation of the designed desalination unit. It does not need to work, but its parts and function should be obvious or annotated with labels.
2. Provide students with a range of materials to create their prototype. Remind students that a prototype should be created rapidly and is not meant to look 'nice'.
3. After a prototype has been created, ask students to see if it works and get feedback from others.
4. Students then use the feedback to prototype again.

Ask students to fill in the Prototype part of **Learning journal template 4 (Prototype and test page)**. See the **Journal tip** for further student guidance.

PROMPTS

- What worked?
- How could it be improved?
- What else do you need to know, do or have?
- What other suggestions do you have?

MORE VOCABULARY

- feedback – information about, for example, a person's performance or the design of a product, which can be used to make improvements
- prototype – an initial version of a model of a product or process that is used to develop a final model

TOP TIP!

The Prototype stage is often very messy. It is important that students are focusing on their ideas, rather than the end product. Provide them with lots of materials to help them build a scale model of the desalination unit – recycling depots can be a useful source of resources. Students may add labels to prototypes to explain some of the main features. Photographing and annotating pictures of prototypes can be useful.

To gain feedback, students could ask each other some of the following questions:

- What is the main feature of your prototype?
- How does your prototype work?
- Which aspects work best? What will you keep?
- Which aspects need changing? How might you do this?
- What other materials might you need?

JOURNAL TIP

Remind students to highlight the main features of their prototype. If students are creating an electronic journal, they can insert a photo of their prototype and annotate it.

USEFUL APPS/LINKS

- App for creating interactive links (for example, between descriptions, videos, images and websites and a main image), such as ThingLink
- App for making notes using text, drawings, images, weblinks and audio, such as Notability

ASSESSMENT

Observe students as they make changes to their designs. Are they able to consider feedback, make modifications and move rapidly through this process? Or do they have difficulties with holding on to an idea and accepting feedback?

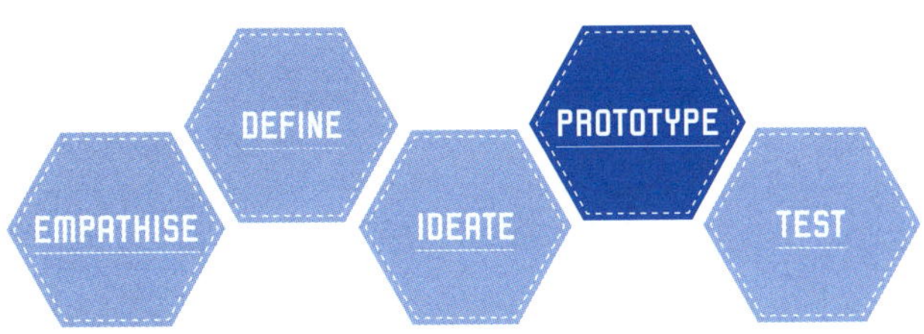

TEST

At this stage of the design thinking process, students test their prototype to see how it meets the requirements of the user – in this case, the island villagers. Students check to see if their prototype meets the criteria set at the start of the design process.

ACTIVITY: TEST FEEDBACK

1. Students take their last prototype and consider the initial criteria and the needs of the island villagers.
2. Ask students to check whether or not their design works. If not, what do they need to do to make it work?
3. Provide the opportunity to cycle through the prototyping and testing stages again.

Ask students to fill in the Test part of **Learning journal template 4 (Prototype and test page)**. See the **Journal tip** for further student guidance.

PROMPTS

- Does your prototype do what you wanted it to do? Are there other features you could add?
- What needs to be changed?
- What works well?

MORE VOCABULARY

- evaluate – assess something, perhaps considering what worked and what didn't
- feature – a specific aspect of something, such as size, shape, colour and quality
- feedback – information about, for example, a person's performance or the design of a product, which can be used to make improvements
- prototype – an initial version of a model of a product or process that is used to develop a final model
- review – consider an idea, process or product and decide what needs to be changed and what works

JOURNAL TIP

Ask students to think about why it is important to test their ideas before they build their final design.

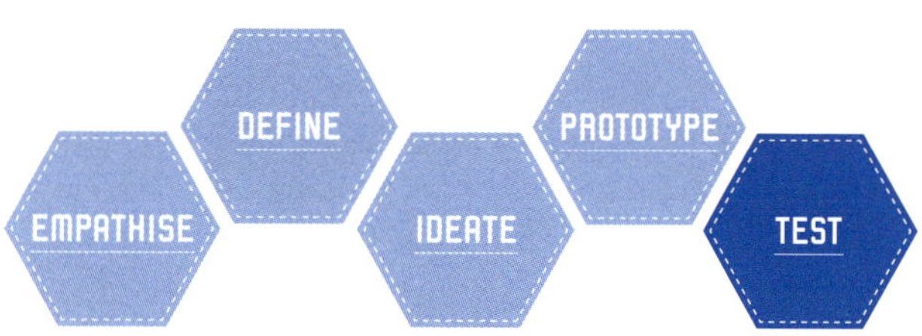

SHARE AND EVALUATE

At this stage of the investigation, students are provided with an opportunity to share their final design, as well as the processes involved in the investigation. Students evaluate their learning journals and their solutions.

ACTIVITY 1: BRING THE DESIGNS TOGETHER

1. Students can create an iMovie or use Adobe Spark Video to demonstrate the process and thinking behind the designs. There should be an element of narration, where they are sharing their story about points of view, insights, prototyping and solutions.
2. Students should include their learning journals with the desalination plant so others can see the different stages of the design process.

ACTIVITY 2: EVALUATE AND GIVE FEEDBACK

1. Provide students with **Generic reproducible 2 (Self-evaluation)** to complete.
2. Ask students to provide feedback to each other about the most interesting features, the aspects that were most difficult and the changes that they would make if they repeated the task.
3. Provide students with opportunities to share their designs with the wider community. This could include inviting someone from an environmental agency (or similar), a family member or friend with relevant experience or an external professional. It may be possible to share some of the video clips with an expert for feedback about the designs.

ASSESSMENT

Ask students to again complete **Generic reproducible 1 (Key vocabulary table)**, using the key vocabulary for this unit: condensation, desalination, distillation, evaporation, potable, states of matter. Compare their table with the one they completed at the Tune-in stage, to demonstrate changes in understanding.

Students complete **Generic reproducible 3 (Responding to the investigation)**. Compare their responses to those on **Generic reproducible 2**.

Teachers and students each complete **Generic reproducible 5 (Design thinking assessment rubric)**. Students compare the teacher feedback with their self-assessment of their design thinking skills.

STEM INVESTIGATIONS

Name: ....

Date: ....

Cut out the cards and organise the words into three categories to describe their state of matter at room temperature: solid, liquid or gas.

OXYGEN	WOOD
STEEL	MILK
WATER	PLASTIC
HONEY	HELIUM
STEAM	ORANGE JUICE
PORCELAIN	WOOL

STEM Investigations, UP, ISBN 978 1 4202 4154 9

EMPATHISE

STEM INVESTIGATIONS

Name: ....

Date: ....

Collect information about what people would do if they had no fresh water. Ask the following question, or write your own question.

What would you do if there was no fresh water?	
NAME	**RESPONSE**

Write a few sentences to summarise some of the things people would do if they had no fresh water.

....

....

....

....

....

....

STEM Investigations, UP, ISBN 978 1 4202 4154 9 © Macmillan Science and Education Australia 2018

Name: ....

Date: ....

Find out about the uses of water, problems with water that happen after natural disasters and how people solve these problems. Write your findings here.

What are some of the important uses of water?

What problems with water need to be solved after natural disasters?

SOLVING WATER PROBLEMS

How do people solve problems with water after natural disasters?

BE THE BEST WEATHER PRESENTER FOR THE JOB

NATURAL WORLD 12

→ INTRODUCTION

The Earth's climate is changing and there have been numerous extreme weather events in recent years. Extreme weather events have an impact on the natural environment and the human population. Their impact is often felt beyond the place that is initially affected. The weather forecast is now a key feature of a news presentation. Presenters use a range of data and tools to inform their audiences.

In this STEM investigation, students will find out about different extreme weather events and their impacts. They will learn about the role of temperature and cloud formation in these events. Students will explore a range of technologies to demonstrate their understanding of different aspects of weather, as well as their ability to engage a younger group of students.

THE CHALLENGE

A group of students have created a school news station. You want to join the team as a weather presenter so you can broadcast stories about local and global weather events. You want students to learn about extreme weather. First, though, you will need to impress the school news selection team.

Your challenge is to put together a practical and fun presentation for younger students. Your presentation should describe extreme weather events and demonstrate ways that they can affect the Earth's surface. It should also explain how temperature and cloud formation can cause differences in weather. As part of this investigation, you will learn all about weather, and the properties and behaviour of solids, liquids and gases.

KEY UNDERSTANDINGS

- Extreme weather can change the Earth's surface.
- Hurricanes, cyclones and droughts are examples of extreme weather events.
- Temperature and cloud formation have an impact on the weather.
- Technology can be used to predict the path and impact of an extreme weather event.

KEY VOCABULARY

climate change
condensation
evaporation
global warming
precipitation
states of matter

KEY SKILLS

- Locate information.
- Generate useful investigative questions.
- Use technology relating to weather.
- Analyse information and provide explanations.
- Develop presentation skills.

KEY ACTIONS

- Gather information about extreme weather events.
- Present information about the weather using suitable technology.
- Create an engaging presentation for younger students.

OVERVIEW OF STAGES

TUNE IN:

Students learn about states of matter relating to weather phenomena. They explore the three main states of matter (solid, liquid and gas) and how they can change, with a focus on condensation and evaporation. Students find out how rain, snowflakes and clouds are formed.

EMPATHISE

Students consider eyewitness accounts of extreme weather events. They consider people's responses and generate questions to learn more.

DEFINE

Students explore different types of extreme weather events, considering their causes, their impact and human responses to the events.

IDEATE

Students generate ideas to create a presentation for a younger audience, to inform and engage them about extreme weather events.

PROTOTYPE

Students choose one or two ideas to develop further. These are created rapidly, using simple materials.

TEST

Students share their presentation ideas and provide feedback to each other. They are given the opportunity to cycle through the Prototype and Test stages again.

SHARE AND EVALUATE:

Final presentations are shared and evaluated.

SUGGESTED SCHEDULE

LESSON	STAGE
1–2	**Tune in**: explore states of matter relating to weather phenomena; explore rain, snowflakes and clouds; and introduce the student challenge
3–4	**Empathise**: consider eyewitness accounts of extreme weather, consider people's responses and generate questions, and write/record in journal
5–6	**Define**: define the main causes, impacts and responses to extreme weather events, and write/record in journal
7	**Ideate**: develop ideas and write/record in journal
8–11	**Prototype** and **Test**: conduct prototyping and testing cycles for presentation, and write/record in journal
12–13	**Share and evaluate**: share and evaluate presentations

CURRICULUM LINKS

The following tables show the key Science, Technologies and Mathematics curricula with which this STEM investigation is aligned.

SCIENCE

YEAR	STRAND	SUB-STRAND AND CONTENT
5	Science Understanding	Chemical sciences: • Solids, liquids and gases have different observable properties and behave in different ways
6	Science Understanding	Earth and space sciences: • Sudden geological changes and extreme weather events can affect Earth's surface
5 & 6	Science as a Human Endeavour	Use and influence of science: • Scientific knowledge is used to solve problems and inform personal and community decisions
6	Science as a Human Endeavour	Nature and development of science: • Science involves testing predictions by gathering data and using evidence to develop explanations of events and phenomena

TECHNOLOGIES

YEAR	STRAND	CONTENT
5 & 6	Design and Technologies Processes and Production Skills	• Generate, develop and communicate design ideas and processes for audiences using appropriate technical terms and graphical representation techniques • Select appropriate materials, components, tools, equipment and techniques, and apply safe procedures to make designed solutions • Negotiate criteria for success that include sustainability to evaluate design ideas, processes and solutions • Develop project plans that include consideration of resources when making designed solutions individually and collaboratively

MATHEMATICS

YEAR	STRAND	SUB-STRAND
5 & 6	Measurement and Geometry	Using units of measurement

AC

OTHER CURRICULUM LINKS

GENERAL CAPABILITIES

- Literacy
- Numeracy
- Information and Communication Technology (ICT) Capability
- Critical and Creative Thinking

ASSESSMENT

The following resources are provided for assessing students at different stages of the STEM investigations:

- Generic reproducible 1 (Key vocabulary table), for assessing understanding of vocabulary
- Generic reproducible 2 (Self-evaluation), for student self-evaluation of the learning process
- Generic reproducible 3 (Define graphic organiser), for assessing student engagement in the challenges, and the collaboration and skills involved in the design thinking stages
- Generic reproducible 5 (Design thinking assessment rubric), for evaluating student engagement in the design thinking stages
- Learning journal templates 1, 2, 3 and 4, for incorporating student reflection and evaluation

→ GETTING READY FOR THE INVESTIGATION

You can prepare yourself and students for this STEM investigation in the following ways:

- Identify groups of students who will work well together.
- Review the **Key science knowledge** that supports this investigation, and look at the **Useful links**.
- Investigate the **Useful apps**.
- Gather materials (including ice cubes) for exploring states of matter with different weather phenomena during the Tune-in session.
- Start collecting additional materials for prototyping (as shown on the **Materials needed** list).
- Determine where prototypes will be kept between lessons.
- Create a wall space where students can share their ideas in the Ideate stage.
- Organise the class into pairs.
- Start thinking about:
  - if experiments will be teacher demonstrations with assistance, or group experiments
  - equipment needed for experiments
  - safety considerations when using materials such as borax
  - additional staffing when completing experiments
  - perhaps arranging a visit or contact with someone associated with a bureau of meteorology or similar organisation
  - the audience for the presentations
  - how the presentation will be evaluated.

USEFUL APPS

- App for creating semantic maps (links between different words and/or concepts), such as Popplet
- App for creating interactive links (for example, between descriptions, videos, images and websites and a main image), such as ThingLink
- App for making notes using text, drawings, images, weblinks and audio, such as Notability
- App for creating multimedia presentations, such as Adobe Spark Video or iMovie
- App for creating surveys, such as Typeform
- App for making dynamic presentations, such as Prezi
- App for making podcasts, such as Podbean

USEFUL LINKS

- Information about states of matter, such as at chem4kids.com/files/matter_states.html
- Information and interactives about global climate change, such as at climatekids.nasa.gov/climate-change-meaning or science.org.au/learning/general-audience/science-booklets-0/science-climate-change/1-what-climate-change
- Hurricane/cyclone information for students, such as at abc.net.au/btn/story/s4645345.htm
- Bushfire information for students, such as at abc.net.au/btn/story/s4620405.htm

RESOURCES PROVIDED

- Generic reproducibles 1, 2, 3, 4, 5, 6
- Reproducibles 12.1, 12.2, 12.3
- Learning journal templates 1, 2, 3, 4 (on disc)

MATERIALS NEEDED

- Sticky notes (half a pad per pair)
- Paper
- Coloured card
- Pens and markers
- Sticky tape
- White pipe-cleaners
- Cardboard
- String
- Wide-mouthed jar
- Boiling water
- Borax
- Wooden pencil
- Gloves
- Drinking glass
- Plastic plate
- Ice cubes
- Glass jar with lid
- Hairspray

KEY SCIENCE KNOWLEDGE

This section provides an overview of the key science concepts and vocabulary needed for this unit.

THE THREE MAIN STATES OF MATTER

Matter is anything with mass that takes up space. Atoms and molecules, which are extremely tiny particles, make up matter. The three main **states of matter** are solid, liquid and gas. The state of matter of a substance changes with temperature and pressure. Each state has different observable properties. For a substance to change from one state to another, energy needs to be put in or removed, usually by heating or cooling.

Solids have atoms or molecules that sit tightly together. They have a definite shape and size, but they are not necessarily hard. They are very difficult to compress. Rocks, hard-boiled eggs and sherbet are all solids.

Liquids contain atoms or molecules that can move more than solids. Liquids have a fixed volume, will flow and take on the shape of their container. They can be slightly compressed. Water, milk and honey are examples of liquids.

Gases have no fixed shape or volume. The atoms are moving rapidly and can spread out. Gases can be compressed. Air molecules in a room take up its shape, helium-filled balloons can be squashed and fumes from rotting apples move into their surroundings.

HOW CLOUDS FORM

When water **evaporates**, it moves into the air as invisible vapour. Clouds form when the water vapour **condenses** into water droplets (liquid) that clump together, sometimes with tiny ice crystals (solid). If clouds combine and are sufficiently large and too heavy to stay up in the atmosphere, **precipitation** will fall as rain, snow or hail.

CLIMATE CHANGE AND EXTREME WEATHER

Climatology is the study of climate relating to weather conditions and patterns over long periods of time. **Climate change** is changes in weather patterns over long periods of time.

Global warming is related to but is not the same as climate change. It is the increased surface temperature of the Earth, some of which is natural and some of which is caused by human activities that produce greenhouse gases.

Increases in the Earth's surface temperature can melt glaciers, snow caps and ice shelves, warm oceans and change ocean currents. Climatologists say that extreme weather events such as droughts, floods, bushfires and severe storms occur more often because of human-induced global warming.

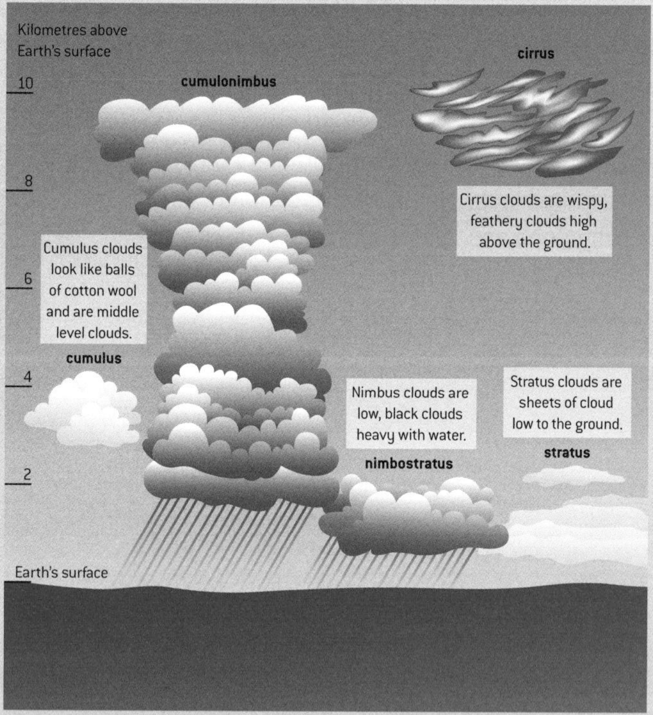

There are many different types of clouds. Clouds with 'nimbus' or 'nimbo' in their names are rain clouds.

KEY VOCABULARY

climate change – a change, over a long time period, in global or regional weather patterns
condenses – changes from a gas into a liquid (for example, steam into water)
evaporates – changes from a liquid into a gas (for example, water into steam)
global warming – the increasing surface temperature of the Earth, both naturally and because of human activities
precipitation – rain, snow or hail
states of matter – the different arrangements that particles can take (for example, solid, liquid and gas)

→ TUNE IN

1. Ask students to complete **Generic reproducible 1 (Key vocabulary table)** using the key vocabulary for this unit. This reproducible will also be used at the end of the unit, to demonstrate changes in understanding.
2. Watch a video clip about extreme weather (see **Useful apps/links**). List different types of extreme weather.
3. Explore different states of matter. Provide students with **Reproducible 12.1 (Which state of matter?)**. Have them record 5 to 10 different examples for each state. Students should 'pair' and 'share' their tables. Have them move their 'unsure' substances to the correct category.
4. Have students make generalisations about the properties of each state of matter.
5. Before engaging in the challenge, students need to have an understanding of states of matter, how a substance changes from one state to another, and how this can be applied to weather.

Additional care needs to be taken when working with borax. Assist students to pour the hot water.

ACTIVITY 1: MAKING SNOWFLAKES

1. Cut a pipe-cleaner into three even sections (see **Materials needed** list). Twist them together in the centre to form a shape like an asterisk (*). Make sure the points are the same length.
2. Attach one end of a piece of string to a pipe-cleaner spoke and the other end to the centre of a pencil. The string length should be about two-thirds of the height of the wide-mouthed jar.
3. Find out the volume of the jar, then carefully pour very hot water into it, so it is three-quarters full. Ask students to stand back to avoid any splashes.
4. You will need to wear gloves for this step. For each cup of water add three tablespoons of borax, one tablespoon at a time. Stir until the mixture is mostly dissolved.
5. Put the pipe-cleaner snowflake into the jar so that the pencil is resting on its rim and the snowflake is suspended in the middle of the solution. Leave the snowflake overnight. Ask students to predict what will happen and which change of state will be observed. Ask 'Why do crystals form when the solution cools?'

ACTIVITY 2: MAKING RAIN

1. Half fill a drinking glass and place a plate on top. You should notice the water vapour condensing inside the glass. Ask students to explain what is happening.
2. Put some ice on the plate and observe. Students should describe what they see and elaborate their understanding to explain how rain is formed. For example, 'Water vapour (gas) rises in the atmosphere. It then cools (condenses) and forms tiny water droplets (liquid) called rain.'

ACTIVITY 3: CLOUDS IN A JAR

1. Pour very hot water into a glass jar so it is one-third full. Invert the lid and place it on top of the jar for about 1 minute.
2. Take the lid off, spray some hairspray into the jar and immediately replace the inverted lid.
3. Wait another minute before putting some ice into the inverted lid. Ask students to describe what they see.
4. After a few minutes, take the lid off the jar. You should have clouds in the jar.
5. Discuss the terms 'changes of state' and 'weather'.

6. Introduce the STEM investigation and challenge to the students. Provide them with the student card and read the information together. Ask students to think about some of the extreme weather events they have heard about or experienced.
7. Introduce the design thinking process by reviewing the stages on the student card.
8. Explain that students will keep a journal about their learning at the different stages of the design.

TOP TIP! During the Tune-in stage, conduct vocabulary activities to highlight and develop key vocabulary knowledge. Activities could include drawing semantic webs, creating a word wall or paired discussions.

USEFUL APPS/LINKS

- Extreme weather video clips, such as at youtube.com/watch?v=yr0YxLt9SCI

→ EMPATHISE

During the Empathise stage of the design thinking process, students focus on finding out about different points of view. To empathise with others, they need to research some of the experiences that people have had with extreme weather conditions, or their reactions to reports. Students will take notes, ask questions, draw diagrams and take photos where relevant.

ACTIVITY 1: REACTIONS TO WEATHER EVENTS

1. Students find out about people's experiences of extreme weather conditions. They watch two video clips about different extreme weather events (see **Useful apps/links**).
2. Provide students with **Reproducible 12.2 (Extreme weather event responses)** to make notes about the different responses people had to the events. Write a short summary about the key information gathered.

ACTIVITY 2: SHARE PERSONAL EXPERIENCES

As a class, list different types of extreme weather in your country and globally. Ask small groups of students to share experiences they or family and friends have had in extreme weather, such as a wind storm, thunderstorm or heat wave. Be mindful that some students may have had very stressful experiences. Have them consider the following questions:

- What emotions did you feel during and after the event?
- What made you feel that way?
- What would you do differently if you experienced a similar situation in the future?
- What would you do the same?

ACTIVITY 3: QUESTION TIME

1. Find an organisation or individual with whom students can communicate about extreme weather events. Have pairs of students generate macro and micro questions and ask them to write two of these in an email or letter, or for a teacher-moderated online discussion. You could invite a speaker for a question and answer session, face to face or online.
2. If students have the opportunity to ask real-time questions, ask them to choose one question for their guest expert. If they are emailing, writing a letter or engaged in an online discussion, provide students with scaffolding for writing.

Ask students to consider the different responses of people to extreme weather events and how they coped.

PROMPTS

- What were some common responses of people to extreme weather events?
- What are some examples of extreme weather?
- What are some of the things people would do differently?
- How did people cope after the event had stopped?

MORE VOCABULARY

- empathise – understand and consider another person's or group's point of view
- point of view – an opinion, attitude or judgement considered in a particular way

JOURNAL TIP

Ask students to complete **Learning journal template 1 (Empathise page)** while they are completing the different tasks. Remind them to date their notes and include photos of relevant information or pictures.

USEFUL APPS/LINKS

- Hurricane/cyclone information, such as at abc.net.au/btn/story/s4645345.htm
- Bushfire information, such as at abc.net.au/btn/story/s4620405.htm

ASSESSMENT

This stage of the design thinking process offers opportunities to observe students collecting information, developing questions, and recording their notes and thinking in their journal.

TOP TIP! Encourage empathy and sensitivity to students who may have been involved in traumatic events such as bushfires, floods and storms. It might be possible to organise a member of the community who has experienced an extreme weather event to talk to the class. Students could develop a set of interview questions that can be given to them prior to their presentation. Alternatively, it might be possible to video-conference with a climate change scientist or meteorologist.

EMPATHISE DEFINE IDEATE PROTOTYPE TEST

→ DEFINE

The main focus of this stage of the design thinking process is to reframe the challenge. The initial challenge is quite open, so at this stage students learn how to define what needs to be done. This includes noting insights that have been generated.

ACTIVITY 1: CONSIDER OBSERVATIONS

1. Students consider the information they gathered in the Empathise stage. They may work in pairs or small groups. Provide them with a whiteboard, large sheet of paper and/or sticky notes to collate some of the key information they have gathered about different types of events and how people have responded.
2. Students should discuss one section of **Learning journal template 2 (Define page)** at a time, write their responses, then continue discussing their ideas for the next section, until the task is complete. This provides students with opportunities to hear others' responses and also provides the teacher with input points.
3. Discuss the different types of extreme weather events. Provide students with the opportunity to research further. Ask them to write down other information they would like to know, such as the causes of different types of extreme weather events, the impact, preventative measures and responses to events. Provide them with **Generic reproducible 4 (Key question table)** to assist them to record their questions, findings and sources.

ACTIVITY 2: CONSIDER INSIGHTS

Students think of at least one insight they have gained from the process; for example, people are very resilient.

Students add this insight to **Learning journal template 2** and then write a brief explanation of what needs to be created.

When considering insights, students could think about the following:

- What was something unexpected that you saw or found out? How was it unexpected?
- How will you choose the extreme weather event you would like to focus on?
- Is there any other information that you need or would like to know? How will you find out?

ACTIVITY 3: CONSIDER CONSTRAINTS

At this stage, let students know the constraints of the challenge, by describing the time frame, the types of technology available, the length of their presentation, key compulsory components, the audience and how the presentation will be evaluated.

Students can then update **Learning journal template 2**.

PROMPTS

- What did you discover?
- What were the most important pieces of information that you gathered?
- What was something new that you learned?
- What other information do you need?

MORE VOCABULARY

- define – state the meaning of something
- insight – an accurate understanding of someone or something

JOURNAL TIP

Discuss the term 'insight'. Explain that it relates to something students have learned about the people and their responses to the surveys, as well as information gathered through research or excursions. You could refer to **Learning journal template 2**.

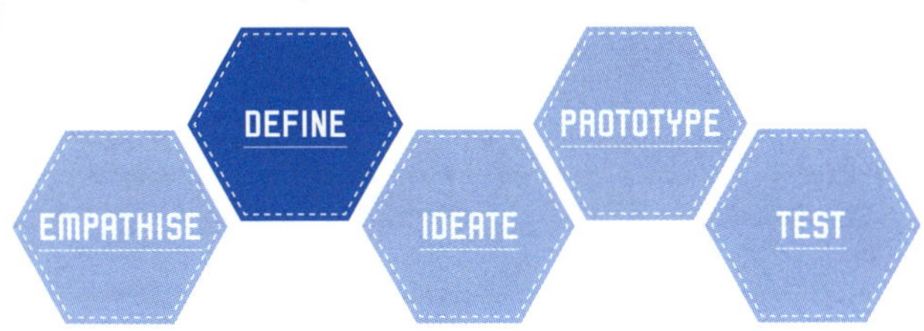

→ IDEATE

The Ideate stage of the design thinking process is all about generating lots of ideas. Students need to be flexible in their thinking and able to move beyond obvious ideas. At this stage, ideas are not judged, just generated and gathered.

ACTIVITY: GENERATE IDEAS

1. Ask groups of students to draw or write their ideas about their extreme weather event, what they will include and how they might do this, considering useful technology. They need to think of some ways, using everyday items, to model cloud formation for different conditions. Students need to consider what form their presentation will take, such as a presentation and/or demonstration.
2. Each new idea should be written or drawn on a separate piece of paper or sticky note.
3. Ask students to group ideas on a wall or board.
4. Ask students to look at the different ideas and provide feedback to each other. It is important that students don't defend their ideas at this stage. They should just be listening to the feedback.
5. After the initial feedback, ask students to come up with more ideas. Encourage them to be creative and even radical. Provide students with **Reproducible 12.3 (Presentation plan)** to collate some of their ideas.
6. Ask students to choose four of their ideas to write in their journal. Students use **Learning journal template 3 (Ideate page)** to do this. Ask students to choose one idea to explore further and explain the reasoning behind their choice.

TOP TIP!

At this stage, students may have produced a series of annotated drawings about what their presentation might include and how their presentation will look. They may have a collection of sticky notes, which they can organise into related ideas.

Encourage students to view and read others' ideas before giving feedback. Feedback could be within small groups or between partners. Considering others' ideas is an important part of this process, so students can build on their own ideas as they continue to ideate.

At each stage of this activity, ask students to discuss their thoughts before writing their responses. This will help them to think through their ideas and select their final ideas to develop.

PROMPTS

- How do these ideas relate to being a weather presenter?
- How might you test your design?
- How can you make it informative for younger children?
- How can you make it interesting for younger children?
- What if you had to use different technology or resources?

MORE VOCABULARY

- feedback – information about, for example, a person's performance or the design of a product, which can be used to make improvements
- ideate – generate many ideas without making judgements about the ideas

JOURNAL TIP

When choosing four ideas to include in the journal, students should try to choose ideas that aren't related.

USEFUL APPS/LINKS

- Tools for creating ideas, such as at creatingminds.org/tools/tools_ideation.htm
- Tips for creativity and innovation, such as at designorate.com/creativity-innovation-in-education

ASSESSMENT

At the Ideate stage, assessment could include observations about the number and diversity of student ideas, and their ability to provide feedback and create additional ideas. Reflection in the journal should provide an insight into some of the reasoning behind student choices.

EMPATHISE | DEFINE | IDEATE | PROTOTYPE | TEST

PROTOTYPE

At this stage of the design thinking process, students are asked to create a physical prototype of a solution. It is the stage where students need to get their ideas out of their head and presented in a way that engages other students and helps them to understand the concept. When students create, it helps them to think and solve problems and disagreements. Students can role-play, make storyboards or use sticky notes when they prototype. The most important feature is that viewers can interact with whatever is produced.

Encourage students to photograph or film during the prototyping and testing stages. This can be used to show the learning behind the design thinking process.

ACTIVITY: TRANSFORM IDEAS INTO PROTOTYPES

1. Students review the ideas generated at the Ideate stage. Provide them with an A3 copy of **Generic reproducible 6 (In the frame)** so they can organise their ideas into two sections: 'least relevant' and 'most relevant'. Students continue to cycle through this activity until they have an idea to start prototyping.
2. Provide students with access to a range of materials and technology for their prototyping. Remind students that a prototype should be created rapidly and is not meant to look 'nice'. A prototype might be a storyboard, mind map or a role-play. It will also include ideas for a presentation script.
3. After a prototype has been created, ask students to seek feedback from others.
4. Students then use the feedback to prototype again.

Ask students to fill in the Prototype part of **Learning journal template 4 (Prototype and test page)**. See the **Journal tip** for further student guidance.

PROMPTS

- What worked?
- How could it be improved?
- What else do you need to know, do or have?
- What other suggestions do you have?

MORE VOCABULARY

- feedback – information about, for example, a person's performance or the design of a product, which can be used to make improvements
- prototype – an initial version of a model of a product or process that is used to develop a final model

JOURNAL TIP

Remind students to highlight the main features of their prototype. If students are creating an electronic journal, they can insert a photo of their prototype and annotate it.

USEFUL APPS/LINKS

- App for creating interactive links (for example, between descriptions, videos, images and websites and a main image), such as ThingLink
- App for making notes using text, drawings, images, weblinks and audio, such as Notability
- App for creating multimedia presentations, such as Adobe Spark Video or iMovie
- App for making dynamic presentations, such as Prezi
- App for making podcasts, such as Podbean

ASSESSMENT

Observe students as they make changes to their designs. Are they able to consider feedback, make modifications and move rapidly through this process? Or do they have difficulties with holding on to an idea and accepting feedback?

TOP TIP!

The Prototype stage is often very messy. It is important that students are focusing on their ideas, rather than the end product. Provide them with lots of materials. Students may add labels to prototypes to explain some of the main features. Photographing and annotating pictures of prototypes can be useful.

To gain feedback, students could ask each other some of the following questions:

- What is the main feature of your presentation?
- How does it show the science behind weather?
- Which aspects of the presentation work best? What will you keep?
- Which aspects need changing? How might you do this?
- What other materials, information or technology might you need?

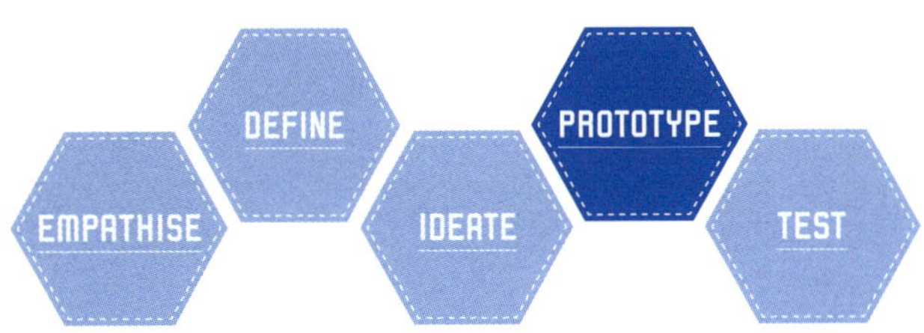

→ TEST

At this stage of the design thinking process, students test their prototype to see how it meets the criteria in the challenge. Students check to see if their prototype meets the criteria set at the start of the design process.

ACTIVITY: TEST FEEDBACK

1. Students take their last prototype and consider the initial needs of their audience.
2. Ask students to check whether or not their presentation design meets audience needs and what they need to do to ensure that it is informative and engaging.
3. Provide the opportunity to cycle through the prototyping and testing stages again.

Ask students to fill in the Test part of **Learning journal template 4 (Prototype and test page)**. See the **Journal tip** for further student guidance.

PROMPTS

- Does your presentation do what you wanted it to do?
- Does it have additional features that might help students to understand and remember?

MORE VOCABULARY

- evaluate – assess something, perhaps considering what worked and what didn't
- feature – a specific aspect of something, such as size, shape, colour and quality
- feedback – information about, for example, a person's performance or the design of a product, which can be used to make improvements
- prototype – an initial version of a model of a product or process that is used to develop a final model
- review – consider an idea, process or product and decide what needs to be changed and what works

JOURNAL TIP

Ask students to think about why it is important to test their ideas before they finalise their presentation.

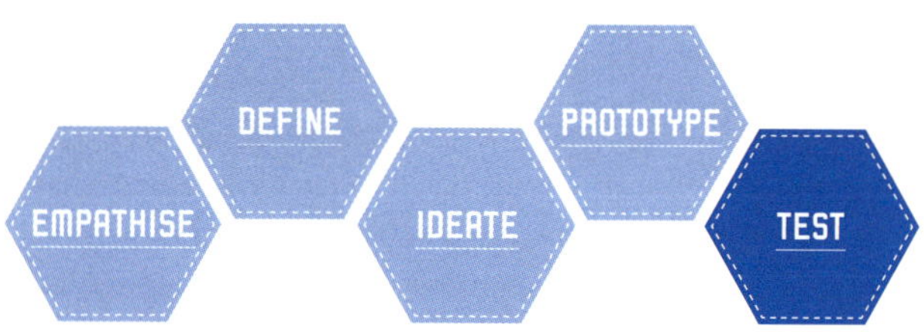

→ SHARE AND EVALUATE

At this stage of the investigation, students are provided with an opportunity to share their final design, as well as the processes involved in the investigation. Students evaluate their learning journals and their solutions.

ACTIVITY 1: BRING THE DESIGNS TOGETHER

1. Provide students with time to create final presentations. Students can create an iMovie or use Adobe Spark Video to demonstrate the process and thinking behind the designs. There should be an element of narration, where they are sharing their story about points of view, insights, prototyping and solutions.
2. Students may wish to create a podcast or a dynamic presentation (see **Useful apps/links**).
3. Students should include their learning journals with the display so others can see the different stages of the design process.

ACTIVITY 2: EVALUATE AND GIVE FEEDBACK

1. Provide students with **Generic reproducible 2 (Self-evaluation)** to complete.
2. Ask students to provide feedback to each other about the most interesting features, the difficult aspects and any changes they would make.
3. Provide students with opportunities to share their designs with the wider community. This could include inviting someone from a weather bureau or media organisation, or a friend or family member with relevant experience. It may be possible to share some of the videos with an expert for feedback about the designs.

USEFUL APPS/LINKS

- App for making dynamic presentations, such as Prezi
- App for making podcasts, such as Podbean

ASSESSMENT

Ask students to complete **Generic reproducible 1 (Key vocabulary table)** again, using the key vocabulary. Compare their table with the one they completed at the Tune-in stage, to demonstrate changes in understanding.

Students complete **Generic reproducible 3 (Responding to the investigation)**. Compare their responses to those on **Generic reproducible 2 (Self-evaluation)**.

Teachers and students each complete **Generic reproducible 5 (Design thinking assessment rubric)**. Students compare the teacher's feedback with their self-assessment of their design thinking skills.

WHICH STATE OF MATTER?

Name: ....

Date: ....

Discuss the three main states of matter: solid, liquid and gas.
Write 5 to 10 examples of each state of matter in the columns below.
Put substances that you are not sure about in the 'unsure' column.

SOLID	LIQUID	GAS	UNSURE

STEM Investigations, UP, ISBN 978 1 4202 4154 9 © Macmillan Science and Education Australia 2018

EMPATHISE

STEM INVESTIGATIONS

Name: ....

Date: ....

Watch two videos of eyewitnesses describing their experiences in an extreme weather event. Name or briefly describe each event and note other information that you have learned from the eyewitnesses.

EXTREME WEATHER EVENT 1	EXTREME WEATHER EVENT 2
Event name/description:	Event name/description:
Notes about eyewitness experiences:	Notes about eyewitness experiences:

STEM Investigations, UP, ISBN 978 1 4202 4154 9 © Macmillan Science and Education Australia 2018

IDEATE

STEM INVESTIGATIONS

Name: ....

Date: ....

Use this table to help you plan your presentation.

Weather event:
Age of audience:
Length of presentation:
Type of presentation:
Technology to use:
Important information to include:
Useful weather technology to use and explain:
Key science concepts to explain:

HELP ANIMALS CROSS THE NEW ROAD SAFELY

SUSTAINABLE WORLD 13

→ INTRODUCTION

The threat that vehicles pose to wildlife is a global one. Millions of animals are killed each year by vehicles. Most of these are small- to medium-sized animals that play an important part in their local ecosystems. Continued urbanisation is fragmenting animal habitats, which means that animals are increasingly at risk of injury or death because they graze on roadside vegetation or must cross roads to find food, shelter or a mate. The effects on individual species in an area can impact food webs and whole ecosystems.

In this STEM investigation, students are asked to create a product or process that assists animals to cross a road safely. Students will find out why so many animals are killed on the roads, the impact of this and what can be done to reduce the number of animals being killed.

Choose an appropriate local area for students to study. Provide students with a map.

THE CHALLENGE

A small rural town is connected to a highway by a gravel road through a forested area. The forested area is home to large populations of small animals. The gravel road is bumpy, so cars travel fairly slowly and the animals usually hear oncoming traffic. Roadkill rates are very low. Now, the local council wants to upgrade the road. Cars will move faster and almost silently on the new surface, endangering local animals and possibly affecting the forest ecosystem.

Your challenge is to find a way for the road designers to help an animal in your local area to cross the road. Look at a map and consider the physical features of the area. Think about the types of animals that live in the forest ecosystem. Why might they cross the road and when? As part of your challenge, you will learn about animal habitats, food webs and ecosystems, and investigate what animals need to survive.

KEY UNDERSTANDINGS

- A food web explains how plants and animals are interconnected.
- Ecosystems are communities of living things connecting with non-living things such as air and water.
- The connections between plants and animals are important.
- Reducing the numbers of particular animals can have a negative impact on ecosystems.
- Millions of animals are killed by vehicles every year.

KEY VOCABULARY

ecosystem

food web

habitat

migrate

nocturnal

KEY SKILLS

- Talk about food webs.
- Identify direct and indirect impacts of roads on animals.
- Describe some examples of how animals are being protected from vehicles.
- Consider different points of view.

KEY ACTIONS

- Explore the impact of roads on animals.
- Interview others to find out their point of view and experiences of roadkill.
- Design a product or process to assist an animal to cross the road safely.

→ OVERVIEW OF STAGES

TUNE IN:

- Learn about why animals move around their habitats.
- Find out about food webs and ask students to create their own.
- Investigate the direct and indirect impacts of roads on animals.
- Explore some of the solutions other people have created for animals in their local areas.

EMPATHISE

Students find out about some of the issues involved with roads and animals' habitats. They learn about others' reactions to seeing or hearing about animals killed by vehicles.

DEFINE

Students determine what the main issues are and choose an animal from their local area to design a product or process to protect the animal from vehicles.

IDEATE

Students generate ideas about how to protect animals from vehicles, considering the context. They sketch and label their designs.

PROTOTYPE

Students transform some of their ideas into physical representations (models). These are created rapidly, using simple materials. Students can role-play, make storyboards or use sticky notes when they prototype.

TEST

As a class, prototypes are tested by explaining the process to peers or experts. Students share their prototypes and provide feedback to each other. They are given the opportunity to cycle through the Prototype and Test stages again.

SHARE AND EVALUATE:

Final prototypes are shared and evaluated, with opportunities for expert feedback.

→ SUGGESTED SCHEDULE

LESSON	STAGE
1–2	**Tune in**: explore food webs, find out about how roads fragment habitat and disrupt food webs, and discover some of the solutions that people have created so far
3–5	**Empathise**: learn about others' responses to the impact of roads on animals, consider different case studies and write/record in journal
6	**Define**: define the main issues and write/record in journal
7	**Ideate**: develop ideas and write/record in journal
8–10	**Prototype** and **Test**: conduct prototyping and testing cycles, and write/record in journal
11–13	**Share and evaluate**: share and evaluate designs and prototypes

→ CURRICULUM LINKS

The following tables show the key Science, Technologies and Mathematics curricula with which this STEM investigation is aligned.

SCIENCE

YEAR	STRAND	SUB-STRANDS AND CONTENT
5	Science Understanding	Biological sciences: • Living things have structural features and adaptations that help them to survive in their environment
6	Science Understanding	Biological sciences: • The growth and survival of living things are affected by physical conditions of their environment
5 & 6	Science as a Human Endeavour	Nature and development of science: • Science involves testing predictions by gathering data and using evidence to develop explanations of events and phenomena
	Science Inquiry Skills	Questioning and predicting Processing and analysing data and information Communicating

TECHNOLOGIES

YEAR	STRAND	CONTENT
5 & 6	Design and Technologies Processes and Production Skills	• Generate, develop and communicate design ideas and processes for audiences using appropriate technical terms and graphical representation techniques • Develop project plans that include consideration of resources when making designed solutions individually and collaboratively

MATHEMATICS

YEAR	STRAND	SUB-STRANDS
5 & 6	Number and Algebra	Number and place value Fractions and decimals

→ OTHER CURRICULUM LINKS

GENERAL CAPABILITIES

- Literacy
- Numeracy
- Information and Communication Technology (ICT) Capability
- Critical and Creative Thinking

→ ASSESSMENT

The following resources are provided for assessing students at different stages of the STEM investigations:

- Generic reproducible 1 (Key vocabulary table), for assessing understanding of vocabulary
- Generic reproducible 2 (Self-evaluation), for student self-evaluation of the learning process
- Generic reproducible 3 (Responding to the investigation), for assessing student engagement in the challenge, and the collaboration and skills involved in the design thinking stage
- Generic reproducible 5 (Design thinking assessment rubric), for evaluating student engagement in the design thinking stages
- Learning journal templates 1, 2, 3 and 4, for incorporating student reflection and evaluation

GETTING READY FOR THE INVESTIGATION

You can prepare yourself and students for this STEM investigation in the following ways:

- Identify groups of students who will work well together.
- Review the **Key science knowledge** that supports this investigation, and look at the **Useful links**.
- Investigate the **Useful apps**.
- Gather materials for the habitat experiment.
- Start collecting additional materials for prototyping (as shown on the **Materials needed** list).
- Determine where prototypes will be kept between lessons.
- Create a wall space where students can share their ideas in the Ideate stage.
- Organise the class into pairs.
- Start thinking about:
  - » organising a guest speaker or expert
  - » how materials will be cut and any related safety issues
  - » finding images of plants and animals from forest environments.

USEFUL APPS

- App for creating a learning journal, such as Book Creator
- App for creating semantic maps (links between different words and/or concepts), such as Popplet
- App for creating interactive links (for example, between descriptions, videos, images and websites and a main image), such as ThingLink
- App for creating multimedia presentations, such as Adobe Spark Video and iMovie
- Survey app such as Typeform (free for small surveys)

USEFUL LINKS

- Information about wildlife crossings, such as at faunacrossings.com.au
- Solutions to wildlife crossing infrastructure, such as at arc-solutions.org/new-solutions
- Fauna-sensitive road design guidelines, such as at tinyurl.com/y8sgorae
- Koala tunnels and bridges , such as at tinyurl.com/y9pnm763
- Purpose-built crossings (a bridge for crabs and a penguin underpass), such as at tinyurl.com/ycj8lkmp

RESOURCES PROVIDED

- Generic reproducibles 1, 2, 3, 4, 5, 6
- Reproducibles 13.1, 13.2, 13.3
- Learning journal templates 1, 2, 3, 4 (on disc)

MATERIALS NEEDED

- Sticky notes (half a pad per pair)
- Paper
- Coloured card
- Pens and markers
- Sticky tape
- Masking tape
- Pipe-cleaners
- Cardboard
- Straws
- Plastic pipes
- Hot glue guns and glue

KEY SCIENCE KNOWLEDGE

This section provides an overview of the key science concepts and vocabulary needed for this unit.

HABITATS, FOOD WEBS AND ECOSYSTEMS

A **habitat** is the natural environment of a living thing, which provides food, water, shelter and areas to reproduce and raise young. A forest is one type of habitat.

- Forest habitats support many forest-dwelling or forest-dependent animal and plant species.
- Coniferous forests occur in the northern hemisphere, and mainly consist of cone-bearing fir trees.
- Temperate forests are found in both the northern and southern hemispheres.
- Rainforests can be tropical or cool to temperate, with tropical forests found close to the equator.

Each type of forest contains particular species of plants and animals.

Food webs show the feeding relationships among and between plants and animals. Plants are the basic food sources that sustain most life forms; they make food by photosynthesis. Herbivores obtain energy by eating plants, and carnivores obtain energy by eating the herbivores. Food webs can be disrupted if something affects them. For example, if there are too many carnivores the herbivores reduce or die out, then the plants thrive and the carnivores move out or starve.

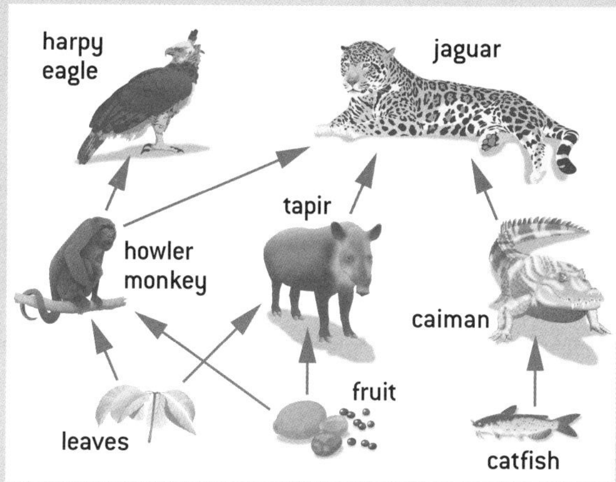

A food web shows the feeding relationships between living things. These arrows point to what each plant or animal is eaten by.

Ecosystems are food webs plus the non-living things in a natural environment that plants and animals need, such as air and water. Like food webs, they can be altered. If plants reduce in numbers or die, for example, due to drought or polluted water, the animals have to move elsewhere to find food and water.

Animals move about to find food, water, shelter and to reproduce. If a road divides a forest habitat, animals must go across it to do these things. Construction of roads removes habitat, which may include food sources and shelter. Roads can act as a barrier, isolating groups of animals from different food sources, mates for reproduction or other animal groups.

Roads are dangerous places for animals.

ANIMAL MOVEMENT

For some animals, food sources change with the seasons, so they need to **migrate** to other places. For non-flying animals, roads can be a considerable challenge, as their usual green 'corridors' have been fragmented. **Nocturnal** animals are particularly vulnerable, because they are active at night, when road visibility is poor.

KEY VOCABULARY

ecosystem – a community of living things, including plants and animals, and the non-living things that they need, such as air and water

food web – a set of feeding relationships among and between plants and animals

habitat – the natural environment of a living thing

migrate – move from one place to another with the seasons, for example, to breed or find food

nocturnal – active during the night

→ TUNE IN

1. Ask students to complete **Generic reproducible 1 (Key vocabulary table)** using the key vocabulary for this unit: ecosystem, food web, fragmented, habitat, migrate, nocturnal. This reproducible will also be used at the end of the unit, to demonstrate changes in understanding.
2. Ask students to complete a mind map to illustrate what they know about forests and the plants and animals that live in them. This will also be used at the end of the unit, to demonstrate changes in understanding.
3. Watch a video clip about rainforests or dry sclerophyll forests (see **Useful apps/links**).
4. Discuss the types of plants and animals featured in the video. What are the characteristics of the forest habitat?

ACTIVITY 1: FOREST ANIMALS AND PLANTS

1. Prepare a slideshow of various plants and animals (native as well as introduced).
2. Ask students to identify and list the animals and plants that can be found in their local forest or parkland. Why did they think these would be there?
3. In pairs, students use their local animal and plant list to construct a food web. The arrows should point to the recipient of the energy gain.
4. Ask students what happens if part of a food web is changed or removed (for example, the major predator or some of the plants). Students discuss using their food web and present their findings.
5. Ask students to write the names of the plants and animals onto pieces of paper or card. Review the terms 'indigenous' and 'non-indigenous'. Link them to the word 'native'. Students sort the plants and animals into indigenous and non-indigenous species and then check their selections.
6. Discuss why the death of native animals may be particularly problematic.

ACTIVITY 2: MODEL A FOREST HABITAT

1. Ask student pairs to research one of the animals from the food web and determine what food it needs, where it finds water and shelter, and where it raises its young. What plants and other natural features (living and non-living) are part of its habitat? Use **Reproducible 13.1 (Animal needs)** to gather information.
2. Have each student pair construct a diorama that models this habitat.
3. Each group presents their diorama to the class and explains what is represented.

ACTIVITY 3: DIRECT AND INDIRECT IMPACTS

1. Ask students to think about the direct and indirect impacts of a road on the animals in a natural environment. Direct impacts include injury or death of smaller animals, particularly nocturnal ones, due to poor visibility to drivers. Indirect impacts include fragmentation of green 'corridors' and of animal groups. Encourage them to relate the impacts to food webs and ecosystems.
2. Make a list of current road features for animal safety (positive and negative). Use **Reproducible 13.2 (Road features)** as a guide. Make sure students consider the 'barrier effect', which reduces animals' ability to move between environments. Encourage students to think about ways to improve the safety features (see **Useful apps/links**).

5. Introduce the STEM investigation and challenge to the students. Provide them with the student card and read the information together. Identify the area that the students will be studying, and give them a printed map or access to Google Maps. Ask students to think about the types of animals they might want to design a safe road crossing for, as well as their habitat.
6. Introduce the design thinking process by reviewing the stages on the student card.
7. Explain that students will keep a journal about their learning at the different stages of the design.

TOP TIP! During the Tune-in session, conduct vocabulary activities to highlight and develop key vocabulary knowledge. Activities could include drawing semantic webs, creating a word wall or paired discussions. Check the **Key vocabulary** definitions or read the **Key science knowledge** for a refresher on the key terms and concepts.

USEFUL APPS/LINKS

- Descriptions of rainforest and dry sclerophyll forest, such as at gullivermedia.com.au/resources-for-schools/for-schools.php and steveparish-natureconnect.com.au/nature-centre/dry-sclerophyll-forests
- Fauna-sensitive road design guidelines, such as at tinyurl.com/y8sgorae

→ EMPATHISE

During the Empathise stage of the design thinking process, students focus on finding out about different points of view. To empathise with others, they find out their opinions and experiences of roadkill. They gather insights from case studies and also consider their own points of view. Students will observe, take notes, ask questions, draw diagrams and take photos where relevant.

ACTIVITY 1: INTERVIEW

1. Students interview a partner to find out their experiences and reactions to seeing animals that have been injured or killed by a vehicle. If a student hasn't experienced this, they can be asked to consider how they might feel.
2. Provide students with **Reproducible 13.3 (Student interview)**. This will help guide students through the interview process and assist them to take notes.
3. Students take turns interviewing another student.

ACTIVITY 2: OBSERVE

1. Look at some case studies about issues to do with vehicles injuring or killing animals and about attempts to protect local wildlife (see **Useful apps/links**).
2. Students discuss their responses to the information.

ACTIVITY 3: EMPATHISE

1. Ask students to consider other students' responses to animal injury and death due to roads and vehicles.
2. Provide students with **Learning journal template 1 (Empathise page)**. Ask:
   - » What are some of the animals injured or killed by vehicles?
   - » What were the main points that you learned?
   - » How did people react when they found out the number of animals being injured or killed by vehicles?
   - » What information surprised you?

MORE VOCABULARY

- empathise – understand and consider another person's or group's point of view
- point of view – an opinion, attitude or judgement considered in a particular way

JOURNAL TIP

Ask students to complete **Learning journal template 1 (Empathise page)** while they are completing the different tasks. Remind them to date their notes and include photos and drawings of relevant information.

USEFUL APPS/LINKS

- Areas where roadkill rates are high, such as at sbs.com.au/news/article/2016/04/01/tas-roadkill-problem-worst-experts
- Attempts by young people to protect local wildlife, such as at scientificamerican.com/article/roadkill-endangers-endangered-wildlife

ASSESSMENT

This stage of the design thinking process offers opportunities to observe students collecting information, developing questions, and recording their notes and thinking in their journal.

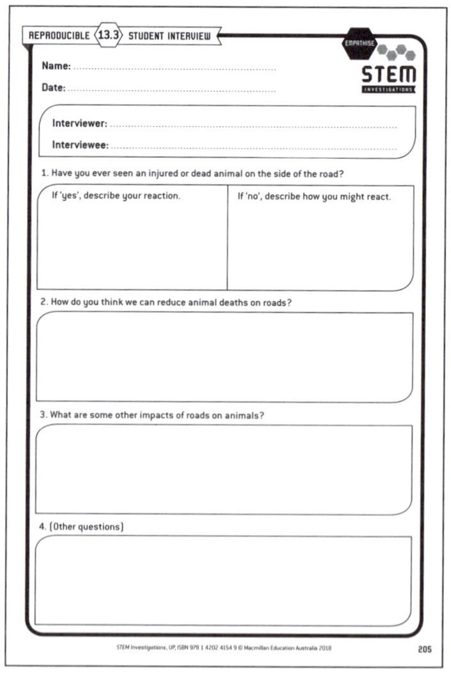

REPRODUCIBLE 13.3 STUDENT INTERVIEW

EMPATHISE

STEM INVESTIGATIONS

Name: ....

Date: ....

Interviewer: ....

Interviewee: ....

1. Have you ever seen an injured or dead animal on the side of the road?

If 'yes', describe your reaction.	If 'no', describe how you might react.

2. How do you think we can reduce animal deaths on roads?

3. What are some other impacts of roads on animals?

4. (Other questions)

STEM Investigations, UP, ISBN 978 1 4202 4154 9 © Macmillan Education Australia 2018 205

Reproducible 13.3 (Student interview)

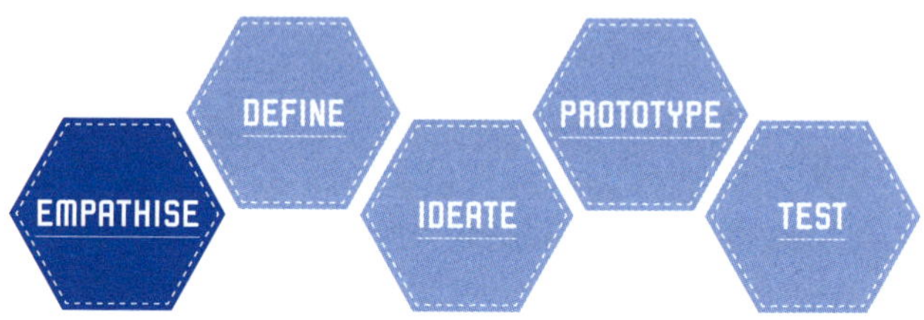

→ DEFINE

The main focus of this stage of the design thinking process is to reframe the challenge. The initial challenge is quite open, so at this stage students learn how to define what needs to be done. This includes noting insights that have been generated.

ACTIVITY 1: CONSIDER OBSERVATIONS

1. Students consider the information they gathered in the Empathise stage. They may work in pairs or small groups. Provide them with a whiteboard, large sheet of paper and/or sticky notes to collate some of the key information they have gathered about the number and types of animals affected, and the responses of other people, including how they feel about this issue.
2. Students should discuss one section of **Learning journal template 2 (Define page)** at a time, write their responses, and then continue discussing their ideas for the next section, until the task is complete. This provides students with opportunities to hear others' responses and also provides the teacher with input points.
3. Discuss the information gathered about animals that are injured or killed on the roads. Provide students with the opportunity to research further. Ask them to write other information they would like to know, such as different ways that people, groups and organisations have helped to reduce the number of deaths, road construction information and which animals in their local area may be affected. Provide them with **Generic reproducible 4 (Key question table)** to assist them to record their questions, findings and sources.

ACTIVITY 2: CONSIDER INSIGHTS

1. Students think of at least one insight they have gained from the process; for example, the issue is a global one, small- to medium-sized animals are at greatest risk, and people are trying to address the issue in many ways.
2. Students add this insight to **Learning journal template 2 (Define page)**. They should then relate the insight to their design. When considering insights, students could think about the following:
   » What was something unexpected that you saw or found out? How was it unexpected?
   » How will you decide on the most important aspect of the road crossing design?
   » Is there any other information that you need or would like to know? How will you find out?

ACTIVITY 3: CONSIDER CONSTRAINTS

At this stage, let students know the constraints of the challenge, by describing the schedule, maximum size of designs and materials to access. Students can then update **Learning journal template 2**.

PROMPTS

- What did you discover?
- What were the most important pieces of information that you gathered?
- What was something new that you learned?
- What other information do you need?

MORE VOCABULARY

- define – state the meaning of something
- insight – an accurate understanding of someone or something

JOURNAL TIP

Discuss the term 'insight'. Explain that it relates to something students have learned about the people and their responses to the surveys, as well as information gathered through research or excursions. You could refer to **Learning journal template 2**.

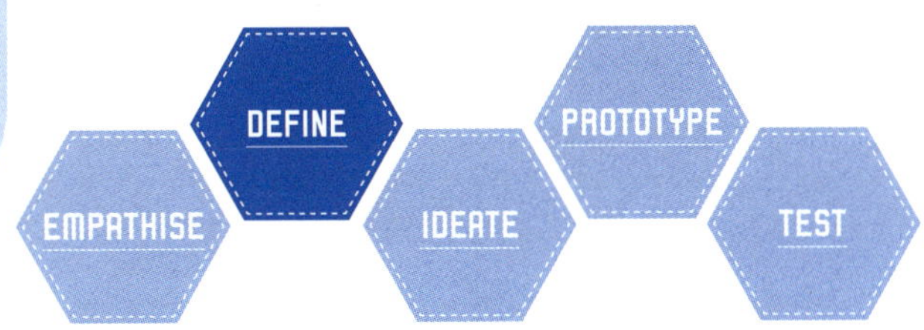

→ IDEATE

The Ideate stage of the design thinking process is all about generating lots of ideas. Students need to be flexible in their thinking and able to move beyond obvious ideas. At this stage, ideas are not judged, just generated and gathered.

ACTIVITY: GENERATE IDEAS

1. Ask groups of students to draw or write their ideas. Each new idea should be written or drawn on a separate piece of paper or sticky note.
2. Ask students to group ideas on a wall or board.
3. Ask students to look at the different ideas and provide feedback to each other. It is important that students don't defend their ideas at this stage. They should just be listening to the feedback.
4. After the initial feedback, ask students to come up with more ideas. Encourage them to be creative and even radical.
5. Ask students to choose four of their ideas to write in their journal. Students use **Learning journal template 3 (Ideate page)** to do this. Ask students to choose one idea to explore further and explain the reasoning behind their choice.

TOP TIP!

At this stage, students may have produced a series of annotated drawings about how to create a safe crossing for an animal. They may have a collection of sticky notes, which they can organise into related ideas.

Encourage students to view and read others' ideas before giving feedback. Feedback could be within small groups or between partners. Considering others' ideas is an important part of this process, so students can build on their own ideas as they continue to ideate.

At each stage of this activity, ask students to discuss their thoughts before writing their responses. This will help them to think through their ideas and select their final ideas to develop.

PROMPTS

- How do your chosen ideas relate to the animal you are designing this road crossing for?
- How might you test your design?
- How can you make it accessible for the animal?
- How can you make it possible to build?
- What if you had to use different materials?

MORE VOCABULARY

- feedback – information about, for example, a person's performance or the design of a product, which can be used to make improvements
- ideate – generate many ideas without making judgements about the ideas

JOURNAL TIP

When choosing four ideas to include in the journal, students should try to choose four ideas that aren't related, to show a range of ideas.

USEFUL APPS/LINKS

- Tools for creating ideas, such as at creatingminds.org/tools/tools_ideation.htm
- Tips for creativity and innovation, such as at designorate.com/creativity-innovation-in-education/

ASSESSMENT

At the Ideate stage, assessment could include observations about the number and diversity of students' ideas, and their ability to provide feedback and create additional ideas. Reflection in the journal should provide an insight into some of the reasoning behind students' choices.

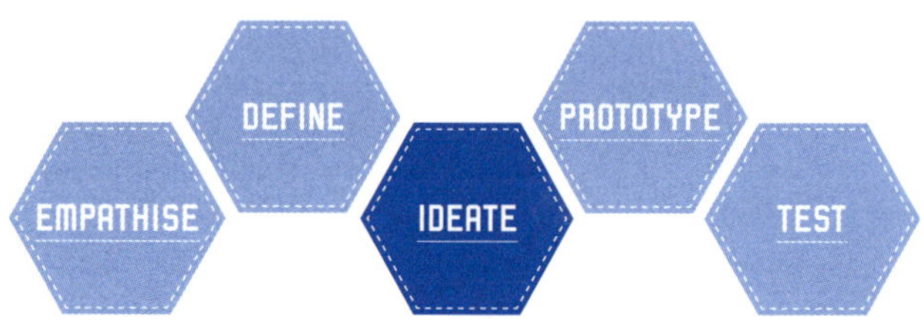

→ PROTOTYPE

At this stage of the design thinking process, students are asked to create a physical prototype of a solution. It is the stage where students need to get their ideas out of their head and presented in a way that engages other students and helps them to understand the ideas. When students create, it helps them to think and solve problems and disagreements. Students can role-play, make storyboards or use sticky notes when they prototype. The most important feature is that viewers can interact with whatever is produced.

Encourage students to photograph or film during the prototyping and testing stages. This information can be used to show the learning behind the design thinking process in action.

ACTIVITY: TRANSFORM IDEAS INTO PROTOTYPES

1. Students review the ideas generated at the Ideate stage. Provide them with an A3 copy of **Generic reproducible 6 (In the frame)** so they can organise their ideas into two sections: least relevant and most relevant. Students continue to cycle through this activity until they have an idea to start prototyping.
2. Provide students with a range of materials to use to create their prototype. Remind students that a prototype should be created rapidly and is not meant to look 'nice'.
3. After a prototype has been created, ask students to see if it works and get feedback from others.
4. Students then use the feedback to prototype again.

Ask students to fill in the Prototype part of **Learning journal template 4 (Prototype and test page)**. See the Journal tip for further student guidance.

TOP TIP!

The Prototype stage is often very messy. It is important that students are focusing on their ideas, rather than the end product. Provide them with lots of materials – recycling depots can be a useful source of resources. Students may add labels to prototypes to explain some of the main features. Photographing and annotating pictures of prototypes can be useful.

To gain feedback, students could ask each other some of the following questions:

- What is the main feature of your prototype?
- How does your prototype work?
- Which aspects work best? What will you keep?
- Which aspects need changing? How might you do this?
- What other materials might you need?

PROMPTS

- What worked?
- How could it be improved?
- What else do you need to know, do or have?
- What other suggestions do you have?

MORE VOCABULARY

- feedback – information about, for example, a person's performance or the design of a product, which can be used to make improvements
- prototype – an initial version of a model of a product or process that is used to develop a final model

JOURNAL TIP

Remind students to highlight the main features of their prototype. If students are creating an electronic journal, they can insert a photo of their prototype and annotate it.

USEFUL APPS/LINKS

- App for creating interactive links (for example, between descriptions, videos, images and websites and a main image), such as ThingLink
- App for making notes using text, drawings, images, weblinks and audio, such as Notability

ASSESSMENT

Observe students as they make changes to their designs. Are they able to consider feedback, make modifications and move rapidly through this process? Or do they have difficulties with holding onto an idea and accepting feedback?

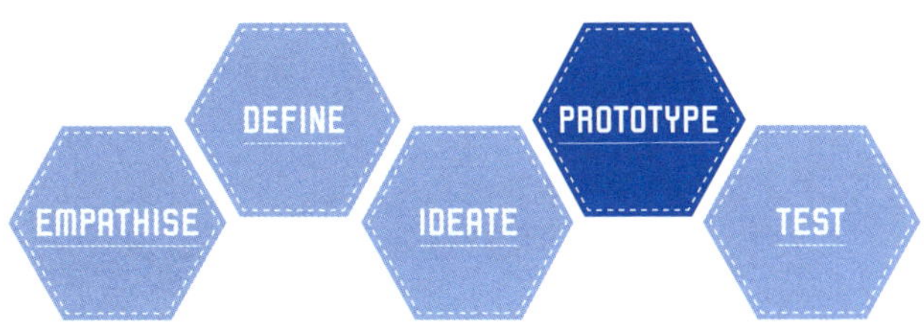

TEST

At this stage of the design thinking process, students test their prototype to see how it meets the criteria in the challenge. Students check to see if their prototype meets the criteria set at the start of the design process.

ACTIVITY: TEST FEEDBACK

1. Students take their last prototype and consider the initial needs of the animal they have chosen, as well as the location.
2. Ask students to think about how they will check whether or not their design works. If not, what do they need to do to make it work? This may need to include feedback from an expert, such as a member of an environment research organisation.
3. Provide the opportunity to cycle through the prototyping and testing stages again.

Ask students to fill in the Test part of **Learning journal template 4 (Prototype and test page)**. See the **Journal tip** for further student guidance.

PROMPTS

- Does your prototype do what you wanted it to do?
- Are there other features you could add?
- What needs to be changed?
- What works well?

MORE VOCABULARY

- evaluate – assess something, perhaps considering what worked and what didn't
- feature – a specific aspect of something, such as size, shape, colour and quality
- feedback – information about, for example, a person's performance or the design of a product, which can be used to make improvements
- prototype – an initial version of a model of a product or process that is used to develop a final model
- review – consider an idea, process or product and decide what needs to be changed and what works

JOURNAL TIP

Ask students to think about why it is important to test their ideas before they build their final design.

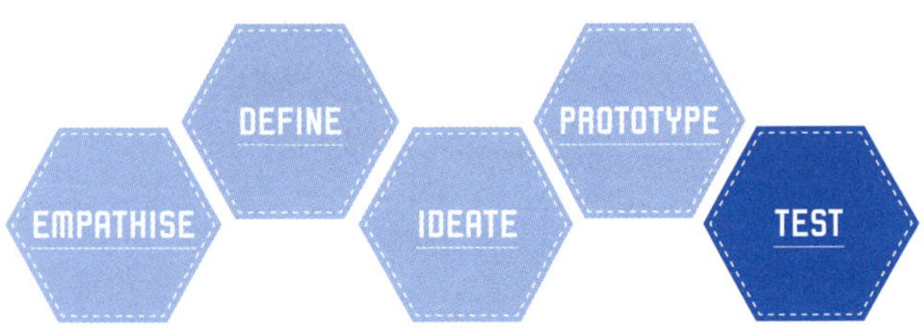

SHARE AND EVALUATE

At this stage of the investigation, students are provided with an opportunity to share their final design, as well as the processes involved in the investigation. Students evaluate their learning journals as well as their solutions.

ACTIVITY 1: BRING THE DESIGNS TOGETHER

1. Students can create an iMovie or use Adobe Spark Video to demonstrate the process and thinking behind the designs. There should be an element of narration, where they are sharing their story about points of view, insights, prototyping and solutions.
2. Students should include their learning journals with the display.

ACTIVITY 2: EVALUATE AND GIVE FEEDBACK

1. Provide students with **Generic reproducible 2 (Self-evaluation)** to complete.
2. Ask students to provide feedback to each other about the most interesting features, the aspects that were most difficult and the changes that they would make if they repeated the task.
3. Provide students with opportunities to share their designs with the wider community. It may be possible to organise for a member of the local council or a politician to view the designs and provide feedback about their viability for the area.

ASSESSMENT

Ask students to again complete **Generic reproducible 1 (Key vocabulary table)** using the key vocabulary for this unit: ecosystem, food web, fragmented, habitat, migrate, nocturnal. Compare their table with the one they completed at the Tune-in stage, to demonstrate changes in understanding.

Students complete **Generic reproducible 3 (Responding to the investigation)**. Compare their responses to those on **Generic reproducible 2**.

Teachers and students each complete **Generic reproducible 5 (Design thinking assessment rubric)**. Students compare the teacher feedback with their self-assessment of their design thinking skills.

STEM INVESTIGATIONS

Name: ....

Date: ....

Animal: ....

FOOD	
WATER SOURCE	
TYPES OF SHELTER	
PLANTS IN HABITAT	
OTHER	

STEM Investigations, UP, ISBN 978 1 4202 4154 9 © Macmillan Science and Education Australia 2018

Name: ....

Date: ....

STEM INVESTIGATIONS

POSITIVE FEATURES

ROAD FEATURES

NEGATIVE FEATURES

STEM Investigations, UP, ISBN 978 1 4202 4154 9 © Macmillan Science and Education Australia 2018

EMPATHISE

STEM INVESTIGATIONS

Name: ....

Date: ....

Interviewer: ....

Interviewee: ....

1. Have you ever seen an injured or dead animal on the side of the road?

If 'yes', describe your reaction.	If 'no', describe how you might react.

2. How do you think we can reduce animal deaths on roads?

3. What are some other impacts of roads on animals?

4. (Other questions)

CREATE SUSTAINABLE GARDEN BEDS AT SCHOOL

SUSTAINABLE WORLD 14

→ INTRODUCTION

Environmental sustainability is about using resources in a way that minimises impact on the ability to use those resources in the future. Being sustainable includes reducing the use of non-renewable resources, recycling and reusing.

In this STEM investigation, students are asked to create a sustainable kitchen garden bed to grow food for students to use or sell. They are asked to find out about sustainable gardening practices and how these can be applied to a school or home garden.

THE CHALLENGE

The student sustainability club at your school has a new project. They already collect organic scraps for compost and worm farm bins. Now, they want to reuse waste and other materials to create sustainable, low-cost garden beds that require very little water. Can you help?

Your challenge is to design four garden beds on a tight budget that includes the cost of soil and seeds. Each garden bed must include one recycled item, and needs its own irrigation system. Think creatively and sustainably. Do you have old crates that could be reused as herb gardens? Can you get your irrigation system to work at night, when it is cooler? Which kinds of plants will grow best together? As part of your challenge, you will learn about sustainable practices and calculating capacity and volume.

KEY UNDERSTANDINGS

- Environmental sustainability is about using resources carefully to make sure they are still available in the future.
- Being sustainable includes reducing, reusing and recycling materials.
- The choices we make about using materials can have an impact on the health of the environment.

KEY VOCABULARY

capacity
environmental sustainability
irrigation
organic waste
recycling
volume

KEY SKILLS

- Describe environmental sustainability.
- Explain and describe reusing, recycling and reducing.
- Identify ways of being sustainable.
- Explain how irrigation systems can use water more efficiently.

KEY ACTIONS

- Gather information about sustainable growing practices, including composting.
- Design an irrigation system.
- Create a garden bed from reused and recycled materials.

→ OVERVIEW OF STAGES

TUNE IN:

Students learn about sustainable practices – in particular, reducing, recycling and reusing materials. They explore differences between organic and non-organic waste, and find out about composting. Students also learn about volume in order to plan and construct a garden bed.

EMPATHISE

Students find out what needs to be considered when using organic waste in a garden.

DEFINE

Students find out about the types and amount of organic waste generated, and how much is thrown away. Students consider the link between composting and sustainability.

IDEATE

Students generate ideas about how to create a sustainable garden bed. They sketch and label their designs.

PROTOTYPE

Students choose one or two ideas to transform into physical representations (models). These are created rapidly, using simple materials.

TEST

As a class, prototypes are tested. Students share their prototypes and provide feedback to each other. They are given the opportunity to cycle through the Prototype and Test stages again.

SHARE AND EVALUATE:

Final prototypes are shared and evaluated, with opportunities for expert feedback investigated. Students consider whether or not their designs could be scaled up to create a functioning kitchen garden bed.

→ SUGGESTED SCHEDULE

LESSON	STAGE
1–2	**Tune in**: explore sustainability (including reducing, recycling and reusing), composting, plant cycles, and organic and non-organic waste
3–5	**Empathise**: interview others about sustainability, composting and organic waste, audit organic waste generation at home, and write/record in journal
6	**Define**: define the main issues and write/record in journal
7	**Ideate**: develop ideas and write/record in journal
8–10	**Prototype** and **Test**: conduct prototyping and testing cycles, and write/record in journal
11–13	**Share and evaluate**: share and evaluate designs and prototypes

→ CURRICULUM LINKS

The following tables show the key Science, Technologies and Mathematics curricula with which this STEM investigation is aligned.

SCIENCE

YEAR	STRAND	SUB-STRANDS AND CONTENT
5	Science Understanding	Biological sciences: • Living things have structural features and adaptations that help them to survive in their environment
6	Science Understanding	Biological sciences: • The growth and survival of living things are affected by physical conditions of their environment
5 & 6	Science as a Human Endeavour	Use and influence of science: • Scientific knowledge is used to solve problems and inform personal and community decisions
	Science Inquiry Skills	Planning and conducting: • Evaluating

TECHNOLOGIES

YEAR	STRAND	CONTENT
5 & 6	Design and Technologies Knowledge and Understanding	• Investigate how and why food and fibre are produced in managed environments and prepared to enable people to grow and be healthy
	Design and Technologies Processes and Production Skills	• Critique needs or opportunities for designing, and investigate materials, components, tools, equipment and processes to achieve intended designed solutions • Generate, develop and communicate design ideas and processes for audiences using appropriate technical terms and graphical representation techniques • Select appropriate materials, components, tools, equipment and techniques and apply safe procedures to make designed solutions • Negotiate criteria for success that include sustainability to evaluate design ideas, processes and solutions • Develop project plans that include consideration of resources when making designed solutions individually and collaboratively

MATHEMATICS

YEAR	STRAND	SUB-STRANDS
5 & 6	Measurement and Geometry	Using units of measurement

→ OTHER CURRICULUM LINKS

GENERAL CAPABILITIES

- Literacy
- Numeracy
- Information and Communication Technology (ICT) Capability
- Critical and Creative Thinking

→ ASSESSMENT

The following resources are provided for assessing students at different stages of the STEM investigations:

- Generic reproducible 1 (Key vocabulary table), for assessing understanding of vocabulary
- Generic reproducible 2 (Self-evaluation), for student self-evaluation of the learning process
- Generic reproducible 3 (Responding to the investigation), for assessing student engagement in the challenge, and the collaboration and skills involved in the design thinking stages
- Generic reproducible 5 (Design thinking assessment rubric), for evaluating student engagement in the design thinking stages
- Learning journal templates 1, 2, 3 and 4, for incorporating student reflection and evaluation

→ GETTING READY FOR THE INVESTIGATION

You can prepare yourself and students for this STEM investigation in the following ways:

- Identify groups of students who will work well together.
- Review the **Key science knowledge** that supports this investigation, and look at the **Useful links**.
- Investigate the **Useful apps**.
- Gather materials for creating a garden bed.
- Start collecting additional materials for prototype and full-scale models (if completed) (as shown on the **Materials needed** list).
- Determine where prototypes will be kept between lessons.
- Create a wall space where students can share their ideas in the Ideate stage, as well as their wondering questions about sustainability.
- Organise the class into pairs.
- Start thinking about:
  - » whether or not students will build a full-scale model, including the safe handling of soil and organic waste
  - » who might be available to mentor students regarding sustainable practices and construction techniques
  - » whether it is possible to find sponsorship for creation of the garden beds.

USEFUL APPS

- App for creating a learning journal, such as Book Creator
- App for creating semantic maps (links between different words and/or concepts), such as Popplet
- App for creating interactive links (for example, between descriptions, videos, images and websites and a main image), such as ThingLink
- App for creating multimedia presentations, such as Adobe Spark Video and iMovie
- App for creating surveys, such as Typeform (free for small surveys)
- App that allows students to independently document what they are learning at school, such as SeeSaw
- App for conversation with students and teachers, such as Today's Meet
- App for creating three-dimensional designs, such as SketchUp
- App for idea collection and sharing, such as Padlet

USEFUL LINKS

- Information and activity about structural features of a plant, such as at splash.abc.net.au/home#!/media/1496591/plant-scan
- Information about caring for a garden, such as at compostrocks.com.au
- Guidelines for designing a drip irrigation system, such as at mysmartgarden.org.au/en/Resources/Water/Drip-Irrigation-Design-Guidelines
- Information about volume and capacity, such as at splash.abc.net.au/home#!/topic/496722/volume-and-capacity
- A junior maths dictionary, such as at amathsdictionaryforkids.com

RESOURCES PROVIDED

- Generic reproducibles 1, 2, 3, 4, 5, 6, 9
- Reproducibles 14.1, 14.2, 14.3
- Learning journal templates 1, 2, 3, 4 (on disc)

MATERIALS NEEDED

- Sticky notes (half a pad per pair)
- Paper
- Coloured card
- Pens and markers
- Sticky tape
- Pipe-cleaners
- Wooden craft sticks
- Balsa wood
- Straws
- Scissors
- Craft knives and cutting boards
- Cardboard
- Recycled materials, such as plastic piping, wooden crates, plastic bottles, plastic sheeting
- Soil
- Compost
- Seeds and plants

KEY KNOWLEDGE

This section provides an overview of the key science and maths concepts and vocabulary needed for this unit.

Environmental sustainability is about a way of using resources that can be continued into the future. Examples include making less waste, using less water and energy, and recycling. Unsustainable practices include cutting down old forests, using petrol-powered cars and overfishing.

STRUCTURAL FEATURES OF PLANTS

Structural features of a plant include roots, flowers, stem and leaves. The root structures are designed to pull water and minerals from the soil. The stem transports food and water and acts as a support structure. Leaves are all about photosynthesis, creating food molecules and absorbing carbon dioxide for the plant. These parts are connected by the vascular system of xylem and phloem that spreads through the entire plant.

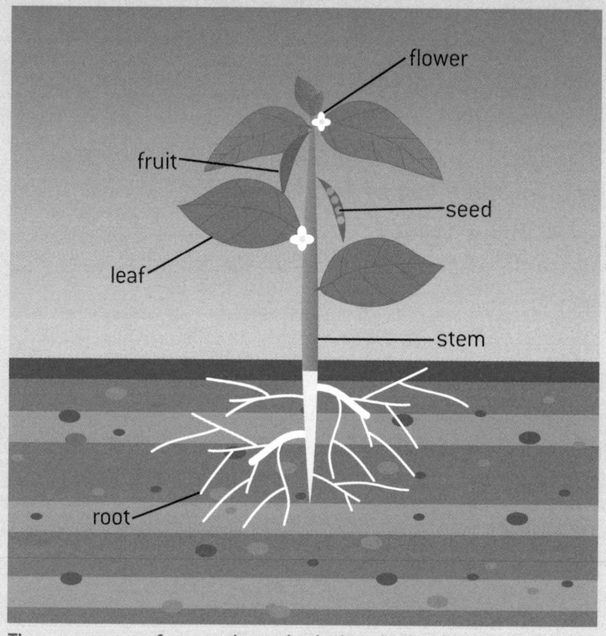

The structure of most plants includes the leaf, stem and roots.

COMPOSTING

Compost made from **organic waste** can be used to improve soil, adding important nutrients and minerals. These nutrients and minerals can be taken up by plants through their root structures. Composting organic waste is a form of environmental sustainability.

AREA, VOLUME AND CAPACITY

Area is the size of a surface. Area = length × width. Some examples of units of area are square metres and hectares. **Volume** is the amount of space occupied by a three-dimensional object. Volume = length × width × height. Some examples of units of volume are cubic metres and litres. **Capacity** is the maximum amount a container can hold. It can have many different units of measurement.

When you are building a container such as a garden bed, you need to determine what area your plants will need (including an **irrigation** system to water them) and how deep they need the soil to be. You can then calculate what capacity the garden bed must have and the volume of soil and organic waste required to fill the garden bed.

COMPOSTABLE MATERIALS

Green materials	Brown materials
fruit scraps	pine needles
vegetable scraps	straw
coffee grounds	shredded newspaper
fresh grass clippings	dead leaves
weeds	dried plant cuttings
fresh plant cuttings	wood chips

A successful compost heap needs a mix of green (nitrogen-rich) materials and brown (carbon-rich) materials. The recommended ratio is 25 parts brown to 1 part green.

KEY VOCABULARY

capacity – the maximum amount a container can hold
environmental sustainability – careful use of resources so that they are available in the future
irrigation – the supply of certain amounts of water to plants at particular times, to grow crops
organic waste – material from animals and plants that is thrown away (for example, horse manure and food scraps)
recycling – making an object that includes something that has been used before
volume – the amount of space taken up by a solid

TUNE IN

1. Ask students to complete **Generic reproducible 1 (Key vocabulary table)** using the key vocabulary for this unit: capacity, environmental sustainability, irrigation, organic waste, recycling, volume. This reproducible will also be used at the end of the unit, to demonstrate changes in understanding.
2. Provide students with pictures of items that are thrown away, both organic and non-organic. Discuss the terms 'organic' and 'non-organic', then ask students to sort the images into the two categories. Students can think of additional items to add to this classification activity.
3. Provide information and statistics about organic waste. Provide students with time to find out more facts and create an information wall or electronic collection, using an app for idea collection and sharing (see **Useful apps/links**).
4. Watch a video clip about how much general waste there is in the world. Discuss students' responses.
5. Provide students with some information and statistics about organic waste. Students create a 'Did you know?' wall with facts about organic waste, incorporating local, national and global information. Add to the wall as the investigation progresses. Before engaging in the challenge, students need to have an understanding of sustainability, including reducing, recycling and reusing resources; volume and area; and the plant life cycle.

ACTIVITY 1: ENVIRONMENTAL SUSTAINABILITY

1. Ask students to consider the question, 'What is a sustainable use of organic waste?' Students use a student–teacher conversation app (see **Useful apps/links**) and brainstorm ideas about organic waste and how it can be used at school.
2. Collect information on how much organic waste can be collected at school in one day by completing an audit. Gather information about how much was gathered for each year level and the different types of organic waste collected. Use this information to calculate how much organic waste is gathered in a week and a school year.
3. Ask students to find out about how organic waste can be reduced so that less ends up in landfill.
4. Ask students to complete **Generic reproducible 9 (See, think, wonder)**, considering the information collected about organic waste creation at school. Provide space for key questions from the 'I wonder' section to be displayed in the classroom. Students can add information that answers the questions as the investigation continues.

ACTIVITY 2: VOLUME

1. Brainstorm the concepts of area, volume and capacity during a maths lesson. Provide students with two copies of **Reproducible 14.1 (Area, volume and capacity)**. Students work in pairs, then display their ideas.
2. Give pairs of students a piece of paper and ask them to create a box. Ask them to estimate the volume and area of the box. Then give students centimetre cubes and ask them to work out how many cubes the box can hold. Video-record students' understandings using a student documenting app (see **Useful apps/links**). Ask students to share their strategies.

ACTIVITY 3: PLANT CYCLE AND PLANT NEEDS

1. View a video clip or diagram about the plant cycle and plant needs. Discuss the key needs of plants, such as water, nutrients from soil and sunlight.
2. Discuss the different stages of the plant cycle and ask students to share their experiences of growing plants.
3. Ask students to create an animation of the plant cycle or plant needs.

6. Introduce the STEM investigation and challenge. Provide students with the student card and read the information together. Walk around the school looking for potential garden beds and items that can be recycled. Organise students into groups of four. Encourage students to think about cost-effective recycling ideas.
7. Introduce the design thinking process by reviewing the stages on the student card.
8. Explain that students will keep a journal about their learning at the different stages of the design. Allow students time to research irrigation systems and plant produce based on location, climate and season.

USEFUL APPS/LINKS

- App for idea collection and sharing, such as Padlet
- App for conversation with students and teachers, such as Today's Meet
- App that allows students to independently document what they are learning at school, such as SeeSaw

→ EMPATHISE

During the Empathise stage of the design thinking process, students focus on finding out about different points of view. To empathise with others, they need to research some of the experiences that people have had with organic waste in their homes. Students will observe others, taking notes, asking questions and taking photos where possible.

ACTIVITY 1: ORGANIC WASTE AUDIT

1. Ask students to audit their organic waste at home. Provide them with **Reproducible 14.2 (Organic waste audit)** for recording information.
2. Compare amounts and types of organic waste, including paper, between households. Students can take photographs or make lists of the rough amounts of different types of waste.

> Be mindful of the potential hazards associated with organic waste and the precautions that may need to be taken if students are collecting or handling it.

ACTIVITY 2: COMPOST SURVEY

1. Students create a survey, using pen and paper, or a survey app, such as Typeform or Survey Monkey. Information to be collected could include what people know about composting, which organic waste composts the quickest/slowest and ways organic waste can be used. Provide students with **Reproducible 14.3 (Compost survey plan)** to help them plan their survey.
2. Students collate information from their survey and create a short summary of their findings. Encourage students to consider further questions they have that result from their survey findings.
3. Ask students to review the information they have gathered.

PROMPTS

- What types of organic waste were found?
- What was the most common type of waste?
- What were some of the differences between households?
- Were there any surprising results?

MORE VOCABULARY

- empathise – understand and consider another person's or group's point of view
- point of view – an opinion, attitude or judgement considered in a particular way

JOURNAL TIP

Ask students to complete **Learning journal template 1 (Empathise page)** while they are completing the different tasks. Remind them to date their notes and include drawings or photos of relevant information.

USEFUL APPS/LINKS

- App for creating surveys, such as Typeform or Survey Monkey

ASSESSMENT

This stage of the design thinking process offers opportunities to observe students collecting information, developing questions, and recording their notes and thinking in their journal.

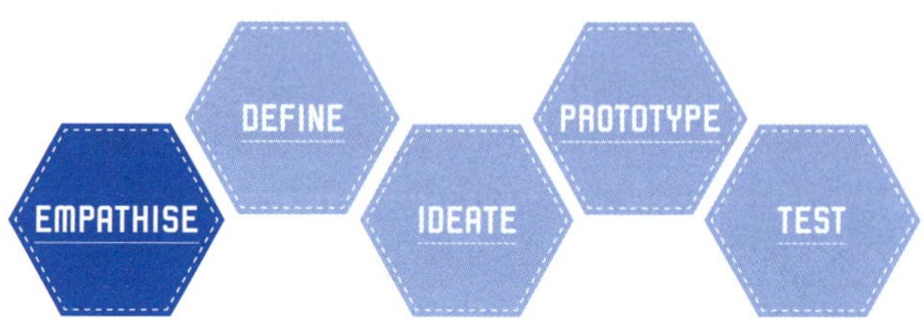

DEFINE

The main focus of this stage of the design thinking process is to reframe the challenge. The initial challenge is quite open, so at this stage students learn how to define what needs to be done. This includes noting insights that have been generated.

ACTIVITY 1: CONSIDER OBSERVATIONS

1. Students consider the information they gathered in the Empathise stage. They may work in pairs or small groups. Provide them with a whiteboard, large sheet of paper and/or sticky notes to collate some of the key information they have gathered about the types and amounts of organic waste generated by people, as well as their understandings about composting and environmental sustainability.
2. Students should discuss one section of **Learning journal template 2 (Define page)** at a time, write their responses, and then continue discussing their ideas for the next section, until the task is complete. This provides students with opportunities to hear others' responses and also provides the teacher with input points.
3. Discuss the information collected about organic waste, and composting in particular. Provide students with the opportunity to research further. Ask them to write other information they would like to know, such as how to irrigate garden beds and some important design considerations. Provide them with **Generic reproducible 4 (Key question table)** to assist them to record their questions, findings and sources.

ACTIVITY 2: CONSIDER INSIGHTS

Students think of at least one insight they have gained from the process; for example, the foods that are most commonly wasted, or what environmental sustainability means.

Students add this insight to **Learning journal template 2 (Define page)**. They should then relate the insight to their design.

When considering insights, students could think about the following:

- What was something unexpected that you saw or found out? How was it unexpected?
- How will you decide on the most important aspect of the garden bed?
- Is there any other information that you need or would like to know? How will you find out?

ACTIVITY 3: CONSIDER CONSTRAINTS

At this stage, let students know the constraints of the challenge, by describing the safety precautions students need to take if handling organic waste, the time frame, the materials available for prototyping and how the final solutions will be shared. Students can then update **Learning journal template 2 (Define page).**

PROMPTS

- What did you discover?
- What were the most important pieces of information that you gathered?
- What was something new that you learned?
- What other information do you need?

MORE VOCABULARY

- define – state the meaning of something
- insight – an accurate understanding of someone or something

JOURNAL TIP

Discuss the term 'insight'. Explain that it relates to something students have learned about the people and their responses to the surveys, as well as information gathered through research or excursions. You could refer to **Learning journal template 2**.

EMPATHISE DEFINE IDEATE PROTOTYPE TEST

→ IDEATE

The Ideate stage of the design thinking process is all about generating lots of ideas. Students need to be flexible in their thinking and able to move beyond obvious ideas. At this stage, ideas are not judged, just generated and gathered.

ACTIVITY: GENERATE IDEAS

1. Ask groups of students to draw or write their ideas. Each new idea should be written or drawn on a separate piece of paper or sticky note.
2. Ask students to group ideas on a wall or board.
3. Ask students to look at the different ideas and provide feedback to each other. It is important that students don't defend their ideas at this stage. They should just be listening to the feedback.
4. After the initial feedback, ask students to come up with more ideas. Encourage them to be creative and even radical.
5. Ask students to choose four of their ideas to write in their journal. Students use **Learning journal template 3 (Ideate page)** to do this. Ask students to choose one idea to explore further and explain the reasoning behind their choice.

TOP TIP!

At this stage, students may have produced a series of annotated drawings about garden beds and irrigation. They may have a collection of sticky notes, which they can organise into related ideas.

Encourage students to view and read others' ideas before giving feedback. Feedback could be within small groups or between partners. Considering others' ideas is an important part of this process, so students can build on their own ideas as they continue to ideate.

At each stage of this activity, ask students to discuss their thoughts before writing their responses. This will help them to think through their ideas and select their final ideas to develop.

PROMPTS

- How do your chosen ideas relate to sustainable use of organic waste?
- How might you test your design?
- How can you make it easy to use?
- How can you use recycled materials?
- What if you had to use different materials?

MORE VOCABULARY

- feedback – information about, for example, a person's performance or the design of a product, which can be used to make improvements
- ideate – generate many ideas without making judgements about the ideas

JOURNAL TIP

When choosing four ideas to include in the journal, students should try to choose ideas that aren't related.

USEFUL APPS/LINKS

- Tools for creating ideas, such as at creatingminds.org/tools/tools_ideation.htm
- Tips for creativity and innovation, such as at designorate.com/creativity-innovation-in-education/

At the Ideate stage, assessment could include observations about the number and diversity of students' ideas, and their ability to provide feedback and create additional ideas. Reflection in the journal should provide an insight into some of the reasoning behind students' choices.

→ PROTOTYPE

At this stage of the design thinking process, students are asked to create a physical prototype of a solution. It is the stage where students need to get their ideas out of their head and presented in a way that engages other students and helps them to understand the ideas. When students create, it helps them to think and solve problems and disagreements. Students can role-play, make storyboards or use sticky notes when they prototype. The most important feature is that viewers can interact with whatever is produced.

Encourage students to photograph or film during the prototyping and testing stages. This information can be used to show the learning behind the design thinking process in action.

ACTIVITY: TRANSFORM IDEAS INTO PROTOTYPES

1. Students review the ideas generated at the Ideate stage. Provide them with an A3 copy of **Generic reproducible 6 (In the frame)** so they can organise their ideas into two sections: least relevant and most relevant. Students continue to cycle through this activity until they have an idea to start prototyping.
2. Provide students with a range of materials to use to create their prototype. Remind students that a prototype should be created rapidly and it is not meant to look 'nice'.
3. After a prototype has been created, ask students to see if it works and get feedback from others.
4. Students then use the feedback to prototype again.

Ask students to fill in the Prototype part of **Learning journal template 4 (Prototype and test page)**. See the **Journal tip** for further student guidance.

TOP TIP!

The Prototype stage is often very messy. It is important that students are focusing on their ideas, rather than the end product. Provide them with lots of materials – recycling depots can be a useful source of resources. Students may add labels to prototypes to explain some of the main features. Photographing and annotating pictures of prototypes can be useful.

To gain feedback, students could ask each other some of the following questions:

- What is the main feature of your prototype?
- How does your prototype work?
- Which aspects work best? What will you keep?
- Which aspects need changing? How might you do this?
- What other materials might you need?

PROMPTS

- What worked?
- How could it be improved?
- What else do you need to know, do or have?
- What other suggestions do you have?

MORE VOCABULARY

- feedback – information about, for example, a person's performance or the design of a product, which can be used to make improvements
- prototype – an initial version of a model of a product or process that is used to develop a final model

JOURNAL TIP

Remind students to highlight the main features of their prototype. If students are creating an electronic journal, they can insert a photo of their prototype and annotate it.

USEFUL APPS/LINKS

- App for creating interactive links (for example, between descriptions, videos, images and websites and a main image), such as ThingLink
- App for making notes using text, drawings, images, weblinks and audio, such as Notability

ASSESSMENT

Observe students as they make changes to their designs. Are they able to consider feedback, make modifications and move rapidly through this process? Or do they have difficulties with holding onto an idea and accepting feedback?

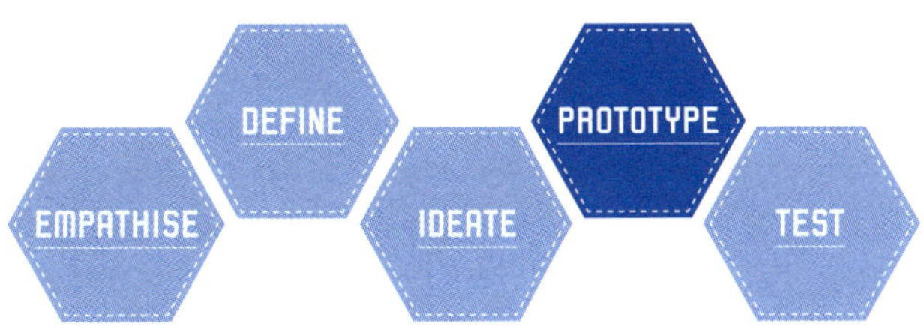

→ TEST

At this stage of the design thinking process, students test their prototype to see how it meets the criteria in the challenge. Students check to see if their prototype meets the criteria set at the start of the design process.

ACTIVITY: TEST FEEDBACK

1. Students take their last prototype and consider the initial needs of their audience.
2. Ask students to check whether or not their design works. If not, what do they need to do to make it work?
3. Provide the opportunity to cycle through the prototype and test stages again.

Ask students to fill in the Test part of **Learning journal template 4 (Prototype and test page)**. See the **Journal tip** for further student guidance.

PROMPTS

- Does your prototype do what you wanted it to do?
- Are there other features you could add?
- What needs to be changed?
- What works well?

MORE VOCABULARY

- evaluate – assess something, perhaps considering what worked and what didn't
- feature – a specific aspect of something, such as size, shape, colour and quality
- feedback – information about, for example, a person's performance or the design of a product, which can be used to make improvements
- prototype – an initial version of a model of a product or process that is used to develop a final model
- review – consider an idea, process or product and decide what needs to be changed and what works

JOURNAL TIP

Ask students to think about why it is important to test their ideas before they build their final design.

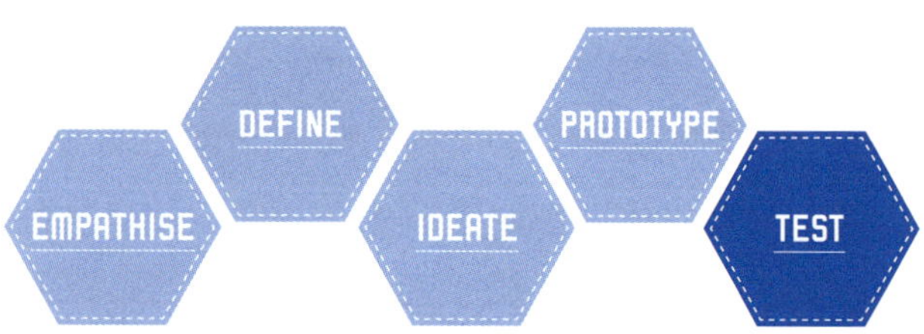

→ SHARE AND EVALUATE

At this stage of the investigation, students are provided with an opportunity to share their final design, as well as the processes involved in the investigation. Students evaluate their learning journals and their solutions.

ACTIVITY 1: BRING THE DESIGNS TOGETHER

1. Students can create an iMovie or use Adobe Spark Video to demonstrate the process and thinking behind the designs. There should be an element of narration, where they are sharing their points of view, insights, prototyping and solutions.
2. Students should include their learning journals with the display so others can see the different stages of the design process.

ACTIVITY 2: EVALUATE AND GIVE FEEDBACK

1. Provide students with **Generic reproducible 2 (Self-evaluation)** to complete.
2. Ask students to provide feedback to each other about the most interesting features, the aspects that were most difficult and the changes that they would make if they repeated the task.
3. Provide students with opportunities to share their designs with the wider community. It may be possible to share some of the video clips with an expert for feedback about their designs.

It may be possible to build one or more of the designs as a full-scale model. Consider how designs will be judged and who will make the final decisions. It may be possible to gather sponsorship for the garden.

ASSESSMENT

Ask students to again complete **Generic reproducible 1 (Key vocabulary table)** using the key vocabulary for this unit: capacity, environmental sustainability, irrigation, organic waste, recycle, volume. Compare their table with the one they completed at the Tune-in stage, to demonstrate changes in understanding.

Students complete **Generic reproducible 3 (Responding to the investigation)**. Compare their responses to those on **Generic reproducible 2**.

Teachers and students each complete **Generic reproducible 5 (Design thinking assessment rubric)**. Students compare the teacher's feedback with their self-assessment of their design thinking skills.

Name: ....

Date: ....

Group name: ....

STEM INVESTIGATIONS

CONCEPT:

Where I see it:

Problem:

Key maths words and units:

Definition:

Name: ....

Date: ....

TYPE OF ORGANIC WASTE	AMOUNT OF ORGANIC WASTE

 STEM Investigations, UP, ISBN 978 1 4202 4154 9 © Macmillan Science and Education Australia 2018

EMPATHISE

STEM INVESTIGATIONS

Name: ....

Date: ....

Group name: ....

What do you want to know?

1)	2)	3)

Question:

1)	2)	3)

Type of answer:

1)	2)	3)

- Multiple choice
- Short answer
- Ranking
- Yes/no
- Rating
- Other

PLAN AND DESIGN A SOLAR-PANEL UNIFORM

→ INTRODUCTION

Renewable energy technology continues to be developed because of the finite supplies and environmental impacts of non-renewable energy. One of the limitations of solar-powered devices has been the large size of solar panels. Australian researchers have now developed lightweight solar panels that can be worn on uniforms. This provides the opportunity to use the Sun's energy where weight or access to power might be difficult, for example, in aircraft or for medical or communication devices while on the move or in remote areas.

In this STEM investigation, students will learn about energy and how it can be used. They explore the possibilities for wearable solar panels and consider the needs of people living in remote communities.

THE CHALLENGE

Researchers have developed lightweight solar panels that are designed to be worn on uniforms. This technology could help people working in remote areas that do not have electricity. You are part of a junior think-tank team that is investigating who could best use this technology.

Your challenge is to investigate the different occupations that could benefit from solar-panel clothing, and then design a useful uniform for one occupation. Think about the needs of the user. Consider how energy could be stored so that it can be used at night or when there is little light. As part of your investigation, you will find out how solar energy is converted to electrical energy.

KEY UNDERSTANDINGS

- Energy is the ability for an object to do work.
- Potential energy is energy available to do something, such as in a battery.
- Kinetic energy is energy that is doing something.
- An electrical circuit is a continuous loop in which electrical energy flows.
- Energy can be moved (transferred) from one place to another.
- Energy can be changed from one form of energy to another (for example, potential energy can become kinetic energy).
- Solar energy is renewable.

KEY VOCABULARY

electrical circuit
energy
energy transformation
photovoltaic cell
renewable
solar panel

KEY SKILLS

- Gather and evaluate information.
- Consider important points about solar energy.
- Create electrical circuits.

KEY ACTIONS

- Experiment with circuits.
- Explore energy transformations.
- Design a solar-panel uniform.

→ OVERVIEW OF STAGES

TUNE IN:

Students learn about energy. They find out about different types of energy, especially potential and kinetic energy. Students learn about the transfer of energy from one object to another and explore energy transformations.

EMPATHISE

Students find out about some of the challenges of living in remote areas. They learn about different occupations, as well as equipment that relies on electrical energy. They consider the problems caused when there is no electricity for equipment.

DEFINE

Students consider the latest in wearable technology and its links to solar-powered energy. They create a design brief to help guide their investigation.

IDEATE

Students generate ideas for creating solar-panel uniforms. They sketch and label their designs.

PROTOTYPE

Students choose one or two ideas to transform into detailed sketches or models. These are created rapidly, using simple materials.

TEST

As a class, prototypes are tested. Students share their prototypes and provide feedback to each other. They are given the opportunity to cycle through the Prototype and Test stages again.

SHARE AND EVALUATE:

Final prototypes are shared and evaluated, with opportunities for expert feedback investigated. Students consider whether or not their designs could potentially be created to meet the demands of people living and working in remote areas.

→ SUGGESTED SCHEDULE

LESSON	STAGE
1–2	**Tune in**: learn about energy, explore energy transfer and transformations, and introduce the student challenge
3–5	**Empathise**: learn about challenges related to living in remote areas, find out about the importance and impact of equipment that relies on electrical energy, and write/record in journal
6	**Define**: define the main issues and write/record in journal
7	**Ideate**: develop ideas and write/record in journal
8–10	**Prototype** and **Test**: conduct prototyping and testing cycles and write/record in journal
11–13	**Share and evaluate**: share and evaluate designs and prototypes

CURRICULUM LINKS

The following tables show the key Science, Technologies and Mathematics curricula with which this STEM investigation is aligned.

SCIENCE

YEAR	STRAND	SUB-STRAND AND CONTENT
6	Science Understanding	Physical sciences: • Electrical energy can be transferred and transformed in electrical circuits and can be generated from a range of sources • Energy from a variety of sources can be used to generate electricity
5 & 6	Science as a Human Endeavour	Use and influence of science: • Scientific knowledge is used to solve problems and inform personal and community decisions

TECHNOLOGIES

YEAR	STRAND	CONTENT
5 & 6	Design and Technologies Knowledge and Understanding	• Investigate how electrical energy can control movement, sound or light in a designed product or system
	Design and Technologies Processes and Production Skills	• Critique needs or opportunities for designing, and investigate materials, components, tools, equipment and processes to achieve intended designed solutions • Generate, develop and communicate design ideas and processes for audiences using appropriate technical terms and graphical representation techniques • Select appropriate materials, components, tools, equipment and techniques, and apply safe procedures to make designed solutions • Negotiate criteria for success that include sustainability to evaluate design ideas, processes and solutions • Develop project plans that include consideration of resources when making designed solutions individually and collaboratively

MATHEMATICS

YEAR	STRAND	SUB-STRAND
5 & 6	Measurement and Geometry	Using units of measurement Location and transformation

OTHER CURRICULUM LINKS

GENERAL CAPABILITIES

- Literacy
- Numeracy
- Information and Communication Technology (ICT) Capability
- Critical and Creative Thinking

CROSS-CURRICULUM PRIORITIES

- Sustainability

ASSESSMENT

AC

The following resources are provided for assessing students at different stages of the STEM investigations:

- Generic reproducible 1 (Key vocabulary table), for assessing understanding of vocabulary
- Generic reproducible 2 (Self-evaluation), for student self-evaluation of the learning process
- Generic reproducible 3 (Define graphic organiser), for assessing student engagement in the challenges, and the collaboration and design skills involved in the design thinking stages
- Generic reproducible 5 (Design thinking assessment rubric), for evaluating student engagement in the design thinking stages
- Learning journal templates 1, 2, 3 and 4, for incorporating student reflection and evaluation

GETTING READY FOR THE INVESTIGATION

You can prepare yourself and students for this STEM investigation in the following ways:

- Identify groups of students who will work well together.
- Review the **Key science knowledge** that supports this investigation, and look at the **Useful links**.
- Investigate the **Useful apps**.
- Gather materials for the cotton reel car and electrical alarm activities for the Tune-in session.
- Start collecting additional materials for prototyping (as shown on the **Materials needed** list).
- Determine where prototypes will be kept between lessons.
- Create a wall space where students can share their ideas in the Ideate stage.
- Organise the class into pairs.
- Start thinking about:
  - » sourcing information for the electrical circuits
  - » inviting someone to speak about solar energy
  - » making connections with a school in a remote area
  - » time constraints for the task
  - » gathering a panel of advisors or mentors to assist students when completing circuits
  - » finding experts to provide feedback to students
  - » how, when and where the designs will be shared and evaluated.

USEFUL APPS

- App for creating semantic maps (links between different words and/or concepts), such as Popplet or Inspiration
- App for creating interactive links (for example, between descriptions, videos, images and websites and a main image), such as ThingLink
- App for making notes using text, drawings, images, weblinks and audio, such as Notability
- App for creating multimedia presentations, such as Adobe Spark Video, Prezi or iMovie
- App for creating surveys, such as Survey Monkey or Typeform
- App for drawing shapes, inserting images and making annotations or adding to the inserted image, such as Drawisland

USEFUL LINKS

- Information about electricity for students, such as at bbc.co.uk/education/topics/zq8wxnb
- Information about energy and electricity for students, with interactive activities, such as at sciencekids.co.nz/physics.html
- Information about electricity generation for teachers, such as at thoughtco.com/what-is-electricity-4019643
- Information about photovoltaic cells, such as at youtube.com/watch?v=he_JjrXEfN0
- Information about solar-powered clothing, such as at engineersaustralia.org.au/portal/news/clothing-future-could-generate-and-store-solar-power
- Internet issues in remote areas (for example, the Australian outback), such as at abc.net.au/btn/story/s4716377.htm
- Some of the loneliest jobs in the world, such as at mnn.com/money/green-workplace/stories/6-of-the-loneliest-jobs-in-the-world

RESOURCES PROVIDED

- Generic reproducibles 1, 2, 3, 4, 5, 6
- Reproducibles 15.1, 15.2, 15.3
- Learning journal templates 1, 2, 3, 4 (on disc)

MATERIALS NEEDED

- Sticky notes (half a pad per pair)
- Paper
- Coloured card
- Pens and markers
- Sticky tape
- Pipe-cleaners
- Cardboard
- Cotton reels
- 2 washers per group
- 2 small sticks (a little longer than matchsticks) per group
- Rubber bands
- Copper wire
- Wooden pegs
- Electronic buzzers (9 V maximum)
- 9 V battery connected to a snap-type battery holder, one per group
- D battery
- 2 long, large-eyed sewing needles
- Sandpaper
- Blu-Tack
- Strong, small circular magnet
- Electrical tape
- Thick whiteboard marker

KEY SCIENCE KNOWLEDGE

This section provides an overview of the key science concepts and vocabulary needed for this unit.

WHAT IS ENERGY?

Energy can be described as the ability for an object to do work or to cause movement. It is *not* a mass or a force. It is measured in joules and has many different forms. We experience energy in forms such as light, heat and sound, and as electrical and chemical energy.

The energy of motion is called kinetic energy. The energy moving in an **electrical circuit** is kinetic energy. Potential energy is stored energy. A battery not connected to a circuit is storing chemical energy. The charge has the ability to move, but it is not moving, so we say this energy is stored energy (has the potential to move). Some sources of energy, such as energy from the wind and the Sun, are **renewable** – the energy does not run out.

ENERGY TRANSFORMATIONS

The law of conservation of energy states that energy cannot be created or destroyed, but is changed between different forms.

Energy transformations happen when energy is changed from one form of energy into a different form. These transformations happen in many different ways, such as in our bodies, in moving vehicles and in all the electrical appliances in our homes.

Solar panels transform light energy into electrical energy. Each panel is made from groups of **photovoltaic cells**. These cells work differently to solar hot water systems – solar hot water involves a transfer of the sun's heat energy to water, but there is no energy transformation. Photovoltaic cells are often made of wafers of silicon. These are specially coated and arranged so that when light strikes them, negative particles are knocked free and become part of an **electrical circuit**.

The very latest photovoltaic cells are much thinner and lighter than earlier ones. The cells are made at the same time as the plastic that supports them, so they are flexible and can be used on clothing and on portable electronic devices.

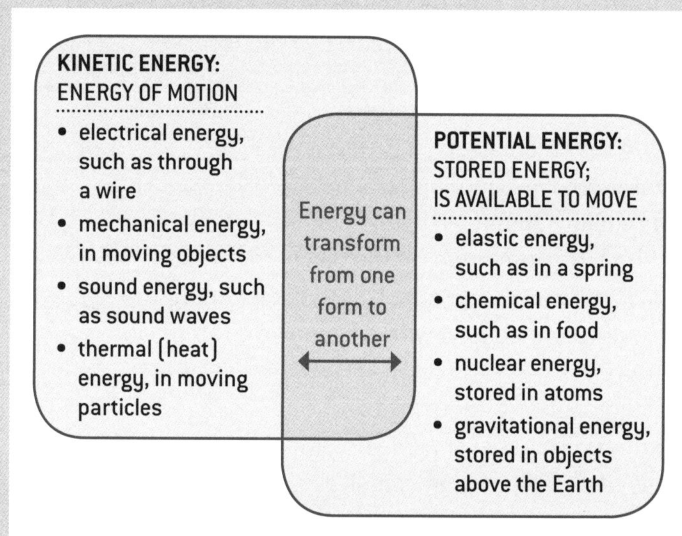

The various energy types can transform from one form to another.

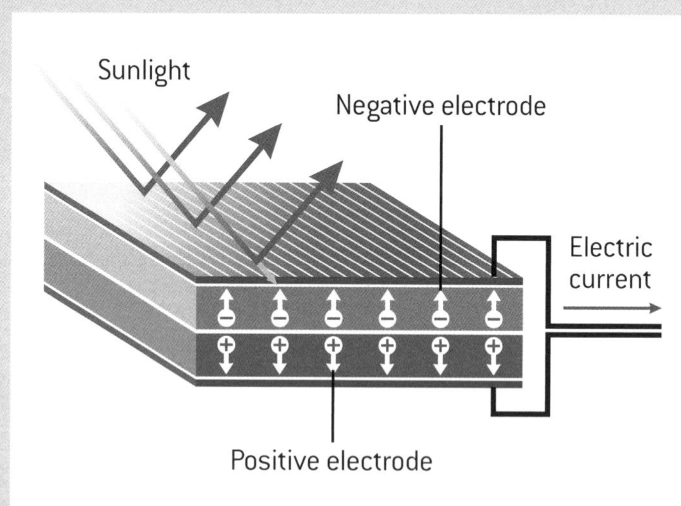

Photovoltaic cells use light energy in an electrical circuit.

KEY VOCABULARY

electrical circuit – a continuous loop in which electrical energy flows
energy – the ability to cause movement or do work; two main types are kinetic and potential energy
energy transformation – the conversion of one form of energy into a different form
photovoltaic cell – a device that transforms light energy into electrical energy
renewable – able to be used for an unlimited time without running out
solar panel – a group of photovoltaic cells

TUNE IN

1. Ask students to complete **Generic reproducible 1 (Key vocabulary table)** using the key vocabulary for this unit. This reproducible will also be used at the end of the unit, to demonstrate changes in understanding.
2. Have students work in small groups of about three to brainstorm the word 'energy' and come up with a definition. An image could be displayed in the room to initiate discussion about forms of energy (see **Useful apps/links**).
3. Watch one or two video clips about energy (see **Useful apps/links**). Students should make comparisons between these videos and their understanding. Discuss and decide on a definition for energy. Write it on a large poster or board and ask students to annotate it with everyday examples of energy. This could also be done digitally using Lino or Padlet. Students need to understand energy transfers and transformations.

ACTIVITY 1: COTTON REEL CAR

1. Place a rubber band through the centre of a cotton reel and loop it over one of the sticks to secure it. Thread the other end of the rubber band through the washers and then loop this end over the second rubber band.
2. Hold the cotton reel firmly and wind the washer-end stick in a circular motion until the band is tight. Ask students to predict what will happen when the cotton reel car is placed on the ground and released.
3. Release the car on the ground. Ask students to describe and explain what they observe.

USEFUL APPS/LINKS

- Video clips about energy, such as at youtube.com/watch?v=8qGyD9Y7SJA and youtube.com/watch?v=Q4M-q8fiJ2I
- Information about photovoltaic cells and solar energy storage, such as at youtube.com/watch?v=he_JjrXEfN0

ACTIVITY 2: ELECTRICAL ALARM

1. Wrap a piece of wire around a peg leg (see **Materials needed** list), leaving about 3 cm of wire sticking out. Repeat this on the other peg leg. The wires should not touch but the peg legs must touch when the legs are squeezed together. Ask students what the action of squeezing the peg legs together is doing.
2. Connect the black wire of the battery holder to the black wire of the buzzer.
3. Connect the red wire from the battery holder to one wire on the peg leg. Connect the red wire from the buzzer to the wire on the other peg leg. Ask students what will happen when the peg legs are squeezed together.
4. Squeeze the peg legs together. Have students describe and explain what they observe.

4. To evaluate learning, look at some images of energy being transformed from one form to another and have students identify the types of energy. Focus on images involving electrical energy transformations and discuss their effectiveness. Refer to the diagram in **Key science knowledge**.
5. Before engaging in the challenge, students need to understand how solar energy can be used to generate electrical energy and be stored. Darken the room and bring in an already charged solar-powered light to discuss how solar energy can be used to generate electrical energy. Discuss ideas about photovoltaic cells, energy storage and using batteries (see **Useful apps/links**).
6. Introduce the STEM investigation and challenge to the students. Provide them with the student card and read the information together. Ask students to think about what is meant by a uniform and to start considering some of the issues in remote areas.
7. Introduce the design thinking process by reviewing the stages on the student card. Explain that students will keep a journal about their learning at the different stages of the design.

TOP TIP! During the Tune-in stage, conduct vocabulary activities to highlight and develop key vocabulary knowledge. Throughout the investigation, quiz students about energy transfers and transformations they have observed. Activities could include drawing semantic webs, creating a word wall or paired discussions.

→ EMPATHISE

During the Empathise stage of the design thinking process, students focus on finding out about different points of view. To empathise with others, they need to research some of the challenges associated with living in remote areas. Students will take notes, ask questions, draw diagrams and take photos where relevant.

ACTIVITY 1: REMOTE AREA CHALLENGES

1. Find out about some of the challenges associated with living in a remote area. Provide students with some resources (see **Useful apps/links**).
2. Discuss some of the information presented.
3. Ask students to consider the different uses of electricity. Students create a class wall using sticky notes. After they have collected ideas, ask them to reorganise the information into categories and name each category (for example, communication, food and drink, entertainment/leisure).
4. Ask students to consider their responses to different scenarios relating to limited or no access to services or objects that require electricity. Provide them with **Reproducible 15.1 (What if...?)** for recording their thoughts. Discuss the responses.

ACTIVITY 2: FIND OUT ABOUT OCCUPATIONS

1. Students find out about occupations that rely on electrical energy. These occupations might need to have equipment that is specific to their job, such as an X-ray machine or more general equipment, such as a mobile phone.
2. Ask students to survey students, parents, family members and friends to find out about different occupations and the types of electrical equipment those occupations might use. They could use a survey app or create a simple pen and paper survey.
3. After students have collected information, provide them with **Reproducible 15.2 (Electrical equipment problems)** to consider some of the issues that may arise when equipment is not able to be used.

Ask students to consider the information they have collected and determine the most important insights they have found out.

PROMPTS

- What are some of the occupations that rely on electricity?
- What are some of the potential issues with not having access to electricity?
- What are some of the types of electrical equipment needed by different occupations?
- What is one interesting insight you found out?

MORE VOCABULARY

- empathise – understand and consider another person's or group's point of view
- point of view – an opinion, attitude or judgement considered in a particular way

JOURNAL TIP

Ask students to fill out **Learning journal template 1 (Empathise page)** while they are completing the different tasks. Remind them to date their notes and include photos of relevant information or pictures.

USEFUL APPS/LINKS

- Outback internet issues, such as at abc.net.au/btn/story/s4716377.htm
- Some of the loneliest jobs in the world, such as at mnn.com/money/green-workplace/stories/6-of-the-loneliest-jobs-in-the-world
- App for creating surveys, such as Survey Monkey or Typeform

ASSESSMENT

This stage of the design thinking process offers opportunities to observe students collecting information, developing questions, and recording their notes and thinking in their journal.

EMPATHISE DEFINE IDEATE PROTOTYPE TEST

→ DEFINE

The main focus of this stage of the design thinking process is to reframe the challenge. The initial challenge is quite open, so at this stage students learn how to define what needs to be done. This includes noting insights that have been generated.

ACTIVITY 1: CONSIDER OBSERVATIONS

1. Students consider the information they gathered in the Empathise stage, in pairs or small groups. Provide them with a whiteboard, large sheet of paper and/or sticky notes to collate some of the key information. Ask them to consider some of the issues with living in a remote community and the types of jobs that rely on electricity.
2. Students should discuss one section of **Learning journal template 2 (Define page)** at a time, write their responses, then continue discussing their ideas for the next section, until the task is complete. This provides students with opportunities to hear others' responses and also provides the teacher with input points.
3. Discuss the term 'wearable technology'. Watch a video clip about solar-powered clothing (see **Useful apps/links**) and discuss its advantages.
4. Explore which occupations might benefit most from solar-panel technology. Ask students to write other information they would like to know, such as current uses for solar-panel uniforms and how to create an electric circuit for solar panels. Provide **Generic reproducible 4 (Key question table)** to assist them to record their questions, findings and sources.

ACTIVITY 2: CONSIDER INSIGHTS

Students think of at least one insight they have gained from the process; for example, electricity is needed for simple and complex tasks, such as lighting, phones and medical equipment.

Students add this insight to **Learning journal template 2 (Define page)** and then write a brief explanation of what needs to be created.

When considering insights, students could think about the following:

- What was something unexpected that you saw or found out? How was it unexpected?
- How will you decide which is the most useful type of device to create?
- Is there any other information that you need or would like to know? How will you find out?

ACTIVITY 3: CONSIDER CONSTRAINTS

At this stage, let students know the constraints of the challenge, by describing the time frame, available materials, how and when designs will be shared, and whether annotated designs or working models will be created. Provide students with **Reproducible 15.3 (Solar-panel uniform design brief)** for recording the specifications of the challenge. Students can then update **Learning journal template 2**.

PROMPTS

- What did you discover?
- What were the most important pieces of information that you gathered?
- What was something new that you learned?
- What other information do you need?

MORE VOCABULARY

- define – state the meaning of something
- insight – an accurate understanding of someone or something

JOURNAL TIP

Discuss the term 'insight'. Explain that it relates to something students have learned about the people and their responses to the surveys, as well as information gathered through research or excursions. You could refer to **Learning journal template 2**.

USEFUL APPS/LINKS

The advantages of solar-powered clothing, such as at youtube.com/watch?v=rhUqDy4tg50

EMPATHISE DEFINE IDEATE PROTOTYPE TEST

→ IDEATE

The Ideate stage of the design thinking process is all about generating lots of ideas. Students need to be flexible in their thinking and able to move beyond obvious ideas. At this stage, ideas are not judged, just generated and gathered.

ACTIVITY: GENERATE IDEAS

1. Ask groups of students to draw or write their ideas. Each new idea should be written or drawn on a separate piece of paper or on a sticky note.
2. Ask students to group ideas on a wall or board.
3. Ask students to look at the different ideas and provide feedback to each other. It is important that students don't defend their ideas at this stage. They should just be listening to the feedback.
4. After the initial feedback, ask students to come up with more ideas. Encourage them to be creative and even radical.
5. Ask students to choose four of their ideas to write in their journal. Students use **Learning journal template 3 (Ideate page)** to do this. Ask students to choose one idea to explore further and explain the reasoning behind their choice.

TOP TIP!

At this stage, students may have produced a series of annotated drawings, about using wearable solar-powered clothes. They may have a collection of sticky notes, which they can organise into related ideas.

Encourage students to view and read others' ideas before giving feedback. Feedback could be within small groups or between partners. Considering others' ideas is an important part of this process, so students can build on their own ideas as they continue to ideate.

At each stage of this activity, ask students to discuss their thoughts before writing their responses. This will help them to think through their ideas and select their final ideas to develop.

PROMPTS

- How do these ideas relate to the challenges of living or working in a remote community?
- How might you test your design?
- How can you make it more useful?
- How can you make it easy to wear or incorporate into clothing?
- What if you had to use different materials?

MORE VOCABULARY

- feedback – information about, for example, a person's performance or the design of a product, which can be used to make improvements
- ideate – generate many ideas without making judgements about the ideas

JOURNAL TIP

When choosing four ideas to include in the journal, students should try to choose ideas that aren't related.

USEFUL APPS/LINKS

- Tools for creating ideas, such as at creatingminds.org/tools/tools_ideation.htm
- Tips for creativity and innovation, such as at designorate.com/creativity-innovation-in-education

ASSESSMENT

At the Ideate stage, assessment could include observations about the number and diversity of students' ideas, and their ability to provide feedback and create additional ideas. Reflection in the journal should provide an insight into some of the reasoning behind students' choices.

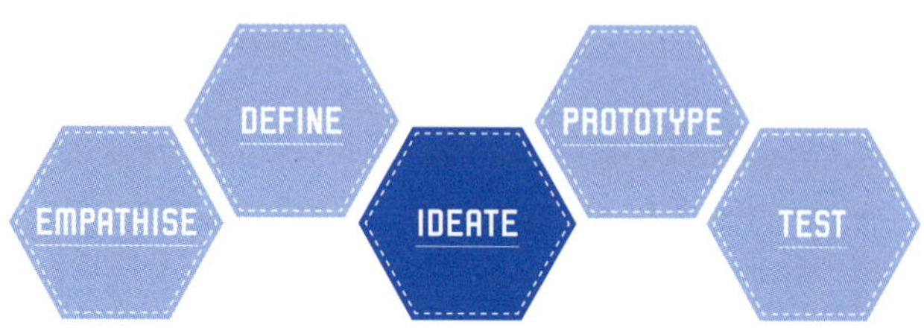

PROTOTYPE

At this stage of the design thinking process, students are asked to create a physical prototype of a solution. It is the stage where students need to get their ideas out of their head and presented in a way that engages other students and helps them to understand the concept. When students create, it helps them to think and solve problems and disagreements. Students can role-play, make storyboards or use sticky notes when they prototype. The most important feature is that viewers can interact with whatever is produced.

Encourage students to photograph or film during the prototyping and testing stages. This information can be used to show the learning behind the design thinking process in action.

ACTIVITY: TRANSFORM IDEAS INTO PROTOTYPES

1. Students review the ideas generated at the Ideate stage. Provide them with an A3 copy of **Generic reproducible 6 (In the frame)** so they can organise their ideas into two sections: 'least relevant' and 'most relevant'. Students continue to cycle through this activity until they have an idea to start prototyping.
2. Provide students with a range of materials to create their prototype. Remind students that a prototype should be created rapidly and is not meant to look 'nice'.
3. After a prototype has been created, ask students to see if it works and get feedback from others.
4. Students then use the feedback to prototype again.

TOP TIP!

During the Prototype stage, it is important that students are focusing on their ideas, rather than the end product. Provide them with lots of materials. Students may add labels to prototypes to explain some of the main features. Photographing and annotating pictures of prototypes can be useful.

To gain feedback, students could ask each other some of the following questions:

- What is the main feature of your prototype?
- How does it work?
- Which aspects work best? What will you keep?
- Which aspects need changing? How might you do this?
- What other materials might you need?

Ask students to fill in the Prototype part of **Learning journal template 4 (Prototype and test page)**. See the **Journal tip** for further student guidance.

PROMPTS

- What worked?
- How could it be improved?
- What else do you need to know, do or have?
- What other suggestions do you have?

MORE VOCABULARY

- feedback – information about, for example, a person's performance or the design of a product, which can be used to make improvements
- prototype – an initial version of a model of a product or process that is used to develop a final model

JOURNAL TIP

Remind students to highlight the main features of their prototype. If students are creating an electronic journal, they can insert and annotate a photo of their prototype.

USEFUL APPS/LINKS

- App for creating interactive links (for example, between descriptions, videos, images and websites and a main image), such as ThingLink
- App for making notes using text, drawings, images, weblinks and audio, such as Notability
- App for drawing shapes, inserting images and making annotations or adding to the inserted image, such as Drawisland

ASSESSMENT

Observe students as they make changes to their designs. Are they able to consider feedback, make modifications and move rapidly through this process? Or do they have difficulties with holding on to an idea and accepting feedback?

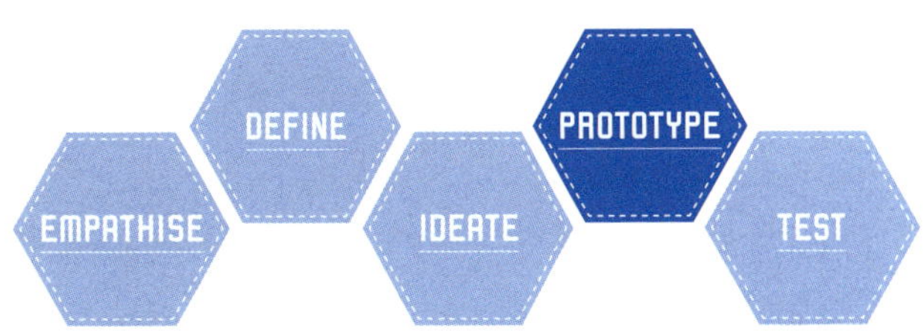

→ TEST

At this stage of the design thinking process, students test their prototype to see how it meets the criteria in the challenge. Students check to see if their prototype meets the criteria set at the start of the design process.

ACTIVITY: TEST FEEDBACK

1. Students take their last prototype and consider the initial needs of their audience.
2. Ask students to check whether or not their design works. If not, what do they need to do to make it work?
3. Provide the opportunity to cycle through the prototyping and testing stages again.

Ask students to fill in the Test part of **Learning journal template 4 (Prototype and test page)**. See the **Journal tip** for further student guidance.

PROMPTS

- Does your prototype do what you wanted it to do?
- Are there other features that need to be added?

MORE VOCABULARY

- evaluate – assess something, perhaps considering what worked and what didn't
- feature – a specific aspect of something, such as size, shape, colour and quality
- feedback – information about, for example, a person's performance or the design of a product, which can be used to make improvements
- prototype – an initial version of a model of a product or process that is used to develop a final model
- review – consider an idea, process or product and decide what needs to be changed and what works

JOURNAL TIP

Ask students to think about why it is important to test their ideas before they build their final design.

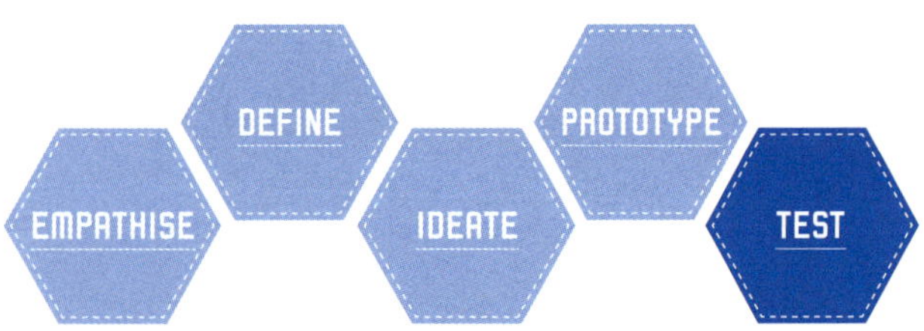

→ SHARE AND EVALUATE

At this stage of the investigation, students are provided with an opportunity to share their final design, as well as the processes involved in the investigation. Students evaluate their learning journals and their solutions.

ACTIVITY 1: BRING THE DESIGNS TOGETHER

1. Provide students with time to create final designs. Students can create an iMovie or use Adobe Spark Video or Prezi to demonstrate the process and thinking behind the designs. There should be an element of narration, where they are sharing their story about points of view, insights, prototyping and solutions.
2. Students should include their learning journals with the display so others can see the different stages of the design process.

ACTIVITY 2: EVALUATE AND GIVE FEEDBACK

1. Provide **Generic reproducible 2 (Self-evaluation)** for students to complete.
2. Ask students to provide feedback to each other about the most interesting features, the difficult aspects and the changes they would make.
3. Provide students with opportunities to share their designs. This could include inviting someone from a technology company, or connecting with someone from a remote community or a friend or family member with relevant experience. It may be possible to share some of the videos with an expert for feedback.

ASSESSMENT

Ask students to again complete **Generic reproducible 1 (Key vocabulary table)** using the key vocabulary for this unit. Compare their table with the one they completed at the Tune-in stage, to demonstrate changes in understanding.

Students complete **Generic reproducible 3 (Responding to the investigation)**. Compare their responses to those on **Generic reproducible 2**.

Teachers and students each complete **Generic reproducible 5 (Design thinking assessment rubric)**. Students compare teacher feedback with their self-assessment of their design thinking skills.

EMPATHISE

STEM INVESTIGATIONS

Name: ....

Date: ....

Write how you might react and feel if the following things happened.

WHAT IF ...?

There is not enough electricity to access the internet.	You can use electricity for only an hour each day.
There is only enough electricity to use two electrical devices. (Which two would you choose?)	(Create your own 'what if' question here.)

EMPATHISE

STEM INVESTIGATIONS

Name: ....

Date: ....

List some equipment that relies on electrical energy, including energy from batteries. Think about some of the problems that would occur if you couldn't use this equipment. Look at the example in the first row.

Electrical equipment	What might happen if it doesn't work?
Mobile phone	Cannot make or receive phone calls Cannot connect with other people by messaging or social media Cannot use navigation apps to work out your location

STEM Investigations, UP, ISBN 978 1 4202 4154 9 © Macmillan Science and Education Australia 2018

DEFINE

STEM INVESTIGATIONS

Name: ....

Date: ....

Use this flowchart to help you plan your solar-panel uniform design.

Purpose of design	→	
Name of design	→	
Description of how it works	→	
Main features	→	
Benefits of design	→	
Other	→	

STEM Investigations, UP, ISBN 978 1 4202 4154 9 © Macmillan Science and Education Australia 2018

EXPLORE – AND COLONISE – OUTSIDE YOUR WORLD

→ INTRODUCTION

Humans have long been fascinated by space travel and places beyond the Earth. Technological advances have allowed us to gather considerable data about the planets. As the Earth's population grows and the demands on its resources increase, discussions about the possibility of colonising another planet or moon continue.

In this STEM investigation, students consider the different options available for colonisation beyond the Earth and design a living pod for their chosen planet. They explore the basic requirements for living things, key features of planets in our solar system and important structural aspects of designing a living pod.

THE CHALLENGE

For your school's annual science show, your teacher has chosen the theme 'Explore outside your world'. You decide to investigate how another planet or moon could support a human colony. This project will be a chance to demonstrate your problem-solving and design skills.

Your challenge is to first identify the most suitable planet or moon for colonisation. To do this, you will need to investigate the requirements for humans to survive on another planet. You will then create a flowchart that will help you to choose the best planet to colonise. Your flowchart will show each planet's characteristics, such as its atmosphere and its distance from the Sun and the Earth. Lastly, you will design a living pod and present it at the science show.

KEY UNDERSTANDINGS

- All living things need an energy source, nutrients and water.
- The Earth is part of our solar system.
- Each planet has unique features.
- Some structures are stronger than others.

KEY VOCABULARY

atmosphere
biosphere
colonisation
orbit
organism
sustainable

KEY SKILLS

- Locate, categorise and summarise information.
- Compare and evaluate information.
- Use logic to create flowcharts.

KEY ACTIONS

- Research different planets.
- Create a flowchart to work out which planet to colonise.
- Design and share a living pod for humans colonising another planet.

→ OVERVIEW OF STAGES

TUNE IN:

Students learn about the solar system and the Earth's unique features. They explore the features of different planets and compare them with the Earth. Students find out about the difference between living and non-living things. They also explore the strength of different structures when considering the design of a living pod for the colonisation of a planet.

EMPATHISE

Students find out about some potential issues with basic requirements for living on different planets. They use and create flowcharts to assist with future decision making.

DEFINE

Students consider the issues relating to the planet they have chosen and create criteria for the living pod they will design.

IDEATE

Students generate ideas for how to create a living pod that will allow humans to live on another planet. They sketch and label their designs.

PROTOTYPE

Students choose one or two ideas to transform into physical representations (models). These are created rapidly, using simple materials.

TEST

As a class, prototypes are tested. Students share their prototypes and provide feedback to each other. They are given the opportunity to cycle through the Prototype and Test stages again.

SHARE AND EVALUATE:

Final prototypes are shared and evaluated, with opportunities for expert feedback investigated.

→ SUGGESTED SCHEDULE

LESSON	STAGE
1–2	**Tune in**: consider the solar system and the Earth's uniqueness, explore different planets and compare to the Earth, consider living and non-living things, explore the strength of different structures and introduce the student challenge
3–5	**Empathise**: find out about issues relating to basic requirements for different planets, create flowcharts and write/record in journal
6	**Define**: define the main issues, create design criteria for a living pod and write/record in journal
7	**Ideate**: develop ideas and write/record in journal
8–10	**Prototype** and **Test**: conduct prototyping and testing cycles and write/record in journal
11–13	**Share and evaluate**: share and evaluate designs and prototypes

CURRICULUM LINKS

The following tables show the key Science, Technologies and Mathematics curricula with which this STEM investigation is aligned.

SCIENCE

YEAR	STRAND	SUB-STRAND AND CONTENT
5	Science Understanding	Earth and space sciences: • The Earth is part of a system of planets orbiting around a star (the Sun)
	Science as a Human Endeavour	Use and influence of science: • Scientific knowledge is used to solve problems and inform personal and community decisions
	Science Inquiry Skills	Processing and analysing data and information: • Questioning and predicting • Communicating
6	Science Understanding	Biological sciences: • The growth and survival of living things are affected by physical conditions of their environment

TECHNOLOGIES

YEAR	STRAND	CONTENT
5 & 6	Design and Technologies Processes and Production Skills	• Generate, develop and communicate design ideas and processes for audiences using appropriate technical terms and graphical representation techniques • Select appropriate materials, components, tools, equipment and techniques, and apply safe procedures to make designed solutions • Negotiate criteria for success that include sustainability to evaluate design ideas, processes and solutions • Develop project plans that include consideration of resources when making designed solutions individually and collaboratively • Critique needs or opportunities for designing, and investigate materials, components, tools, equipment and processes to achieve intended designed solutions
	Digital Technologies Processes and Production Skills	• Design, modify and follow simple algorithms involving sequences of steps, branching and iteration (repetition)

MATHEMATICS

YEAR	STRAND	SUB-STRANDS
5	Measurement and Geometry	Using units of measurement Shape
6	Measurement and Geometry	Shape

OTHER CURRICULUM LINKS

GENERAL CAPABILITIES

- Literacy
- Numeracy
- Information and Communication Technology (ICT) Capability
- Critical and Creative Thinking

CROSS-CURRICULUM PRIORITIES

- Sustainability

ASSESSMENT

The following resources are provided for assessing students at different stages of the STEM investigations:

- Generic reproducible 1 (Key vocabulary table), for assessing understanding of vocabulary
- Generic reproducible 2 (Self-evaluation), for student self-evaluation of the learning process
- Generic reproducible 3 (Define graphic organiser), for assessing student engagement in the challenges, and the collaboration and skills involved in design thinking
- Generic reproducible 5 (Design thinking assessment rubric), for evaluating student engagement in the design thinking stages
- Learning journal templates 1, 2, 3 and 4, for incorporating student reflection and evaluation

→ GETTING READY FOR THE INVESTIGATION

You can prepare yourself and students for this STEM investigation in the following ways:

- Identify groups of students who will work well together.
- Review the **Key science knowledge** that supports this investigation, and look at the **Useful links**.
- Investigate the **Useful apps**.
- Gather materials for comparing living and non-living things during the Tune-in session.
- Start collecting additional materials for prototyping (as shown on the **Materials needed** list).
- Determine where prototypes will be kept between lessons.
- Create a wall space where students can share their ideas in the Ideate stage.
- Organise the class into pairs.
- Start thinking about:
  - » learning how to use and create different flowcharts
  - » who to connect with for student feedback (for example, educational services attached to a space organisation)
  - » organising a science fair.

USEFUL APPS

- App for creating semantic maps (links between different words and/or concepts), such as Popplet
- App for creating interactive links (for example, between descriptions, videos, images and websites and a main image), such as ThingLink
- App for making notes using text, drawings, images, weblinks and audio, such as Notability
- App for creating multimedia presentations, such as Adobe Spark Video or iMovie
- App for creating different diagrams like flowcharts, such as Creately
- Website for creating flowcharts, such as Draw.io
- App for exploring the solar system, such as SolarWalk

USEFUL LINKS

- Facts about planets, moons and other bodies, such as at solarsystem.nasa.gov/planets or nssdc.gsfc.nasa.gov/planetary/factsheet
- Virtual exploration of planets and the solar system, such as at splash.abc.net.au/home#!/digibook/618096/solar-system-and-space-exploration
- Design tool for designing the living pod, such as at tinkercad.com
- Short video tutorial for Tinkercad, such as at youtube.com/watch?v=KCaenAGeK_Q
- Virtual voyage to the planets, such as at abc.net.au/tv/voyage

RESOURCES PROVIDED

- Generic reproducibles 1, 2, 3, 4, 5, 6
- Reproducibles 16.1, 16.2, 16.3
- Learning journal templates 1, 2, 3, 4 (on disc)

MATERIALS NEEDED

- Sticky notes (half a pad per pair)
- Paper
- Coloured card
- Pens and markers
- Sticky tape
- Pipe-cleaners
- Cardboard
- Living things, such as pot plants
- Non-living things, such as ice blocks, plastic flowers
- Images of living and non-living things

KEY SCIENCE KNOWLEDGE

This section provides an overview of the key science concepts and vocabulary needed for this unit.

ESSENTIAL REQUIREMENTS FOR LIFE

All **organisms** require certain things to survive in their environment. They need nutrients (such as oxygen, protein and carbohydrates), an energy source (such as sunlight) and water.

Humans can only survive within a certain range of temperatures and pressures. The Earth is considered to be a 'Goldilocks' planet. Its distance from the Sun and its **atmosphere** mean that the temperature is not too hot and not too cold, which allows large bodies of liquid water to exist. Conditions are 'just right' for the Earth's living organisms.

OUR SOLAR SYSTEM

A solar system is made up of a star and all the bodies that orbit around it, such as asteroids, planets and moons. In our solar system, the Sun is the star, and eight planets **orbit** around it: Mercury, Venus, Earth, Mars, Jupiter, Saturn, Uranus and Neptune. Our solar system also contains planets' moons, meteorites, asteroid belts, dwarf planets and their moons, and many other things (such as 'space junk') that are stuck in orbit around the Sun.

The Earth's atmosphere protects humans from extreme temperatures and pressures. From space it looks like a thin blue layer above the Earth's surface.

LIVING IN A SPACE COLONY

For successful space **colonisation**, humans must create a suitable **biosphere**. This biosphere must produce oxygen and water, grow food and provide shelter from extreme temperatures. A biosphere can consist of one large structure or many pods.

Due to the distance and potential travel time between a new colony and the Earth, humans must be able to live in their biosphere for an indefinite amount of time. This means that they must live in a **sustainable** way, consuming only the amount of food, water and oxygen that they produce.

STRONG STRUCTURES

Students can choose many different shapes when designing their living pods. The strength that the shapes give a structure is important so that a pod can withstand extreme weather conditions.

Biosphere 2 is a science research facility in Arizona, USA. It was built to experiment with the idea of a sustainable biosphere.

KEY VOCABULARY

atmosphere – a mixture of gases surrounding a planet
biosphere – an area where life can be supported, such as a structure made by humans to support an ecosystem
colonisation – the setting up of a settlement in a new place
orbit – move in a regular and repeating pattern around another object in space
organism – a living thing
sustainable – able to be continued so that a resource doesn't run out

→ TUNE IN

1. Ask students to complete **Generic reproducible 1 (Key vocabulary table)** using the key vocabulary for this unit. This reproducible will also be used at the end of the unit, to demonstrate changes in understanding.
2. Use the think–pair–share method to brainstorm key vocabulary about the solar system. Have students each generate a list and work in pairs to expand their list further, then come together to create a class word list.
3. Identify categories within the list, such as 'features', 'requirements for life' and 'planets and moons'.
4. Around the classroom, spread large sheets of paper with a different category and key vocabulary on each. Have students move from category to category to write any known definitions and additional words.
5. Regroup as a class and identify/define unknown words. Display around the class for use in the unit.

ACTIVITY 1: THE SOLAR SYSTEM

1. List the planets and ask students to order them correctly. They can also consider distance from the Sun.
2. Display a diagram of the solar system showing the shape of the orbits of the planets around the Sun. Identify the Earth and ask, 'What makes the Earth special?'
3. Students choose one planet to research and compare to the Earth (see **Useful apps/links**).
4. Have students compare the two planets and identify the key characteristics and features. Ask, 'How far from the Sun is it? What is its atmosphere? What is the planet made from?'
5. Students present their findings as a table, class spreadsheet or wall display.

ACTIVITY 2: REQUIREMENTS FOR LIFE

1. Show students a variety of items (see **Materials needed** list) and ask them to characterise the items as living or non-living.
2. Have pairs of students define 'living thing', then create a class definition. Challenge students by providing examples that do not fit into their definitions, particularly with plants.
3. Prompt students to consider the requirements of living organisms. Consider all living organisms, not just humans and animals.
4. Show photos of different environments containing life, and determine the common requirements for life (nutrients, an energy source and water).

ACTIVITY 3: THE STRONGEST STRUCTURE

1. Find images (such as bridges, arches and beehives) to display shapes in structures.
2. Have students hypothesise which shape makes the strongest structure. Pairs of students create a structure made of that shape using only straws and tape (for joining corners).
3. Students can test the strength of their structure to withstand external forces such as wind (from a fan or hairdryer) and weights.

6. Provide students with the student card and read the information together. Reflect on the initial brainstorm of key vocabulary and add language and definitions. Students will need to create design criteria based on the requirements for life. Ask students to consider the features of different planets and moons and why the Earth is so special.
7. Introduce the design thinking process by reviewing the stages on the student card. Explain that students will keep a journal about their learning at the different stages of the design.
8. Before engaging in the challenge, students need to have an understanding of the solar system, essential requirements for life, the difference between living and non-living things, and the impact of shapes on structural strength and design.

TOP TIP! During the Tune-in stage, conduct vocabulary activities to highlight and develop key vocabulary knowledge. Activities could include drawing semantic webs, creating a word wall or paired discussions. Check the **Key vocabulary** or read the **Key science knowledge** for a refresher on the key terms and concepts.

USEFUL APPS/LINKS

- App for exploring the solar system, such as SolarWalk
- Facts about planets, moons and other bodies, such as at solarsystem.nasa.gov/planets or nssdc.gsfc.nasa.gov/planetary/factsheet
- Virtual exploration of planets and the solar system, such as at splash.abc.net.au/home#!/digibook/618096/solar-system-and-space-exploration
- Virtual voyage, such as at abc.net.au/tv/voyage

EMPATHISE

During the Empathise stage of the design thinking process, students focus on finding out about different aspects of the challenge. To empathise with the people who would potentially colonise another planet, they need to consider liveability issues and the criteria for choosing a planet to colonise. Students will take notes, ask questions, and draw and create flowcharts, taking photos where relevant.

ACTIVITY 1: FIND OUT THE REQUIREMENTS FOR LIFE

Review the basic requirements for life. Organise students into groups of three or four and provide them with A3 copies of **Reproducible 16.1 (Planet placemat)** (one for each planet). Students refer to the collated information about each planet, then write their ideas about what some of the issues might be and which basic requirements might be difficult to meet. Provide students with a limited time (for example, three minutes) for each placemat. Rotate groups through the different planets, ensuring each group completes at least four different placemats.

ACTIVITY 2: CONSIDER WHICH PLANET IS BEST

1. Students need to consider which planet has the best conditions for colonisation. To do this, they need to create a flowchart to help with the decision-making process. Demonstrate how to create a simple flowchart with yes/no responses.
2. Provide students with the opportunity to make simple flowcharts with a partner. Start by creating a flowchart showing the steps taken to complete an everyday activity, such as making a sandwich.
3. When students are familiar with the basic structure of a flowchart, they can brainstorm key questions to include in their flowcharts to help them make their decision. Demonstrate how to include other elements of logic on the flowchart, such as 'if ... then ...' statements. Students use **Reproducible 16.2 (Flowchart plan)** to plan a simple flowchart. Explore flowcharts using pen and paper, or a flowchart app (see **Useful apps/ links**).
4. Ask students to include the following in their flowchart: atmospheric pressure, climate, distance from the Sun and composition of the planet. They may wish to include other criteria.

Ask students to consider the information they have gathered through researching and commenting. Use the **Prompts** to start a class discussion.

PROMPTS

- Which basic living requirements might be difficult to find out about for each planet?
- What level of atmospheric pressure is acceptable?
- What are some of the features common to several planets, if any?
- How did you organise your flowchart?

MORE VOCABULARY

- empathise – understand and consider another person's or group's point of view
- point of view – an opinion, attitude or judgement considered in a particular way

JOURNAL TIP

Ask students to complete **Learning journal template 1 (Empathise page)** while they are completing the different tasks. Remind them to date their notes and include photos or drawings of relevant information.

USEFUL APPS/LINKS

- App for creating different diagrams like flowcharts, such as Creately
- Website for creating flowcharts, such as Draw.io

ASSESSMENT

This stage of the design thinking process offers opportunities to observe students collecting information, developing questions, and recording their notes and thinking in their journal.

TOP TIP! Computational thinking skills are analytical thinking skills that help to solve problems. They include the use of algorithms and programs to think about different ideas and data. Flowcharts are a tool that students can use to create basic algorithms, in order to make a decision or demonstrate a sequence of steps.

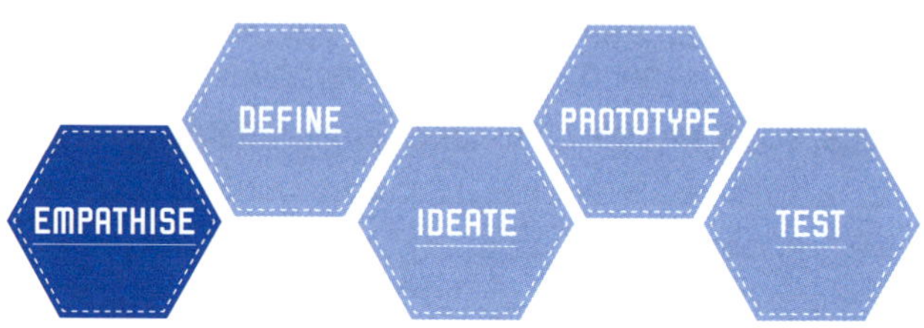

→ DEFINE

The main focus of this stage of the design thinking process is to reframe the challenge. The initial challenge is quite open, so at this stage students learn how to define what needs to be done. This includes noting insights that have been generated.

ACTIVITY 1: CONSIDER OBSERVATIONS

1. Students consider the information they gathered in the Empathise stage. They may work in pairs or small groups. Provide them with a whiteboard, large sheet of paper and/or sticky notes to collate some of the key information they have gathered, especially in relation to the flowchart. They should focus on one of the planets identified as suitable for colonisation and some of the issues relating to requirements essential for life.
2. Students should discuss one section of **Learning journal template 2 (Define page)** at a time, write their responses, then continue discussing their ideas for the next section, until the task is complete. This provides students with opportunities to hear others' responses and also provides the teacher with input points.
3. Discuss the need to design a living pod for the chosen planet. Ask students to create some design criteria for biosphere requirements such as source of oxygen, access to food and water, protection from the weather and ways to keep healthy. Students use **Reproducible 16.3 (Living pod requirements)** to record the criteria. Provide them with the opportunity to research life in space. Ask them to write other information they would like to know, for example, current information about space travel and life in space, such as on the International Space Station. Provide them with **Generic reproducible 4 (Key question table)** to assist them to record their questions, findings and sources.

ACTIVITY 2: CONSIDER INSIGHTS

Students think of at least one insight they have gained from the process; for example, it is important to find a way to provide water and food sources.

Students add this insight to **Learning journal template 2 (Define page)** and then write a brief explanation of what needs to be created.

When considering insights, students could think about the following:

- What was something unexpected that you found out? How was it unexpected?
- How will you decide on the most important aspect of creating a biosphere for colonising a planet?
- Is there any other information that you need or would like to know? How will you find out?

ACTIVITY 3: CONSIDER CONSTRAINTS

At this stage, let students know the constraints of the challenge, by describing the timeframe, the materials available, how and when the designs will be shared and technology options. Students can then update **Learning journal template 2**.

PROMPTS

- What did you discover?
- What were the most important pieces of information that you gathered?
- What was something new that you learned?
- What other information do you need?

MORE VOCABULARY

- define – state the meaning of something
- insight – an accurate understanding of someone or something

JOURNAL TIP

Discuss the term 'insight'. Explain that it relates to something students have learned about information gathered through research. You could refer to **Learning journal template 2**.

EMPATHISE DEFINE IDEATE PROTOTYPE TEST

→ IDEATE

The Ideate stage of the design thinking process is all about generating lots of ideas. Students need to be flexible in their thinking and be able to move beyond obvious ideas. At this stage, ideas are not judged, just generated and gathered.

ACTIVITY: GENERATE IDEAS

1. Ask groups of students to draw or write their ideas relating to creating a biosphere. Each new idea should be written or drawn on a separate piece of paper or sticky note.
2. Ask students to group ideas on a wall or board.
3. Ask students to look at the different ideas and provide feedback to each other. It is important that students don't defend their ideas at this stage. They should just be listening to the feedback.
4. After the initial feedback, ask students to come up with more ideas. Encourage them to be creative and even radical.
5. Ask students to choose four of their ideas to write in their journal. Students use **Learning journal template 3 (Ideate page)** to do this. Ask students to choose one idea to explore further and explain the reasoning behind their choice.

TOP TIP!

At this stage, students may have produced a series of annotated drawings about a biosphere. They may have a collection of sticky notes, which they can organise into related ideas.

Encourage students to view and read others' ideas before giving feedback. Feedback could be within small groups or between partners. Considering others' ideas is an important part of this process, so students can build on their own ideas as they continue to ideate.

At each stage of this activity, ask students to discuss their thoughts before writing their responses. This will help them to think through their ideas and select their final ideas to develop.

PROMPTS

- How do these ideas relate to the criteria, including essential requirements for life?
- How might you test your design?
- How can you make it portable?
- How can you make it adapt to potential changes in environmental conditions?
- What if you had to use different materials?

MORE VOCABULARY

- feedback – information about, for example, a person's performance or the design of a product, which can be used to make improvements
- ideate – generate many ideas without making judgements about the ideas

JOURNAL TIP

When choosing four ideas to include in the journal, students should try to choose four ideas that aren't related.

USEFUL APPS/LINKS

- Tools for creating ideas, such as at creatingminds.org/tools/tools_ideation.htm
- Tips for creativity and innovation, such as at designorate.com/creativity-innovation-in-education

ASSESSMENT

At the Ideate stage, assessment could include observations about the number and diversity of students' ideas, and their ability to provide feedback and create additional ideas. Reflection in the journal should provide an insight into some of the reasoning behind students' choices.

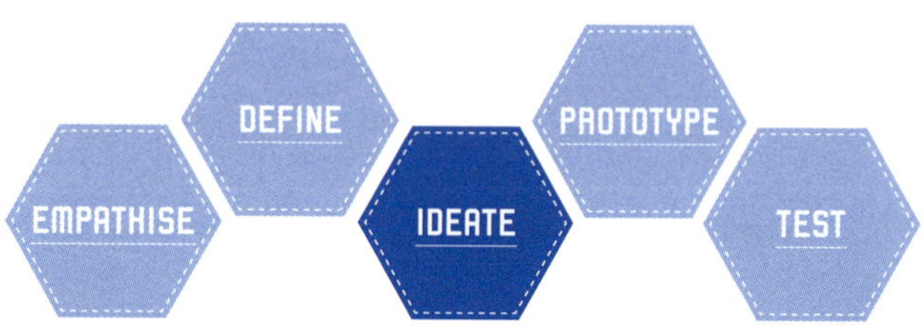

→ PROTOTYPE

At this stage of the design thinking process, students are asked to create a physical prototype of a living pod. It is the stage where students need to get their ideas out of their head and presented in a way that engages other students and helps them to understand the concept. When students create, it helps them to think and solve problems and disagreements. Students can role-play, make storyboards or use sticky notes when they prototype. The most important feature is that viewers can interact with whatever is produced.

Encourage students to photograph or film during the prototyping and testing stages. This information can be used to show the learning behind the design thinking process in action.

ACTIVITY: TRANSFORM IDEAS INTO PROTOTYPES

1. Students review the ideas generated at the Ideate stage. Provide them with an A3 copy of **Generic reproducible 6 (In the frame)** so they can organise their ideas into two sections: 'least relevant' and 'most relevant'. Students continue to cycle through this activity until they have an idea to start prototyping.
2. Provide students with a range of materials to use to create their prototype. Remind students that a prototype should be created rapidly and is not meant to look 'nice'.
3. After a prototype has been created, ask students to see if it works and get feedback from others.
4. Students then use the feedback to prototype again.

Ask students to fill in the Prototype section of **Learning journal template 4 (Prototype and test page)**. See the **Journal tip** for further student guidance.

TOP TIP!

The Prototype stage is often very messy. It is important that students are focusing on their ideas, rather than the end product. Provide them with lots of materials – recycling depots can be a useful source of resources. Students may add labels to prototypes to explain some of the main features. Photographing and annotating pictures of prototypes can be useful.

To gain feedback, students could ask each other some of the following questions:

- What is the main feature of your prototype?
- How does it work?
- Which aspects work best? What will you keep?
- Which aspects need changing? How might you do this?
- What other materials might you need?

PROMPTS

- What worked?
- How could it be improved?
- What else do you need to know, do or have?
- What other suggestions do you have?

MORE VOCABULARY

- feedback – information about, for example, a person's performance or the design of a product, which can be used to make improvements
- prototype – an initial version of a model of a product or process that is used to develop a final model

JOURNAL TIP

Remind students to highlight the main features of their prototype. If students are creating an electronic journal, they can insert a photo of their prototype and annotate it.

USEFUL APPS/LINKS

- App for creating interactive links (for example, between descriptions, videos, images and websites and a main image), such as ThingLink
- App for making notes using text, drawings, images, weblinks and audio, such as Notability

ASSESSMENT

Observe students as they make changes to their designs. Are they able to consider feedback, make modifications and move rapidly through this process? Or do they have difficulties with holding on to an idea and accepting feedback?

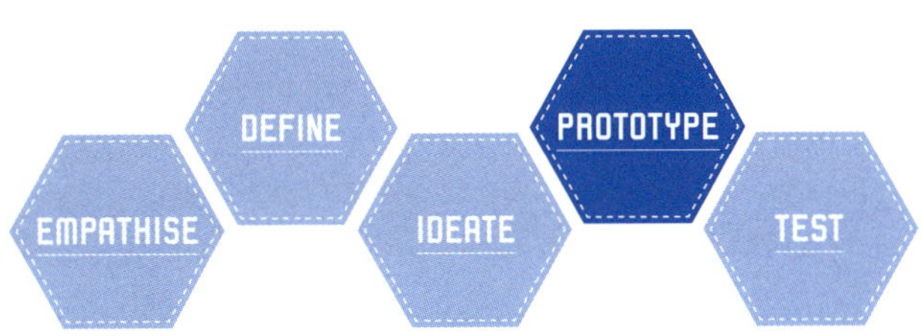

→ TEST

At this stage of the design thinking process, students test their prototype to see how it meets the criteria in the challenge. This may involve gathering independent feedback because the planetary conditions can't be re-created for the living pods. Students review the criteria and continue to cycle through the prototyping and testing stages.

ACTIVITY: TEST FEEDBACK

1. Students take their last prototype and consider the main needs of the people who would be using the living pod.
2. Ask students to check whether or not their design might work. If not, what do they need to do to make it viable?
3. Provide the opportunity to cycle through the prototyping and testing stages again.

Ask students to fill in the Test part of **Learning journal template 4 (Prototype and test page)**. See the **Journal tip** for further student guidance.

PROMPTS

- Does your prototype do what you wanted it to do?
- Does it have additional features?
- Are there features that need to be removed?

MORE VOCABULARY

- evaluate – assess something, perhaps considering what worked and what didn't
- feature – a specific aspect of something, such as size, shape, colour and quality
- feedback – information about, for example, a person's performance or the design of a product, which can be used to make improvements
- prototype – an initial version of a model of a product or process that is used to develop a final model
- review – consider an idea, process or product and decide what needs to be changed and what works

JOURNAL TIP

Ask students to think about why it is important to test their ideas before they build their final design.

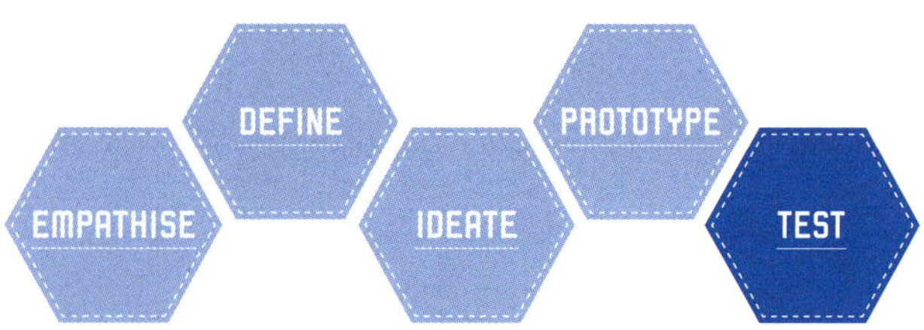

→ SHARE AND EVALUATE

At this stage of the investigation, students are provided with an opportunity to share their final design, as well as the processes involved in the investigation. Students evaluate their learning journals and their solutions.

ACTIVITY 1: BRING THE DESIGNS TOGETHER

1. Students can create an iMovie or use Adobe Spark Video to demonstrate the process and thinking behind the designs. There should be an element of narration, where they are sharing their story about points of view, insights, prototyping and solutions.
2. Students should include their learning journals with the display so others can see the different stages of the design process.

ACTIVITY 2: EVALUATE AND GIVE FEEDBACK

1. Provide students with **Generic reproducible 2 (Self-evaluation)**.
2. Ask students to provide feedback to each other about the most interesting features, the aspects that were most difficult and the changes that they would make if they repeated the task.
3. Provide students with opportunities to share their designs with the wider community, through a science expo or online gallery. It may be possible to share some of the videos with an expert for feedback about the designs.

ASSESSMENT

Ask students to complete **Generic reproducible 1 (Key vocabulary table)** again, using the key vocabulary for this unit. Compare their table with the one they completed at the Tune-in stage, to demonstrate changes in understanding.

Students complete **Generic reproducible 3 (Responding to the investigation)**. Compare their responses to those on **Generic reproducible 2**.

Teachers and students each complete **Generic reproducible 5 (Design thinking assessment rubric)**. Students compare the feedback they are given by the teacher with their self-assessment of their design thinking skills.

EMPATHISE

STEM INVESTIGATIONS

Names: ....

Date: ....

Name of planet: ....

What might be one issue with living on this planet? Which basic living requirement might be most difficult to provide?	What might be another issue with living on this planet? Which other basic living requirement might be difficult to provide?
What might be another issue with living on this planet? Which other basic living requirement might be difficult to provide?	What might be another issue with living on this planet? Which other basic living requirement might be difficult to provide?

STEM Investigations, UP, ISBN 978 1 4202 4154 9 © Macmillan Science and Education Australia 2018

Name: ....

Date: ....

Think of some questions you need to ask about a planet and what type of answer might be given. This should help you to plan your flowchart.

QUESTION	TYPE OF ANSWER		
	Yes/no	Number	Words
	☐	☐	☐
	☐	☐	☐
	☐	☐	☐
	☐	☐	☐
	☐	☐	☐
	☐	☐	☐
	☐	☐	☐

DEFINE

STEM INVESTIGATIONS

Name: ....

Date: ....

What are the essential requirements for life?

What are the key features of the planet for which you are designing the living pod?

What does your living pod need to include or do?

- [ ] oxygen source
- [ ] water source
- [ ]
- [ ]
- [ ]
- [ ]
- [ ]
- [ ]
- [ ]
- [ ]
- [ ]
- [ ]
- [ ]
- [ ]

STEM Investigations, UP, ISBN 978 1 4202 4154 9

IMAGINE HUMANS OF THE FUTURE – ON FILM

→ INTRODUCTION

Living organisms continue to adapt to changes within their environments. Animals have physical or behavioural adaptations that have allowed them to survive in their changing environments. An example of a physical adaptation is additional fat stores that help an animal survive in a cold climate. Staying in a burrow during the day in a hot climate and hunting for food at night when it is cooler is a behavioural adaptation. Humans have also changed over time, for example, gaining more sweat glands when more activity was required to hunt for food.

In this STEM investigation, students are asked to find out about possible adaptations that could occur in humans of the future. They are asked to imagine a considerably hotter Earth in the distant future and to use scientific information to create a stop-motion animation that gives a snapshot of a future human.

This STEM challenge is easily differentiated for students by encouraging different groups to use different degrees of complexity when investigating. Students could also be provided with opportunities to test different materials as well as designs.

THE CHALLENGE

Your favourite Hollywood director is holding a competition for fans. She wants to produce a sci-fi blockbuster, set 50 000 years in the future, about humans who have adapted to life on a much warmer Earth. All the human adaptations must be based on science and linked to real-world adaptations. The best 'future human' design wins a prize.

Your challenge is to design a human who could live on an Earth that is 6°C warmer than today, in a world of extreme heat waves and superstorms. You will need to make a stop-motion animation that shows how your new human would look and move. As part of your challenge, you will learn about body structures and behaviours that help animals to live in harsh environments on Earth today.

KEY UNDERSTANDINGS

- Scientists predict an increase in temperatures and changes to climate in the future.
- Adaptation is change that helps an animal or plant to survive in its environment.
- Evolution explains how living things, including humans, have changed over time.
- Physical adaptations are changes to the physical structure of an animal, for example, a thicker layer of skin.
- Behavioural adaptations are changes in behaviour, such as hibernation in winter.

KEY VOCABULARY

adaptation

behavioural

biomechanics

evolution

physical

structural feature

KEY SKILLS

- Make careful observations.
- Consider different points of view.
- Develop research skills.
- Apply scientific knowledge.

KEY ACTIONS

- Find out about animal adaptations to harsh climates, especially dry and hot environments.
- Learn about physical adaptations to dry and hot environments.
- Find out about how humans sit, walk and stand.
- Explore ways to adapt a future human's physical structure to a hotter climate.
- Create a stop-motion animation of a human of the future.

OVERVIEW OF STAGES

TUNE IN:

Students view science fiction trailers, collect science fiction characters and play an adaptation game. They explore simple biomechanics of movement, learn about stop-motion animation and make a zoetrope.

EMPATHISE

Students interview each other to find out others' opinions about science fiction films and characters.

DEFINE

Students consider the main issues that relate to future humans and the key features of a science fiction film.

IDEATE

Students generate creative ideas for human adaptations, based on animal adaptations.

PROTOTYPE

Students transform some of their ideas into physical representations. These are created rapidly, using simple materials. Students can role-play, make storyboards or use sticky notes when they prototype.

TEST

Students share their prototypes and provide feedback to each other. Students check which ideas work best, then choose a final design to build. Students check which ideas the audience responded to best.

SHARE AND EVALUATE:

The final prototype is used to create a stop-motion animation. A storyboard is used to plan the sequence of the animation. Final animations are shared and evaluated, with opportunities for expert feedback.

SUGGESTED SCHEDULE

LESSON	STAGE
1–4	**Tune in**: pre-test key vocabulary, watch science fiction trailers, play an adaptations game, explore simple biomechanics of movement, learn about stop-motion animation and make a zoetrope
5	**Empathise**: interview people about science fiction movies and characters, and write/record in journal
6	**Define**: define the main issues relating to human adaptation in the future, and write/record in journal
7–8	**Ideate**: develop ideas for a human of the future, and write/record in journal
9–11	**Prototype** and **Test**: conduct prototyping and testing, and write/record in journal
12–14	**Share and evaluate**: share and evaluate designs and prototypes

CURRICULUM LINKS

The following tables show the key Science, Technologies and Mathematics curricula with which this STEM investigation is aligned.

SCIENCE

YEAR	STRAND	SUB-STRANDS AND CONTENT
5	Science Understanding	Biological sciences: • Living things have structural features and adaptations that help them to survive in their environment
6	Science Understanding	Biological sciences: • The growth and survival of living things are affected by the physical conditions of their environment Earth and space sciences: • Sudden geological changes or extreme weather conditions can affect Earth's surface
5 & 6	Science as a Human Endeavour	Nature and development of science: • Science involves testing predictions by gathering data and using evidence to develop explanations of events and phenomena
5 & 6	Science Inquiry Skills	Questioning and predicting Processing and analysing data and information Communicating

TECHNOLOGIES

YEAR	STRAND	CONTENT
5 & 6	Design and Technologies Processes and Production Skills	• Generate, develop and communicate design ideas and processes for audiences using appropriate technical terms and graphical representation technique • Develop project plans that include consideration of resources when making designed solutions individually and collaboratively
	Digital Technologies Processes and Production Skills	• Design a user interface for a digital system, generating and considering alternative designs • Implement digital solutions as simple visual programs involving branching, iteration (repetition), and user input

MATHEMATICS

YEAR	STRAND	CONTENT
5 & 6	Measurement and Geometry	Using units of measurement Geometric reasoning
	Statistics and Probability	Chance Data representation and interpretation

OTHER CURRICULUM LINKS

GENERAL CAPABILITIES

- Literacy
- Numeracy
- Personal and Social Capability
- Information and Communication Technology (ICT) Capability
- Critical and Creative Thinking

ASSESSMENT

The following resources are provided for assessing students at different stages of the investigation:

- Generic reproducible 1 (Key vocabulary table), for assessing understanding of vocabulary
- Generic reproducible 2 (Self-evaluation), for student self-evaluation of the learning process
- Generic reproducible 3 (Responding to the investigation), for assessing student engagement in the challenges, and the collaboration and skills involved in the design thinking stages
- Generic reproducible 5 (Design thinking assessment rubric), for evaluating student engagement in the design thinking stages
- Learning journal templates 1, 2, 3 and 4, for incorporating student reflection and evaluation

GETTING READY FOR THE INVESTIGATION

You can prepare yourself and students for this STEM investigation in the following ways:

- Identify groups of students who will work well together.
- Review the **Key science knowledge** that supports this investigation, and look at the **Useful links**.
- Investigate the **Useful apps** for stop-motion animations.
- Gather materials for creating future humans and animations.
- Start collecting additional materials for prototyping (as shown on the **Materials needed** list).
- Determine where prototypes will be kept between lessons.
- Create a wall space where students can share their ideas in the Ideate stage and create a collection of science fiction characters.
- Organise the class into pairs or groups of three.
- Create display space for information about adaptations.
- Start thinking about:
  - » student experience with stop-motion animation apps and tasks
  - » timing for movie making
  - » criteria for the animation, including length and actions for the human to demonstrate
  - » managing cutting when making the zoetrope
  - » who students might interview to find out about science fiction movie preferences.

USEFUL APPS

- App for making notes using text, drawings, images, weblinks and audio, such as Notability
- App for creating interactive links (for example, between descriptions, videos, images and websites and a main image), such as ThingLink
- App for creating a learning journal, such as Book Creator
- App for creating semantic maps (links between different words and/or concepts), such as Popplet
- App for creating multimedia presentations, such as Adobe Spark Video and iMovie
- App for making simple animations, such as PowerPoint and KeyNote
- Animation app, such as Stop Motion Studio and iMotion
- Survey app, such as Typeform (free for small surveys)

USEFUL LINKS

- Types of animal and plant adaptations, such as at bbc.co.uk/nature/adaptations
- Adaptations to heat, such as at bbc.co.uk/nature/adaptations/Thermophile
- Adaptations to fire, such as at bbc.co.uk/nature/adaptations/Fire_ecology
- An adaptation game, such as at desertmuseumdigitallibrary.org/kids/Games/Adaptations.html
- Instructions for making a zoetrope, such as at wikihow.com/Make-a-Zoetrope
- Information about animation apps, such as at makerspaceforeducation.com/stop-motion-animation.html
- Biomechanics of walking, such as at footeducation.com/page/biomechanics-of-walking-gait
- Online video of illuminated dancers, such as at youtube.com/watch?v=kmK06mhkUjU

RESOURCES PROVIDED

- Generic reproducibles 1, 2, 3, 4, 5, 6, 7
- Reproducibles 17.1, 17.2, 17.3
- Learning journal templates 1, 2, 3, 4 (on disc)

MATERIALS NEEDED

- Sticky notes (half a pad per pair)
- Paper
- Coloured card
- Pens and markers
- Sticky tape
- Pipe-cleaners
- Cardboard
- Reusable modelling product, such as Plasticine
- Soft, bendable wire
- Circular paper box, such as the lid from a cylindrical ice-cream carton
- LEGO
- Stiff black card
- White paper
- Scissors
- Craft knife
- Marbles
- Wide masking tape
- Digital camera or device with in-built camera
- Any of the animation apps in the **Useful apps** list

KEY SCIENCE KNOWLEDGE

This section provides an overview of the key science concepts and vocabulary needed for this unit.

ADAPTATION AND EVOLUTION

Adaptation is change that helps a plant or animal survive in its environment. An adaptation may be **physical** or **behavioural**. A physical adaptation is a structural change. An example of this is the fat stores under a seal's skin, which insulates it from cold water. A behavioural adaptation is a change in behaviour. An example of this is a bear hibernating in winter, when food is limited.

Animals in dry environments have physical adaptations to prevent loss of water and store water. A camel is physically adapted to its environment: it needs less water than other animals and stores energy in its hump as fat. Animals in hot environments have heat-tolerant adaptations, such as large ears to dissipate heat.

Evolution is an explanation of the change in characteristics in a living population over a long time. Humans have evolved over time from apelike ancestors. This evolution took millions of years. Some individual human populations have adapted to their specific environments. The people of Tibet have adapted to life at high altitudes, where the air contains very little oxygen. Part of their physical adaptation includes an increased breathing rate and increased lung capacity.

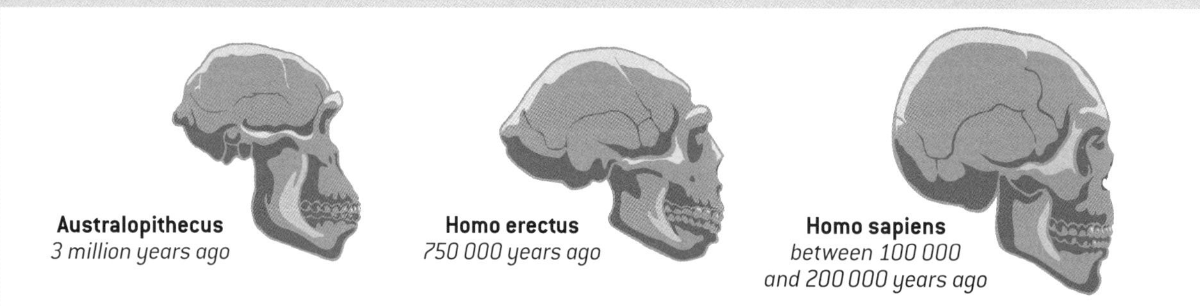

The shape of the human skull has changed a lot over time.

Animals with **structural features** that are well suited to their environments are more likely to survive and to breed. This means that the number of animals with these features increases gradually over generations.

Sitting and standing might seem to be simple actions but there are quite complex **biomechanics** behind these movements. A combination of joint actions and muscle contraction and extension allows us to control our bodies in order to walk and sit.

The action of walking has several phases:

- **heel strike:** placing the heel of one foot on the ground
- **early flatfoot:** point when the whole foot is on the ground
- **late flatfoot:** point when the heel begins to rise
- **toe off:** the toes begin to leave the ground
- **swing phase:** the foot swings forward to take another step

The ankle joint and nearby transverse tarsal joint have a critical role in walking. See the **Useful apps/links** or visit a similar website about the biomechanics of walking.

A fennec fox has very large ears to help heat escape and keep its body cool.

KEY VOCABULARY

adaptation – a change that helps a plant or animal survive in its environment
behavioural – relating to how someone or something acts
biomechanics – the structure and function of living things
evolution – a scientific explanation for certain changes in living things over a long time
physical – relating to the body
structural feature – a feature (for example, shape or size) relating to a physical part of a person, animal, plant or object

→ TUNE IN

1. Ask students to complete **Generic reproducible 1 (Key vocabulary table)** using the key vocabulary for this unit. This reproducible will also be used at the end of the unit, to demonstrate changes in understanding.
2. Watch some age-appropriate science fiction trailers. Discuss the characters, their physical features and students' response to the characters.
3. Discuss with students the differences between science fiction and non-science fiction television programs and movies. Students create a display of science fiction characters and annotate their features. Add to the display as the investigation continues.
4. Before engaging in the challenge, students need to have an understanding of: adaptation; types of physical and behavioural adaptation; evolution; the simple mechanics of human movement; and how to make a stop-motion animation. To this end, set up the following three activities (or similar).

ACTIVITY 1: ANIMAL ADAPTATION

1. Discuss the term 'adaptation'. Provide students with some examples of adaptation, such as those of the desert hopping mouse (large ears) or camel (hump).
2. Provide students with a link to an adaptation game (see **Useful apps/links**). Students look at the picture of a particular animal and choose the adaptation they think is linked to the animal. They can repeat this several times with different animals.
3. Provide students with **Reproducible 17.1 (Animal adaptations)**. Ask students to choose an animal and provide six different types of adaptations, with only one matching the animal. Students write each adaptation on a sticky note and stick it on top of a square. They write whether the adaptation is correct or not under the sticky note, so other students can check their answer. Students could create an electronic version of this activity.

USEFUL APPS/LINKS

- Online video of illuminated dancers, such as at youtube.com/watch?v=kmKO6mhkUjU
- Instructions for making a zoetrope, such as at wikihow.com/Make-a-Zoetrope
- An adaptation game, such as at desertmuseumdigitallibrary.org/kids/Games/Adaptations.html

ACTIVITY 2: HOW BODY PARTS MOVE

1. Watch the video showing illuminated dancers (see **Useful apps/links**). Discuss the different ways that the dancers move. Start the video at 1 minute 40 seconds and finish at 3 minutes.
2. In pairs, students stick large, round stickers on their hips, knees, ankles, heels and toes. Students take turns observing their partner (side view) and noting how their body parts move as they sit, stand and walk. They might wish to video the actions to refer to later, when they create their animation.

ACTIVITY 3: STOP-MOTION ANIMATION

1. Discuss the concept of stop-motion animations. Show students a video of a stop-motion animation.
2. A zoetrope is a pre-film animation device that can be used to explore the components and effects of a stop-motion animation. Provide students with the materials and instructions to make a zoetrope (see **Useful apps/links**).
3. Discuss the changes made to each image in the zoetrope, and how this links to using a PowerPoint animation or stop-motion app.

5. Introduce the STEM investigation and challenge to the students. Provide them with the student card and read through the information together. Ask students to think about the types of adaptations they might need to learn about, especially considering the predicted future environment. Students also start to think about the types of materials they may wish to use to create their future human.
6. Introduce the design thinking process by reviewing the stages on the student card. Explain that students will keep a journal about their learning at the different stages of the design.

TOP TIP!

During the Tune-in session, conduct vocabulary activities to highlight and develop key vocabulary knowledge. Activities could include drawing semantic webs, creating a word wall or paired discussions. Check the **Key vocabulary** definitions or read over the **Key science knowledge** for a refresher on the key terms and concepts.

→ EMPATHISE

During the Empathise stage of the design thinking process, students focus on finding out about different points of view. To empathise with others, they need to engage in observation, interact with others and immerse themselves in the experiences that others have. Students will observe others, taking notes, asking questions and taking photos where possible. Students interview people to find out what they think about different science fiction films and characters.

ACTIVITY 1: SCIENCE FICTION FILMS

1. Students interview two different people about science fiction films and characters using **Reproducible 17.2 (Science fiction interview)**. Students should ask the following questions:
   - » Which types of films do you like? Why?
   - » Would you prefer a funny or serious film? Why?
   - » Would you prefer an optimistic or pessimistic film? Why?
   - » What might the world be like in 50 000 years?
   - » Which types of science fiction characters do you like or dislike? Why?
2. Students are allocated 10 minutes to conduct each interview and make notes.

ACTIVITY 2: SIMILAR AND DIFFERENT OPINIONS

1. Students consider the information collected in the interviews. They consider what they have noticed, then share their information with a partner. Students note similarities and differences in the interviews.
2. Provide students with **Generic reproducible 7 (Double bubble)** to note the similarities and differences between the two interviews they conducted.
3. Students can complete a class Google Doc to share some of their insights or make a wall display.

ACTIVITY 3: EMPATHISE

Ask students to think about some of the responses. They create a short PowerPoint or album with pictures of science fiction characters. Students ask people to choose a feeling word to respond to each character. Students write some of these words on **Learning journal template 1 (Empathise page)**.

PROMPTS

- What types of characters did people like?
- What types of characters did people dislike?
- Which type of film did most people want?
- Which types of films were the least popular?
- What did you learn about other people's opinions?

MORE VOCABULARY

- empathise – understanding and considering another person's or group's point of view
- point of view – an opinion, attitude or judgement considered in a particular way

JOURNAL TIP

Ask students to complete **Learning journal template 1 (Empathise page)** while they are completing the different tasks. Remind them to date their notes and include photos or pictures of relevant information.

USEFUL APPS/LINKS

- PowerPoint or KeyNote for simple presentation of images
- *Dr Who* website: doctorwho.tv
- Science fiction characters, such as at comicvine.gamespot.com/profile/the_poet/lists/cvs-top-100-science-fiction-and-fantasy-characters/38638/

ASSESSMENT

This stage of the design thinking process offers opportunities to observe students collecting information, developing questions, and recording their notes and thinking in their journal.

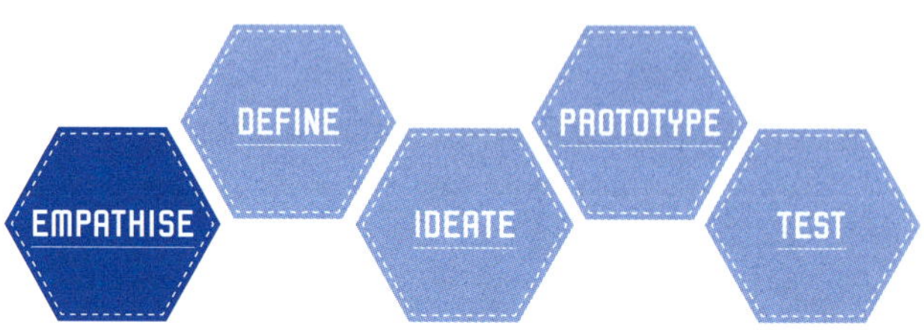

→ DEFINE

The main focus of this stage of the design thinking process is to reframe the challenge. The initial challenge is quite open, so at this stage students learn how to define what needs to be done. This includes noting insights that have been generated.

ACTIVITY 1: CONSIDER OBSERVATIONS

1. Students consider the information they gathered in the Empathise stage about people's preferences about science fiction characters. They may work in pairs or small groups. Provide them with a whiteboard, large sheet of paper and/or sticky notes to collate some of their key information. Students sort the feedback from their interviews. They discuss some of the common observations in pairs, then join with another pair to share again.
2. Students should discuss one section of **Learning journal template 2 (Define page)** at a time, write their responses and then continue discussing their ideas for the next section, until the task is complete. This provides students with opportunities to hear others' responses and it provides the teacher with input points.
3. Discuss the exploration of how humans move in the Tune-in sessions. Provide students with the opportunity to research further so they have a better understanding of how their human of the future will move. Ask them to write other information they would like to know, such as predicted changes in climate and subsequent adaptations to consider.
4. Provide students with **Generic reproducible 4 (Key question table)** to assist them to record their questions, findings and sources. Provide time for students to share some of the key information they have collected.

ACTIVITY 2: CONSIDER INSIGHTS

Students think of at least one insight they have gained from the process; for example, people wanted an optimistic film and a character with superhuman powers. Students add this insight to **Learning journal template 2 (Define page)**.
They should then relate the insight to their design.

When considering insights, students could think about the following:

- What was something unexpected that you saw or found out? How was it unexpected?
- How will you decide on the most important aspect of the future human's structural features?
- Is there any other information that you need or would like to know? How will you find out?

ACTIVITY 3: CONSIDER CONSTRAINTS

At this stage, let students know the constraints of the challenge, by describing what the future human needs to be able to demonstrate, such as sitting, standing and walking. Discuss also the length of the animation, the inclusion of narration or text explanation, the schedule for the investigation and the materials available. Students can then update **Learning journal template 2**.

PROMPTS

- What did you discover?
- What were the most important pieces of information that you gathered?
- What was something new that you learned?
- What other information do you need?

MORE VOCABULARY

- define – state the meaning of something
- insight – an accurate understanding of someone or something

JOURNAL TIP

Discuss the term 'insight'. Explain that it relates to something students have learned about the people they interviewed and the information they gathered. You could refer to **Learning journal template 2**.

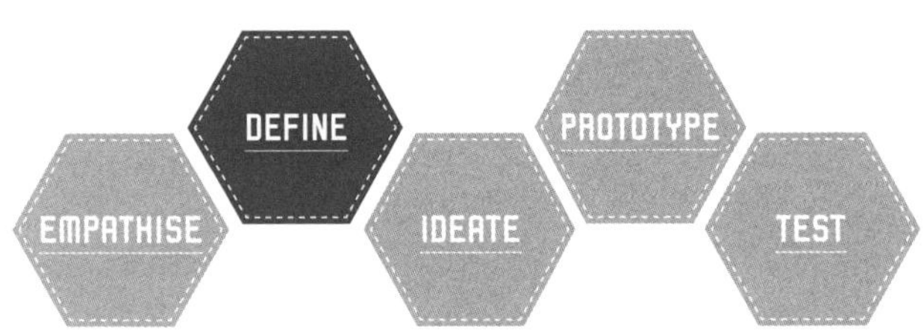

→ IDEATE

The Ideate stage of the design thinking process is all about generating lots of ideas. Students need to be flexible in their thinking and be able to move beyond obvious ideas. At this stage, ideas are not judged, just generated and gathered.

ACTIVITY: GENERATE IDEAS

1. Ask groups of students to draw or write their ideas.
2. Each new idea should be written or drawn on a separate piece of paper or sticky note.
3. Ask students to group ideas on a wall or board.
4. Ask students to look at the different ideas and provide feedback to each other. It is important that students don't defend their ideas at this stage. They should just be listening to the feedback.
5. After the initial feedback, ask students to come up with more ideas. Encourage them to be creative and even radical.
6. Ask students to choose four of their ideas to write in their journal. Students use **Learning journal template 3 (Ideate page)** to do this. Ask students to choose one idea to explore further and explain the reasoning behind their choice.

TOP TIP!

At this stage, students may have produced a series of drawings that are annotated. They may have a collection of sticky notes, which they can organise into related ideas.

Encourage students to view and read others' ideas before giving feedback. Feedback could be within small groups or between partners. Considering others' ideas is an important part of this process, so students can build on their own ideas as they continue to ideate.

At each stage of this activity, ask students to discuss their thoughts before writing down their responses. This will help them to think through their ideas and select their final ideas to develop.

PROMPTS

- How do your chosen ideas relate to how humans move?
- How do these ideas relate to some of the adaptations that may occur in a future human?
- How might you test your design?
- How can you change the way your future human moves?
- How can you show the different adaptations of your future human?
- What would you do if you had to use different materials?

MORE VOCABULARY

- feedback – information about, for example, a person's performance or the design of a product, which can be used to make improvements
- ideate – generate many ideas without making judgements about the ideas

JOURNAL TIP

When choosing four ideas to include in the journal, students should try to choose ideas that aren't related, to show a range of ideas.

USEFUL APPS/LINKS

- Tools for creating ideas, such as at creatingminds.org/tools/tools_ideation.htm
- Tips for creativity and innovation, such as at designorate.com/creativity-innovation-in-education/

ASSESSMENT

At the Ideate stage, assessment could include observations about the number and diversity of students' ideas, and their ability to provide feedback and create additional ideas. Reflection in the journal should provide an insight into some of the reasoning behind students' choices.

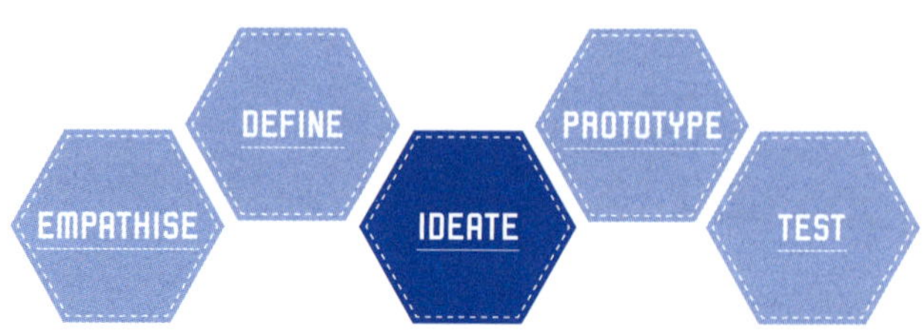

PROTOTYPE

At this stage of the design thinking process, students are asked to create a physical prototype of a solution. It is the stage where students need to get their ideas out of their head and presented in a way that engages other students and helps them to understand the concept. When students create, it helps them to think and solve problems and disagreements. Students can role-play, make a storyboard or use sticky notes when they prototype. The most important feature is that viewers can interact with whatever is produced.

ACTIVITY: TRANSFORM IDEAS INTO PROTOTYPES

1. Students review the ideas generated at the Ideate stage. Provide them with an A3 copy of **Generic reproducible 6 (In the frame)** so they can organise their ideas into two sections: least relevant and most relevant. Students continue to cycle through this activity until they have an idea to start prototyping.
2. Provide students with a range of materials to use to create their prototype. Remind students that a prototype should be created rapidly and is not meant to look 'nice'.
3. After a prototype has been created, ask students to see if it works and get feedback from others.
4. Students then use the feedback to prototype again.

Ask students to fill in the Prototype part of **Learning journal template 4 (Prototype and test page)**. See the **Journal tip** for further student guidance.

PROMPTS

- What worked?
- How could it be improved?
- What else do you need to know, do or have?
- What other suggestions do you have?

MORE VOCABULARY

- feedback – information about, for example, a person's performance or the design of a product, which can be used to make improvements
- prototype – an initial version of a model of a product or process that is used to develop a final model

JOURNAL TIP

Remind students to highlight the main features of their prototype. If students are creating an electronic journal, they can insert a photo of their prototype and annotate it.

USEFUL APPS/LINKS

- App for creating interactive links (for example, between descriptions, videos, images and websites and a main image), such as ThingLink
- App for making notes using text, drawings, images, weblinks and audio, such as Notability

ASSESSMENT

Observe students as they make changes to their designs. Are they able to consider feedback, make modifications and move rapidly through this process? Or do they have difficulties with holding onto an idea and accepting feedback?

TOP TIP!

The Prototype stage is often very messy. It is important that students are focusing on their ideas, rather than the end product. Provide them with lots of materials for prototyping their future human, like LEGO, modelling clay and recycled materials such as cardboard tubes and boxes (recycling places can be a useful source of resources). Students may add labels to prototypes to explain some of the main features and adaptations. Photographing and annotating pictures of prototypes can be useful.

To gain feedback, students could ask each other some of the following questions:

- What is the main adaptation of your future human?
- How does your prototype move?
- Which features work best? What will you keep?
- Which features need changing? How might you do this?
- What other materials might you need?

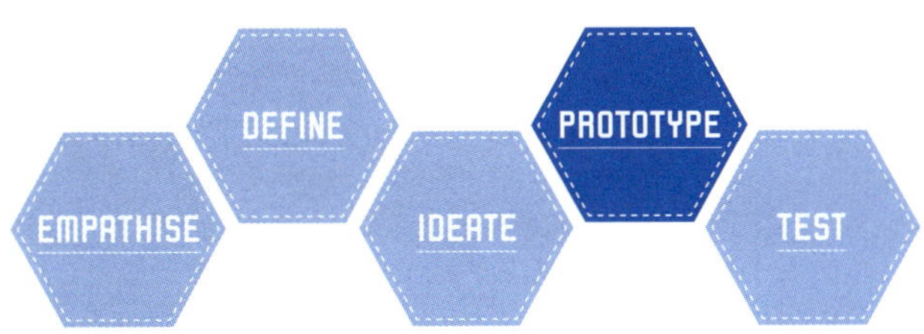

→ TEST

At this stage of the design thinking process, students test their prototype of a future human to see if it meets the original criteria. Students should be able to demonstrate how it moves and it should have clear adaptations.

ACTIVITY: TEST FEEDBACK

1. Students take their last prototype and consider the feedback provided in the initial survey of people and their responses to science fiction films and characters.
2. Ask students to check whether or not their design is able to demonstrate movement. If not, what do they need to do to make it work?
3. Provide the opportunity to cycle through the Prototype and Test stages again.
4. Students complete their final design.

Ask students to fill in the Test part of **Learning journal template 4 (Prototype and test page)**. See the **Journal tip** for further student guidance.

PROMPTS

- Does your prototype do what you wanted it to do?
- Does it have additional features that need changing or removing?
- Are there other features you could add?
- What works well?

MORE VOCABULARY

- evaluate – assess something, perhaps considering what worked and what didn't
- feature – a specific aspect of something, such as size, shape, colour, quality
- feedback – information about, for example, a person's performance or the design of a product, which can be used to make improvements
- prototype – an initial version of a model of a product or process that is used to develop a final model
- review – consider an idea, process or product and decide what needs to be changed and what works

JOURNAL TIP

Ask students to think about why it is important to test their ideas before they build their final design.

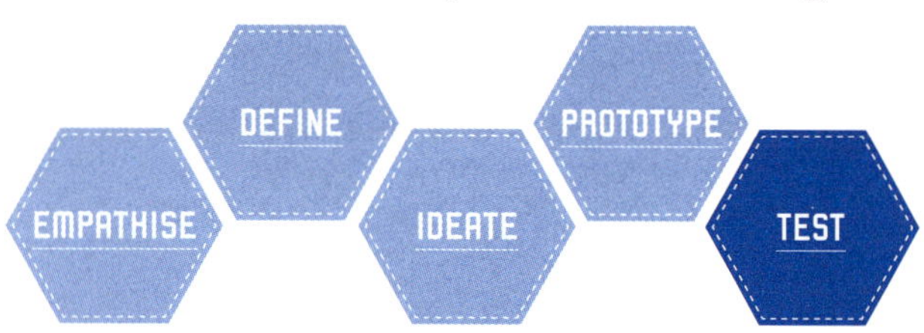

→ SHARE AND EVALUATE

At this stage of the investigation, students are provided with an opportunity to share their final design, as well as the processes involved in the investigation. Students evaluate their learning journals and their solutions.

ACTIVITY 1: BRING THE DESIGNS TOGETHER

1. Students can create an iMovie or use Adobe Spark Video using their final design. There should be an element of narration, where they are sharing their points of view, insights, prototyping and end product.
2. Provide students with **Reproducible 17.3 (Storyboard)** to plan the sequence of their animation.
3. Students film and edit their animations, with clear guidelines for time management.
4. Students should include their learning journals with the animations so others can see the different stages of the design process.

ACTIVITY 2: EVALUATE AND GIVE FEEDBACK

1. Provide students with **Generic reproducible 2 (Self-evaluation)** to complete.
2. Ask students to provide feedback to each other about the most interesting features, the aspects that were most difficult and the changes that they would make.
3. Provide students with opportunities to share their designs with the wider community. It may be possible to share some of the videos with an expert for feedback about the designs. Animations could be shared on a school website or class blog. Look out for animation competitions too.

ASSESSMENT

Ask students to again complete **Generic reproducible 1 (Key vocabulary table)** using the key vocabulary for this unit. Compare their table with the one they completed at the Tune-in stage, to demonstrate changes in understanding.

Students complete **Generic reproducible 3 (Responding to the investigation)**. Compare their responses to those on **Generic reproducible 2**.

Teachers and students each complete **Generic reproducible 5 (Design thinking assessment rubric)**. Students compare the feedback from the teacher with their self-assessment of their design thinking skills.

STEM INVESTIGATIONS

Name: ....

Date: ....

Choose an animal that has adapted to its environment. Draw or stick a picture of it in the box provided. Write six possible adaptations, one per sticky note and then stick them in each of the rectangles. Only one of them should be true. Write if the adaptation is correct or not under each sticky note.

Animal name:

....

Picture:

EMPATHISE

STEM INVESTIGATIONS

Name: ....

Date: ....

Use this table to record your two interviews.

QUESTIONS	INTERVIEW 1	INTERVIEW 2
Which types of films do you like? Why?		
Would you prefer a funny or serious film? Why?		
Would you prefer an optimistic or pessimistic film? Why?		
What might the world be like in 50 000 years?		
Which types of science fiction characters do you like or dislike? Why?		

STEM Investigations, UP, ISBN 978 1 4202 4154 9 © Macmillan Science and Education Australia 2018

Name: ....

Date: ....

STEM INVESTIGATIONS

Use this storyboard to plan the sequence for your animation.
In each frame, draw or write about what your future human does.
Make an extra copy of this storyboard if you need more frames.

STEM Investigations, UP, ISBN 978 1 4202 4154 9 © Macmillan Science and Education Australia 2018

THINK UP AN EXCITING DISH THAT REPRESENTS YOU

→ INTRODUCTION

Cooking shows and competitions are very popular, with contestants exploring both simple and complex recipes. Molecular gastronomy is the study of the physical and chemical processes that occur when ingredients are transformed. It combines the use of edible ingredients with laboratory techniques and equipment. Many chefs, particularly those in the best restaurants, continue to explore the science and possibilities of cooking.

Food is very connected with culture and identity. This STEM investigation combines the science of cooking with the artistic expression of identity. Students will learn about changes in states of matter, in relation to food. They will find out about different cooking techniques and the science behind them. Students will create a dish that demonstrates their understanding of food transformations and represents aspects of their personality.

THE CHALLENGE

Every year your family competes to come up with the craziest and most delicious ideas for a celebration dinner. The winner gets to cook their dish on New Year's Eve. This year the theme has been set as 'Me on a plate'. You are interested in molecular gastronomy – using science to transform the tastes and textures of food – and you're keen to cook!

Your challenge is to design a unique dish that uses science to transform ingredients in a surprising way. The dish should represent your personality, too. You will need to pitch your idea to your family. To do this, you should write a recipe, explain the motivation for your dish and present a labelled diagram, showing what the dish will look like and how it should be served. As part of your investigation, you will learn about some of the science behind cooking, including chemical reactions.

KEY UNDERSTANDINGS

- There are three main states of matter: solid, liquid and gas.
- Foods can be solid, liquid or gas.
- Changes can be reversible or irreversible.
- A chemical reaction creates at least one new substance.
- Personal hygiene is very important when handling food.

KEY VOCABULARY

chemical reaction
freezing point
irreversible
melting point
molecular gastronomy
reversible

KEY SKILLS

- Locate information.
- Follow instructions.
- Collate and evaluate information.
- Apply scientific concepts about change that are specific to food.

KEY ACTIONS

- Learn about molecular gastronomy.
- Experiment with cooking techniques that demonstrate change.
- Interview family and friends about special meals.
- Plan and create a meal.
- Explain the design of the meal and the idea behind it.

→ OVERVIEW OF STAGES

TUNE IN:

Students learn about states of matter and the properties of solids, liquids and gases. They explore some of the ways that states of matter can change. They make observations about states of matter. Students are introduced to chemical changes in food and molecular gastronomy.

EMPATHISE

Students find out about some of the trends in cooking. They interview others to find out what constitutes a good meal.

DEFINE

Students consider others' opinions about food and learn about different cooking techniques.

IDEATE

Students generate ideas for how to create a meal that reflects their personality and incorporates interesting flavours, textures and presentation.

PROTOTYPE

Students choose one or two ideas to create. They may focus on a particular component of a dish, as well as create a model of its final presentation.

TEST

Prototypes are tested, either at home or at school. Feedback is collected from others so adjustments can be made.

SHARE AND EVALUATE:

Final dish ideas are shared, through a presentation that incorporates the recipe, photographs and an explanation of the ideas and science processes behind the dish.

→ SUGGESTED SCHEDULE

LESSON	STAGE
1–2	**Tune in**: learn about states of matter, explore chemical changes in cooking and introduce the student challenge
3–4	**Empathise**: find out about cooking trends, interview others to find out what constitutes a good meal and write/record in journal
5–6	**Define**: define the main issues and expectations, explore different cooking techniques and write/record in journal
7	**Ideate**: develop ideas for creating a dish and write/record in journal
8–11	**Prototype** and **Test**: conduct prototyping and testing cycles and write/record in journal
12–13	**Share and evaluate**: share and evaluate dish ideas

CURRICULUM LINKS

The following tables show the key Science, Technologies and Mathematics curricula with which this STEM investigation is aligned.

SCIENCE

YEAR	STRAND	SUB-STRAND AND CONTENT
5	Science Understanding	Chemical sciences: • Solids, liquids and gases have different observable properties and behave in different ways
6	Science Understanding	Chemical sciences: • Changes to materials can be reversible or irreversible
5 & 6	Science as a Human Endeavour	Use and influence of science: • Scientific knowledge is used to solve problems and inform personal and community decisions

TECHNOLOGIES

YEAR	STRAND	CONTENT
5 & 6	Design and Technologies Processes and production skills	• Generate, develop and communicate design ideas and processes for audiences using appropriate technical terms and graphical representation techniques • Select appropriate materials, components, tools, equipment and techniques, and apply safe procedures to make designed solutions • Develop project plans that include consideration of resources when making designed solutions individually and collaboratively

MATHEMATICS

YEAR	STRAND	CONTENT
5 & 6	Measurement and Geometry	Using units of measurement
	Number and Algebra	Number and place value

OTHER CURRICULUM LINKS

AC

GENERAL CAPABILITIES

- Literacy
- Numeracy
- Information and Communication Technology (ICT) Capability
- Critical and Creative Thinking

ASSESSMENT

The following resources are provided for assessing students at different stages of the STEM investigations:

- Generic reproducible 1 (Key vocabulary table), for assessing understanding of vocabulary
- Generic reproducible 2 (Self-evaluation), for student self-evaluation of the learning process
- Generic reproducible 3 (Define graphic organiser), for assessing student engagement in the challenges, and the collaboration and skills involved in the design thinking stages
- Generic reproducible 5 (Design thinking assessment rubric), for evaluating student engagement in the design thinking stages
- Learning journal templates 1, 2, 3 and 4, for incorporating student reflection and evaluation

GETTING READY FOR THE INVESTIGATION

You can prepare yourself and students for this STEM investigation in the following ways:

- Identify groups of students who will work well together.
- Review the **Key science knowledge** that supports this investigation, and look at the **Useful links**.
- Investigate the **Useful apps**.
- Gather materials for exploring states of matter during the Tune-in session.
- Start collecting additional materials for prototyping (as shown on the **Materials needed** list).
- Determine where prototypes will be kept between lessons.
- Create a wall space where students can share their ideas in the Ideate stage.
- Organise the class into pairs.
- Start thinking about:
  - if the task will be an individual or group challenge
  - if the cooking components can be completed at school or need to be completed at home
  - access to cooking and science equipment
  - students with allergies – avoid using any foods that may be a problem for these students
  - a budget for ingredients
  - organising an incursion or excursion
  - creating or developing links with a chef
  - other useful websites about molecular gastronomy
  - how to source special ingredients, such as agar-agar, if needed
  - planning some activities to happen over several days.

USEFUL APPS

- App for creating semantic maps (links between different words and/or concepts), such as Popplet
- App for creating mind maps, such as Inspiration
- App for creating interactive links (for example, between descriptions, videos, images and websites and a main image), such as ThingLink
- App for making notes using text, drawings, images, weblinks and audio, such as Notability
- App for creating multimedia presentations, such as Adobe Spark Video, iMovie, KeyNote and PowerPoint
- App for creating surveys, such as Typeform (free for small surveys)

USEFUL LINKS

- Information about changing states of matter, such as at chem4kids.com/files/matter_changes.html
- Examples of chemical reactions in the kitchen, such as at leaf.tv/articles/examples-of-chemical-reactions-in-the-kitchen and australasianscience.com.au/article/science-and-technology/kitchen-science-chemistry-behind-amazing-meringue-and-perfect-cappucc
- Dairy foods information, such as at legendairy.com.au
- Recipes and menus, such as at kitchengardenfoundation.org.au/uploads/09_resources/the_program_in_action/SAKGF_Recipes_and_Menus.pdf
- Food safety information, such as at health.gov.au/internet/main/publishing.nsf/content/5FFB6A30ECEE9321CA257BF0001DAB17/$File/Food%20Safety%20Fact%20Sheet.pdf and healthykids.nsw.gov.au/recipes/food-safety-and-hygiene.aspx
- Signature dishes, such as at hungryforever.com/9-celebrity-chefs-signature-dishes
- Top recipes and food trends, such as at bbcgoodfood.com/recipes/collection/all-time-top-20 and bbcgoodfood.com/article/food-trends-2017
- Common molecular gastronomy techniques, such as at organicauthority.com/foodie-buzz/molecular-gastronomy-techniques-explained.html

RESOURCES PROVIDED

- Generic reproducibles 1, 2, 3, 4, 5, 6
- Reproducibles 18.1, 18.2, 18.3, 18.4, 18.5
- Learning journal templates 1, 2, 3, 4 (on disc)

MATERIALS NEEDED

- Sticky notes (half a pad per pair)
- Paper
- Coloured card
- Pens and markers
- Sticky tape
- Cardboard
- Sugar
- Milk
- Honey
- Butter
- Pasta
- Apple
- Jelly
- 8 clear containers
- Plastic syringes and plastic piping (if making fruit spaghetti)
- Blender
- Ice
- Fruit
- Agar-agar

KEY SCIENCE KNOWLEDGE

This section provides an overview of the key science concepts and vocabulary needed for this unit.

MATTER

Matter is made of tiny particles called atoms. Atoms can join together to form molecules; for example, water molecules are a combination of hydrogen and oxygen atoms. Matter can be one type of atom or molecule or it can be two or more types. The arrangement of the atoms and molecules in matter determine its state. The main states of matter are solid, liquid and gas.

CHANGES OF STATE DUE TO HEATING AND COOLING

The state of matter of a substance changes with temperature and pressure. For example, at room temperature and normal air pressure water is a liquid, but at 0°C it will become a solid and at 100°C a gas.

Changes in state are physical changes and can be caused by adding or removing heat. Bonds between the atoms or molecules of a substance become 'looser' when energy is applied. At a temperature specific to that substance, the substance changes from solid to liquid (**melting point**) or liquid to gas (boiling point). These changes are **reversible** – a gas condenses to a liquid when cooled, and reducing the temperature of a liquid to its **freezing point** changes the liquid to a solid.

See **STEM Investigation 11: Use sea water to save the village**, for more information on changing states of matter.

CHANGES DUE TO CHEMICAL REACTIONS

During a chemical reaction, atoms or molecules in one or more substances rearrange to form one or more other substances. Most chemical reactions are **irreversible**, which means the reacted substances cannot return to their original form. For example, when bread is toasted (applying energy as heat) the sugars (carbohydrates) in the bread break down to form carbon, turning the bread brown.

SCIENCE AND COOKING

Even basic cooking is an example of science in action, from boiling an egg to toasting bread. **Molecular gastronomy** uses physical changes of state and chemical reactions to transform ingredients even further. 'Molecular' refers to the makeup of the ingredients, and 'gastronomy' refers to the art or science of good eating.

SOLID

Solids have atoms or molecules that sit tightly together. They have a definite shape and size. They are very difficult to compress.

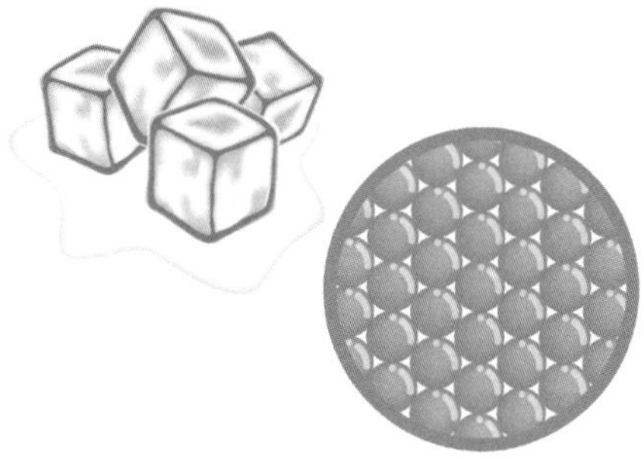

LIQUID

Liquids contain atoms or molecules that can move more than solids. They have a fixed volume, will flow and take on the shape of their container. They can be slightly compressed.

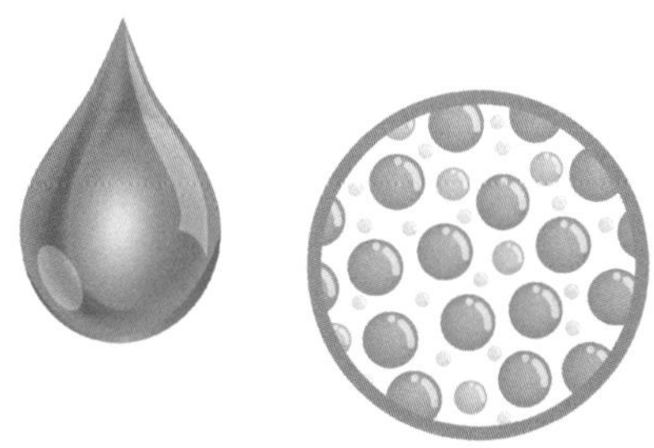

GAS

Gases have no fixed shape or volume. The atoms are moving rapidly and can spread out. They can be compressed.

KEY VOCABULARY

chemical reaction – rearrangement of atoms or molecules in one or more substances to form one or more other substances
freezing point – the temperature at which something changes in state from liquid to solid
irreversible – unable to be changed back to the original form
melting point – the temperature at which something changes in state from solid to liquid
molecular gastronomy – a branch of food science that investigates and explores physical changes and chemical changes of ingredients in cooking
reversible – able to be changed back to the original form

→ TUNE IN

1. Ask students to complete **Generic reproducible 1 (Key vocabulary table)** using the key vocabulary for this unit. This reproducible will also be used at the end of the unit, to demonstrate changes in understanding.
2. Before engaging in the challenge, students need to have an understanding of the properties of solids, liquids and gases; some changes in states of matter and chemical reactions that occur when cooking; and the field of molecular gastronomy.

ACTIVITY 1: INTRODUCING STATES OF MATTER

1. Prepare seven clear containers with the following foods as examples of different states of matter. An eighth container will contain only air (a mixture of gases).
   - sugar (solid)
   - milk (liquid)
   - honey, uncreamed (liquid)
   - apple (solid)
   - butter (soft solid)
   - pasta (solid)
   - jelly (a gel – part solid and part liquid)
2. Discuss how we make observations, using a simple object such as a rock. Note things such as colour, shape, texture, hardness and behaviour.
3. Provide students with **Reproducible 18.1 (States of matter)** to record observations.
4. In small groups, students move around the samples and record observations. They decide whether samples are a solid, liquid or gas. Each group reports back to the class and a class table is collated.
5. Discuss the observable properties. How were decisions made about the state of matter?
6. Write a class definition for solids, liquids and gases that will be referred back to.
7. Remind students that this is initial thinking and they will be exploring further.

TOP TIP! During the Tune-in stage, conduct vocabulary activities to highlight and develop key vocabulary knowledge. Activities could include drawing semantic webs, creating a word wall or paired discussions. Check the **Key vocabulary** or read the **Key science knowledge** for a refresher on the key terms and concepts.

ACTIVITY 2: INTRODUCTION TO COOKING

1. Show a video about kitchen chemical changes (see **Useful apps/links**).
2. Working with partners, students decide if different cooking processes are reversible or irreversible reactions. Students complete **Reproducible 18.2 (Reversible or irreversible?)**. For each cooking process, students tick the boxes they think apply and then state whether the process is reversible or irreversible.

ACTIVITY 3: MOLECULAR GASTRONOMY

1. Show students a video that provides examples of molecular gastronomy techniques (see **Useful apps/links**).
2. Provide students with **Reproducible 18.3 (Molecular gastronomy ingredients)**. Students choose one ingredient mentioned in one of the videos and fill in the following boxes:
   - food ingredient
   - usual ways this ingredient is used
   - unusual ways this ingredient has been used.
3. Students then choose an ingredient not mentioned in the video and complete a brainstorm, filling in the following boxes:
   - food ingredient
   - usual ways this ingredient is used
   - unusual ways this ingredient might be used.

3. Introduce the STEM investigation and challenge to the students. Provide them with the student card and read the information together. Ask students to think about the foods they like and how particular foods or dishes might reflect their own personality. Introduce the design thinking process by reviewing the stages on the student card.
4. Explain that students will keep a journal about their learning at the different stages of the design.

USEFUL APPS/LINKS

- Chemical changes in the kitchen, such as at youtube.com/watch?v=37pir0ej_SE
- Molecular gastronomy techniques, such as at youtube.com/watch?v=vbvQIKzSmkQ or youtube.com/watch?v=4nPMLNaBWNI

→ EMPATHISE

During the Empathise stage of the design thinking process, students focus on finding out about different points of view. To empathise with others, they need to research some of the experiences that people have had. Students will take notes, ask questions, draw diagrams and take photos where relevant. This may include gathering other people's reactions to different images of food.

ACTIVITY 1: FIND OUT ABOUT TRENDS

1. Ask students to find out more about trends in cooking, especially since the increase in the number of cooking shows and competitions on television. Organise students into groups of four and complete a jigsaw task. Set up four tasks, based on the following themes (see **Useful apps/links**):
   - » signature dishes
   - » top recipes
   - » food trends
   - » common molecular gastronomy techniques.
2. Each member of the groups joins a different task group. After they have completed their task, they return to their group to share their findings. Ask students to take notes that they can share with their original group. Discuss some of the unusual and interesting information discovered.

ACTIVITY 2: INTERVIEW OTHERS

Ask students to interview others about what makes a dish special. Ask them to generate questions relating to flavour, ingredients, presentation, texture and any other aspect that they think might be relevant. Provide students with **Reproducible 18.4 (Features of special dishes)** to record their questions and the responses of their interviewees.

Ask students to consider the information gathered about the trends in cooking, as well as others' observations and opinions about good food.

PROMPTS

- What cooking trend was the most unusual?
- What are some of the most popular types of dishes people like to cook?
- What were some of the most important aspects of food?
- How important was the presentation of food to others?

MORE VOCABULARY

- empathise – understand and consider another person's or group's point of view
- point of view – an opinion, attitude or judgement considered in a particular way

JOURNAL TIP

Ask students to complete **Learning journal template 1 (Empathise page)** while they are completing the different tasks. Remind them to date their notes and include photos of relevant information or pictures.

USEFUL APPS/LINKS

- Signature dishes, such as at hungryforever.com/9-celebrity-chefs-signature-dishes
- Top recipes and food trends, such as at bbcgoodfood.com/recipes/collection/all-time-top-20 and bbcgoodfood.com/article/food-trends-2017
- Common molecular gastronomy techniques, such as at organicauthority.com/foodie-buzz/molecular-gastronomy-techniques-explained.html

ASSESSMENT

This stage of the design thinking process offers opportunities to observe students collecting information, developing questions, and recording their notes and thinking in their journal.

EMPATHISE DEFINE IDEATE PROTOTYPE TEST

→ DEFINE

The main focus of this stage of the design thinking process is to reframe the challenge. The initial challenge is quite open, so at this stage students learn how to define what needs to be done. This includes noting insights that have been generated.

ACTIVITY 1: CONSIDER OBSERVATIONS

1. Students consider the information they gathered in the Empathise stage. They may work in pairs or small groups. Provide them with a whiteboard, large sheet of paper and/or sticky notes to collate some of the key information they have gathered. They should focus on the types of cooking techniques and the important aspects of food presentation.
2. Students should discuss one section of **Learning journal template 2 (Define page)** at a time, write their responses, then continue discussing their ideas for the next section, until the task is complete. This provides students with opportunities to hear others' responses and also provides the teacher with input points.
3. Discuss states of matter. Check that students have a good understanding of the different transformations. Provide students with the opportunity to research further and explore different techniques, including butter making, 'creaming' butter and sugar, and making jelly. Perhaps provide students with recipe books to explore some simple techniques. Ask them to write other information they would like to know, such as which foods provide natural colourings and how liquids can be solidified quickly. Provide **Generic reproducible 4 (Key question table)** to assist hem to record questions, findings and sources.

ACTIVITY 2: CONSIDER INSIGHTS

Students think of at least one insight they have gained from the process; for example, ingredients can be changed so they look like something else.

Students add this insight to **Learning journal template 2 (Define page)** and then write a brief explanation of what needs to be created.

When considering insights, students could think about the following:

- What was something unexpected that you saw or found out? How was it unexpected?
- How will you decide on the most important aspect of your dish?
- Is there any other information that you need or would like to know? How will you find out?

ACTIVITY 3: CONSIDER CONSTRAINTS

At this stage, let students know the constraints of the challenge, by describing the time frame, materials available, budget (if relevant), safety issues with equipment and handling food, and how the final dish design will be shared and evaluated. Students can then update **Learning journal template 2**.

PROMPTS

- What did you discover?
- What were the most important pieces of information that you gathered?
- What was something new that you learned?
- What other information do you need?

MORE VOCABULARY

- define – state the meaning of something
- insight – an accurate understanding of someone or something

JOURNAL TIP

Discuss the term 'insight'. Explain that it relates to something students have learned about the people and their survey responses. Refer to **Learning journal template 2**.

USEFUL APPS/LINKS

- Cooking for kids, such as at essentialkids.com.au/recipes/kids-cooking

TOP TIP! Non-domestic food preparation is government regulated. The main focus areas when preparing food are personal hygiene (hand washing, hair tied back, protective clothing and cuts covered), food preparation (separate utensils and handling requirements for raw or ready-to-eat food; being aware of thawing, freezing and cooking guidelines) and food storage (storing cold food below 5°C and serving hot food above 60°C).

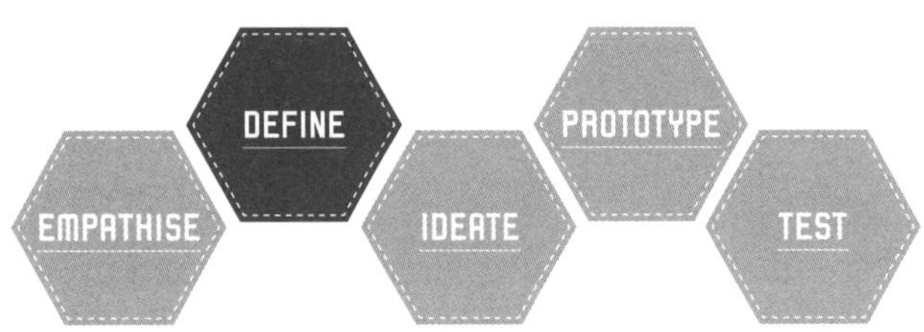

→ IDEATE

The Ideate stage of the design thinking process is all about generating lots of ideas. Students need to be flexible in their thinking and able to move beyond obvious ideas. At this stage, ideas are not judged, just generated and gathered.

ACTIVITY: GENERATE IDEAS

1. Ask groups of students to draw or write their ideas. Ask them to brainstorm ingredients and/or dishes that represent them in some way – perhaps they remind them of good times in the past or future. Ask how they could transform these ingredients in new ways or substitute different ingredients into a familiar dish. Highlight the following ways that a meal could be changed: deconstruction of main ingredients, addition of a new ingredient, different presentation.
2. Each new idea should be written or drawn on a separate piece of paper or sticky note.
3. Ask students to group ideas on a wall or board.
4. Ask students to look at the different ideas and provide feedback to each other. It is important that students don't defend their ideas at this stage. They should just be listening to the feedback.
5. After the initial feedback, ask students to come up with more ideas. Encourage them to be creative and even radical.
6. Ask students to choose four of their ideas to write in their journal. Students use **Learning journal template 3 (Ideate page)** to do this. Ask students to choose one idea to explore further and explain the reasoning behind their choice.

TOP TIP!

At this stage, students may have produced a series of annotated drawings about what they might include in their meal or how it will look. They may have a collection of sticky notes, which they can organise into related ideas.

Encourage students to view and read others' ideas before giving feedback. Feedback could be within small groups or between partners. Considering others' ideas is an important part of this process, so students can build on their own ideas as they continue to ideate.

At each stage of this activity, ask students to discuss their thoughts before writing their responses. This will help them to think through their ideas and select their final ideas to develop.

PROMPTS

- How do these ideas relate to the dish challenge?
- How might you test your design?
- How can you make it look inviting?
- How can you make it taste good?
- What if you had to use different ingredients?

MORE VOCABULARY

- feedback – information about, for example, a person's performance or the design of a product, which can be used to make improvements
- ideate – generate many ideas without making judgements about the ideas

JOURNAL TIP

When choosing four ideas to include in the journal, students should try to choose ideas that aren't related.

USEFUL APPS/LINKS

- Tools for creating ideas, such as at creatingminds.org/tools/tools_ideation.htm
- Tips for creativity and innovation, such as at designorate.com/creativity-innovation-in-education

ASSESSMENT

At the Ideate stage, assessment could include observations about the number and diversity of students' ideas, and their ability to provide feedback and create additional ideas. Reflection in the journal should provide an insight into some of the reasoning behind students' choices.

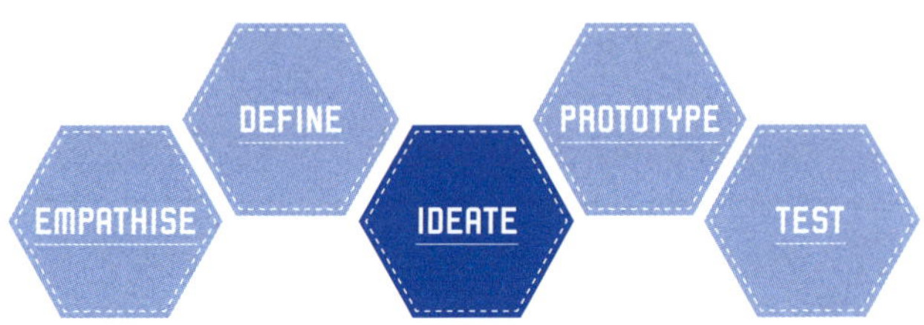

PROTOTYPE

At this stage of the design thinking process, students are asked to create a physical prototype of a solution. It is the stage where students need to get their ideas out of their head and presented in a way that engages other students and helps them to understand the concept. When students create, it helps them to think and solve problems and disagreements. Students can role-play, make storyboards or use sticky notes when they prototype. The most important feature is that viewers can interact with whatever is produced.

Encourage students to photograph or film during the prototyping and testing stages. This information can be used to show the learning behind the design thinking process in action.

ACTIVITY: TRANSFORM IDEAS INTO PROTOTYPES

1. Students review the ideas generated at the Ideate stage. Provide them with an A3 copy of **Generic reproducible 6 (In the frame)** so they can organise their ideas into two sections: 'least relevant' and 'most relevant'. Students continue to cycle through this activity until they have an idea to start prototyping.
2. Decide whether or not students will complete this stage at school, or whether they will be asked to experiment with food at home. Provide students with a range of materials to create their prototype. If experimenting with food at school, consider budget, safety and hygiene issues and time constraints, as well as adult assistance. If students are focusing on how their dish might look, they might find it helpful to draw it or model the dish with modelling clay.
3. After a prototype has been created, ask students to gather feedback from others. This may include friends or family if the meal is prepared at home. Provide students with **Reproducible 18.5 (Food feedback)** for them to record information and feedback relating to different components of their meal.
4. Students then use the feedback to prototype again.

Ask students to fill in the Prototype part of **Learning journal template 4 (Prototype and test page)**. See the **Journal tip** for further student guidance.

PROMPTS

- What worked?
- How could it be improved?
- What else do you need to know, do or have?
- What other suggestions do you have?

MORE VOCABULARY

- feedback – information about, for example, a person's performance or the design of a product, which can be used to make improvements
- prototype – an initial version of a model of a product or process that is used to develop a final model

JOURNAL TIP

Remind students to highlight the main features of their prototype. If students are creating an electronic journal, they can insert a photo of their prototype and annotate it.

USEFUL APPS/LINKS

- App for creating interactive links (for example, between descriptions, videos, images and websites and a main image), such as ThingLink
- App for making notes using text, drawings, images, weblinks and audio, such as Notability

ASSESSMENT

Observe students as they make changes to their designs. Are they able to consider feedback, make modifications and move rapidly through this process? Or do they have difficulties with holding on to an idea and accepting feedback?

TOP TIP!

The Prototype stage is often very messy. It is important that students are focusing on their ideas, rather than the end product. Photographing and annotating pictures of prototypes can be useful.

To gain feedback, students could ask each other some of the following questions:

- What is the main food transformation that has occurred in your dish?
- How does it taste?
- Which aspects work best? What will you keep?
- Which aspects need changing? How might you do this?
- What other ingredients or materials might you need?

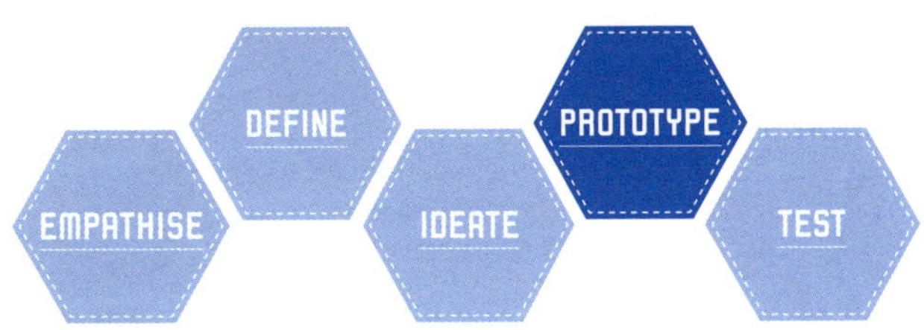

→ TEST

At this stage of the design thinking process, students test their prototype to see how it meets the criteria set at the start of the design process.

ACTIVITY: TEST FEEDBACK

1. Students take their last prototype and consider the initial needs of their audience.
2. Ask students to check whether or not their dish works. If not, what do they need to do to make it work?
3. Provide the opportunity to cycle through the prototyping and testing stages again.

Ask students to fill in the Test part of **Learning journal template 4 (Prototype and test page)**. See the **Journal tip** for further student guidance.

PROMPTS

- Does your dish include all the features that you wanted it to?
- Which cooking techniques did you use? Could you use a different technique?
- Does your dish reflect your personality? How?

MORE VOCABULARY

- evaluate – assess something, perhaps considering what worked and what didn't
- feature – a specific aspect of something, such as size, shape, colour and quality
- feedback – information about, for example, a person's performance or the design of a product, which can be used to make improvements
- prototype – an initial version of a model of a product or process that is used to develop a final model
- review – consider an idea, process or product and decide what needs to be changed and what works

JOURNAL TIP

Ask students to think about why it is important to test their ideas before they create their final presentation.

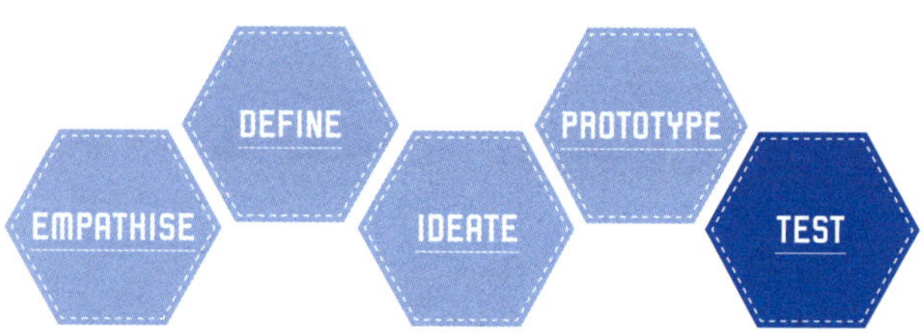

→ SHARE AND EVALUATE

At this stage of the investigation, students are provided with an opportunity to share their final design, as well as the processes involved in the investigation. Students evaluate their learning journals and their solutions.

ACTIVITY 1: BRING THE DESIGNS TOGETHER

1. Provide students with time to create their final presentation, featuring an image of their meal, an explanation of their motivation and the scientific processes involved in the dish.
2. Students can create an iMovie or use Adobe Spark Video to demonstrate the process and thinking behind the designs. There should be an element of narration, where they are sharing their story about points of view, insights, prototyping and solutions.
3. Students should include their learning journals with the display so others can see the different stages of the design process.

ACTIVITY 2: EVALUATE AND GIVE FEEDBACK

1. Provide students with **Generic reproducible 2 (Self-evaluation)** to complete.
2. Ask students to provide feedback to each other about interesting features, difficult aspects and the changes they might make.
3. Provide students with opportunities to share their designs. This could include inviting someone from a cafe or restaurant, or a friend or family member with relevant experience. It may be possible to share some of the videos with an expert for feedback.

ASSESSMENT

Ask students to again complete **Generic reproducible 1 (Key vocabulary table)** using the key vocabulary for this unit. Compare their table with the one they completed at the Tune-in stage, to demonstrate changes in understanding.

Students complete **Generic reproducible 3 (Responding to the investigation)**. Compare their responses to those on **Generic reproducible 2 (Self-evaluation)**.

Teachers and students each complete **Generic reproducible 5 (Design thinking assessment rubric)**. Students compare the feedback they are given by the teacher with their self-assessment of their design thinking skills.

Name: ....

Date: ....

Look at each of the different samples and describe their properties. Decide whether each sample is a solid, liquid or gas. Record your answers in the table.

Sample	Description of properties	Solid	Liquid	Gas
		☐	☐	☐
		☐	☐	☐
		☐	☐	☐
		☐	☐	☐
		☐	☐	☐
		☐	☐	☐
		☐	☐	☐
		☐	☐	☐

STEM Investigations, UP, ISBN 978 1 4202 4154 9

Name: ....

Date: ....

STEM INVESTIGATIONS

Think about these kitchen processes and record what you know about each. Decide if they are reversible or irreversible. The first process has been partly completed for you.

Kitchen process	Was energy added or removed?	Is there a colour change?	Is there a smell?	Are any gases released?	Can the change be undone?	Reversible or irreversible?
Making a cake			Yes		No	Irreversible
Freezing water to make ice cubes						
Making toast						
Boiling an egg						
Melting chocolate						
Making bread						
Boiling water						

STEM Investigations, UP, ISBN 978 1 4202 4154 9 © Macmillan Science and Education Australia 2018

Name: ....

Date: ....

STEM INVESTIGATIONS

Watch a video clip about molecular gastronomy.
Choose one ingredient from the clip and complete the first three boxes.

Food ingredient	Usual ways this ingredient is used	Unusual ways this ingredient is used

Choose an ingredient that hasn't been mentioned in the video clip.
Fill in these boxes.

Food ingredient	Usual ways this ingredient is used	Unusual ways this ingredient is used

EMPATHISE

STEM INVESTIGATIONS

Name: ....

Date: ....

Interview friends or family members about what makes a dish special.
Use the table to write questions and record interview responses.

Feature that might make a dish special	Question	Response
Flavour		
Texture		
Ingredients		
Presentation		
Other		

STEM Investigations, UP, ISBN 978 1 4202 4154 9 © Macmillan Science and Education Australia 2018

PROTOTYPE

STEM INVESTIGATIONS

Name: ....

Date: ....

Use this table to record feedback from others and any changes to your dish.

DESCRIPTION OF DISH		
Part/aspect of dish	First observations and feedback	Changes to make

STEM Investigations, UP, ISBN 978 1 4202 4154 9 © Macmillan Science and Education Australia 2018

COLOUR YOUR COMMUNITY WITH LIGHT

→ INTRODUCTION

Community festivals are held across cultures and countries. Events such as Diwali (the Hindu festival of lights) are celebrated around the world. In China, the Chinese Lantern Festival marks the first full moon of the Chinese year. Light displays are an integral part of the celebrations. White Night is a global, all-night arts festival showcasing art installations, performers and light displays. These festivals bring communities together, celebrating who we are.

This STEM investigation incorporates an exploration of the properties of light and colour, as well as adding an artistic, aesthetic element. Students consider reflection, refraction and absorption of light. They experiment with colour and design to create a light display to be projected on a wall.

THE CHALLENGE

Your local community is holding a Festival of Light to celebrate midwinter. There will be a lantern parade and bonfire, but the main attraction will be light projections and art installations across the town. The local librarian has asked your class to use your knowledge of the properties of light to light up a section of the local library.

Your challenge is to design a large, colourful art installation using a light source and materials such as glass prisms, glass bottles and mirrors. You will need to measure the area you want to light up, come up with different ways of dispersing light, and predict how your design would look. As part of your investigation, you will learn about the properties of light, and about reflection, refraction and absorption.

KEY UNDERSTANDINGS

- Light travels in a straight line unless something makes it change direction.
- Light can be absorbed.
- Light can be reflected.
- Light can be refracted.
- When light is reflected (for example, from a mirror), its path is changed but it does not enter the new material.
- When light is refracted, it changes direction. This happens when light passes through a transparent material.
- Light can be used to direct attention.
- Light can be used to engage.

KEY VOCABULARY

absorption
dispersion
opaque
reflection
refraction
transparent

KEY SKILLS

- Make careful observations.
- Develop interviewing skills.
- Gather information.
- Explain different properties of light.

KEY ACTIONS

- Interview others.
- Experiment with the behaviour of light – reflection, refraction and absorption.
- Create an art installation focusing on light and colour.

OVERVIEW OF STAGES

TUNE IN:

Students learn about the different properties of light, including reflection, refraction and absorption. They explore the ability to see light, experiment with shadows, and consider colour filters.

EMPATHISE

Students find out about how people respond to light displays. They find out about different light festivals and record people's responses to the images and videos.

DEFINE

Students consider some of the issues associated with organising a light display. This includes the need to create a video clip of their display, because they will not have access to professional laser equipment.

IDEATE

Students generate ideas for components of their light display, as well as how the display might look.

PROTOTYPE

Students choose one or two ideas to transform into physical representations (models). These are created rapidly, using simple materials.

TEST

Students test their prototypes and share them for feedback. They also provide feedback to each other. They are given the opportunity to cycle through the Prototype and Test stages again.

SHARE AND EVALUATE:

The final light displays are created using videoing apps. They are shared and evaluated, with opportunities for expert feedback.

SUGGESTED SCHEDULE

LESSON	STAGE
1–2	**Tune in**: explore different properties of light and introduce the student challenge
3–4	**Empathise**: find out about people's responses to light displays and art installations, interview and record responses, and write/record in journal
5–6	**Define**: define the main issues with creating a light display and write/record in journal
7	**Ideate**: develop ideas and write/record in journal
8–10	**Prototype** and **Test**: conduct prototyping and testing cycles and write/record in journal
11–14	**Share and evaluate**: share and evaluate light displays

CURRICULUM LINKS

The following tables show the key Science, Technologies and Mathematics curricula with which this STEM investigation is aligned.

SCIENCE

YEAR	STRAND	SUB-STRAND AND CONTENT
5	Science Understanding	Physical sciences: • Light from a source forms shadows and can be absorbed, reflected and refracted
5 & 6	Science as a Human Endeavour	Use and influence of science: • Scientific knowledge is used to solve problems and inform personal and community decisions

TECHNOLOGIES

YEAR	STRAND	CONTENT
5 & 6	Design and Technologies Processes and Production Skills	• Critique needs or opportunities for designing, and investigate materials, components, tools, equipment and processes to achieve intended designed solutions • Generate, develop and communicate design ideas and processes for audiences using appropriate technical terms and graphical representation techniques • Select appropriate materials, components, tools, equipment and techniques, and apply safe procedures to make designed solutions • Negotiate criteria for success that include sustainability to evaluate design ideas, processes and solutions • Develop project plans that include consideration of resources when making designed solutions individually and collaboratively

MATHEMATICS

YEAR	STRAND	CONTENT
5 & 6	Measurement and Geometry	Using units of measurement Geometric reasoning

OTHER CURRICULUM LINKS

GENERAL CAPABILITIES

- Literacy
- Numeracy
- Information and Communication Technology (ICT) Capability
- Critical and Creative Thinking

ASSESSMENT

The following resources are provided for assessing students at different stages of the STEM investigations:

- Generic reproducible 1 (Key vocabulary table), for assessing understanding of vocabulary
- Generic reproducible 2 (Self-evaluation), for student self-evaluation of the learning process
- Generic reproducible 3 (Define graphic organiser), for assessing student engagement in the challenges, and the collaboration and skills involved in the design thinking stages
- Generic reproducible 5 (Design thinking assessment rubric), for evaluating student engagement in the design thinking stages
- Learning journal templates 1, 2, 3 and 4, for incorporating student reflection and evaluation

→ GETTING READY FOR THE INVESTIGATION

You can prepare yourself and students for this STEM investigation in the following ways:

- Identify groups of students who will work well together.
- Review the **Key science knowledge** that supports this investigation, and look at the **Useful links**.
- Investigate the **Useful apps**.
- Gather materials for exploring the properties of light during the Tune-in session.
- Start collecting additional materials for prototyping (as shown on the **Materials needed** list).
- Determine where prototypes will be kept between lessons.
- Create a wall space where students can share their ideas in the Ideate stage.
- Organise the class into pairs.
- Start thinking about:
  - » organisation of materials
  - » software to use to record the installation
  - » time constraints
  - » location and use of a laser beam
  - » access to artists/librarians
  - » creating a theme or focus for the installation
  - » opportunities to present the installation at school, such as a school twilight fair or parent information evening
  - » whether each group is creating a standalone light display, or whether each group's light display will be collated into a class light display.

USEFUL LINKS

- Information about light, such as at sciencekids.co.nz/light.html
- Information about light for students, such as at synopsys.com/optical-solutions/learn/optics-for-kids/what-is-light.html
- Information about light for teachers as an extra resource in the form of lessons, such as at physicsclassroom.com/Physics-Interactives/Light-and-Color
- Information about festivals like Diwali, Chinese Lantern Festival, White Night, Field of Light and Berlin's Festival of Lights, such as at kidzworld.com/article/27580-all-about-diwali, youtube.com/watch?v=qG6QSYMhAB0 and youtube.com/watch?time_continue=90&v=KCEeuxJEk6c (from 1 minute into the clip)

USEFUL APPS

- App for creating semantic maps (links between different words and/or concepts), such as Popplet
- App for creating interactive links (for example, between descriptions, videos, images and websites and a main image), such as ThingLink
- App for making notes using text, drawings, images, weblinks and audio, such as Notability
- App for creating multimedia presentations, such as Adobe Spark Video or iMovie
- App for creating surveys, such as Typeform
- App for drawing shapes, inserting images, making annotations or adding to an inserted image, such as Drawisland

RESOURCES PROVIDED

- Generic reproducibles 1, 2, 3, 4, 5, 6
- Reproducibles 19.1, 19.2, 19.3
- Learning journal templates 1, 2, 3, 4 (on disc)

MATERIALS NEEDED

- Sticky notes (half a pad per pair)
- Paper
- Coloured card
- Pens and markers
- Sticky tape
- Scissors
- Pipe-cleaners
- Cardboard
- Mirror
- Laser light
- Spray bottle with water
- A2 sheets of white paper
- Lamp
- Device for recording video such as a digital camera, iPad or smartphone
- Glass or Perspex prism
- Non-LED torch
- Rubber band
- Red, blue and green cellophane
- A5 white cards
- Objects of the following colours: red, green, blue, yellow, magenta, cyan

Do not let students handle the laser light. Laser light can be dangerous. Do not look directly at the laser light.

KEY SCIENCE KNOWLEDGE

This section provides an overview of the key science concepts and vocabulary needed for this unit.

WHAT IS LIGHT?

Light is a form of energy. It is different from other types of energy, such as sound waves, because it does not need a medium, such as air, to travel through. For example, light from the Sun travels through space to reach the Earth.

White light is the narrow band of energy that is visible to us and is made up of the different colours of the rainbow. Light travels at very high speeds – nothing can travel faster than light. Light travels in a straight line unless something causes it to change direction.

REFLECTION, ABSORPTION AND 'SEEING' COLOURS

Light **reflection** occurs when light bounces off a surface. Most surfaces reflect some light. When light hits a shiny surface, the angle it makes with the surface is the same size as the angle it makes when the light bounces off, so we see a reflected image. This is regular reflection. On rough surfaces, the light reflects at many different angles, so a reflected image is not formed. This is diffuse reflection.

Light reflection affects how we see colour. For example, an orange basketball reflects orange light to our eyes and absorbs the other colours of visible light.

Light **absorption** occurs when light meets a surface and light energy is transferred into the material. **Opaque** materials often have this property. The absorbed light is usually converted into heat. Absorption of light depends on an object's colour, texture and material. A shiny or white surface will absorb less light than a dull black surface, and so it heats up more slowly.

Kaleidoscopes reflect light to create symmetrical patterns

REFRACTION AND DISPERSION

Light **refraction** occurs when light travels from one **transparent** substance, such as air, to another, such as water. When this happens, light bends. If you put a pencil in a glass of water and look at it from the side of the glass, the pencil will appear to be bent.

Dispersion is the separation of white light into individual colours (known as a spectrum). Each colour bends by a different amount when it is refracted by transparent materials. You sometimes see this when sunlight refracts through water droplets in the sky to form a rainbow.

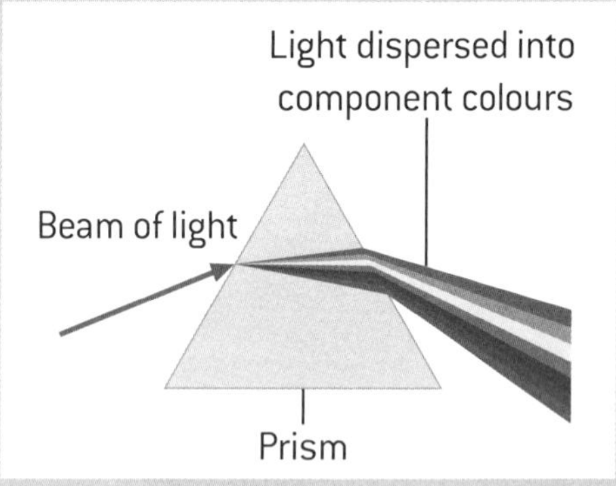

Dispersion of light

KEY VOCABULARY

absorption – the taking in of light by a material

dispersion – refraction of white light into its different colours (spectrum), such as through a triangular prism

opaque – not able to been seen through; for example, a brick is opaque

reflection – the bouncing of light off a surface

refraction – the bending of light, which occurs when light travels from one transparent material (such as air) to another (such as water)

transparent – able to be seen through; for example, glass is transparent

→ TUNE IN

1. Ask students to complete **Generic reproducible 1 (Key vocabulary table)** using the key vocabulary for this unit. This reproducible will also be used at the end of the unit, to demonstrate changes in understanding.
2. Watch one or two video clips about art installations using light (see **Useful apps/links**). Students should make comparisons between these videos and their understanding of light and art installations.
3. Before engaging in the challenge, students need to understand that the reason we are able to see is because light reflects off objects to our eyes. They also need to understand how shadows are formed, that light travels in straight lines and that visible light is made up of different colours.

ACTIVITY 1: 'SEEING' LIGHT

1. Place a mirror on a wall, then darken the room. Ask students why it is dark (the absence of light). Explain that dark objects absorb light rather than reflect it.
2. At an angle, shine a laser onto the mirror, being careful not to let the reflected light shine in students' eyes. You can see where the light is reflected but you cannot see the beam of light between the laser and mirror. Ask students why they cannot see the beam.
3. Using a spray bottle, mist water droplets into the laser beam path. Ask students why they can see the beam. (Light needs a medium to reflect off for us to see it.)

ACTIVITY 2: SHADOW PUPPET PLAY

1. Students form groups of three. They need a screen (A2 sheet of white paper) and a lamp.
2. Have them write a 1-minute play of a familiar story, such as a fairytale. Provide students with **Reproducible 19.1 (Shadow puppets)** to help them organise their play. They then act out the play using shadow puppets. One student will be the narrator.
3. Ask students to describe what they observe and explain how they know light travels in straight lines.

ACTIVITY 3: ABSORPTION AND REFLECTION

1. Have students make coloured light filters for a non-LED torch by cutting three squares of green, red and blue cellophane. Use a rubber band to secure the squares.
2. In a darkened room, have students use each coloured filter to shine light onto different coloured objects, making sure the reflected light (if any) strikes a piece of white A5 card. For example, shining red light onto a red apple will reflect red light. However, shining green light onto a red apple will reflect no light – it has been absorbed.
3. Ask students to record what they observe using **Reproducible 19.2 (Coloured light)**. Ask students to explain the difference between absorption and reflection of light.

4. Introduce the STEM investigation and challenge. Provide students with the student card and read the information together. Ask them to think about ways they can demonstrate absorption, dispersion, reflection and refraction of light. Encourage students to think about innovative ways to showcase different properties of light. Have students discuss and evaluate their ideas.
5. Introduce the design thinking process by reviewing the stages on the student card.
6. Explain that students will keep a journal about their learning at the different stages of the design.

TOP TIP! During the Tune-in stage, conduct vocabulary activities to highlight and develop key vocabulary knowledge. Activities could include creating a word wall or paired discussions.

USEFUL APPS/LINKS

- Art installations using light, such as at youtube.com/watch?v=3toJ9PwF3ss and youtube.com/watch?v=8VwJMw_fLvI

→ EMPATHISE

During the Empathise stage of the design thinking process, students focus on finding out about different points of view. To empathise with others, they need to interview others about their experiences of light-based art installations and also make observations about how other people respond to different experiences. Students will take notes, ask questions, draw diagrams and take photos where relevant.

ACTIVITY 1: FIND OUT OPINIONS AND EXPERIENCES

1. Ask students to create a short survey or set of interview questions to find out other people's opinions and experiences of art installations and light displays. Students' questions should focus on the impact of light and colour on the interviewee.
2. Modes of interviewing could include a school-, home-based or email interview, or an online survey.

ACTIVITY 2: EXPLORE LIGHT FESTIVALS

1. Ask students to gather information about light displays around the world. Provide students with some initial sources to explore (see **Useful apps/links**). These could be set up on a class Padlet.
2. Ask students to choose some images and video clips to share. Ask them to record their initial responses on **Reproducible 19.3 (Light festivals)**.
3. Explain that light displays use laser beams, projectors and mini mirrors (see **Useful apps/links**).
4. Ask students to consider the types of light displays that inspired them and the people they interviewed.

PROMPTS

- What feature of light displays was most popular?
- What are some of the well-known light festivals?
- What were some images that you liked in the videos?
- What new information did you learn?

MORE VOCABULARY

- empathise – understand and consider another person's or group's point of view
- point of view – an opinion, attitude or judgement considered in a particular way

JOURNAL TIP

Students complete **Learning journal template 1 (Empathise page)** while they are completing the different tasks. Remind them to date their notes and include photos or pictures of relevant information.

USEFUL APPS/LINKS

- Diwali traditions and fun facts, such as at kidzworld.com/article/27580-all-about-diwali and bbc.co.uk/newsround/15451833
- Chinese Lantern Festival pictures, activities and foods, such as at bbc.co.uk/newsround/38130998, chinahighlights.com/festivals/mid-autumn-festival.htm and hutong-school.com/how-celebrate-chinese-lantern-festival
- White Night highlights and news, such as at whitenightmelbourne.com.au and abc.net.au/news/2017-02-19/white-night-lights-up-melbourne/8283788
- Field of Light installation at Uluru, such as at youtube.com/watch?v=qG6QSYMhAB0 and abc.net.au/news/2016-03-22/uluru-lights-up-with-spectacular-art-installation/7266890
- Video clip of the Berlin Festival of Lights, such as at youtube.com/watch?time_continue=90&v=KCEeuxJEk6c (from 1 minute into the video)
- Information for teachers about lasers, such as at laserist.org/technology.htm

ASSESSMENT

This stage of the design thinking process offers opportunities to observe students collecting information, developing questions, and recording their notes and thinking in their journal.

EMPATHISE DEFINE IDEATE PROTOTYPE TEST

→ DEFINE

The main focus of this stage of the design thinking process is to reframe the challenge. The initial challenge is quite open, so at this stage students learn how to define what needs to be done. This includes noting insights that have been generated.

ACTIVITY 1: CONSIDER OBSERVATIONS

1. Students consider the information they gathered in the Empathise stage. They may work in pairs or small groups. Provide them with a whiteboard, large sheet of paper and/or sticky notes to collate some of the key information they have gathered about people's responses to light displays.
2. Students should discuss one section of **Learning journal template 2 (Define page)** at a time, write their responses, then continue discussing their ideas for the next section, until the task is complete. This provides students with opportunities to hear others' responses and also provides the teacher with input points.
3. Discuss some of the practicalities of the challenge. Students will need to consider how they will use light to create different images without professional equipment. Ask students to think about how they could record the images they create and project their video. Ask students to write other information they would like to know, such as creating shadows, lighting effects and useful videoing techniques or apps. Provide them with **Generic reproducible 4 (Key question table)** to assist them to record their questions, findings and sources.

ACTIVITY 2: CONSIDER INSIGHTS

Students think of at least one insight they have gained from the process; for example, colour can have a strong impact on people's emotions. They add this insight to **Learning journal template 2 (Define page)** and write a brief explanation of what needs to be created.

When considering insights, students could think about the following:

- What was something unexpected that you saw or found out? How was it unexpected?
- How will you decide on the most important aspect of your light display?
- Is there any other information that you need or would like to know? How will you find out?

At this stage, let students know the constraints of the challenge, by providing the dimensions of the space to be used for the light display and describing the time frame, materials available (including technology), the audience and how the display will be evaluated. Students then update **Learning journal template 2**.

PROMPTS

- What did you discover?
- What were the most important pieces of information that you gathered?
- What was something new that you learned?
- What other information do you need?

MORE VOCABULARY

- define – state the meaning of something
- insight – an accurate understanding of someone or something

JOURNAL TIP

Discuss the term 'insight'. Explain that it relates to something students have learned about the people and their responses to the surveys, as well as information gathered through research or excursions. You could refer to **Learning journal template 2**.

EMPATHISE DEFINE IDEATE PROTOTYPE TEST

→ IDEATE

The Ideate stage of the design thinking process is all about generating lots of ideas. Students need to be flexible in their thinking and able to move beyond obvious ideas. At this stage, ideas are not judged, just generated and gathered. Consider if there is to be a theme or message associated with the light display. Does it relate to an event, culture, issue or interest?

ACTIVITY: GENERATE IDEAS

1. Ask groups of students to draw or write their ideas about what the light display might include and look like. Students should consider colours as well as images. Each new idea should be written or drawn on a separate piece of paper or sticky note.
2. Ask students to group ideas on a wall or board.
3. Ask students to look at the different ideas and provide feedback to each other. It is important that students don't defend their ideas at this stage. They should just be listening to the feedback.
4. After the initial feedback, ask students to come up with more ideas. Encourage them to be creative and even radical.
5. Ask students to choose four of their ideas to write in their journal. Students use **Learning journal template 3 (Ideate page)** to do this. Ask students to choose one idea to explore further and explain the reasoning behind their choice.

TOP TIP!

At this stage, students may have produced a series of annotated drawings about a light display. They may have a collection of sticky notes, which they can organise into related ideas.

Encourage students to view and read others' ideas before giving feedback. Feedback could be within small groups or between partners. Considering others' ideas is an important part of this process, so students can build on their own ideas as they continue to ideate.

At each stage of this activity, ask students to discuss their thoughts before writing their responses. This will help them to think through their ideas and select their final ideas to develop.

PROMPTS

- How do these ideas relate to the light display challenge?
- How might you test your design?
- How can you make sure it will fit the space?
- How can you make sure it will incorporate different colours and properties of light?
- What if you had to use different materials?

MORE VOCABULARY

- feedback – information about, for example, a person's performance or the design of a product, which can be used to make improvements
- ideate – generate many ideas without making judgements about the ideas

JOURNAL TIP

When choosing four ideas to include in the journal, students should try to choose four ideas that aren't related.

USEFUL APPS/LINKS

- Tools for creating ideas, such as at creatingminds.org/tools/tools_ideation.htm
- Tips for creativity and innovation, such as at designorate.com/creativity-innovation-in-education

ASSESSMENT

At the Ideate stage, assessment could include observations about the number and diversity of students' ideas, and their ability to provide feedback and create additional ideas. Reflection in the journal should provide an insight into some of the reasoning behind students' choices.

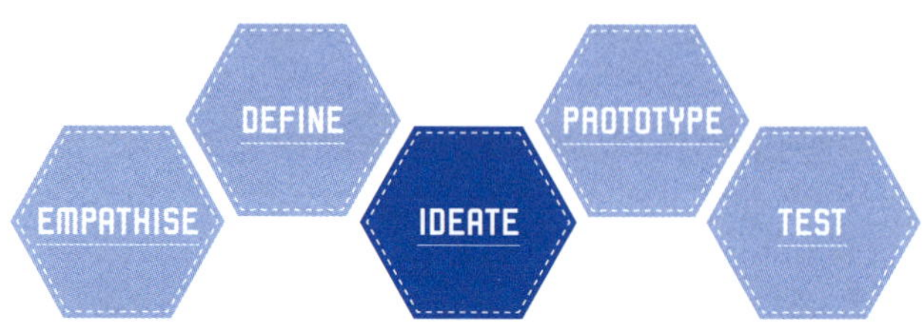

→ PROTOTYPE

At this stage of the design thinking process, students are asked to create a physical prototype. It is the stage where students need to get their ideas out of their head and presented in a way that engages other students and helps them to understand the concept. When students create, it helps them to think and solve problems and disagreements. Students can role-play, make storyboards or use sticky notes when they prototype. The most important feature is that viewers can interact with whatever is produced.

Encourage students to photograph or film during the prototyping and testing stages. This information can be used to show the learning behind the design thinking process in action.

ACTIVITY: TRANSFORM IDEAS INTO PROTOTYPES

1. Students review the ideas generated at the Ideate stage. Provide them with an A3 copy of **Generic reproducible 6 (In the frame)** so they can organise their ideas into two sections: 'least relevant' and 'most relevant'. Students continue to cycle through this activity until they have an idea to start prototyping.
2. Encourage students to prototype one element of their light display at a time. They will need time to experiment with the different ways that light can be used to generate interesting shapes, patterns, colours and images. Provide students with a range of materials to use to create their prototype. Remind students that a prototype should be created rapidly and is not meant to look 'nice'.
3. After a prototype has been created, ask students to see if it works and get feedback from others.
4. Students then use the feedback to prototype again.

Ask students to fill in the Prototype part of **Learning journal template 4 (Prototype and test page)**. See the **Journal tip** for further student guidance.

PROMPTS

- What worked?
- How could it be improved?
- What else do you need to know, do or have?
- What other suggestions do you have?

MORE VOCABULARY

- feedback – information about, for example, a person's performance or the design of a product, which can be used to make improvements
- prototype – an initial version of a model of a product or process that is used to develop a final model

JOURNAL TIP

Remind students to highlight the main features of their prototype. If students are creating an electronic journal, they can insert a photo of their prototype and annotate it.

USEFUL APPS/LINKS

- App for creating interactive links (for example, between descriptions, videos, images and websites and a main image), such as ThingLink
- App for making notes using text, drawings, images, weblinks and audio, such as Notability

ASSESSMENT

Observe students as they make changes to their designs. Are they able to consider feedback, make modifications and move rapidly through this process? Or do they have difficulties with holding on to an idea and accepting feedback?

TOP TIP!

The Prototype stage is often very messy. It is important that students are focusing on their ideas, rather than the end product. Provide them with lots of materials. Students may add labels to prototypes to explain some of the main features. Photographing and annotating pictures of prototypes can be useful.

To gain feedback, students could ask each other some of the following questions:

- What is the main feature of your prototype?
- How does it work? Can you explain which properties of light you have used?
- Which aspects work best? What will you keep?
- Which aspects need changing? How might you do this?
- What other materials might you need?

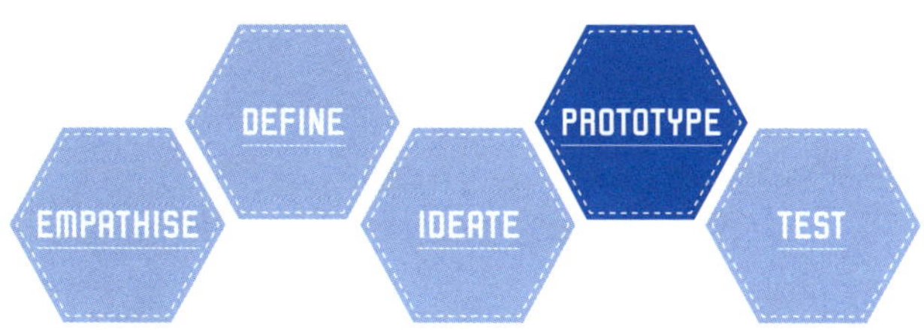

→ TEST

At this stage of the design thinking process, students test their prototype to see how it meets the criteria set at the start of the design process.

ACTIVITY: TEST FEEDBACK

1. Students take their last prototype and consider the initial needs of their audience.
2. Ask students to check whether or not their design works. If not, what do they need to do to make it work?
3. Provide the opportunity to cycle through the prototyping and testing stages again.

Ask students to fill in the Test part of **Learning journal template 4 (Prototype and test page)**. See the **Journal tip** for further student guidance.

PROMPTS

- Does your prototype do what you wanted it to do?
- Are there other features that you could add?

MORE VOCABULARY

- evaluate – assess something, perhaps considering what worked and what didn't
- feature – a specific aspect of something, such as size, shape, colour and quality
- feedback – information about, for example, a person's performance or the design of a product, which can be used to make improvements
- prototype – an initial version of a model of a product or process that is used to develop a final model
- review – consider an idea, process or product and decide what needs to be changed and what works

JOURNAL TIP

Ask students to think about why it is important to test their ideas before they build their final design.

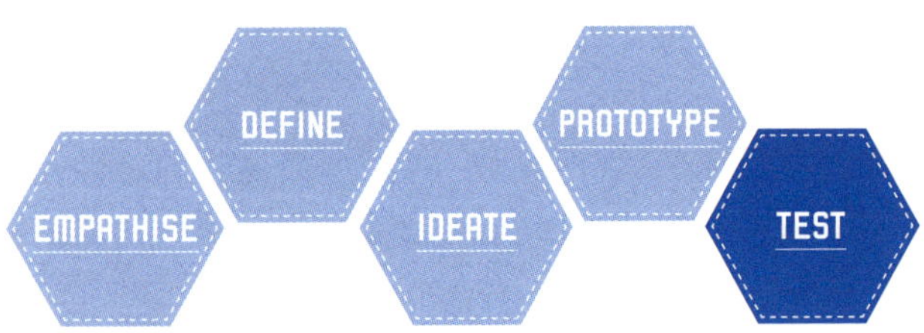

→ SHARE AND EVALUATE

At this stage of the investigation, students are provided with an opportunity to share their final design, as well as the processes involved in the investigation. Students evaluate their learning journals and their solutions.

ACTIVITY 1: BRING THE DESIGNS TOGETHER

1. Provide students with time to create final designs. They will need to video record the different components of their light display and then edit to create a video for projection.
2. Students can also create an iMovie or use Adobe Spark Video to demonstrate the process and thinking behind the designs. There should be an element of narration, where they are sharing their story about points of view, insights, prototyping and solutions.
3. Students should include their learning journals with the display so others can see the different stages of the design process.

ACTIVITY 2: EVALUATE AND GIVE FEEDBACK

1. Provide students with **Generic reproducible 2 (Self-evaluation)** to complete.
2. Ask students to provide feedback to each other about interesting features, difficult aspects and the changes that they might make.
3. Provide students with opportunities to share their designs. This could include inviting someone from a local gallery, library or council or similar, or a friend or family member with relevant experience. It may be possible to share some of the videos with an expert for feedback.

ASSESSMENT

Ask students to again complete **Generic reproducible 1 (Key vocabulary table)** using the key vocabulary for this unit. Compare their table with the one they completed at the Tune-in stage, to demonstrate changes in understanding.

Students complete **Generic reproducible 3 (Responding to the investigation)**. Compare their responses to those on **Generic reproducible 2 (Self-evaluation)**.

Teachers and students each complete **Generic reproducible 5 (Design thinking assessment rubric)**. Students compare the feedback they are given by the teacher with their self-assessment of their design thinking skills.

Name: ....

Date: ....

STEM INVESTIGATIONS

Plan your short story here. Include the characters, the main event of the story, how the story ends and the types of shadows you need to create.

Setting

Main characters

Main event

Ending

Types of shadows needed (such as characters, background, equipment)

Other

STEM Investigations, UP, ISBN 978 1 4202 4154 9 © Macmillan Science and Education Australia 2018

STEM INVESTIGATIONS

Name: ....

Date: ....

Write your observations about the different coloured light filters and the different coloured objects.

Object	Colour of object	Coloured light filter used	Colour of light reflected on screen	Other

EMPATHISE

STEM INVESTIGATIONS

Name: ....

Date: ....

Choose some images and videos about light festivals to share with others. Record their initial responses.

Image or video clip (describe it or include link)	Person 1 response	Person 2 response	Person 3 response

SHINE A NEW LIGHT ON STUDENT WORK

→ INTRODUCTION

A trip to a museum or art gallery is often an interactive experience, whether it involves listening to a podcast, using apps to manipulate displays or engaging with exhibitions in a multimodal way. Within the school environment, displays are more likely to be static.

In this STEM investigation, students are asked to consider how their learning can be presented using engaging and possibly interactive elements, with a particular focus on using light.

This STEM challenge is easily differentiated for students by encouraging different degrees of complexity when using light sources, and reflection and refraction of light. Introducing electrical circuits provides opportunities to create simple lighting solutions, as well as more elaborate displays.

THE CHALLENGE

Your school principal wants to hold an exhibition to showcase what students have been learning. The audience will be families, friends and other students. The principal wants to display the student work in a way that engages and entertains the audience.

Your challenge is to design and create a new way to display student work. You must use lighting in your design. Think about any great displays you have seen in the community, for example, at museums, galleries or festivals. How have these displays used light? As part of your investigation, you will learn about the properties of light and investigate how they can be used to make interesting and fun student displays.

KEY UNDERSTANDINGS

- Light travels in a straight line unless something makes it change direction.
- Light can be absorbed.
- Light can be reflected.
- Light can be refracted.
- When light is reflected, it bounces back towards its source, for example, from a mirror.
- When light is refracted, it changes direction, for example, as it moves from one transparent material into another.
- Light can be used to direct attention.
- Light can be used to engage.

KEY VOCABULARY

absorption

circuit

opaque

reflection

refraction

transparent

KEY SKILLS

- Make careful observations.
- Consider different points of view.
- Develop interviewing skills.
- Create electric circuits.*
- Transform an idea into something that can be seen.

KEY ACTIONS

- Interview other students.
- Experiment with lights – reflection, refraction and absorption.
- Experiment with circuits.*
- Explore ways of using sound and light to engage others.
- Design a way to make displays more interesting.

*This can be incorporated as an extension.

→ OVERVIEW OF STAGES

TUNE IN:

- Share pictures and short online videos of different types of displays.
- Discuss students' experiences of visiting and interacting with displays and exhibitions.
- Explore different properties of light, including absorption, reflection and refraction.
- Provide students with the STEM investigation challenge card.

EMPATHISE

Students observe and interview others about their responses and interactions with different types of student work displays or community displays, if practical.

DEFINE

Students consider the main issues with school displays and how they would prefer to see their work or the work of others displayed. The parameters of the challenge are defined.

IDEATE

Students generate creative ideas for displays.

PROTOTYPE

Students transform some of their ideas into physical representations, incorporating light. These are created rapidly, using simple materials.

TEST

Students share their prototypes and provide feedback to each other.

SHARE AND EVALUATE:

Final prototypes are shared and evaluated, with several designs chosen for further development and implementation.

→ SUGGESTED SCHEDULE

LESSON	STAGE
1–2	**Tune in:** share information about displays and discuss students' experiences; explore absorption, reflection, refraction, sources of light and reflectors of light; introduce the student challenge
3–5	**Empathise:** observe a display or exhibition; interview, empathise and write/record in journal
6	**Define:** define the main issues and write/record in journal
7	**Ideate:** develop ideas and write/record in journal
8–10	**Prototype** and **Test:** conduct prototyping and testing cycles, and write/record in journal
11–13	**Share and evaluate:** share and evaluate designs and prototypes

CURRICULUM LINKS

SCIENCE

YEAR	STRAND	SUB-STRANDS AND CONTENT
5	Science Understanding	Physical sciences: • Light from a source forms shadows and can be absorbed, reflected and refracted
6*	Science Understanding	Physical sciences: • Electrical energy can be transferred and transformed in electrical circuits, and can be generated from a range of sources
5	Science as a Human Endeavour	Use and influence of science: • Scientific knowledge is used to solve problems and inform personal and community decisions

* This element could be included if working with a Year 6 group.

TECHNOLOGIES

YEAR	STRAND	CONTENT
5 & 6	Design and Technologies Knowledge and Understanding	• Investigate how electrical energy can control movement, sound or light in a designed product or system
	Design and Technologies Processes and Production Skills	• Generate, develop and communicate design ideas and processes for audiences using appropriate technical terms and graphical representation techniques • Select appropriate materials, components, tools, equipment and techniques, and apply safe procedures to make designed solutions • Negotiate criteria for success that include sustainability to evaluate design ideas, processes and solutions • Develop project plans that include consideration of resources when making designed solutions individually and collaboratively

MATHEMATICS

YEAR	STRAND	CONTENT
5	Measurement and Geometry	Using units of measurement Geometric reasoning
6	Measurement and Geometry	Geometric reasoning

OTHER CURRICULUM LINKS

AC

GENERAL CAPABILITIES

- Literacy
- Numeracy
- Information and Communication Technology (ICT) Capability
- Critical and Creative Thinking

ASSESSMENT

The following resources are provided for assessing students at different stages of the investigation:

- Generic reproducible 1 (Key vocabulary table), for assessing understanding of vocabulary
- Generic reproducible 2 (Self-evaluation), for student self-evaluation of the learning process
- Generic reproducible 3 (Responding to the investigation), for assessing student engagement in the challenges, and the collaboration and skills involved in the design thinking stages
- Generic reproducible 5 (Design thinking assessment rubric), for evaluating student engagement in the design thinking stages
- Learning journal templates 1 and 3, for incorporating student reflection and evaluation

GETTING READY FOR THE INVESTIGATION

You can prepare yourself and students for this STEM investigation in the following ways:

- Identify current student displays in the school for students to observe and review.
- Visit an interactive display with students, such as at a local library, art gallery or museum.
- Review the **Key science knowledge** that supports this investigation, and look at the **Useful links**.
- Investigate the **Useful apps**.
- Gather materials for the three explorations of light during the Tune-in session.
- Start collecting additional materials for prototyping (as shown on the **Materials needed** list).
- Determine where prototypes will be kept between lessons.
- Create a wall space where students can share their ideas in the Ideate stage.
- Organise the class into pairs.
- Start thinking about:
  - creating a student display about this investigation in which students can incorporate some of their ideas
  - who will view this student display – other students, families, friends and/or teachers
  - which students might benefit from the extension option
  - speaking with staff or parents who may be interested in assisting, especially during the creation of circuits.

USEFUL APPS

- App for creating semantic maps (links between different words and/or concepts), such as Popplet
- App for creating interactive links (for example, between descriptions, videos, images and websites and a main image), such as ThingLink
- App for making notes using text, drawings, images, weblinks and audio, such as Notability

USEFUL LINKS

- Information about light, such as at sciencekids.co.nz/light.html
- Copper tape circuit instructions, such as at makezine.com/projects/simple-paper-circuit/

RESOURCES PROVIDED

- Generic reproducibles 1, 2, 3, 5
- Reproducibles 20.1, 20. 2, 20.3
- Learning journal templates 1, 3 (on disc)

MATERIALS NEEDED

- Sticky notes (half a pad per pair)
- Mirrors (one per pair)
- Light sources, such as LEDs, torches or lamps (one per pair)
- Range of transparent and opaque materials, such as cellophane, cardboard, different fabrics, Perspex, foil
- Opaque bag
- Paper
- Coloured card
- Pens and markers
- Large glass jars (one per pair)
- Water jug
- Sticky tape
- Copper tape*
- Coin cell batteries for circuits* – 1 per circuit

* These materials are only needed if incorporating electrical circuits into this investigation (Year 6 only).

Swallowing coin cell batteries can be fatal. Warn students and monitor them carefully during battery use.

KEY SCIENCE KNOWLEDGE

This section provides an overview of the key science concepts and vocabulary needed for this unit.

WHAT IS LIGHT?

Light is a form of energy. It is made up of both particles and waves. Light travels in straight lines and at high speeds. The closer you are to a light source, the brighter the light will be. The further away you are from a light source, the dimmer the light will be. Light travels in a straight line unless something makes it change direction.

Light **absorption** occurs when light hits an **opaque** surface. Energy is then transferred to the material the light is shining on. If a surface is not smooth or shiny, light is more likely to be absorbed. Dark surfaces absorb more light than pale surfaces. For example, if you shine a torch on a black piece of material, the material will not reflect the light, it will absorb it. If the torch is shone for long enough, the temperature of the material will begin to increase as the light energy is transformed into heat energy.

Light **reflection** occurs when light bounces off a surface. This happens when a surface is smooth or shiny, such as a mirror. For example, if you are driving your car at night and a car is driving behind you, you may see their headlights reflected in your rearview mirror. When light hits a mirror, the angle it makes with the mirror is the same size as the angle it makes when the light bounces off.

Reflection of light

Light **refraction** occurs when light travels from one **transparent** material, such as air, to another, such as water. When this happens, light bends. If you put a pencil in a glass of water and look at it from the side of the glass, the pencil will appear to be broken.

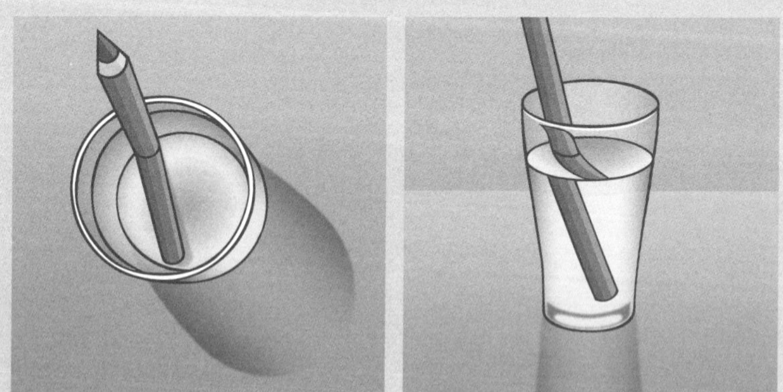

Refraction of light

KEY VOCABULARY

absorption – the taking in of light by a material
circuit – a complete path in which an electrical current can flow
opaque – not able to be seen through, for example, a brick
reflection – the bouncing of light off a surface
refraction – the bending of light, which occurs when light travels from one transparent material (for example, air) to another (for example, water)
transparent – able to be seen through, for example, glass

→ TUNE IN

1. Ask students to complete **Generic reproducible 1 (Key vocabulary table)** using the key vocabulary for this unit: absorption, circuit, opaque, reflection, refraction and transparent. This reproducible will also be used at the end of the unit, to demonstrate changes in understanding.
2. Watch the online video of shadow puppets (see **Useful apps/links**).
3. Discuss how light is used to create the characters and objects in the performance.
4. Look at some of the images at the White Night Melbourne website (see **Useful apps/links**). Discuss how light has been used in effective and engaging ways.
5. Explore different properties of light. Before beginning the challenge, students need to understand how light travels in a straight line, and about absorption, reflection and refraction. Set up the following three activities (or similar) for students.

ACTIVITY 1: ABSORPTION

1. Shine a light into an opaque bag. Ask students to describe what they see when they look into the bag.
2. Place a piece of foil in the bag and shine a torch into the bag. Ask students to describe what they see.
3. Place different types of materials in the bag and have students make observations.
4. Discuss the terms 'light source' (for example, a torch) and 'reflector' (for example, aluminium foil).

ACTIVITY 2: REFLECTION

1. Ask students to form pairs and for one student to draw a small symbol onto a sticky note and place the note on their partner's back (without them seeing the symbol).
2. Provide each pair with a mirror and ask students to use their mirror to find out which symbol is on their back.
3. Discuss how the mirrors reflect light, allowing the symbols to be seen from different angles.
4. Discuss situations when reflected light can be useful, for example, the rear-view mirror in a car.

ACTIVITY 3: REFRACTION

1. Draw a picture of a sailing boat on a piece of card and stand it upright. Make sure the boat has an obvious front and back.
2. Place a large glass or jar in front of the picture. Ask students to note which way the boat is facing.
3. Fill the glass or jar with water. Ask students to describe which direction the boat is now facing. (It should be facing in the opposite direction.)
4. Discuss the term 'refraction' and explain how light changes direction when it passes through transparent material.

6. Introduce the STEM investigation and challenge to the students. Provide them with the student card and read the information together. Ask students to think about times when they have visited an exhibition or engaged in an interactive activity. Make a list of features that were positive and negative. Encourage students to think about how light was or was not used effectively. Encourage students to discuss their experiences.
7. Introduce the design thinking process by reviewing the stages on the student card.
8. Explain that students will keep a journal about their learning at the different stages of the design.

TOP TIP! During the Tune in session, conduct vocabulary activities to highlight and develop key vocabulary knowledge. Activities could include drawing semantic webs, creating a word wall or paired discussions. Check the **Key vocabulary** definitions or read the **Key science knowledge** if you need a refresher on the key terms and concepts.

USEFUL APPS/LINKS

- Online video of shadow puppets, such as at youtube.com/watch?v=EAQxNVQF_I0
- Images from a light festival, such as White Night Melbourne, at whitenightmelbourne.com.au, or Vivid Sydney, at vividsydney.com

EMPATHISE

During the Empathise stage of the design thinking process, students focus on considering different points of view. To empathise with others, they need to engage in observation, interact with others and immerse themselves in the experiences that others have. Students will observe others, taking notes, asking questions and taking photos where possible. Students will then be encouraged to interact with others by constructing and then taking part in interviews. They are also encouraged to try to experience a situation from another's point of view.

ACTIVITY 1: OBSERVE

1. Take students to a local exhibition or display. Ask them to note how people interact with the display. Provide them with **Reproducible 20.1 (Observation graphic organiser)**.
   » What do people do at an exhibition?
   » How long do they spend at different parts of the exhibition?
   » What types of emotions can you notice from people's expressions and body language?
   » How do you know when a person is interested? What do they do?
   » How do you know when someone is not interested? What do they do?
   » Which exhibition features seem to be the most interesting? Why? How do you know?
   » Which features seem to be the least interesting? Why? How do you know?
2. Use a table to record information, or use an app such as Popplet.

ACTIVITY 2: INTERVIEW

Organise students into pairs. Students interview each other, using **Reproducible 20.2 (Display interview graphic organiser)** to organise questions and take notes. The first stage of the interview is to find out what makes an experience entertaining, interesting and repeatable. The second stage is to find out how the student being interviewed felt about different experiences.

ACTIVITY 3: EMPATHISE

Ask students to consider the responses to the interview. Have them look at a display and consider some of the feedback provided. Is it possible for them to think like the other student – to put themselves in the other student's shoes? Discuss.

PROMPTS

- How do people show that they are interested? What do they do?
- What are the main features of an interesting display?

MORE VOCABULARY

- empathise – understand and consider another person's or group's point of view
- observe – notice; watch someone or something very carefully
- point of view – an opinion, attitude or judgement considered in a particular way

JOURNAL TIP

Ask students to complete **Learning journal template 1 (Empathise page)** while they are completing the different tasks. Remind them to date their notes and include photos of relevant information or pictures.

USEFUL APPS/LINKS

- App to gather information when making observations, such as Popplet
- A short video about reflection, such as at bbc.co.uk/guides/zqdxb82

ASSESSMENT

This stage of the design thinking process offers opportunities to observe students collecting information, developing questions, and recording their notes and thinking in their journal.

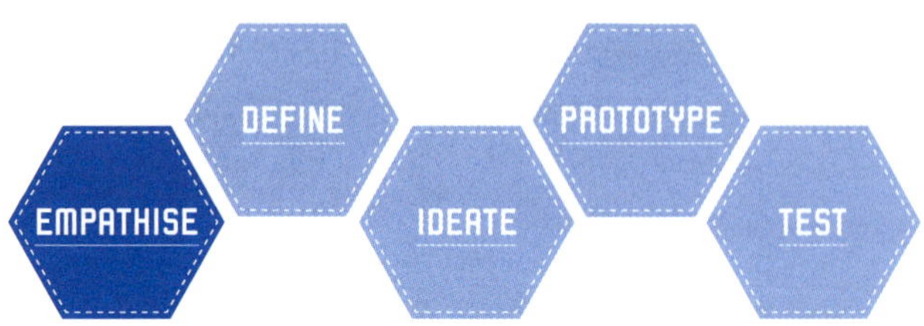

→ DEFINE

The main focus of this stage of the design thinking process is to reframe the challenge. The initial challenge is quite open, so at this stage students learn how to define what needs to be done. This includes noting insights that have been generated.

ACTIVITY 1: CONSIDER OBSERVATIONS

1. Students consider the observations they made and information they gathered in the Empathise stage. They may work in pairs or small groups. Provide them with a whiteboard, large sheet of paper and/or sticky notes to collate some of the key information they have gathered. They should refer to the information they have recorded on **Reproducible 20.1 (Observation)** and **Reproducible 20.2 (Display interview)**. When this has been done, students should transfer the main findings to **Reproducible 20.3 (Define)**.
2. Students should discuss one section of **Reproducible 20.3** at a time, write their responses, then continue discussing their ideas for the next section, until the task is complete. This provides students with opportunities to hear others' responses and it provides the teacher with input points.

ACTIVITY 2: CONSIDER INSIGHTS

Students should think of at least one insight they have gained from the process; for example, choice of colour is very important. Students add this insight to **Reproducible 20.3**. They should then explain how this relates to their display.

When considering insights, students could think about the following:

- What was something unexpected that you saw or found out? How was it unexpected?
- How will you decide on the most important aspect of the display?
- Is there any other information that you need or would like to know? How will you find out?

ACTIVITY 3: CONSIDER CONSTRAINTS

At this stage, let students know the constraints of the challenge, by describing the display space (including size, shape and existing lighting conditions), the work to be displayed and the available materials. Students can then update **Reproducible 20.3**.

PROMPTS

- What did you discover?
- What were the most important pieces of information that you gathered?
- What was something new that you learned?
- What did you learn about your partners' point of view?

MORE VOCABULARY

- define – state the meaning of something
- insight – an accurate understanding of someone or something

JOURNAL TIP

Discuss the term 'insight'. Explain that it relates to something students have learned about the people they observed or interviewed.

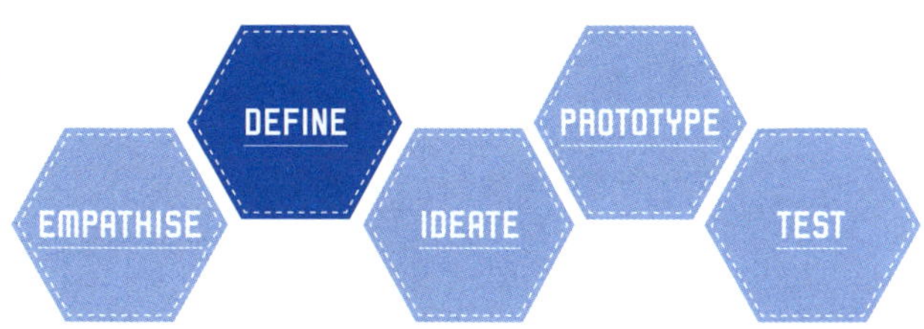

→ IDEATE

The Ideate stage of the design thinking process is all about generating lots of ideas. Students need to be flexible in their thinking and be able to move beyond obvious ideas. At this stage, ideas are not judged, just generated and gathered.

ACTIVITY: GENERATE IDEAS

1. Ask groups of students to draw or write their ideas.
2. Each new idea should be written or drawn on a separate piece of paper or sticky note.
3. Ask students to group ideas on a wall or board.
4. Ask students to look at the different ideas and provide feedback to each other. It is important that students don't defend their ideas at this stage. They should just be listening to the feedback.
5. After the initial feedback, ask students to come up with more ideas. Encourage them to be creative and even radical.
6. Ask students to choose four of their ideas to write in their journal. Students use **Learning journal template 3 (Ideate page)** to do this. Ask students to choose one idea to explore further and explain the reasoning behind their choice.

TOP TIP!

At this stage, students may have produced a series of drawings that are annotated. They may have a collection of sticky notes, which they can organise into related ideas.

Encourage students to view and read others' ideas before giving feedback. Feedback could be within small groups or between partners. Considering others' ideas is an important part of this process, so students can build on their own ideas as they continue to ideate.

At each stage of this activity, ask students to discuss their thoughts before writing their responses. This will help them to think through their ideas and select their final ideas to develop.

PROMPTS

- How do your chosen ideas relate to what your audience wants?
- How might you add sound to your idea?
- How can you make it smaller?
- How can you make it a different shape?
- What if you had to use different materials?

MORE VOCABULARY

- feedback – information about, for example, a person's performance or the design of a product, which can be used to make improvements
- ideate – generate many ideas without making judgements about the ideas

JOURNAL TIP

When choosing four ideas to include in the journal, students should try to choose ideas that aren't related.

USEFUL APPS/LINKS

- Tools for creating ideas, such as at creatingminds.org/tools/tools_ideation.htm
- Tips for creativity and innovation, such as at designorate.com/creativity-innovation-in-education/

ASSESSMENT

At the Ideate stage, assessment could include observations about the number and diversity of students' ideas, and their ability to provide feedback and create additional ideas. Reflection in the journal should provide an insight into some of the reasoning behind students' choices.

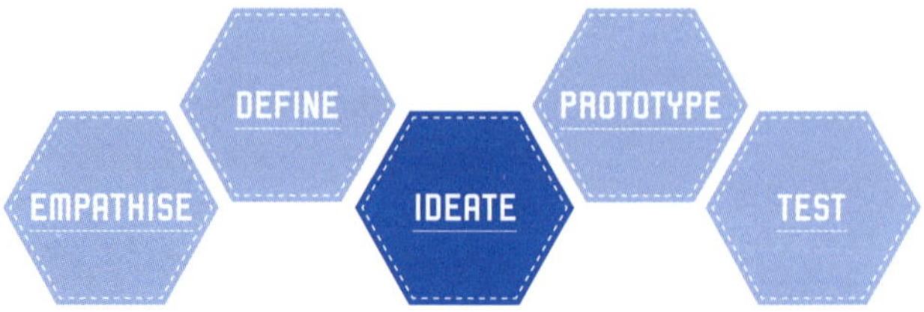

→ PROTOTYPE

At this stage of the design thinking process, students are asked to create a physical prototype of a solution; in this case, a display including light features. It is the stage where students need to get their ideas out of their head and presented in a way that engages other students and helps them to understand the concept. When students create, it helps them to think and solve problems and disagreements. Students can role-play, make storyboards or use sticky notes when they prototype. The most important feature is that viewers can interact with whatever is produced.

Encourage students to photograph or film during prototyping and testing. This information can be used to show the learning behind the design thinking process in action.

ACTIVITY: TRANSFORM IDEAS INTO PROTOTYPES

1. Ask students to choose one idea, or perhaps one aspect of that idea, to prototype.
2. Provide students with a range of materials to create their prototype. Remind students that a prototype should be created rapidly and is not meant to look 'nice'.
3. After a prototype has been created, ask students to see if it works and get feedback from others.
4. Students then use the feedback to prototype again.

TOP TIP!

The Prototype stage is often very messy. It is important that students are focusing on their ideas, rather than the end product. Provide them with lots of materials – recycling depots can be a useful source of resources. Students may add labels to prototypes to explain some of the main features. Photographing and annotating pictures of prototypes can be useful.

To gain feedback, students could ask each other some of the following questions:

- What is the main feature of your prototype?
- How does your prototype work?
- Which aspects work best? What will you keep?
- Which aspects need changing? How might you do this?
- What other materials might you need?

PROMPTS

- What worked?
- How could it be improved?
- What else do you need to know, do or have?
- What other suggestions do you have?

MORE VOCABULARY

- feedback – information about, for example, a person's performance or the design of a product, which can be used to make improvements
- prototype – an initial version of a model of a product or process that is used to develop a final model

JOURNAL TIP

Remind students to highlight the main features of their prototype. If students are creating an electronic journal, they can insert a photo of their prototype and annotate it.

USEFUL APPS/LINKS

- App that can be used for a learning journal, allowing students to draw, link, type and record information, such as Notability
- App that can be used to create an interactive annotation of the prototype, such as ThingLink

ASSESSMENT

Observe students as they make changes to their designs. Are they able to consider feedback, make modifications and move rapidly through this process? Or do they have difficulties with holding on to an idea and accepting feedback?

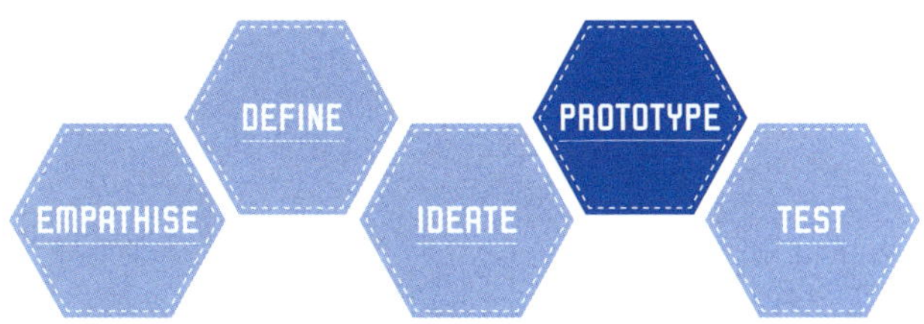

TEST

At this stage of the design thinking process, students test their prototype to see if it meets the requirements of the audience or user. Students check to see if their prototype meets the criteria set at the start of the design process.

ACTIVITY: TEST FEEDBACK

1. Students take their last prototype and consider the initial needs of their audience.
2. Ask students to check whether or not their design works. If not, what do they need to do to make it work?
3. Provide the opportunity to cycle through the prototype and test stages again.

PROMPTS

- Does your prototype do what you wanted it to do?
- Does it have features that your audience might like?
- What is your audience's reaction?

MORE VOCABULARY

- evaluate – assess something, perhaps considering what worked and what didn't
- feature – a specific aspect of something, such as size, shape, colour, quality
- feedback – information about, for example, a person's performance or the design of a product, which can be used to make improvements
- prototype – an initial version of a model of a product or process that is used to develop a final model
- review – consider an idea, process or product and decide what needs to be changed and what works

JOURNAL TIP

Ask students to think about why it is important to test their ideas before they build their final design.

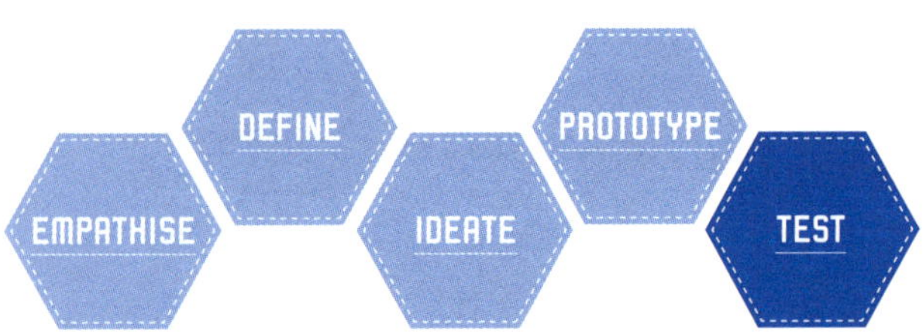

SHARE AND EVALUATE

At this stage of the investigation, students are provided with an opportunity to share their final design, as well as the processes involved in the investigation. Students evaluate their learning journals and their solutions.

ACTIVITY 1: BRING THE DESIGNS TOGETHER

1. Provide students with time to create a class display about light that incorporates the solutions created by the different groups and showcases their designs.
2. Students should include their learning journals with the display so that others can see the different stages of the design process.

ACTIVITY 2: EVALUATE AND GIVE FEEDBACK

1. Provide students with **Generic reproducible 2 (Self-evaluation assessment)** to complete.
2. Ask students to provide feedback to each other about the most interesting features, the aspects that were most difficult and the changes that they would make if they repeated the task.
3. Provide students with opportunities to use elements of their displays in other parts of the school.

ASSESSMENT

Ask students to again complete **Generic reproducible 1 (Key vocabulary table),** using the key vocabulary for this unit: absorption, circuit, opaque, reflection, refraction, transparent. Compare their table with the one they completed at the Tune-in session, to demonstrate changes in understanding.

Students complete **Generic reproducible 3 (Responding to the investigation)**. Compare their responses to those they gave in **Generic reproducible 2**.

Teachers and students each complete **Generic reproducible 5 (Design thinking assessment rubric)**. Students compare the feedback they are given by the teacher with their self-assessment of their design thinking skills.

EMPATHISE

STEM INVESTIGATIONS

Name: ....

Date: ....

Try to answer some of these questions when you are making your observations.

What do people do when they are looking at an exhibition or display?

How long do people spend in different parts of the exhibition or display?

What types of emotion can you notice from people's facial expressions and body language?

How do you know when a person is interested? What do they do?

How do you know when a person is not interested? What do they do?

Which features of the exhibition or display appear to be the most interesting? Why? How do you know?

Which features of the exhibition or display appear to be the least interesting? Why? How do you know?

EMPATHISE

STEM INVESTIGATIONS

Name: ....

Date: ....

What are some exhibitions, displays or events that you have been to?

Think about the features that made the experience interesting.
Describe them to me.

What makes you want to look at something again?
Describe some of the important features.

How did you feel when you were visiting these exhibitions, displays or events?
Tell me some words to describe how you felt.

STEM Investigations, UP, ISBN 978 1 4202 4154 9 © Macmillan Science and Education Australia 2018

DEFINE

STEM INVESTIGATIONS

Name: ....

Date: ....

Make a list of your main findings after you have observed others and interviewed someone.

Write down at least one insight. (This is something that you have learned.)

What do you need to think about when designing a display or exhibition? List details such as the size, shape and existing lighting in the display space, what you'll be displaying, and the materials you can use.

STEM Investigations, UP, ISBN 978 1 4202 4154 9

Name: ....

Date: ....

STEM INVESTIGATIONS

Read each of the topic words. If you do not know the meaning of the word, put a tick in the 'don't know' column. If you are not sure of the meaning, put a tick in the 'not sure' column. If you know the meaning of the word, write it in a sentence.

Topic word	Not sure	Don't know	I know this word. (Write the word in a sentence to show its meaning.)

STEM Investigations, UP, ISBN 978 1 4202 4154 9 © Macmillan Science and Education Australia 2018

Name: ....

Date: ....

STEM INVESTIGATIONS

What was your challenge question?

What information did you already know?

What new information or ideas have you learned?

Describe your solution.

What improvements could you make to your solution?

Which part of your investigation are you most pleased with? Why?

What questions do you still have about the challenge?

STEM Investigations, UP, ISBN 978 1 4202 4154 9

STEM INVESTIGATIONS

Name: ....

Date: ....

I enjoyed learning about this investigation topic.

A LOT — A LITTLE — NOT MUCH

Explain why.

....

....

I would like to learn more about this topic.

A LOT — A LITTLE — NOT MUCH

Explain why.

....

....

I found the activities in this investigation interesting.

A LOT — A LITTLE — NOT MUCH

Explain why.

....

....

I found the group work in this investigation enjoyable.

A LOT — A LITTLE — NOT MUCH

Explain why.

....

....

I feel confident using the design thinking process to create solutions to problems.

A LOT — A LITTLE — NOT MUCH

Explain why.

....

....

DEFINE

STEM INVESTIGATIONS

Name: ....

Date: ....

Use this table to create questions to help you find information that relates to your key (or main) question. Write down some notes. Record where you found this information. This can be used for a bibliography later if needed.

KEY QUESTION:		
Micro-question	Notes	Source of information

Name: ....

Date: ....

STEM INVESTIGATIONS

DESIGN THINKING STAGE/ ASSOCIATED SKILLS		ESTABLISHED	CONSOLIDATING	EMERGING
Empathise	**Observation skills**	Able to make detailed observations about people's points of views or world views. ☐	Make some observations about people's points of view or world views. ☐	Needs assistance to make observations about people's points of view or world views. ☐
	Insights	Able to identify and describe insights that have been inferred from observations with no guidance. Demonstrates empathy. ☐	Able to identify and describe insights that have been inferred from observations with some guidance. Some evidence of empathy. ☐	Needs considerable guidance to identify and describe. Able to describe insights that have been inferred from observations. Little or no evidence of empathy. ☐
Define	**Describing task**	Able to describe the main features of the challenge in detail and include some original approaches. ☐	Able to describe the main features of the challenge – needs more detail and originality. ☐	Needs assistance to describe the main features of the challenge and include detail. ☐
	Reframing of challenge	Uses clear and precise language to reframe the challenge. Uses verbs to describe the actions. ☐	Needs some guidance to choose clear and precise language to reframe the challenge. ☐	Needs guidance to choose precise language to reframe the challenge. Unable to reframe without assistance. ☐
Ideate	**Range of ideas**	Clear evidence of divergent thinking. Able to generate more than ten original ideas without assistance. ☐	Some evidence of divergent thinking. Able to generate at least five original ideas without assistance. ☐	Needs assistance to generate ideas. Divergent thinking not evident. ☐
	Organisation of ideas	Ideas are well organised and clearly articulated. ☐	Ideas show some level of organisation and are able to be explained in simple terms. ☐	Ideas do not show evidence of organisation and guidance is needed to explain the ideas. ☐
Prototype	**Use of materials**	Uses a range of materials in novel ways. ☐	Uses a range of materials in expected ways. ☐	Uses a limited range of materials in expected ways. ☐
	Annotation of designs	Provides a detailed record of the development of prototypes, including annotation of designs. ☐	Provides some evidence of recording development of prototypes, including annotation of designs. ☐	Little or no evidence of recording development of prototypes, including annotation of designs. ☐
	Flexible thinking	Clear evidence of flexibility of thinking through changes made to prototypes. ☐	Some evidence of flexibility of thinking through changes made to prototypes. ☐	Little evidence of flexibility of thinking through minimal changes made to prototypes. ☐
Test	**Questioning and feedback**	Asks probing questions and tests prototypes thoroughly. Listens carefully to feedback and responds appropriately. ☐	Shows evidence of testing prototypes and responding to feedback. Needs prompts to ask questions for feedback. ☐	Needs guidance to test prototypes and prompts to ask questions for feedback. ☐
Teamwork	**Collaboration**	Able to work productively as part of a team. Listens to others' opinions, and understands and fulfils role within the group. ☐	Needs guidance to work productively as part of a team. Listens to others' opinions, and understands and fulfils role within the group, with prompting. ☐	Needs considerable supervision to work productively as part of a team. May have difficulties listening to and acknowledging others' opinions. Needs assistance to complete role in group. ☐
Sharing	**Narration**	Able to provide an engaging narrative that explains the challenge, points of view and insights gained, prototyping and the end solution. ☐	Able to provide a simple narrative that explains the challenge, points of view and insights gained, prototyping and the end solution. ☐	Needs guidance and scaffolding to provide a simple narrative that explains the challenge, points of view and insights gained, prototyping and the end solution. ☐

STEM Investigations, UP, ISBN 978 1 4202 4154 9 © Macmillan Science and Education Australia 2018

PROTOTYPE

STEM INVESTIGATIONS

Name: ....

Date: ....

Brainstorm ideas. Write the most relevant ideas in the middle of the frame. Write the least relevant ideas in the outer part of the frame.

LEAST RELEVANT IDEAS

MOST RELEVANT IDEAS

Name: ....

Date: ....

DIFFERENCES	SIMILARITIES	DIFFERENCES

STEM Investigations, UP, ISBN 978 1 4202 4154 9

Name: ....

Date: ....

Your teacher will provide you with a list of words to record on the hexagons or ask you to create your own words. Cut out the hexagons and use them to make connections between the important words, information and concepts about the issue you are investigating.

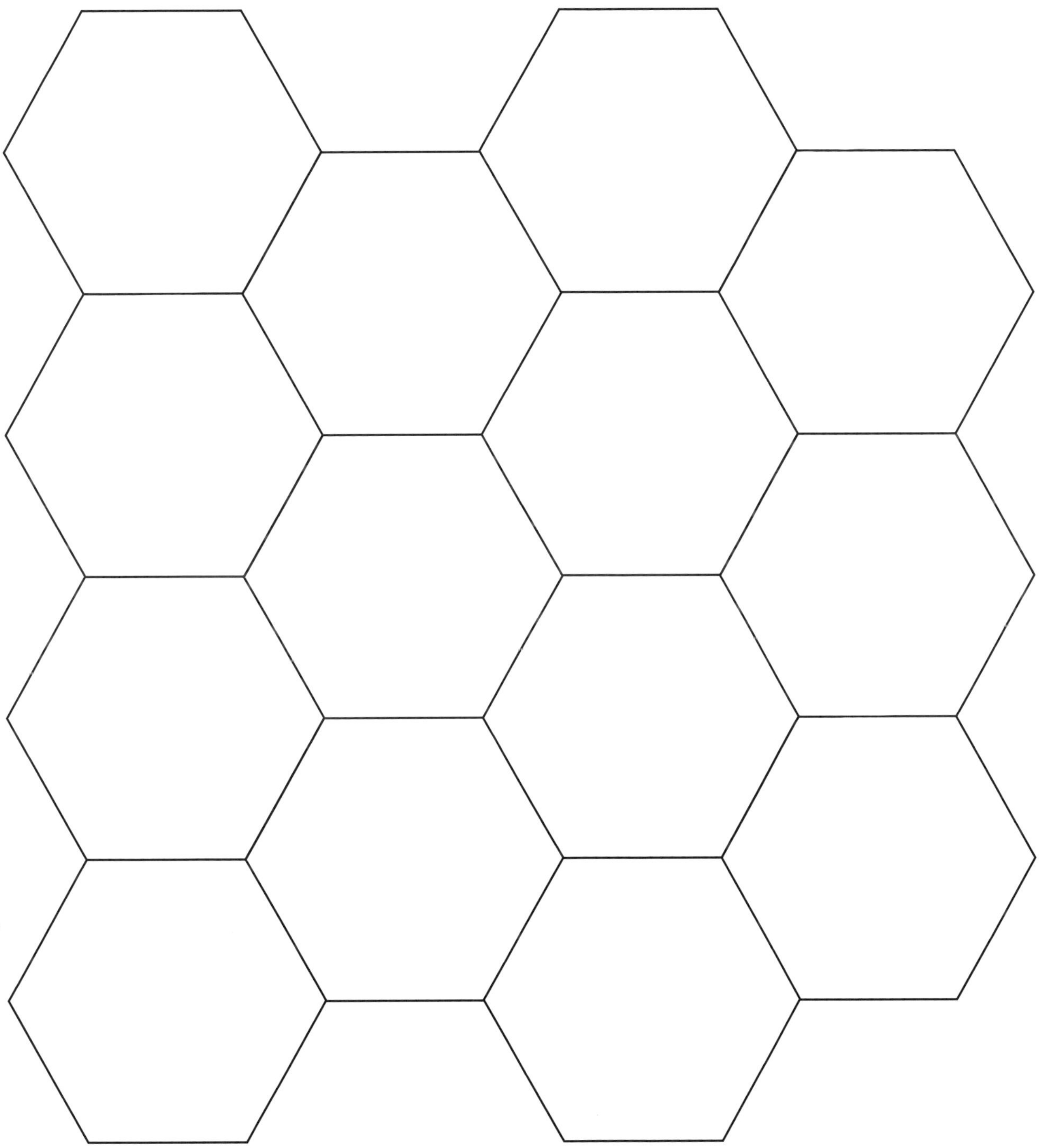

STEM Investigations, UP, ISBN 978 1 4202 4154 9 © Macmillan Science and Education Australia 2018

Name: ....

Date: ....

STEM INVESTIGATIONS

Think about the following three questions in relation to your investigation:

- What do I see?
- What do I think about?
- What does it make me wonder?

I SEE ...	I THINK ...	I WONDER ...

STEM Investigations, UP, ISBN 978 1 4202 4154 9 © Macmillan Science and Education Australia 2018

Name: ....

Date: ....

STEM INVESTIGATIONS

Group members:

STEM challenge:

End product (This is what is going to be produced/made.):

Tasks to be done to complete the end product:

Give each person in the group tasks to do. Tick each task after it has been completed.

Group member:	→	Task:
Group member:	→	Task:
Group member:	→	Task:
Group member:	→	Task:

TEMPLATE: STUDENT INTERVIEW

Name: ....

Date: ....

Interview a friend, family member or a person in the community to find out their experiences, knowledge and opinion.

QUESTION	INTERVIEWEE
What do you know about...?	
What is your experience with...?	
How do you feel about...?	
How would you...?	

STEM Investigations, UP, ISBN 978 1 4202 4154 9 © Macmillan Science and Education Australia 2018

Name: ....

Date: ....

I SEE ...	I THINK ...	I WONDER ...

GRAPHIC ORGANISER: PROTOTYPE AND TEST

PROTOTYPE TEST

Name: ....

Date: ....

What needed to be included in your prototype?

What did you do to check your prototype?

Write at least one change you made when you were prototyping.

What was the most important change you made? Why was it important?

STEM Investigations, UP, ISBN 978 1 4202 4154 9